The
Foreign Policy
of Peru

Ronald Bruce St John

Lynne Rienner Publishers ▬ Boulder & London

Published in the United States of America in 1992 by
Lynne Rienner Publishers, Inc.
1800 30th Street, Boulder, Colorado 80301

and in the United Kingdom by
Lynne Rienner Publishers, Inc.
3 Henrietta Street, Covent Garden, London WC2E 8LU

Library of Congress Cataloging-in-Publication Data
St John, Ronald Bruce.
    The foreign policy of Peru / Ronald Bruce St John.
       p.   cm.
  Includes bibliographical references and index.
  ISBN 1-55587-304-9
  1. Peru—Foreign relations. 2. Peru—History—War of
Independence, 1820–1829. 3. Peru—History—1829–ＩＩ. Title.
F3433.S7   1992
327.85—dc20   91–40509
                                         CIP

British Cataloguing in Publication Data
A Cataloguing in Publication record for this book
is available from the British Library.

To Carol

Contents

Preface   xi

1   Introduction   1

2   Setting the Stage, 1821–1827   7
    Foreign Policy of the Protectorate   8
    Boundary Issues   10
    Pan-Americanism Versus Regionalism   11
    Nascent Peruvian Nationalism   14
    Social and Economic Continuity at Independence   15
    Impact of the Great Powers   17
    End of the Bolivarian Regime   18

3   Search for National Identity, 1827–1845   23
    Regional Clashes   23
    Commercial Rivalry with Bolivia   26
    Foreign Policy of Orbegoso   28
    Trade, Claims, and Tariffs   30
    Creation of the Peru-Bolivia Confederation   31
    Dissolution of the Peru-Bolivia Confederation   34
    Foreign Policy of the Restoration   38

4   End of the Beginning, 1845–1862   45
    Improved Foreign Policy Machinery   45
    Diplomacy of Guano   46
    Promotion of Continental Solidarity   48
    Claims, Trade, and Development   51
    Limited Continuity Under Echenique   54
    Ecuador and the Search for Collective Security   57
    Continued Emphasis on National Integrity   60
    Polynesian Labor Trade   61

5   Rivalry in the Pacific, 1862–1872   67
    Spanish Threat to National Integrity   67
    Search for Continental Solidarity   72
    Abortive Attempts at Settlement   73
    Continental Solidarity Thwarts Spanish Intervention   75
    Fresh Attempts at Settlement   78
    Deterioration in Relations with Chile and Bolivia   80
    Renewed Emphasis on National Integrity and Nonintervention   81
    Economic Consequences of the Spanish Intervention   83

6   Road to War, 1872–1879   89
    Growing Economic Crisis   89
    Foreign and Domestic Policy   92
    Renewed Interest in Immigration   93
    García y García Mission   94
    Treaty of Mutual Benefits   97
    Peru-Bolivia Defensive Alliance   98
    Treaty of Sucre   100
    Diplomacy of the Prado Government   101
    Ten-Centavo Tax   102
    Peruvian Response   104

7   War of the Pacific, 1879–1885   109
    Alliance Diplomacy   109
    Allied Military Defeats   113
    Search for Peace   116
    Diplomacy of the United States   118
    Peace Settlements   123
    Aftermath of War   124

8   Postwar Reconstruction and Regeneration, 1885–1908   131
    Grace Contract   131
    Abortive Attempts to Hold a Plebiscite   133
    Claims Talks with the United States   135
    Territorial Dispute with Ecuador   136
    First Pan-American Conference   138
    Military Reform Under Piérola   139
    Improving Relations with the United States   140
    Chile Strengthens Its Diplomatic Position   141
    Territorial Agreements with Bolivia, Brazil, and Colombia   144
    Third Pan-American Conference   147

9   Leguía and the Delimitation of Peru, 1908–1930   151
    Foreign Policy of the First Leguía Administration   151
    Billinghurst, Pardo, and World War I   155
    Foreign Policy of the *Oncenio*   158
    Long Road to Settlement with Chile   160
    Controversial Salomón-Lozano Treaty   165
    Limited Progress on Other Issues   166

10 New Horizons for the Foreign Policy of Peru, 1930–1962   171
    Foreign Policy Issues in the 1931 Election Campaign   172
    Leticia Affair   173
    Continuity and Change Under Benavides   176
    World War II and Its Aftermath   181
    Export-led Growth and Peruvian Nationalism   184
    Ambivalent Relations with the United States   188

11 Search for Autonomy, 1962–1991   193
    Belaúnde and the International Petroleum Company   193
    Revolution in Foreign Policy   198
    Second Belaúnde Administration   206
    Aprista Foreign Policy   209
    Foreign Policy of Fujimori   213

12 Conclusions   221

    Bibliography   233
    Index   255
    About the Book and Author   269

Preface

In terms of both scope and departure, this is the first book of its kind to be published on the foreign policy of the Republic of Peru. It approaches Peru as a case study in the general issue area of Third World foreign policy in the hopes of rendering the Peruvian experience intelligible and of drawing from it conclusions of a wider comparative experience. In the process, it provides a detailed analysis of the internal and external forces that have influenced Peru's foreign policy since independence in 1824. In addition, the substantive content of individual foreign policies and the subsequent consequences of foreign policy behavior are also explored.

Intended for both Peruvians and non-Peruvians, this book should enable the latter to understand better the behavior of Peruvians they observe, the books by Peruvians they read, and the Peruvians they meet. I hope that intelligent, perceptive, and honest Peruvians will recognize its observations as accurate and its interpretations and analyses as meaningful and enlightening. For both groups, it should serve in some small way to further mutual understanding on the private individual level and the official governmental level. In a study such as this, these should be among the most important tests of validity.

I have assumed some familiarity on the reader's part with the chief events and personalities in Peruvian affairs since 1824. For example, I do not provide details of the various clauses of the Herrera–Da Ponte Ribeyro Convention or give a day-by-day account of the Arica Conference, but I do explore the meaning of the convention and the implications of the conference. In theory, this assumption should mean the present work could be purely thematic and analytical, dispensing altogether with a chronological format. Tempted to adopt such a structure, I have concluded that it would be less than ideal for an audience of advanced undergraduate and graduate students, as well as for fellow academicians and other specialists who wish to familiarize themselves with the growing literature pertinent to the study of Peru's foreign policy. For this reason, I have organized the book around chronological chapters, many of which contain thematic sections relevant to the broader subject.

Working within the constraints of compressed narrative and analysis, I have occasionally fallen back upon terms of historical shorthand such as "Washington," "Lima," the "Ministry of Foreign Affairs," and so on. These should be understood as referring to the leading decisionmakers in the respective governments and not implying that those places were either individuals or monolithic structures.

In undertaking this study of Peru's foreign policy, I have tried to distill more than twenty years of observation, investigation, and reflection, which began in 1968 when I spent a year in Lima researching and writing a doctoral dissertation. My initial visit to Peru was made possible by a generous grant from the Shell Foundation, and I would again like to acknowledge its assistance and support. In the intervening years, I have been able to return to Peru on several occasions to expand my research and study. Although any observer not born into a culture may miss many of its nuances, I hope that my distance from the subject will compensate for potential distortions. As a citizen of an advanced, industrial state, I have tried to remain as objective as possible without either suspending my own moral and intellectual judgments or going to the extreme of being patronizing.

I owe special thanks to numerous Peruvian friends and acquaintances who have facilitated access to materials and information in many different ways. The staffs in the Sala de Investigaciones de la Biblioteca Nacional, the Archivo de la Cámara de Diputados, and the Archivo General del Ministerio de Relaciones Exteriores have been especially generous of their time and talent over a prolonged period. Other libraries that have been of much assistance over the years include the Biblioteca Central de la Universidad Nacional Mayor de San Marcos, the Archivo Histórico de la Biblioteca Municipalidad de Lima, and the Biblioteca del "Instituto Riva-Agüero" de la Pontificia Universidad Católica.

I would also like to acknowledge a few individuals whose inspiration, counsel, or scholarship have made important contributions to this work. They include Jorge Basadre, Fernando Belaúnde Terry, John A. Houston, Frank V. Ortiz, Terrence S. Tarr, Alberto Ulloa Sotomayor, Pedro Ugarteche, and Víctor Villanueva. In particular, I would like to thank David P. Werlich, professor of history at Southern Illinois University, for reading the entire text and offering many perceptive and helpful comments. Hélan Jaworski C., a member of the Peruvian Academy, also read parts of the text and offered guidance and encouragement over a lengthy period. During the past two decades, I have published several articles that dealt with selected aspects of the present work, and I would like to thank the editors who have allowed various earlier approximations of parts of the present material to appear under their auspices. Finally, I would like to thank my wife and two sons for the support they have given me. A work of this sort requires an enormous amount of time and energy, much of which would otherwise have been theirs. For this reason, I gratefully dedicate this volume to my wife, Carol.

Of course, none of these institutions or individuals bears any responsibility for errors of omission or inaccuracies found in the present work. I have aspired to the traditional principles of sound scholarship, which include clarity, accuracy, completeness, and adequate documentation; I ask the reader to judge it on the basis of these criteria.

—*Ronald Bruce St John*

The
Foreign Policy
of Peru

ONE

Introduction

For most of Peru's independent existence, its foreign policy has been characterized by two opposing tendencies. On the one hand, Peruvian diplomacy has been marked by a sense of solidarity with that of its sister republics in South America. Peru's participation in the 1826 Panama Conference and in the formation of the 1836 Peru-Bolivia Confederation reflected an early interest in establishing a continental or regional system of cooperation and defense capable of preserving political independence and guaranteeing the peace. At the Lima Conference in 1847–1848, delegates from Bolivia, Chile, Colombia, Ecuador, and Peru concluded agreements that called for a defensive alliance and an eventual confederation. This enthusiasm for both regional and continental cooperation and development distinguished Peru's foreign policy into the twentieth century, as evidenced by Peru's current active participation in the Organization of American States and the Andean Common Market.

On the other hand, bitter territorial disputes quickly developed between Peru and its neighbors. Often involving vast tracts of land and considerable potential wealth, many of these disputes were in reality boundary disputes that resulted from Spain's failure to delineate carefully its administrative units during the colonial era. Other irredentist issues arose from challenging the validity of treaty settlements previously ratified by the parties to a dispute. One of the most difficult of the latter was the Tacna-Arica question, which plagued Peru-Chile relations for over four decades after the end of the War of the Pacific. Emotionally charged and highly involved, territorial issues complicated and disrupted inter-American relations throughout the period under discussion. Major issues on the contemporary Peruvian foreign policy agenda still include Ecuadorian access to the Amazon River and the Bolivian quest for a sovereign outlet to the Pacific Ocean.

The traditional literature on the foreign policy of Peru has used these two opposing tendencies to divide the subject into three broad periods, with the turning points being the War of the Pacific and World War II. Although these general divisions remain useful today, a closer look suggests that the nation's foreign policy varied considerably in content, approach, and objectives within each period. For example, the period from the declaration of

1

independence in 1821 to the War of the Pacific in 1879 has customarily been described as one in which the government played a broad, active role in the continental arena. In reality, the first two decades of independence were a time of great internal strife, bordering on civil war, in which successive Peruvian caudillos struggled to determine whether Peru would remain an independent state or join some type of subregional confederation. It was only after 1845, during the Castilla administrations, that a Peruvian government first articulated foreign policy objectives at the outset of its term and then pursued them over a sustained period. This process continued to a limited degree after 1862, but the focus of diplomacy narrowed considerably in the decade preceding the War of the Pacific, when selected subregional issues were again the dominant external concerns.

Reacting to wartime losses, Peru in the aftermath of the War of the Pacific sought to regain the continental prestige it enjoyed before 1879 by concentrating on resolution of its territorial disputes. It took little interest in extracontinental affairs, where its only diplomatic relationships of continuing significance were with Great Britain and the United States. More to the point, North American trade and investment eclipsed that of Great Britain, and US interests came to play an increasingly influential socioeconomic as well as political role in Peru. Peru joined the League of Nations in 1919 and participated in several postwar continental conferences, but it took few diplomatic initiatives in these arenas or elsewhere that were not directly related to territorial questions. At the outset of World War II, most Peruvian scholars and diplomats were still emphasizing that the international expression of Peru had been fundamentally territorial in the past and would remain so in the future.

Nevertheless, with the 1942 resolution of the Ecuadorian dispute, the scope of foreign policy began to expand. Increasingly, Peru was called upon to accommodate to the conflicting demands of the inter-American system and the wider international system. This adjustment was complicated, first by the widening influence of the United States in Peru and elsewhere in and out of Latin America, and later by the growing involvement of Peru in the world beyond the inter-American system. In the postwar period, Peru participated in multilateral conferences on mineral resources and maritime fishing. Supporting regional economic integration, it joined the Latin American Free Trade Association and the subregional Andean Pact. The government also broadened its search for financial and technical assistance to include private investment sources and agencies of the United Nations and the Organization of American States. In the process, the economic and political presence and influence of the US government in Peru and throughout Latin America declined considerably. Peru expanded its political and economic relations with the Soviet Union and its Eastern European allies as well as with other socialist states, diversified its trade and armament sources, and pursued a more active role in Third World multilateral diplomacy.

The nineteenth-century and early-twentieth-century work of respected Peruvian scholars like Arturo García Salazar, Víctor M. Maúrtua, Pedro Paz Soldán y Unanue, Francisco Tudela y Varela, and Alberto Ulloa Sotomayor, largely reflected the traditional focus on inter-American relations and territorial issues. They generally approached their subjects chronologically and emphasized regional or bilateral relations as well as the boundary disputes. The literature on the foreign policy of Peru became increasingly abundant in the second half of the twentieth century, but much of it continued to be largely descriptive or polemical in approach. Often legalistic or moralistic in tone, issue-oriented monographs have suffered from being unnecessarily narrow in scope while containing little or no documentation. With a few notable exceptions, Peruvian scholars have provided little assistance or guidance in the form of policy studies on the nation's external relations. In turn, the literature by non-Peruvian scholars has made only a modest contribution to this highly unsatisfactory situation. Frequently oriented toward bilateral relations or specific policy issues, most of these studies address topics like British or French policy toward Latin American independence, US diplomatic and commercial relations with Peru, or the resolution of the Leticia dispute. As the range of Peru's foreign policy broadened in this century, especially after World War II, scholars in and out of Peru generally continued to concentrate on old concerns and issues, a focus that amplified ongoing problems of direction and balance.

In particular, recent studies have often overstated the importance of external determinants—that is, actors and forces beyond the territorial boundaries of Peru which have influenced the foreign policy process—and understated the impact of internal determinants, similar actors or forces within the nation. This tendency has been especially prevalent among Peruvian scholars but also gained some acceptance among North American and European analysts. External influences have long been important to Peru, as is true with most smaller states, because its domestic structures have proved sensitive to actions taken by outside centers of decisionmaking authority; however, in-depth analysis should not ignore or disparage the equal or greater influence of internal forces. The latter became increasingly numerous and complex as this century progressed, and played a correspondingly larger role in the determination and execution of foreign policy.

The narrow focus of traditional scholarship has also tended to cloud rather than clarify the remarkable depth and breadth of the foreign policy of Peru, especially after the War of the Pacific. Peru in the nineteenth century created a first-rate professional diplomatic service, which it has continued to expand and improve. An impressive symbol of the quality of this service was the naming in 1982 of a career Peruvian diplomat as head of the United Nations. Remarkable, albeit sometimes controversial, diplomatic achievements in the first half of the twentieth century included the Salomón-Lozano treaty (1922), the Tacna-Arica Accord (1929), and the Rio Protocol (1942). After World War II, Peru joined Chile and Ecuador in promoting national sovereignty and jurisdiction over the continental shelf and insular seas to a distance of 200 nautical miles, an innovative position that eventually gained sufficient worldwide backing to be incorporated into prevailing international law. The 1969 Andean Pact also played a pioneering role, particularly in regard to its treatment of foreign investment and regional economic and political cooperation. More recently, Peru has been an activist in the Non-Aligned Movement and hosted the Group of 77. Peru also led the reincorporation of Cuba into the regional diplomatic arena through early reestablishment of diplomatic relations; frustrated a Bolivia-Chile agreement on territorial access to the sea; and made a credible, if eventually unsuccessful, effort to prevent the Malvinas/Falklands War. These are impressive diplomatic credentials for a small- to medium-sized power with limited political and economic resources.

Given the above state of affairs, the author has pursued what many readers will consider to be a revisionist approach to the study of the foreign policy of Peru. Government interactions with a variety of nongovernmental bodies have become increasingly important in the twentieth century; therefore, the subject of foreign policy can no longer be confined to the study of intergovernmental relations. A thorough study of Peru's foreign policy now necessitates the analysis and assessment of the total range of internal and external forces that have influenced its scope and direction. Although this approach does not exclude boundary disputes and bilateral relations, it also embraces the impact of foreign capital and multinational companies as well as the effects of domestic entrepreneurs, political parties, and labor movements. As a result, the ensuing study analyzes both the internal and external determinants of Peru's foreign policy, the substantive content of individual foreign policies, and the subsequent consequences of foreign policy behavior.

In particular, the author has tried to assess the overlap or linkage that has often occurred between foreign and domestic determinants when the two types of variables combined to influence foreign policy. He has also endeavored to place Peru's foreign policy in the context of events in the outside world, especially its relationship to United States foreign and domestic policy. This has seldom been done, but it is an essential aspect of a deeper understanding of Peruvian external affairs. It is also important to recognize fully the freedom of choice open to Peruvian decisionmakers on specific foreign policy issues. The failure to do so has produced distorted analyses that overemphasize the limited policy alternatives faced by Peruvians rather than recognize and explore the wider options actually available. In particular, the occasional claim that the Peruvian ruling class was often only a shadow of the US government and North American investors seems exaggerated; there is little convincing evidence to suggest that external powers or forces dictated major policy decisions for any appreciable period. Generally, these assertions appear to be mostly an attempt to lighten whatever responsibility the native ruling class may have had for the country's present state of affairs.

From the opposite angle, foreign policy has occasionally been used by Peruvian decisionmakers to advance domestic political goals. In common with decisionmakers in most small states, Peruvian decisionmakers have generally viewed domestic well-being as the central policy issue, and thus attempts to influence external events have often been shaped by concerns with domestic problems and internal tensions. Lacking popular support, opportunistic politicians have emphasized foreign policy issues to direct attention away from domestic political crises. Political advantage has also been sought and gained by both government and opposition leaders who underscored issues like the territorial disputes, external intervention, or imperialism by foreign entrepreneurs. The nationalization or expropriation of foreign enterprises has also been designed not only to further domestic economic development but to gain popular political support. Because of Peru's limited resources, questions of internal economic growth and development have long had far more salience for Peruvians than the latest round in the cold war. Finally, Peru's foreign policy has been intimately connected with domestic policy and the ideologies, explicit or implicit, that determined internal policy.

International economics and national economic development have often represented the clearest nexus between the foreign and domestic policies of Peru. For that reason, the author has spent a considerable amount of time and effort analyzing the development of Peruvian financial and economic policies since independence. As will become clear, domestic and international economic and financial policies have often played a central role in the formulation and execution of foreign policy. As is the case in any state, the successful pursuit of Peru's policy objectives, either foreign or domestic, has often been the consequence of the more or less efficient utilization of the state's productive economic resources. The crucial importance of this variable is only now being acknowledged by many scholars who devote themselves to Peruvian matters.

The overriding theme of the following chapters is the degree to which the conflicting demands of independence and interdependence, as determined by this constellation of internal and external forces, have determined the content and direction of the foreign policy of Peru since 1824. Systematic analysis will reveal the full extent to which it has been distinguished by a strong linkage between external and internal concerns, with both domestic objectives and domestic political considerations strongly influencing, if not actually dictating, many aspects of the nation's international posture. Because violence is integral to the Peruvian political system, internal conflict in particular has frequently disrupted external policy; the latter is often mainly a reflection of the former. In addition, such other factors as the geographical size and location of Peru, the export-led nature of its economy, and the socioeconomic and political relationships that developed with regional and extraregional powers have also strongly influenced its foreign affairs.

TWO

Setting the Stage, 1821–1827

Peru and Upper Peru (Bolivia) were the last kingdoms of the Spanish empire in continental South America to gain their independence. Although some Peruvians had begun to drift toward political dissent as early as 1808–1810, the majority supported the viceregal government over the next decade. Prisoners of their own society, politically active Peruvians were reluctant to find in independence the answer to their complaints. They sought reform as opposed to a violent break from Spain. This duality of response, unrelenting complaints of Spanish tyranny combined with loyalty in the face of extreme crisis, which surfaced in the preindependence era, intensified during the struggle for independence. In September 1821, June 1823, and March 1824, for example, royalist armies drew near or actually occupied Lima and Callao. In each instance, prominent *limeños* deserted the independence movement and sought the protection of the crown. One result of the prevailing ambivalence was that the military phase of the Peruvian war of independence did not commence until 1820, a decade after the outbreak of armed insurrection throughout most of Latin America. Royalist forces were not permanently expelled from the country until late 1824, three years after the rest of the region.

The political, social, and economic legacies of the colonial era had a deleterious impact on early Peruvian attempts to develop, articulate, and pursue a coherent foreign policy. The independence movement lacked a clear ideology because its leadership was divided into liberal and conservative camps. Widespread differences separated these competing ideologies, with a central concern being the appropriate form of government for an independent Peru. Limited national integration and low levels of sociopolitical consensus combined with an emerging nationalism to retard further the development of a broad-based external view. In this milieu, the conflicting ideals and interests of Pan-Americanism and regionalism combined to split the nation in the early years of independence. A multitude of boundary issues inherited from the colonial era also complicated early foreign policy. For decades, these intractable disputes fostered both bilateral and multilateral disputes with Andean neighbors. Moreover, the ideological and commercial interests of the great powers, particularly Great Britain and the United States, further complicated the foreign policy concerns of the new republic. In short, although Peru was eventually successful in winning its independence from Spain, it inherited a multitude of complex, convoluted issues, forces, and movements that had a major impact on its foreign policy for decades to come.[1]

FOREIGN POLICY OF THE PROTECTORATE

The Chilean expedition of José de San Martín landed on the Peruvian coast at Pisco on September 8, 1820, but San Martín did not enter Lima until July 9, 1821. He declared Peru independent on July 28, 1821; and on August 3, he was declared protector of Peru with supreme civil and military powers. He appointed Juan García del Río as the first minister of foreign affairs of Peru, Bernardo Monteagudo as the minister of war and marine, and Hipólito Unánue as the minister of finance. San Martín's proclamation of independence was more a hope for the future than a statement of fact. While a powerful Spanish army still controlled the highlands of Peru, the possession of the Peruvian capital alone hardly made the nation free. Therefore, it could be argued that Peru had no foreign policy at this point because it did not exist as a state. On the other hand, the period of the protectorate was of decisive importance to the future foreign policy of the republic. Forces developed, opinions crystallized, and policies were articulated that were of considerable long-term significance to the external relations of Peru.[2]

San Martín believed Peru needed an ordered, hierarchical society presided over by a monarch. A few weeks before the proclamation of independence, he offered Spanish General José de la Serna the opportunity to organize a regency to be followed by the solicitation of a Spanish prince. San Martín's enthusiasm for a monarchical solution was not diminished by La Serna's response that he was not authorized to accept such a plan. At the end of 1821, San Martín sent Minister of Foreign Affairs García del Río and English entrepreneur and Surgeon General of the Army of the Liberation James Paroissien to Europe to secure European recognition of Peruvian independence, negotiate a loan, and offer the projected throne of Peru to a European prince. San Martín's monarchical plans were eventually defeated by the constituent congress he convened on September 20, 1822. The congress withdrew official support for the García del Río mission after resolving that its powers and instructions were opposed to the public will and detrimental to the true interests of the country.[3]

On July 14, 1822, San Martín embarked at Callao to travel to Ecuador for a fateful conference with Simón Bolívar. The meetings that took place in Guayaquil on July 26–27, 1822, have been amply described elsewhere and will not be detailed here. The first subject covered was the interest of the governments of both Peru and Colombia in Guayaquil. After San Martín recognized the status quo established by Bolívar, the former outlined his plans for the next campaign and requested Colombian troops to help liberate Peru. Bolívar responded with the offer of a Colombian division, a force San Martín felt was totally inadequate. San Martín also reiterated his belief that only a European prince could solve Peru's political problems. Bolívar was totally opposed to San Martín's monarchical designs and emphasized that he would not tolerate a monarchy in Colombia or elsewhere in South America.[4]

When San Martín returned to Lima, he found his protégé Bernardo Monteagudo had been overthrown and deported. The shortcomings of the San Martín administration in both the economic and political spheres had created a flood of resentment among Peruvians. Monteagudo in particular was strongly criticized for his persecution of the Spaniards, open advocacy of a monarchy, social Jacobinism, and because he was Argentinian and thus an outsider. Other factors, including a clash of personalities with Bolívar, impacted on San Martín's decision to withdraw. On the day he returned his powers to the congress, San Martín told his friend and adviser, Tomás Guido, that he and Bolívar did not fit together in Peru. Equally important, the two men were separated by fundamental policy differences like the disagreement occasioned by San Martín's monarchical persuasions. In addition, San Martín hoped that present-day Ecuador would be joined to Peru; Bolívar saw Ecuador, New Granada, and Venezuela as integral parts of Gran Colombia. On September 21, 1822, the day after the opening of the first Peruvian congress, the protector boarded a ship and sailed for Chile. He lived his last years in France, where he died in 1850.[5]

As San Martín had soon learned, the Peruvian independence movement lacked a clear ideology. For the first fifty years of national life, Peruvians were generally split into two ideological camps, liberal and conservative. The liberals, more accurately labeled romantic liberals, expressed faith in the people's ability to govern themselves and rejected any notion of the divine right of kings. Confident in the future, the liberals firmly believed in the value of education and defended civil rights. They also favored local autonomy, civilian rule, legislative supremacy, and limited central government. Peruvian liberals looked to the United States as a model for republican government. The conservatives, on the other hand, were essentially reactionary authoritarians. With little faith in the present and a fear of the future, they looked backward to better days. Rejecting the idea of popular sovereignty and opposed to an extension of suffrage, they preferred executive supremacy and a powerful central government. Although related issues like the preeminence of church or state and the impact of Peru's precolonial and colonial heritages were also important, the most appropriate form of government remained the central issue of the ensuing debate. It was also the ideological issue of most importance to Peruvian foreign policy because it encompassed first the monarchy-versus-republic split and then the issue of centralism versus federalism.[6]

BOUNDARY ISSUES

In 1821 the exact borders of the newly proclaimed republic were a subject of
great dispute. The Spanish government had made little effort to delimit
carefully the boundaries of its possessions because most of the boundaries lay
in remote and sparsely inhabited areas that were of minimal importance to the
crown. With the establishment of independent republics, boundary issues
assumed new importance because there were now questions of territorial
possession such as did not exist when the entire area belonged to Spain. On
July 6, 1822, Bernardo Monteagudo and the Colombian ambassador to Peru,
Joaquín Mosquera, negotiated a confederation and called for a precise
demarcation of limits at an unspecified later date. An article in the 1823
constitution also called for the Peruvian congress to fix the boundaries of the
republic, and on February 17, 1825, Foreign Minister José Faustino Sánchez
Carrión again asked the congress to resolve the nation's borders. In the face
of such appeals, congress appointed a boundary commission, but the
uncertainty of the times made any real progress impossible. The delimitation
of the nation's boundaries remained a significant foreign policy issue for the
next 120 years.[7]

During the struggle for independence, the Peruvian government joined
other Latin American states in accepting the doctrine of *uti possidetis* as the
principal method to establish the boundaries of the newly independent states.
Uti possidetis was generally understood to say that each new state was
entitled to the territory formerly under the jurisdiction of the colonial
administrative area from which it was formed. In the case of Peru, this meant
the limits of the new republic would be defined by the jurisdiction of the
Viceroyalty of Peru, the Audiencia of Lima, and the Audiencia of Cuzco. The
doctrine of *uti possidetis* was of questionable validity under nineteenth-
century international law, and it proved extremely difficult to apply in
practice. The language employed by the Spanish crown to make territorial
changes often lacked clarity. As a result, confusing and sometimes
contradictory legal bases were often the only foundation for significant
reforms of the Spanish colonial system.[8]

Ostensibly bilateral issues, boundary disputes quickly assumed
multilateral dimensions as Peru and its neighbors formed alliances to achieve
their foreign policy objectives. In the north, separate disputes over
ownership of the Amazon Basin involved Peru and Ecuador, Peru and
Colombia, and Colombia and Ecuador. Toward the end of the nineteenth
century, the Chilean government further complicated matters by encouraging
the Amazonian claims of Colombia and Ecuador in an effort to distract Peru
from the Tacna-Arica question. In the south, the relations of Peru, Chile, and
Bolivia were closely intertwined, especially after the conclusion of the 1883
Treaty of Ancón. The question of Tacna-Arica was intimately bound to
Bolivia's search for a Pacific port, and one of the real mysteries of the dispute

was how repeated attempts to resolve the issue could ignore this essential component.

PAN-AMERICANISM VERSUS REGIONALISM

The spring of 1824 marked the nadir of the independence movement in Peru. The royalists held Lima from February to December with only occasional retreats into Callao, which remained in their hands without interruption until January 1826. In fact, the royalists came very close to smashing the independence armies and winning the war. Only the leadership of Bolívar halted the deterioration and reorganized the patriots into an effective fighting force. Headquartered in Trujillo, he watched helplessly as royalist forces occupied most of the rest of the country. At one point, Bolívar actually controlled only Trujillo, but it was the area best suited to his purpose, which was to keep his army intact until reinforcements arrived from Gran Colombia. To achieve that result, he stationed his Peruvian troops in the north and his Colombian troops in the south. This position kept the Peruvians from deserting to the enemy and the Colombians from returning home.

On December 21, 1824, Bolívar called for a reinstallation of the Peruvian congress. Assembling after the decisive patriot victory at Ayacucho, the congress voted Bolívar a gratuity of one million pesos as well as appropriating another million in veterans' benefits. A congressional committee also drew up a policy statement on territorial limits that set no boundaries but recognized that General Antonio José de Sucre's recent advance into Upper Peru had again raised the territorial issue. The congress dismissed as royalist maneuvers the petitions pending for annexation with Upper Peru, and it resolved to charge the latter for the cost of the revolutionary expedition force that eventually confirmed Bolivian independence in April 1825. After approving a variety of other measures, the congress suspended its sessions for a year, which left Bolívar free to organize and govern the devastated country.[9]

In the coming year, Bolívar devoted most of his time and attention to Upper Peru. Both Argentina and Peru claimed the territory, and each side had its own supporters in Bolivia. Other Bolivians hoped to create an independent state, and it was this group that Bolívar encouraged. The liberator feared the presence of a strong, unified state to the south of his confederation of Gran Colombia but desired a buffer between Argentina and Peru. He also dreamed of fashioning a federation of the Andes comprising Gran Colombia, Peru, and Bolivia. The projected general federation called for the division of Gran Colombia and the maintenance of Peru and Bolivia as separate states to ensure the balance required for harmonious federation.[10]

Bolívar's grand design generated considerable opposition in Peru. Some

Peruvians did not want an independent Bolivia while others were opposed to his plan for an Andean federation, especially if Bolívar dominated the union. Nationalists resented his tendency to surround himself with foreign advisers as well as the continuing presence of thousands of Colombian soldiers in Peru. Peruvian military leaders resented the preference he gave to foreign officers. Nationalist elements feared a federation as large as the one Bolívar advocated would result in permanent Colombian hegemony enforced by the presence of a strong Colombian army in Peru and Bolivia. Liberals enamored with democratic institutions disliked his authoritarian rule. Outside Peru, the governments of Argentina, Chile, and the United States were all openly hostile to the idea of a strong, united Andean America. At the end of 1826, the Peruvian congress, after heated debate, adopted Bolívar's life-term constitution and elected him president. His tenure ended before it began. When a serious quarrel broke out between his lieutenants in Gran Colombia, Bolívar turned over his executive powers to a council of government headed by General Andrés Santa Cruz. On September 3, 1826, he departed for Guayaquil, never to return to Peru.[11]

Simón Bolívar was the leading contemporary spokesman for Pan-Americanism, or permanent cooperation among the American states, and he worked hard to implement his dream. As early as 1815, he articulated the idea of a formal union of American states that would consist of a triple federation of Mexico and Central America, the Spanish states of northern South America, and those of southern South America. On July 6, 1822, the governments of Peru and Gran Colombia concluded a treaty calling for a congress of American states in Panama; and on December 7, 1824, Bolívar extended a formal invitation to the governments of Brazil, Central America, Chile, Gran Colombia, Mexico, Peru, and the United Provinces of Buenos Aires. The primary objective of the conference was to form a federation that would reduce discord among the member states, defend the independence of Latin America, and counteract the influence of the Holy Alliance. Bolívar planned to become president of the federation organized by the Panama congress.[12]

The Peruvian delegates to the Panama congress were José María de Pando and Manuel Lorenzo de Vidaurre. Pando was born in Lima but educated in Spain, where he remained until 1824. Soon after his arrival in Panama, Pando was appointed foreign minister of Peru and replaced by Manuel Pérez de Tudela, who, like Vidaurre, had held high judicial positions in the independent government of Peru. The delegation's first set of instructions called for a compact of union, league, and confederation against Spain as well as other foreign rulers. They also urged the conclusion of treaties of commerce, navigation, and friendship, and the determination of the territorial limits of the new states. These instructions were modified in February 1826, when the delegation was told, among other things, that the Peru-Colombia border would be determined at a later date. The Panama congress opened on

June 22, 1826, with official delegations from Peru, Mexico, Colombia, and Central America in attendance. Great Britain sent an observer and the Netherlands an unofficial representative. The United States sent two delegates, but both arrived after the sessions closed on July 15. Four conventions were concluded at Panama, the central one being a treaty of perpetual union, league, and confederation. Of the republics represented, Colombia was the only one to ratify the conventions, and its ratification did not occur until the middle of 1827. The failure of Peru to ratify was not surprising because opposition to Bolívar's political plans was growing as Peruvians increasingly focused on domestic as opposed to international concerns.[13]

Although the Panama congress failed to achieve its objectives, it was important because it marked the formal beginning of the movement for inter-American cooperation. In this sense, it was significant that Peru participated in the conference and supported the general direction of the negotiations. At the same time, Peruvian diplomacy at Panama displayed a bifurcation of interests and concerns that characterized its subsequent policy toward inter-American cooperation. On the one hand, Peru's foreign relations with its sister republics were characterized by a feeling of kindred spirit and solidarity if not interest in formal union. On the other hand, increasingly bitter rivalries with its neighbors over territorial claims and boundaries worked against this centripetal tendency toward unity.

Regionalism was the opposing tendency to Pan-Americanism, and it also influenced early Peruvian foreign policy. In colonial Latin America, nature reinforced the divisions imposed by the conquerors, for the region was in reality a conglomeration of demicountries. There is as much difference between the coastal, sierra, and Amazonian areas of Peru as there is between the pampas of Argentina and the altiplano of Upper Peru. Regionalism, often more a vague feeling of unrest and dissatisfaction than a movement or program, promoted disintegration rather than union and helped to stifle both national and hemispheric unity and to promote particularism. Like Bolivia and Ecuador, Peru was split internally by a sierra-coast division and a north-south rift that pitted Lima against Cuzco, Puno, and Arequipa. The richest and most powerful members of the creole elite lived in Lima; provincial creoles were concentrated in Cuzco, Arequipa, and a few other centers like Tarma and Trujillo. The pride, status, and, probably, wealth of the provincial creoles approached that of the Lima elite, but their political power never equaled their economic and social position. As a result, these provincials understandably resented the domination of Lima. During the struggle for independence, their resentment was often directed as much at Lima as at Spain. In this context, the independence struggle was in part a struggle of the provinces and middle sectors against the capital and elite.[14]

Regionalism as a political movement also contained the seeds of international conflict. Opposition in Peru to the Peru-Bolivia Confederation

(1836–1839), proposed by Santa Cruz, was based in large part on regional considerations. Lima and northern Peru feared they might lose their hegemony over the nation; the mining-bureaucratic oligarchy of Chuquisaca and southern Bolivia feared they might lose their leadership over Bolivia. On the other hand, Peruvians in Arequipa and the southern highlands were much attracted to the sort of decentralized confederation that Santa Cruz had in mind. In Bolivia, Santa Cruz received his greatest support from La Paz. Through confederation, the commercially minded *paceños* would achieve unencumbered access to the Peruvian port of Arica. For similar reasons, Bolivians in the Tarija and Santa Cruz regions opposed the plan because they feared it would focus commercial interest exclusively on Pacific ports and thus impede trade with Argentina and Brazil.

NASCENT PERUVIAN NATIONALISM

The low level of Peruvian nationalism in the 1820s further complicated the often contradictory impact of the opposing movements of Pan-Americanism and regionalism. Peru experienced a number of preindependence revolts, beginning with the 1780 rebellion of Túpac Amaru and culminating in the 1814–1815 rebellion in Cuzco. Collectively, such revolts strongly suggested that a very low level of national identity, defined as a collective identification by a particular and autonomous group, existed in Peru at independence. Compared to Europe, where the concept of nation had long focused on frontiers encompassing the same language and culture, Peruvian boundaries were not fixed for over 100 years after independence. Furthermore, at least three languages were spoken by the Peruvian people, and Peruvian culture was far from homogeneous. Independence provided no immediate answers to this perplexing question of exactly what constituted Peru. On the contrary, it simply accented Peru's social, economic, and political disorganization and reinforced its asymmetrical articulation.[15]

The search for a sense of national identity preoccupied Peruvians for the remainder of the nineteenth century. To a very real extent, Peruvian history became a story of culturally disparate communities struggling to overcome the liabilities of different pasts as they searched for a common future. Not only was Peru split socially and ethnically among proprietors (whites and mestizos), Indian campesinos, and negro slaves but the various mobilizations against neighboring countries and rival caudillos were not seen by all participants as mobilizations against collective threats. Consequently, the dominant groups within regional power blocs found it very difficult to create identities and symbols that integrated the population.[16]

Early expressions of Peruvian nationalism, considered to be a state of mind in which the supreme loyalty of the individual is due the nation-state, probably antedated independence; however, these sentiments were confined to individuals. There was nothing to suggest that the Peruvian masses in 1821 felt their lives, culturally, politically, or economically, depended on the fate of the national body. In fact, Peruvian nationalism probably first expressed itself not against Spaniards but against fellow Americans. After Bolívar had liberated Ecuador, he was eager to pursue the enemy in the south and offered aid to Peruvian leaders. His offer was initially rejected, and he was later denigrated by the Lima press. Nascent Peruvian nationalism also accounted for much of the later opposition to the dictatorship and the life-term constitution of Bolívar. Although the Peruvian nation remained more a hope than a reality, Peruvian nationalists resented the presence of Colombian troops, loyal to Bolívar, whom they saw as a potential threat to Peru. The former colonial aristocracy, expecting to lead and govern the new nation, felt slighted when Colombian friends and advisers of the liberator were put in positions of trust and power. Similarly, such nationalists viewed the proposed federation of the Andes as little more than a legal maneuver designed to perpetuate Colombian hegemony over Peru. In this context, Peruvian nationalism was forged neither by the colonial conflict against Spanish rule nor by the creation of a nation-state by the dominant class. Instead, it emerged in the postindependence period largely as a product of regional conflicts between the new republics that replaced the Spanish American empire.[17]

SOCIAL AND ECONOMIC
CONTINUITY AT INDEPENDENCE

The revolutions that brought independence to Latin America were unlike the classic revolutions of Europe and Asia in that their primary effect was to throw off the yoke of a transatlantic empire rather than to bring about a drastic reconstruction of society. In the specific case of Peru, political independence from Spain left intact the fundamental elements of Peruvian society that had developed and crystallized during more than 300 years of colonial rule. The social structure of Peru at the conclusion of Bolívar's government in 1826 was not fundamentally different from what it had been before the independence era, and its colonial character remained intact well into the nineteenth century.[18]

During the colonial era, the patrimonial government of the Spanish crown had encouraged compartmentalization of colonial society into semiautonomous units. All of these social and economic units were related to the crown, and few lateral relationships developed among them that were not mediated through the imperial apparatus. The role of the representatives of the crown was to arbitrate the conflicts that arose among commercial units, landowners, indigenous communities, and towns. Independence eliminated the minimum of power and authority that had maintained the system but failed to replace it with viable state institutions. Consequently, power and authority tended to fragment and revert to various semiautonomous social, economic, or political units like cities and provinces, extended family groups, and armed bands. In this sense, it was not Peru that gained independence but, rather, a variety of Peruvian communities and personalities. After independence, these local groups formed their own armed units, whose members cohered on the basis of personal loyalties, immediate interests, or regional associations. Such loyalties and interests were usually not complicated by clearly defined political positions or ideological tenets. In part for these reasons, the prevailing social structure made it extremely difficult for the central government to articulate and pursue a viable, coherent foreign policy.[19]

The political institutions adopted at independence also had a negative impact on early external relations. Peru adopted a democratic form of government in the middle 1820s, but from a social point of view, it was incapable of being a democracy because the Spanish colonial system had not prepared the population to function within the legal boundaries of a democratic republic. The composition of Peruvian society thus contributed directly to the political turmoil that debilitated Peru until 1845 and had a damaging impact on the nation's early foreign policy. Constitutional assemblies drafted ten national charters between 1823 and 1860, but none of them was able to withstand the harsh reality of an authoritarian society of unequals.

The state of the Peruvian economy also impacted negatively on the early foreign policy of the Peruvian republic. From the beginning, the San Martín government depended on contributions, forced or voluntary, for half its income. Forced contributions, the bulk of which came from merchants, Spaniards, and other foreigners, constituted most of this revenue. In 1822, for example, a group of English merchants was forced to make a loan of 73,000 pesos, payable, but without interest, on the receipt of customs revenues. The policy of forced contributions was counterproductive because the bitterness it raised was politically damaging to the independence cause. Chronically short of cash, a *junta gubernativa* named in 1822 continued the practice of extorting contributions from local merchants. Afraid the imposition of a heavy tax burden would cause the citizens of Peru to revolt, the new government tried to pass as much as possible of the tax load to foreigners.[20]

The Peruvian government also endeavored, with some success, to raise money abroad. By 1825 its principal external creditors were England, Chile, and Colombia. The English debt was based on loans issued in 1822, 1824, and 1825; when the Peruvian government defaulted in October 1825, the debt was estimated to be five times the government's annual income. No money was paid on these loans until 1849, when the Peruvian government settled with British bondholders. The debt to Colombia, later recognized in an 1829 treaty, was estimated to be 5 million pesos plus the million pesos voted to Bolívar by the 1825 congress. The debt to Chile, consisting of a loan covered by an 1823 treaty together with interest, approached 3 million pesos. On the positive side of the ledger, the Peruvian government claimed a debt from Bolivia of over 700,000 pesos for its contribution to Bolivian independence. The early financial history of Peru revolved around a series of escalating foreign loans to fund these wartime debts, a process that culminated in bankruptcy in the 1870s. It proved ironic that a revolutionary war fought in the 1820s to win independence from Spain initiated a financial dependence on Europe that escalated disastrously over the next fifty years.[21]

By the time Bolívar departed in 1826, the Peruvian economy, like the economies of most of the rest of Latin America, was prostrate. Wartime purchases of munitions, naval stores, and food had drained the country of its currency and saddled it with large commercial and governmental debts. A scarcity of capital affected all sectors of the economy, and capital accumulation was hampered by the importation of cheap industrial goods, primarily from Great Britain. In addition, the policy of forced contributions, the default in 1825, and the ongoing political turmoil after independence combined to discourage foreign investment. The long war of independence had severely dislocated Peruvian trade; and in the process, Peru lost many of its old markets to British, French, and North American merchants. Economic instability and poor planning continued throughout most of the nineteenth century, as evidenced by the fact that there were no federal budgets in the years 1821–1845, 1855–1860, 1865–1868, 1881–1886, and 1896.[22]

IMPACT OF THE GREAT POWERS

Externally, early Peruvian economic policy focused on Great Britain and the United States; the central issues were investment and trade. From the colonial period onward, the interests of both states in Latin America in general and Peru in particular had been fundamentally commercial. Engaged in a prolonged struggle with Napoleon, Great Britain had looked with disfavor upon colonial disturbances that might weaken its Spanish ally. At the same time, British policy indirectly promoted the interests of the insurgents as it urged the Spanish government to maintain its focus on the Napoleonic struggle by resolving the colonial issue through political concessions. Great Britain also told the Spanish government that opening Latin American markets to British merchants was essential to effective British cooperation in driving the French out of the Spanish peninsula. With the defeat of Napoleon, the British government adopted a neutral policy toward the Latin American revolutions. At the same time, it insisted on the continuation of trade with the region and pressed for more autonomy for the colonists and freer access to their markets.[23]

In 1810 the growing interests of the United States in Latin America led to the appointment of three resident agents for commerce and seamen (to Argentina, Chile, and Peru), one of whom was Joel Roberts Poinsett. The agents were instructed that their first duty was to foster the commercial interests of the United States in the region. US representation in Peru was upgraded in July 1817 when John B. Prevost was appointed special agent to Peru and Chile, and Jeremy Robinson was appointed commercial agent to Peru. Robinson resided in Lima and drew his salary from the consular fees he received from US ships visiting Peruvian ports. Peru's struggle for independence opened new opportunities for profit, and small colonies of foreign businessmen and entrepreneurs began appearing after 1822. This led to the appointment of foreign consuls, including William Tudor, representing the US government. In the spring of 1824 Tudor reached Lima, where he became the first commercial representative of a foreign power to be recognized by Peru. The US government granted diplomatic recognition to Peru in 1826, although the Peruvian government did not appoint its first minister plenipotentiary to Washington for another twenty years.[24]

From 1821 to 1826, rivalry in Peru between the United States and Great Britain was minimal and largely focused on opposing political systems. Great Britain was partial to conservative monarchies and desired to bring Europe and the Americas into a common sphere of political action. The United States favored democratic republics and a clear separation of Europe and the Americas. While the English were partial to Bolívar, the agents of the United States advocated a democratic system more open than the liberator was likely to establish. William Tudor, in particular, aggressively advocated republicanism and independence. He encouraged Peruvian leaders to appeal to the United States for support against the consolidating ambitions of Bolívar, and he may even have helped them draft a federal constitution. At the same time, both governments respected the principle of nonintervention, and neither pursued an active campaign on behalf of its own political system.

END OF THE BOLIVARIAN REGIME

When Bolívar returned to Colombia in September 1826, he installed General Andrés Santa Cruz, his former chief of staff, as president of the council of government and commander of the armed forces. In that position, Santa Cruz made no attempt to suppress the opposition to the liberator that had surfaced upon his departure. When the Colombian troops stationed in Lima revolted, in January 1827, the council of government abolished Bolívar's lifelong constitution, and in March 1827 the Colombian troops were sent home. Santa Cruz favored some kind of union between Peru and Bolivia. As early as August 27, 1825, he had indicated in a letter to a friend that he believed Charcas should not separate from Peru. He lamented the fact that the delegates who assembled in Sucre in 1825 to decide the fate of the Upper

Peruvian provinces would almost surely choose independence. A year later, in October 1826, he wrote a friend in Chuquisaca that his satisfaction would be complete if he could see the reunification of Peru and Bolivia because the two regions should never have been separated in the first place. Many opposed the Santa Cruz plan for a federation of Peru and Bolivia, but there was also widespread unionist support based on geographical, ethnic, historical, and economic precedents.[25]

In June 1826 the Peruvian government had appointed Ignacio Ortiz de Zevallos its diplomatic representative to Bolivia and instructed him to seek the reunification of the two states. In an apparent rejection of Bolívar's plan for a federation of the Andes, the Peruvian government pressed first for a merger of the two republics. Failing this, federation was seen as preferable to continued separation. Eager to promote its plan, the Peruvian government declared its willingness to accept the removal of the capital of a united Peru-Bolivia from Lima to another site if the Bolivians insisted. It also indicated that, if necessary, it would consider ceding Bolivia the ports and territories of Arica and Iquique. At the same time, the Peruvian government again pressed Bolivia for partial payment of its war debts.[26]

On November 15, 1826, Ortiz de Zevallos concluded treaties of federation and limits with Bolivia. The first treaty established a league entitled the Federación Boliviana, with Simón Bolívar as life-term president. Once the treaty was ratified, the new federal government was to send ministers to Bogotá to negotiate Colombian adherence to the pact. In the treaty of limits, Peru ceded Tacna, Arica, and Tarapacá to Bolivia in exchange for the territories of Copacabana on Lake Titicaca and Apolobamba in the northern part of the Department of La Paz. Bolivia also agreed to assume 5 million pesos of its debt to Peru, with the understanding that both governments would renounce the right to seek further indemnities. The Bolivian congress approved the two treaties with the stipulation that Colombia become part of the federation. The Peruvian council of government, on the other hand, rejected both treaties outright, denying Santa Cruz's suggestion that they be submitted to the congress. Santa Cruz himself opposed the treaties on the grounds they were vague, subordinated Peru to Colombia, involved inequitable cessions, and dismembered the national territory.[27]

In January 1827 Santa Cruz called a constituent convention to meet on May 1, 1827, to draw up a new constitution and to choose a successor to Bolívar. Santa Cruz hoped this body would express its gratitude by confirming him in the presidency, but the convention instead elected José de la Mar y Cortazar. Even though La Mar was highly regarded by Bolívar, his election marked the end of the Bolivarian regime in Peru. Santa Cruz was an authoritarian capable of imposing order, and he later put his talents at the service of Bolivia. In contrast, La Mar was a weak chief executive, dominated by a liberal majority in the congress, whose tenure served only to encourage regional chieftains with presidential ambitions. In this sense, the election of

La Mar, or perhaps more accurately the failure to elect Santa Cruz, further set the stage for the era of the caudillos in Peru. As soon as possible, General La Mar removed his rival by naming Santa Cruz Peruvian minister to Chile.

By the time La Mar was installed, the goals, capabilities, options, and constraints of Peruvian foreign policy were beginning to clarify. As with most of the South American states, the exact locations of Peruvian boundaries were in dispute and would remain so into the next century. Territorial questions were complicated by the commercial advantages at stake as the Pacific coast nations quarreled over trade routes and seaports. Ideological differences intensified such conflicts, as did the concern for regional hegemony. The Peruvian government shared with its neighbors a profound awareness of their interlocking interests, and bilateral disputes quickly assumed multilateral dimensions as states shifted alliances in search of relative advantages. In short, political independence had been won from Spain, but successive Peruvian governments would find that old and new socioeconomic and political forces continued to constrain their freedom of action. In the prevailing milieu, domestic and regional influences predominated over extracontinental concerns in the formulation of Peruvian foreign policy.

NOTES

1. Timothy E. Anna, *The Fall of the Royal Government in Peru* (Lincoln: University of Nebraska Press, 1979), pp. 42–55; Jorge Basadre, *Historia de la república del Perú, 1822–1933*, 6th ed., 16 vols. (Lima: Editorial Universitaria, 1968), 1:257–270; John Fisher, "Royalism, Regionalism, and Rebellion in Colonial Peru, 1808–1915," *Hispanic American Historical Review* 59, 2 (May 1979): 232–257.

2. Carlos Vazquez Ayllon, "Política exterior del Perú," *Revista de política internacional* 158 (1978): 23.

3. Daniel Michael Gleason, "Ideological Cleavages in Early Republican Peru, 1821–1872" (Ph.D. diss., University of Notre Dame, 1974), p. 14; Francisco Javier de Luna Pizarro, *Escritos Políticos* (Lima: Universidad Nacional Mayor de San Marcos, 1959), pp. 22–25.

4. Vicente Lecuna, "Bolívar and San Martín at Guayaquil," *Hispanic American Historical Review* 31, 3 (August 1951): 371–393; Gerhard Masur, "The Conference of Guayaquil," *Hispanic American Historical Review* 31, 2 (May 1951): 189–229.

5. Jorge Pérez Concha, *Ensayo histórico-crítico de las relaciones diplomáticos del Ecuador con los estados limítrofes*, 2d ed., 3 vols. (Quito: Editorial Casa de la Cultura Ecuatoriana, 1961), 1:48–57; Gerhard Masur, *Simon Bolívar* (Albuquerque: University of New Mexico Press, 1948), pp. 483–485.

6. Víctor Andrés Belaúnde, *Bolívar and the Political Thought of the Spanish American Revolution* (Baltimore: Johns Hopkins University Press, 1938), pp. 201–210; Fredrick B. Pike, "Heresy, Real and Alleged in Peru: An Aspect of the Conservative-Liberal Struggle, 1830–1875," *Hispanic American*

Historical Review 47, 1 (February 1967): 50–74.

7. Alberto Wagner de Reyna, *Los límites del Perú*, 2d ed. (Lima: Ediciones del Sol, 1962), p. 16; Carlos García Bedoya, *Política exterior peruana: Teoría y práctica* (Lima: Mosca Azul Editores, 1981), pp. 50–51.

8. Alberto Wagner de Reyna, *Historia diplomática del Perú, 1900–1945*, 2 vols. (Lima: Ediciones Peruanas, 1964), 1:10–11; B. Checa Drouet, *La Doctrina Americana del Uti Possidetis de 1810* (Lima: Librería e Imprenta Gil, 1936), pp. 137–138.

9. Fredrick B. Pike, *The Modern History of Peru* (New York: Frederick A. Praeger, 1967), p. 61.

10. Augusto Guzmán, *Historia de Bolivia*, 3d ed. (La Paz: Editorial "Los Amigos del Libro," 1976), pp. 142–144; Phillip Taylor Parkerson, "Sub-Regional Integration in Nineteenth Century South America: Andres Santa Cruz and the Peru-Bolivia Confederation, 1835–1839" (Ph.D. diss., University of Florida, 1979), pp. 23–24.

11. Jorge Basadre, *Chile, Perú y Bolivia independientes* (Barcelona: Salvat Editores, 1948), pp. 295–297, 303.

12. J. M. Yepes, *Del congreso de Panamá a la conferencia de Caracas, 1826–1954*, 2 vols. (Caracas: CROMOTIP, 1955), 1:42–52; Oscar Barrenechea y Raygada, *El congreso de Panamá, 1826* (Lima: Ministerio de Relaciones Exteriores, 1942).

13. A copy of the union treaty can be found in Yepes, *Del congreso de Panamá*, 1:117–136.

14. Alberto Flores-Galindo, *Arequipa y el sur andino: ensayo de historia regional (siglos XVIII–XX)* (Lima: Editorial Horizonte, 1977), pp. 12–44; Heraclio Bonilla and Karen Spalding, "La Independencia en el Perú: las palabras y los hechos," in *La independencia en el Perú*, ed. Heraclio Bonilla et al., 2d ed. (Lima: Instituto de Estudios Peruanos, ediciones 14, 1981), pp. 89–97.

15. César Arróspide de la Flor et al., *Perú: Identidad nacional* (Lima: Ediciones CEDEP, 1979), pp. 17–36, 209–234; Jürgen Golte, *Repartos y Rebeliones: Túpac Amaru y las contradicciones de la economía colonial* (Lima: Instituto de Estudios Peruanos, 1980), especially pp. 139–153.

16. Julio Cotler, *Clases, estado y nación en el Perú* (Lima: Instituto de Estudios Peruanos, 1978), pp. 83–84.

17. Heraclio Bonilla, "Clases populares y Estado en el contexto de la crisis colonial," in *La independencia en el Perú*, ed. Heraclio Bonilla et al., 2d ed. (Lima: Instituto de Estudios Peruanos, ediciones 14, 1981), p. 69.

18. José Carlos Mariátegui, *Seven Interpretive Essays on Peruvian Reality* (Austin: University of Texas Press, 1974), pp. 45–48; Stanley J. Stein and Barbara H. Stein, *The Colonial Heritage of Latin America: Essays on Economic Dependence in Perspective* (New York: Oxford University Press, 1970), pp. 114–115.

19. Woodrow Borah, "Colonial Institutions and Contemporary Latin America: Political and Economic Life," *Hispanic American Historical Review* 43, 3 (August 1963): 375–376; Liisa North, *Civil-Military Relations in Argentina, Chile and Peru* (Berkeley: University of California Press, 1966), pp. 1–6.

20. Basadre, *Historia*, 1:14–15; Anna, *Fall of the Royal Government*, pp. 195–196.

21. Laura Randall, *A Comparative Economic History of Latin America, 1500–1914*, vol. 4, *Peru* (Ann Arbor: University Microfilms International, 1977), pp. 72–73; J. Fred Rippy, *British Investments in Latin America, 1822–1949* (New York: Arno Press, 1977), pp. 18–21.

22. Heraclio Bonilla, ed., *Gran Bretaña y el Perú: Informes de los cónsules*

británicos: 1826–1919, 5 vols. (Lima: Instituto de Estudios Peruanos, 1975), 1:1–83; Heraclio Bonilla, *Un siglo a la deriva: ensayos sobre el Perú, Bolivia y la guerra* (Lima: Instituto de Estudios Peruanos, 1980), p. 13.

23. Bonilla and Spalding, "La Independencia," pp. 81–83; J. Fred Rippy, *Rivalry of the United States and Great Britain over Latin America (1808–1830)* (Baltimore: Johns Hopkins University Press, 1929), pp. 4–8.

24. Arthur P. Whitaker, *The United States and the Independence of Latin America, 1800–1830* (New York: W. W. Norton and Company, 1964), p. 65; Louis Clinton Nolan, "The Diplomatic and Commercial Relations of the United States and Peru, 1826–1875" (Ph.D. diss., Duke University, 1935), pp. 49–51, 60–61, 69–70.

25. Lane Carter Kendall, "Andrés Santa Cruz and the Peru-Bolivia Confederation," *Hispanic American Historical Review* 16, 1 (February 1936): 32.

26. Carlos Ortiz de Zevallos Paz Soldán, ed., *La misión de Ortiz de Zevallos en Bolivia, 1826–1827*, vol. 5 of *Archivo diplomático Peruano*, 9 vols. (Lima: Ministerio de Relaciones Exteriores del Perú, 1956), pp. xxv–xxix, 3–13; Alvaro Pérez del Castillo, *Bolivia, Colombia, Chile y el Perú* (La Paz: Editorial "Los Amigos del Libro," 1980), pp. 17–22.

27. Alfonso Crespo, *Santa Cruz: El Condor Indio* (La Paz: Librería y Editorial "Juventud," 1979), pp. 77–82; Ortiz de Zevallos, *La misión*, pp. 25–38, copies of treaties on pp. 75–86.

THREE

Search for National Identity, 1827–1845

The two decades between the departure of Bolívar in 1826 and the election of Castilla in 1845 were a time of enormous internal strife that often bordered on anarchy. Caudillos dominated Peruvian politics in general and the executive branch in particular. In this confused milieu, foreign policy focused on the struggle to define the nation's geographical limits as well as an acceptable political relationship with its neighbors. Bolívar's exit fueled rather than ended ambitions for a union of Andean republics, and rival caudillos fought over whether a federation of the Andes or a direct union of Peru and Bolivia was the best approach. Attempts at regional union were complicated by Chilean efforts to maintain the status quo on the Pacific coast of South America. From 1828 to 1841 Peru or its short-lived successor, the Peru-Bolivia Confederation, were involved in wars with Argentina, Bolivia, Chile, Ecuador, and Gran Colombia. It was only toward the end of the era that Peru finally attained a more or less defined territory and government. The period also marked Peru's growing integration into the world trade network and the initiation of the guano era, a time of short-term prosperity with some serious long-term consequences for the Peruvian economy.

REGIONAL CLASHES

With the liberals in the ascendancy, the constituent congress that assembled in Lima in June 1827 elected José de la Mar president and Manuel Salazar y Baquíjano vice president. Both men had been members of the 1822 *junta gubernativa*. La Mar was a respected general but a reluctant politician. The liberals in the congress rightly judged he would be incapable of challenging legislative control of government. With their man in office, the liberals began to maneuver La Mar in the direction of a war with Gran Colombia. Aided and abetted by their northern counterparts, the liberal warmongers argued that a defeat of Gran Colombia would discredit the increasingly conservative Bolívar, allow the liberals to gain power in Colombia, and strengthen the liberal position in Ecuador as well as in Peru.

Consumed with the colossus to the north, as liberal leader Francisco

Javier de Luna Pizarro called Gran Colombia, the liberals underestimated the threat to the south. Both General Agustín Gamarra in Cuzco and General Antonio Gutierrez de la Fuente, the prefect of Arequipa, strongly opposed La Mar's election. They joined defeated presidential aspirant Santa Cruz in an informal alliance aimed at bringing down the La Mar government and making peace with Gran Colombia. Santa Cruz saw the overthrow of La Mar as the first step toward his ultimate objective: a union of Peru and Bolivia under his leadership. The Gamarra–La Fuente–Santa Cruz alliance was clearly one of convenience. There is nothing to suggest that either Gamarra or La Fuente intended to allow Santa Cruz to take power in Peru or to unite Peru and Bolivia under his leadership. Both men were ambitious rivals, but they regarded Santa Cruz as the most serious threat to their respective aspirations.

Liberal foreign policy first bore fruit in Bolivia, where the Peruvian and Bolivian governments were divided by trade, border, and ideological disputes. Antonio José de Sucre, a Colombian and Bolívar's most loyal partisan, presided over the Bolivian state, supported by Colombian forces that had remained in Bolivia. The La Mar government thus saw itself flanked by a Colombian satellite likely to hurry to Gran Colombia's aid in the event of war. To counter this threat, the Peruvian government in mid-1827 initiated a search for new allies. As one step in the reorientation of its foreign policy, it stifled a recent rapprochement with Brazil and began to court Argentina. In February 1828 the Peruvian minister of foreign affairs instructed Santa Cruz to improve diplomatic ties with the Argentine government. At the same time, he was told to resist Argentine requests for military assistance against Brazil for fear of attracting a powerful enemy.[1]

Taking advantage of a military revolt in Chuquisaca, the Peruvian army crossed the Bolivian frontier on May 1, 1828. The Bolivian armed forces offered little resistance, eventually capitulating in early July. Peruvians viewed the invasion as a preemptive strike to eliminate an enemy in the south before facing a more dangerous one in the north. A secondary consideration was to secure the support of the Bolivian armed forces, which necessitated the replacement of Sucre with a president more sympathetic to Peru. Finally, ideological differences and personal rivalries, especially the animosity that Agustín Gamarra, the commander of the invading army, felt for Sucre, contributed to the decision to invade Bolivia. Peru and Bolivia later concluded the Treaty of Piquiza on July 6, 1828. It provided for the departure of Sucre and all foreign-born troops and for the abrogation of the Bolivian constitution. In a very real sense, the Treaty of Piquiza ended Bolívar's dream of uniting Bolivia, Colombia, and Peru.

War with Gran Colombia followed the Peruvian invasion of Bolivia. The origins of the 1828–1829 clash were numerous and complex. In the first place, both Peru and Gran Colombia claimed the provinces of Jaén and Maynas, which had adhered to Peru in the early 1820s. Peru also coveted the port of Guayaquil, which Gran Colombia had annexed in 1822. Economic issues were involved because Gran Colombia's loans to Peru during the struggle for independence had gone unpaid, and the Colombian government asserted that Peru owed compensation for the auxiliaries provided during the war. On the ideological plane, both the 1827 Peruvian congress and the La Mar government rejected Bolívar's personal leadership, his authoritarian political model, and the Colombian hegemony that they feared he would reassert over Peru. Diplomatic relations between Peru and Gran Colombia deteriorated steadily after 1827, and when mediation attempts failed, the long-expected war erupted at the end of 1828. Peru's navy quickly won control of the sea, and its armed forces occupied Guayaquil on January 19, 1829. The Peruvian army was near the highland center of Cuenca, La Mar's birthplace, when it was stopped at Tarqui by La Mar's nemesis, Marshal Sucre. The battle of Portete de Tarqui, which occurred on February 27, 1829, was not a total military disaster for Peru, but it halted the Peruvian advance and contributed to La Mar's overthrow. In early June 1829, the La Mar government resigned and was replaced by one headed by General Agustín Gamarra. The Ecuadorian war thus produced opposite results to those intended by the liberals in the Peruvian congress. La Mar's defeat facilitated the rise to power of Gamarra, a man who stood for authoritarian rule and executive dominance. Sucre's victory also strengthened Bolívar's hand and led to a temporary suppression of Colombia's liberals.[2]

On September 22, 1829, the Gamarra administration concluded a peace treaty at Guayaquil that replaced a preliminary peace convention inked earlier in the year. The Larrea-Gual treaty differed in several significant respects from the preliminary pact, and most of the changes favored Peru. In the final settlement, the signatories agreed to reduce to peacetime levels military forces in northern Peru and southern Colombia, but the new treaty did not identify specific troop levels as the earlier one had done. Although both parties acknowledged that their territories were generally the territories that had belonged to the viceroyalties of New Granada and Peru prior to independence, the date of August 1809 included in the earlier draft was eliminated. Such wording left open the question of which date to use for the independence of Latin America in general and Peru in particular. Finally, Peru and Colombia did not pledge to refrain from interfering in the domestic affairs of each other or in the domestic affairs of other American states, specifically Bolivia. The governments of Peru and Bolivia were deeply involved in each other's domestic politics for most of the next decade.[3]

The 1829 treaty was a general instrument of friendship and peace and not exclusively one of boundaries. It neither settled the boundary question nor established a boundary line. It merely specified a procedure to be followed. Article VI left the final solution to a joint boundary commission, which was to meet within forty days of treaty ratification and complete its work within six months. Treaty ratifications were exchanged on October 27, 1829, but Gran Colombia's assent was of debatable legality in that it ratified without congressional approval. The joint boundary commission provided for in the treaty never met because Ecuador separated from Gran Colombia in 1830; the latter eventually became present-day Colombia, Ecuador, and Venezuela. Thereafter, the Peruvian government refused to be bound by the treaty. The boundary question was further complicated by a protocol favoring the Colombian position that was allegedly signed by Peruvian Foreign Minister Carlos Pedemonte and the Colombian minister to Peru, Tomás C. Mosquera, on August 11, 1830. Copies of the so-called Pedemonte-Mosquera protocol were not discovered until the end of the nineteenth century. Peruvian scholars universally rejected the validity of the protocol and Ecuadorians struggled to prove its authenticity.

COMMERCIAL RIVALRY WITH BOLIVIA

When Gamarra assumed the presidency, he faced a growing rebellion in the south of Peru. In June 1829 the Cuzco city council deposed the departmental prefect and replaced him with a supporter of Santa Cruz. The council then requested the support Santa Cruz had promised in May 1829 when he crossed southern Peru on his way to become president of Bolivia. Two months later, a group of army officers led by Ramón Castilla launched a preemptive *golpe* in Arequipa to forestall the plans of santacrucistas. The action of the armed forces provoked a hostile response throughout the southern region, especially in Puno, where the prefect issued a proclamation condemning the *golpe*. Fearing a fate similar to his colleagues in Arequipa, the prefect then requested Bolivian protection against a possible *golpe* by progovernment forces. Santa Cruz initially agreed to defend Puno from Arequipan aggression, but he recanted when Gamarra accused him of interference in Peruvian internal affairs. Santa Cruz denied direct involvement in the events in southern Peru and suggested Gamarra send a diplomatic representative to La Paz to discuss the problems existing between the two countries.[4]

In September 1829 the Peruvian government named Mariano Alejo Alvarez, a personal friend of Santa Cruz, as minister plenipotentiary to Bolivia. Alvarez was instructed to negotiate a commercial treaty and a defensive alliance, obtain guarantees that the Bolivian president would no longer interfere in Peruvian internal affairs, and discuss with Santa Cruz the question of reunification. The Alvarez mission was a complete failure. Supported by Gamarra, the Peruvian diplomat fomented a revolt against Santa Cruz with the objective of incorporating Bolivia as an integral part of Peru. When the Bolivian government realized what Alvarez was doing, it suspended all communication with the Peruvian legation. President Gamarra recalled Alvarez on August 20, 1830.[5]

In October 1830 Santa Cruz accepted an earlier suggestion of Gamarra's and proposed a summit at Desaguadero. The two presidents met on December

13, 1830, for an inconclusive three-day conference. The Peruvian delegation proposed a bilateral alliance and a commercial treaty reducing duties on goods imported from one country to the other. It also suggested a treaty of limits, in which Peru would receive Copacabana and the Bolivian side of the Desaguadero River in exchange for territory in the province of Tarapacá. The Bolivian delegation responded that any alliance should include Colombia, and any treaty of limits should include the cession to Bolivia of the port of Arica. When Peru refused to consider either point, the conference ended.

After Desaguadero, talks continued between Casimiro Olañeta, the newly appointed Bolivian minister to Peru, and the Peruvian minister to Bolivia, Manuel Ferreyros y de la Mata. Unfortunately, the Olañeta-Ferreyros talks were no more fruitful than the Desaguadero summit. The Peruvian government insisted on a defensive alliance as a sine qua non for further negotiations. Afraid a bilateral alliance might enable Gamarra to dismember Colombia, seize Guayaquil, and annex Bolivia, the Bolivian government agreed with the Peruvian proposal, but only if Colombia was included in the alliance. When Peru refused to deal with Colombia, Olañeta countered with a proposal that centered on the cession of Tacna and Tarapacá to Bolivia. Peru again refused to consider a proposal that would make Arica a Bolivian port because it would mean the end of the Peruvian stranglehold on Bolivian commerce. At this point, the Peruvian Ministry of Foreign Affairs broke off the talks and sent Olañeta his passport.[6]

Even though his motives at Desaguadero and during the Olañeta-Ferreyros talks were unclear, Gamarra appeared to be buying time as opposed to pursuing a negotiated solution. The Peruvian president probably explored an alliance with Bolivia, coupled with a reduction in the size of the Bolivian army, to forestall an alliance between Bolivia and Colombia. At the same time, he was negotiating with the Peruvian congress and other political forces in Lima for an agreement to invade Bolivia. After Desaguadero, Gamarra continued to plan for war, directing the chief of the Peruvian navy to be prepared to raze the Bolivian port of Cobija if war broke out. On December 30, 1830, Santa Cruz informed General Juan José Flores, the president of Ecuador, that Peru planned to invade Bolivia. He also warned Flores that Gamarra planned to annex Guayaquil as well as Potosí. Santa Cruz then proposed a defensive alliance between Ecuador and Bolivia, but Flores refused to act.

Throughout 1831 the Santa Cruz administration focused its attention on Bolivia's principal problem: lack of an adequate outlet to the sea. Pursuing a two-part policy, the regime continued efforts to acquire Arica while trying to develop Cobija. In pursuit of the latter objective, the Bolivian government minimized the tariff on trade through Cobija while increasing the tariff on goods entering Bolivia through Peruvian ports. Gamarra took the strongest possible objection to Santa Cruz's trade measures. He charged they were clearly designed to harm Peruvian trade with Bolivia and to reduce the revenues Peru derived from the port of Arica, and responded by increasing duties on Bolivian trade passing through Peruvian territory. Faced with a growing trade war, both sides tried to resolve the issue during the Olañeta-Ferreyros negotiations. When these efforts failed, the Bolivian government in March 1831 requested Chilean mediation. The Chilean government reluctantly agreed and instructed its minister in Lima, Miguel Zañartu, to offer his good offices. Welcoming Chilean mediation, the Peruvian congress rejected Gamarra's petition for a declaration of war against Bolivia and authorized the government to begin negotiations.[7]

On August 25, 1831, representatives of Peru and Bolivia signed a preliminary peace treaty at Tiquina that provided for a reduction in their armed forces and the withdrawal of both from the frontier. A definitive treaty of peace and friendship was later signed at Arequipa on November 8, 1831. The Treaty of Arequipa reduced Peru's army to 3,000 men and Bolivia's army to 1,600 men; committed the signatories to a policy of nonintervention; prohibited seditious activities by political refugees residing in either republic; and recognized existing boundaries until a commission could resolve their differences. A commercial treaty signed on the same day lowered the duties paid on the goods of one country imported by the other. It also reduced the duties charged by Bolivia on foreign goods imported through Peruvian territory to the same levels as those charged by Peru on goods imported for its own consumption. Both Peru and Bolivia asked Chile to guarantee the November pacts, but the latter declined on the grounds it was unwilling to compromise its policy of neutrality.[8]

In the Treaty of Arequipa, Peru achieved all of its economic objectives. The treaty abolished the discriminatory tariff, lowered the duties on Peruvian products and those of other nations imported by Bolivia through Peruvian territory, and guaranteed that Arica would continue as the principal outlet for Bolivian foreign trade. By destroying the tariff wall erected by Santa Cruz to promote Cobija, the treaty undercut Bolivia's only port and perpetuated the Peruvian stranglehold over Bolivian external trade. Politically, the pact did not prove to be a definitive treaty of peace, but it did arrange a temporary truce between Peru and Bolivia. Bolivian opinion strongly opposed both treaties, and the Bolivian congress eventually rejected the commercial pact. On November 17, 1832, the latter was replaced by a new accord that gave Bolivia additional freedom to regulate its tariffs without threatening its highly vulnerable port at Cobija.[9]

FOREIGN POLICY OF ORBEGOSO

At the end of his term, Gamarra failed in a bid to impose his chosen successor when the congress elected General Luís José de Orbegoso president in December 1833. The election of Orbegoso represented a continuation of the liberal strategy to contain militarism by retaining control over the congress while electing the least dangerous general to the presidency. On January 4, 1834, rebel forces executed a *golpe* in Lima and proclaimed the defeated conservative presidential candidate, General Pedro Pablo Bermúdez, the provisional supreme chief of Peru. Army units in Cuzco, Puno, Ayacucho, and Huancavelica supported Bermúdez, as did former President Gamarra. Arequipa remained loyal to Orbegoso, who soon retook Lima and forced the rebels into the sierra. The 1834 civil war centered on the southern departments of Peru, with the loyalists in Arequipa under constant pressure from Gamarra's supporters in Cuzco and Puno. On January 14, 1834, the military commander of Arequipa requested Bolivian support to put down the revolt, a request repeated by President Orbegoso one month later. Although Santa Cruz sent military forces to the Peruvian frontier, he refused to intervene unless Peru agreed to enact a federation plan. The Peruvian congress rejected the Santa Cruz proposal, but it did authorize Orbegoso to solicit Bolivian aid for the exclusive purpose of ending the civil war. In the end, Bolivian intervention was not required; the rebel forces capitulated at Maquinhuayo on April 24, 1834.

In the spring of 1835 Santa Cruz again sought to reunify Peru and Bolivia by creating an independent state in southern Peru that would federate with Bolivia. President Orbegoso eventually accepted this approach, promising—in exchange for Bolivian assistance—to convoke an assembly of southern departments and then attack rebellious General Felipe Santiago Salaverry in the north. Once peace was restored to Peru, he further agreed to convoke an assembly of northern departments and retire to private life. On June 15, 1835, representatives of the two governments signed the Treaty of La Paz, which called for a Bolivian army to move into Peru to restore order and to protect an assembly of southern departments convened to establish the bases of their reorganization. The army was to remain in Peru until the nation was pacified and the northern departments had also assembled to decide their future course of action.[10]

On June 16, 1835, without waiting for ratification of the treaty, the vanguard of the Bolivian army crossed the Desaguadero River into Peru. Three weeks later, Orbegoso and Santa Cruz met in the Peruvian town of Vilque. Orbegoso again promised to convoke the two assemblies, which would create the federation, and then retire from public life. Santa Cruz strove to maintain Gamarra's support, but the latter refused to work with Orbegoso, defecting to the rebel forces in late July 1835. The long-awaited clash between Gamarra and Santa Cruz finally came at Yanacocha on August 13, 1835. After a two-hour battle, Santa Cruz emerged victorious, and Gamarra fled to Lima, where he was arrested and exiled. Santa Cruz and Salaverry later clashed in February 1836 in a pitched battle at Socabaya, a few miles south of Arequipa. Santa Cruz again emerged victorious; with the obstacles blocking his unionist dreams eliminated, he was finally master of Peru.

TRADE, CLAIMS, AND TARIFFS

In this time of considerable political uncertainty, Peruvian trade policies were both capricious and intimately bound to regional rivalries. The commercial isolation that began during the late stages of colonial rule continued for some two decades after independence. At the same time, the government became increasingly dependent on export-import taxes for public revenue. To illustrate the chaotic nature of early trade policy, the Peruvian government granted Brazil and Ecuador duty-free import areas in 1832 but later enacted special import duties to finance government expenses during the 1834 civil war. Between 1832 and 1835, Peru, Bolivia, Chile, and Ecuador concluded treaties designed to reduce reciprocal tariffs and eliminate discriminatory charges for the import of foreign goods through intermediaries. Because only Chile had a merchant marine, the benefits of the 1835 commercial treaty between Peru and Chile were one-sided; after a change in government, Peru decreed it void in May 1836.[11]

After independence, Peruvian diplomatic relations with both the United States and Great Britain centered on war debts, claims, investment, commerce, and shipping. A variety of circumstances, including smuggling by sea, the paper blockade, detentions, seizures of private property, and postindependence civil disturbances, formed the basis for claims the US government pressed on Peru for some five decades after independence. Of the eighty-one claims presented in conventions from 1826 to 1875, only five were against the United States; Peru was the defendant in the remainder. Forty-nine of the claims against Peru involved the Peruvian government, and forty of these arose in connection with revolutionary activities or disturbances. Eventually, most of the claims were resolved in four conventions negotiated in 1841, 1862, 1863, and 1868.[12]

Commercial rivalry between the United States and Great Britain existed, but as far as commodities were concerned, there was little direct competition. The United States largely exported farm products; Great Britain exported mainly finished goods. In the first half of the nineteenth century, the three countries with which Peru had the most commercial exchange were Great Britain, the United States, and France, in that order. Over half of Peru's external commerce was with Great Britain. During the war for independence, the United States developed a substantial trade with Peru, but after the war, trade slumped quickly and badly. When James Cooley was appointed the first US chargé d'affaires to Peru, he was instructed to focus his attention on the deteriorating state of US commerce with Peru. At the same time, he was told to emphasize that the US government was not interested in preferential tariffs—only in free trade. His efforts initiated a free-trade campaign stretching from 1827 to 1837 that attempted to win allies, modify tariff laws, and increase trade. Great Britain also advocated a system of low duties or complete free trade, but its efforts in that regard were less aggressive and more sporadic. In contrast, the French government relied more on intermittent displays of naval force to promote a healthy respect for the property rights of French retailers based in Peru. In the face of these external pressures, the Peruvian government retained its protectionist position for two decades after independence. It was not until the end of the 1840s that a policy of free trade was fully installed and accepted.[13]

CREATION OF
THE PERU-BOLIVIA CONFEDERATION

On March 16, 1836, delegates from the departments of Arequipa, Puno, Cuzco, and Ayacucho assembled in Sicuani as provided for in the Treaty of La Paz. The following day, the assembly proclaimed the independence of the participating departments from Peru and established the state of South Peru, with Santa Cruz as supreme protector. The delegates also declared their intention to unite with Bolivia and a state to be created from northern Peru in a great confederation, whose bases would later be drawn up in a joint congress named by the three states. General Santa Cruz was present in the town of Sicuani but did not attend the sessions. After approving the Treaty of La Paz, the assembly adjourned on March 22, 1836.

The opening of the northern assembly, originally scheduled by General Orbegoso for July 15, 1836, was delayed until early August. With resistance to the new order crystallizing in the north, the delay was needed to give santacrucista agents time to prepare public opinion in favor of the confederation. Installed on August 3, 1836, in the village of Huaura, the assembly followed the Sicuani pattern. The delegates declared independence, created the state of North Peru with Santa Cruz as supreme protector, and empowered a congress of plenipotentiaries to develop bases for confederation. The assembly also elected Orbegoso president of North Peru, thereby overturning his spring 1835 pledge to Santa Cruz to retire to private life after convening a northern assembly. It then closed its sessions on August 11, 1836, leaving all pending matters subject to the power of the supreme protector.

With the initial preparations completed, the supreme protector decreed the establishment of the Peru-Bolivia Confederation on October 28, 1836. The three member states—North Peru, South Peru, and Bolivia—were asked to name representatives to meet in Tacna on January 24, 1837, to draft a charter of confederation. Santa Cruz personally designated all the representatives, choosing men of ability and proven loyalty. The Tacna site was chosen to avoid the rivalry between Cuzco and Arequipa and to allow Santa Cruz to stay near the coast because he feared the Chilean government might attempt to thwart his plans. The assembly did not convene until April 18, 1837, but a treaty of confederation was signed on May 1.[14]

The Treaty of Tacna created a federal republic comprising three sovereign states. Each was to have its own government, but all were subordinate to a powerful central government made up of three branches with the executive clearly dominant. Headed by the supreme protector of the confederation, the executive branch was given control over the armed forces, foreign affairs, and economic matters of general interest. The member states retained control over their internal affairs and were to deal with one another through their foreign ministries. Santa Cruz was named provisional supreme protector pending the opening of the first general congress. The confederation represents the only serious effort at South American regional integration from the collapse of Gran Colombia until the present time. It bore a remarkable similarity to Bolívar's projected federation of the Andes, a debt Santa Cruz did not deny.

Even though Santa Cruz's military conquest of Peru left no one in either Peru or Bolivia who could effectively dispute his will, internal opposition to the confederation did exist. After years of fighting, Peruvians and Bolivians had developed deep antipathies. Many Bolivians were concerned about their independence, for they feared the pact would subordinate them to Peru. Bolivian critics also asserted that Peru, divided into two states, received more advantages than Bolivia and would exercise a greater physical and moral force in the confederation. Another criticism, voiced by Peruvians and Bolivians alike, was that the treaty gave too much power to the supreme protector and thus was proof of Santa Cruz's tyranny and despotism. Regionalism also fueled internal opposition. Residents of Lima and the north of Peru were afraid they would lose their hegemony over the nation; the mining-bureaucratic oligarchies of Chuquisaca and the south feared they might lose their influence over Bolivia. Finally, even among the unionists, a consensus never developed as to the optimal form union would take.[15]

The Chilean government led external opposition to the Peru-Bolivia confederation. Chilean grievances were complex, long-standing, and deep-seated. During the colonial period, haughty *limeños* had looked down on their parochial neighbors to the south. In addition, the colonial economic system had concentrated coastal trade on Lima-Callao and thus discriminated against Chile in favor of Peru. During the struggle for independence, the Chilean government, at considerable cost, sent an army under San Martín to fight for Peru's liberation. According to Chilean accounts, the Peruvian government showed its ingratitude by treating Chilean soldiers and sailors shabbily and refusing to compensate the Chilean government for the expense of Chilean troops. The treaty that covered war costs, together with the 1-million-peso loan made by Chile to Peru after San Martín's departure, was pigeonholed by successive Peruvian governments, none of which attempted to fulfill the nation's obligations.[16]

After independence, Peru had become Chile's largest export opportunity. Successive Chilean governments sought to regularize trade with Peru by eliminating obstacles like high duties, arbitrary official Peruvian actions and exactions, and US competition in the Peruvian market. Trade remained a problem after 1830, when the Chilean government tried unsuccessfully to negotiate a treaty, along with a loan repayment, that would rationalize commerce with Peru. The issue of trade became increasingly important in the ensuing decade, when Chile's elite—led by the country's most powerful political figure, Diego Portales—moved to make Valparaiso, at the expense of Lima-Callao, the major Pacific port of South America. Farsighted Chileans feared that a confederation between Peru and Bolivia might tip the economic scales in favor of its northern neighbors, stifling Chile's growing economy and causing Lima-Callao to eclipse Valparaiso permanently. In the ongoing struggle, Peru had a trump card, which Santa Cruz eventually played when he enacted discriminatory tariffs that favored ships that bypassed Valparaiso after rounding Cape Horn and proceeded directly to Callao.[17]

Already bad, the volatile diplomatic relations between Peru and Chile deteriorated in 1836. As mentioned earlier, General Orbegoso irritated the Chilean government in May 1836 by declaring null and void the Peru-Chile commercial treaty celebrated in Santiago in January 1835 and ratified by the Salaverry government in June of the same year. Two months later, a group of Chilean exiles led by former President Ramón Freire, who had been living in exile in Peru, launched an armed expedition against Chile in an attempt to seize power. Long concerned about Chilean political exiles plotting in Peru, the Chilean government accused Orbegoso and Santa Cruz of complicity in the abortive *golpe* and broke diplomatic relations. Because the Peruvian government had leased two allegedly deactivated naval ships to the Chilean exiles, albeit through a third party, there was little doubt that elements of the Peruvian government, possibly including Orbegoso, were aware of the plot. Nevertheless, the existing evidence does not substantiate Chilean accusations, largely rejected by Peruvians, that General Santa Cruz was involved in the Freire expedition or even aware of it. In any case, the Chilean government viewed the Freire conspiracy as a harbinger of future Peru-Bolivia involvement in Chilean internal affairs if Chile allowed the confederation to establish itself.[18]

In response to the Freire affair, the Chilean warship *Aquiles* entered Callao on August 21, 1836, and seized three ships of the Peruvian navy. Santa Cruz, desperate to preserve the peace until he had consolidated the Peru-Bolivia confederation, sent Casimiro Olañeta to Chile in search of a diplomatic solution. The Chilean government responded to this peace feeler by sending Mariano Egaña, a member of the Chilean Senate, to Lima. Empowered to declare war, Egaña was instructed to negotiate a peace if he could secure agreement on several key points. These included satisfaction for the jailing of the Chilean chargé d'affaires during the *Aquiles* incident, recognition of the Peruvian debt to Chile, naval limitations, a reciprocal trade treaty, exemption of Chilean nationals from forced loans and service in the

Peruvian army, and the dissolution of the Peru-Bolivia confederation. Egaña reached Callao on October 30, 1836, and departed on November 11, after he concluded that further attempts to negotiate with Santa Cruz would be fruitless. With the return of Egaña, the Chilean government informed Olañeta that the Santiago negotiations were finished and issued him his passport. Chile then rejected third-party offers of mediation, and on December 24, 1836, the Chilean congress complied with the government's request for ratification of a declaration of war.[19]

DISSOLUTION OF
THE PERU-BOLIVIA CONFEDERATION

The history of the Peru-Bolivia confederation now became the history of its war with Chile and Argentina because that conflict prevented the supreme protector from consolidating the union so skillfully orchestrated in 1836–1837. The first stage of the dispute was a diplomatic offensive that focused on a search for allies. As early as March 1836, Bolivian diplomatic reports indicated that official opinion in Argentina was opposed to Bolivian intervention in Peru. Argentine hostility to Santa Cruz increased throughout 1836. The assertions of Santa Cruz that he desired only peace did not reassure the Argentine government any more than they had reassured Chile, and negotiations for an anti–Santa Cruz pact were initiated in August 1836 and intensified in February 1837. The negotiations for an Argentina-Chile alliance against the confederation eventually failed because the parties could not agree on the postwar status of Bolivia. On the other hand, this did not deter Argentine President Juan Manuel de Rosas from his determination to destroy the confederation. On February 13, 1837, Rosas ended all communications with the Peru-Bolivia Confederation; and on May 19, 1837, his government declared war.[20]

In the months following Santa Cruz's successful bid for power in Peru, both the Chilean government and the confederation sent diplomatic missions to Ecuador in search of an alliance. From the beginning, Ecuadorian President Vicente Rocafuerte had maintained a friendly attitude toward the confederation, and on November 20, 1836, he agreed to a treaty of friendship and defensive alliance. The pact was subsequently rejected by the Ecuadorian congress, which also refused an alliance with Chile, preferring that Ecuador observe strict neutrality. In April 1837 Juan García del Río, the itinerant statesman and newly appointed confederation minister to Ecuador, concluded a treaty of peace, commerce, and navigation with Ecuador after the Chilean government had also negotiated a commercial treaty with the Quito government. The García del Río treaty granted most-favored-nation status and provided for conventions to settle both boundary questions and the long-standing Colombian debt to Peru. A month later, the confederation accepted an Ecuadorian offer of mediation, but when Chile refused the offer, the Ecuadorian government retired to the neutral position earlier proclaimed by the Ecuadorian congress.[21]

At this point, the dispute entered a second, more violent phase. On September 15, 1837, a Chilean expeditionary force, known as the First Expedition of Restoration, embarked at Valparaiso under the command of Admiral Manuel Blanco Encalada, a veteran of the war of independence and a former president of Chile. Chile's minimum peace terms remained the familiar ones presented by Egaña in the fall of 1836. In addition, Admiral Blanco and his special negotiator, Antonio José de Irisarri, were instructed to remove Santa Cruz from the presidency of Bolivia. In return for active Argentine support, the Chilean government was willing to bolster Argentina's claim to Tarija, compensating Bolivia with a Pacific seaport through the Peruvian Department of Arequipa. This was the first time that Chile sounded a policy that later recurred again and again in Chilean diplomacy: the solution to Bolivian problems through the appropriation of Peruvian territory.[22]

The Chilean expedition reached Iquique on September 22, 1837, eventually disembarking at Arcinta and Quilca to begin the march on Arequipa. Arriving short of supplies and with his troops and horses exhausted, Blanco found himself a virtual prisoner in Arequipa, surrounded by a hostile force that was growing daily. Realizing a fight could be disastrous, Blanco requested an interview with Santa Cruz, which led to the conclusion of a peace treaty on November 17, 1837. The terms of the Treaty of Paucarpata, given the situation of the Chilean army, were generous, although they fell far short of the Chilean government's minimal expectations. The expeditionary army was allowed safe passage to Chile, and perpetual peace and friendship were established between Chile and the Peru-Bolivia Confederation. Trade relations were established on a most-favored-nation basis pending conclusion of special commercial treaties. Both parties renounced the use of armed force and accepted the principle of nonintervention. Accepting Chilean mediation, the confederation agreed to make peace with Argentina, and Santa Cruz assumed with interest the Peruvian debt to Chile. Admiral Blanco agreed to return the three ships kidnapped from Callao on August 21, a move that would give the confederation naval superiority, as soon as the boats had been used to ferry Chilean troops home. Most important, by signing the treaty with the confederation, Chile granted diplomatic recognition to a political body whose destruction had been the primary objective of the Chilean intervention.[23]

The supreme protector ratified the Treaty of Paucarpata immediately. Extremely pleased with the terms of the agreement, Santa Cruz believed it would end the quarrel with Chile and allow him to consolidate the Peru-Bolivia Confederation. The Chilean government, on the other hand, viewed the treaty as an unmitigated disaster and promptly disassociated itself from the negotiations. On December 18, 1837, Chile formally rejected the terms of the agreement and informed Santa Cruz that a state of war still existed. The Treaty of Paucarpata, instead of being the bloodless victory the supreme protector desired, marked the beginning of the end for his political ambitions.

With the Chilean threat temporarily neutralized, Santa Cruz directed his full attention to the south, where fighting with Argentina had broken out in August 1837. Feeling less magnanimous toward Argentina than he had toward Chile, Santa Cruz intended to round out Bolivia's borders by seizing Humahuaca, which lay well within Argentine territory. After an indecisive engagement on September 13, 1837, the southern front was relatively quiet until the following year. In the interim, the Chilean government made another determined effort to secure an alliance with Argentina. Chile proposed that Argentina invade Bolivia while Chile invaded Peru. Argentina's counterproposal was that both parties invade Bolivia, setting aside the question of Peru. Absent a compromise, the talks were suspended, leaving Argentina to fight alone. The Argentine threat to the confederation finally ended at Montenegro in June 1838, when a confederation force defeated the Argentine army.[24]

In a manifesto explaining its rejection of the Treaty of Paucarpata, the Chilean government underscored its intention to continue the struggle until Santa Cruz and the confederation were destroyed. Convinced that Santiago would soon dispatch a new expedition, Santa Cruz directed his considerable energies toward preparing for the anticipated second invasion. Martial law was again declared and the strength of the army was raised to 17,000 men: 7,000 in North Peru, 5,000 in South Peru and northern Bolivia, and 5,000 on the Argentine frontier. Santa Cruz also declared a blockade of Valparaiso, but it was even less effective than the blockade declared earlier by Chile on Callao, Chorrillos, and Ancón. As Santa Cruz worked to increase the effectiveness of his armed forces, he struggled to contain internal resistance to the confederation. In Bolivia, opposition to the Treaty of Tacna was widespread, especially in Chuquisaca; in June 1838 the Bolivian congress set guidelines for a more liberal pact, in which the powers of the supreme protector would be significantly reduced. In Peru, particularly North Peru, opposition to the confederation also focused on the high degree of centralization called for in the Tacna accords. It was further aggravated by the continuation of the war and an increasing sense of rivalry with Bolivia. As early as February 1838, rumors surfaced in the north of a conspiracy aimed at dissolving the confederation and naming Orbegoso president of Peru.[25]

Matters came to a head on July 30, 1838, only days before the arrival of the Chilean invasion force, when Orbegoso declared North Peru free and independent of all foreign influence but still at war with Chile. Orbegoso's criticisms of the Santa Cruz government and the Treaty of Tacna were varied and generally accurate. They centered on Santa Cruz's near-absolute power, Bolivian domination of the confederation, Peruvian subjugation to foreign rulers, and the failure to give the Peruvian people an adequate opportunity to express an opinion of the new arrangement. Orbegoso had been deeply involved in the formation of the confederation, hence personal ambition may also have played a part in his eventual rejection of the union. Events suggest he was willing to collaborate with Santa Cruz until the latter's power was seriously threatened, at which point Orbegoso deserted the supreme protector.[26]

The second Chilean restoration expedition set sail from Valparaiso on July 10, and arrived off Callao on August 6, 1838. Commanded by General Manuel Bulnes, the expedition included a Peruvian contingent led by Agustín Gamarra. On August 7–8, 1838, the Chilean force disembarked at Ancón, and Bulnes announced his intention to move inland. Orbegoso rejected the Bulnes plan, and when Bulnes moved closer to Lima, hostilities broke out. After a pitched battle, the Chileans occupied Lima and declared Gamarra the provisional president of Peru, a move that generated little popular support. One of Gamarra's first acts was to abolish the provisions of the Santa Cruz commercial code, which had established double duties on foreign goods touching at other Pacific ports before arriving at a port of the Peru-Bolivia Confederation. Threatening Valparaiso's commercial hegemony, the provision had greatly angered the Chilean government. Gamarra also agreed to provision the Chilean expeditionary force and to assume all costs of the war against Santa Cruz. Gamarra tried to persuade Orbegoso, besieged in Callao, to unite with the Chilean army against Santa Cruz but was unsuccessful. Orbegoso continued to oppose both the invaders and Santa Cruz, and to demand they all withdraw from Peru.[27]

Orbegoso's rebellion, the second Chilean invasion, and the mounting opposition in Bolivia to Santa Cruz combined to effect a significant change in the strategic thinking of the supreme protector. Recognizing the widespread opposition to the confederation, Santa Cruz revived a contingency plan that called for either leaving South Peru independent or annexing it to Bolivia. Unaware of Santa Cruz's revised plans, Orbegoso accepted at face value Santa Cruz's assertion that he no longer insisted on maintaining the confederation. With Orbegoso's assistance, Santa Cruz recaptured Lima on November 10, 1838, and received a tumultuous welcome. Santa Cruz and Orbegoso were then unable to reach agreement on fuller cooperation, and Santa Cruz replaced Orbegoso as commandant of the Callao garrison. Orbegoso sailed to exile in Ecuador on December 4, 1838.[28]

After reoccupying Lima, Santa Cruz sought a negotiated settlement even at the expense of dissolving the confederation. In mid-November discussions at the Chilean headquarters in Huacho, Santa Cruz authorized the British chargé d'affaires, Belford H. Wilson, to abandon the confederation to make peace as long as the two states of Peru were not united. Santa Cruz wanted both armies to withdraw from Peru, leaving the governments of North Peru and South Peru, both named by him, to decide the fate of the confederation.

The Chilean representative, Mariano Egaña, argued that the Peruvian authorities would not allow freedom of choice and suggested that the Peruvian people elect a national congress to decide the future of the federal pact. Egaña also opposed a proposal by Wilson to limit the military and naval forces of both the confederation and Chile. Finally, he rejected Wilson's proposal that Chile renounce its right to establish differential tariffs on foreign imports, a measure that could be used to punish Peru and Bolivia. Unable to reach agreement, the representatives broke off the talks at Huacho and military operations resumed.[29]

Bulnes and Santa Cruz finally settled the issue outside Yungay, a village nestled in a magnificent stretch of the Andes north of Lima, on January 20, 1839. There Santa Cruz almost won what is considered by many to have been one of the bloodiest battles fought on Peruvian soil, but at a critical moment a cavalry charge led by Ramón Castilla, a future president of Peru, reversed the tide. Determined to continue the struggle, Santa Cruz retired to Lima and then to southern Peru; however, the walls of the confederation were collapsing around him. A revolt by the Army of the South was quickly followed by pronouncements repudiating the confederation in Chuquisaca, Potosí, La Paz, Oruro, Cochabamba, Santa Cruz, and Tarija. On February 18, 1839, a revolt broke out in Puno that was followed by rebellions later in the month in Cuzco, Tacna, and elsewhere in southern Peru. Recognizing his inability to continue in power, Santa Cruz on February 20, 1839, resigned his authority as supreme protector of the Peru-Bolivia Confederation and president of Bolivia and dissolved the confederation. He sailed from Islay into exile on February 28, 1839.

FOREIGN POLICY OF THE RESTORATION

On March 22, 1839, General Gamarra convened a national congress in the sierra town of Huancayo. Eventually installed on August 15, 1839, the Huancayo assembly named Gamarra restorer of Peru as well as general of land and sea forces. Often termed the Restoration, Gamarra's incumbency proved more a consolidation than a restoration because it was now clear that Peru was to remain Peru and not be subdivided or made part of a supranational confederation. By 1839 politically involved Peruvians, traumatized by four years of war, were increasingly drawn to a more practical form of nationalism that valued peace, stability, order, and liberty. In part, the change was symbolized by the 1839 constitution, an authoritarian, centralized document opposed to international agreements that threatened national unity or autonomy. The existing form of government was declared inalterable, and congressional approval was mandated for all international treaties.

The governments of Peru and Bolivia signed a preliminary peace treaty on August 14, 1839, that required the latter to compensate Peru for a wide range of offenses and damages allegedly incurred after 1835. When Bolivia rejected the treaty on the grounds its concessions and indemnities were onerous and inequitable, it was renegotiated in April 1840. The new treaty sought to return Peru-Bolivia affairs to 1835, with several commercial clauses in effect turning the clock back to 1832. The Bolivian government officially repudiated the Santa Cruz regime and agreed to return all flags and prisoners taken in battle. Both signatories declared peace and agreed to limit their military forces. The question of indemnity was left to Colombian arbitration.[30]

On July 10, 1840, the Peruvian congress proclaimed Gamarra the constitutional president of Peru. For more than a decade, Gamarra had dreamed of annexing the Department of La Paz, if not all of Bolivia, and the defeat of Santa Cruz had only heightened his ambitions. Obsessed with the thought that the exiled Santa Cruz might regain power in Bolivia and reconstruct the confederation, Gamarra was determined to eliminate this possibility by dominating his southern neighbor. Colonel Juan Bautista Arguedas was dispatched to Bolivia with the secret mission of securing signatories to a petition in which Bolivian cities would formally request annexation by Peru. At the same time, Gamarra maintained his forces on a war footing and reminded the Huancayo congress that Peru had numerous reasons for attacking Bolivia. Ongoing intrigue by Santa Cruz, coupled with a June 1841 revolution in Bolivia, eventually gave Gamarra a pretext to act. The Peruvian government declared war on July 6, 1841, and the Peruvian army invaded Bolivia in early October, occupying La Paz by the end of the month. After negotiations broke down, the two armies clashed at Ingavi on November 18, 1841. In a short but intense battle, the Peruvian army was routed and Gamarra was later killed. The Bolivian victory was of considerable long-term significance: it ended Gamarra's dreams of dismemberment, defined Peru's southeastern frontier, and assured the independence of the Republic of Bolivia.[31]

After the battle of Ingavi, a Bolivian force occupied Tacna, and on December 22, a Bolivian column seized the port of Arica. A week later, a Bolivian army commanded by General José Ballivián, the president of Bolivia, crossed the Desaguadero River and marched toward Puno. Opposed to a Peru-Bolivia war for fear it would result in Santa Cruz's return to power, the Chilean government was surprised and concerned by Gamarra's sudden attack on Bolivia. When Bolivia then invaded Peru and seemed about to demand the port of Arica as the price for peace, Chile instructed its chargé d'affaires in Lima to seek Bolivian evacuation and a peace treaty guaranteeing the territorial *status quo ante bellum*. After prolonged negotiations, both antagonists accepted Chilean mediation; a peace treaty was signed at Acora on June 7, 1842. The pact affirmed the belligerents' unalterable friendship and provided for a Bolivian withdrawal from Peru.[32]

Embroiled in Bolivian politics, the Peruvian government also had to contend with fresh aggression from the north. General Juan José Flores, who became Ecuador's president for the second time in 1839, planned to increase Ecuadorian territory at the expense of Peru, New Granada, or both. In late 1839 Flores proposed to Chile a plan to divide Peru into two separate nations and to cede northern Peru to Ecuador. The Chilean government opposed the plan because it feared a partitioned and impotent Peru would become an easy prey for Santa Cruz. Not waiting for the official Chilean response, President Flores directed his chargé d'affaires in Lima to negotiate a boundary settlement with Peru that recognized Ecuadorian rights to Jaén and Maynas. Flores then turned his attention to New Granada, invading its southernmost province of Pasto for the second time in May 1841, and the Ecuadorian diplomatic initiatives with Chile and Peru lapsed temporarily.[33]

Toward the end of 1841, the Quito government renewed its diplomatic efforts, aggressively pressing its case on Peru. Preoccupied with Bolivia, the Gamarra administration hoped to restrain the Flores government by sending Minister Matías León to Quito to negotiate. The subsequent negotiations between León and José Feliz Valdivieso, an early supporter of Flores who was elected president of the Ecuadorian Senate in 1841, continued from November 1841 to January 1842 but did not produce a settlement. Ecuadorian critics later charged, with some reason, that the real objective of the León mission was to occupy the Quito government until Peru's international position improved and Lima could press its case more forcefully. In early 1942 President Flores threatened to occupy Jaén and Maynas by force if Peru did not cede them voluntarily; however, he took no further action after the Peruvian government called his bluff and rejected the ultimatum. Peruvian Foreign Minister Agustín Charún and Ecuadorian Minister Bernardo Daste held additional talks in Lima in April 1842 but achieved no substantive results.[34]

As diplomatic relations between Peru and Ecuador deteriorated, the government of New Granada became increasingly alarmed. Bound to Ecuador by a treaty of alliance and friendship, New Granada had no desire to become involved in a war with Peru. Armed conflict would weaken the ruling conservative regime and encourage the liberals to renew their bid for power. On the other hand, if New Granada remained aloof, a Peruvian victory threatened to increase Peruvian influence over Ecuador at the expense of New Granada. Similarly, an Ecuadorian victory might embolden the Quito government and encourage it to try again to wrestle the Pasto region from New Granada. Faced with this dilemma, New Granada enlisted Chilean support to pressure Peru and Ecuador to avoid an all-out war. Eventually, it was the Treaty of Acora as much as regional diplomacy that reduced the level of tension between Peru and Ecuador. The Ecuadorian government simply lacked the diplomatic and military resources to challenge Peru once the latter had signed its peace treaty with Bolivia and was free to direct its full attention to the north.

For the first two decades after independence, unsettled boundaries, territorial ambitions, the machinations of political refugees, and assorted international intrigues produced serious tensions among the Andean nations. At the same time, the Republic of Peru struggled to define its frontiers, not in the narrow sense of planting boundary markers but in the broader sense of whether Peru would be divided, federate with Bolivia, or stand alone. Like many newly emergent nations, Peru accomplished statehood long before it achieved nationhood; in its early years, it found it difficult to retain the former as it sought to develop the latter. This political struggle was complicated by economic, ideological, and personal conflicts. If Peru were a democracy at all, the prominent pattern of political bargaining was a kind of democracy by violence in which the persistent use of violence, aided and abetted by the prevailing forces of militarism and caudillismo, was the political system or at least a very large part of it. In this sense, the first twenty years of independence were a harbinger of the central role violence was to play in the future political life of the country as well as the debilitating effect this violence would repeatedly have on the nation's external relations. By 1845 statehood had been reconfirmed and the frontiers of Peru had been defined in general terms, but a high level of nationhood or national identity remained to be developed. The ingredients of a foreign policy were surfacing, but a strong executive and a period of relative stability were required to give them coherence and expression.

NOTES

1. Ron L. Seckinger, "South American Power Politics During the 1820s," *Hispanic American Historical Review* 56, 2 (May 1976): 256–261.

2. Juan de Arona [Pedro Paz-Soldán y Unanue], *Páginas diplomáticas del Perú*, 2d ed. (Lima: Talleres Gráficas P. L. Villanueva, 1968), pp. 37–62; Washington Cano, *Historia de los límites del Perú* (Arequipa: Tipografía Quiróz Perea, 1925), pp. 42–44.

3. A copy of the 1829 Larrea-Gual treaty can be found in David H. Zook, Jr., *Zarumilla-Marañón: The Ecuador-Peru Dispute* (New York: Bookman Associates, 1964), pp. 271–279.

4. Dante F. Herrera Alarcón, *Rebeliones que Intentaron Desmembrar el Sur del Perú* (Lima: Imprenta Colegio Militar Leoncio Prado, 1961), p. 119.

5. Carlos Ortiz de Zevallos Paz-Soldán, ed., *La misión Alvarez en Bolivia, 1829–1830*, vol. 6 of *Archivo Diplomático Peruano*, 9 vols. (Lima: Ministerio de Relaciones Exteriores, 1957), pp. 59–89.

6. Carlos Ortiz de Zevallos Paz-Soldán, ed., *Negociación Ferreyros-Olañeta, 1830–1831*, vol. 7 of *Archivo Diplomático Peruano*, 9 vols. (Lima: Ministerio de Relaciones Exteriores, 1958), pp. vii–xxxii; Arona, *Páginas diplomáticas*, pp. 133–142.

7. Carlos Ortiz de Zevallos Paz Soldán, ed., *La misión La Torre en Bolivia (1831–1835)*, vol. 8 of *Archivo Diplomático Peruano*, 9 vols. (Lima: Ministerio de Relaciones Exteriores, 1971), pp. xvii–xviii.

8. Robert N. Burr, *By Reason or Force: Chile and the Balancing of Power in South America, 1830–1905* (Berkeley and Los Angeles: University of California Press, 1965), pp. 26–27. Copies of the peace and commercial treaties can be found in Ortiz de Zevallos, *La misión La Torre*, pp. 3–17.

9. A copy of the November 1832 commercial treaty can be found in Ortiz de Zevallos, *La misión La Torre*, pp. 19–23.

10. A copy of the 1835 Treaty of La Paz can be found in Carlos Ortiz de Zevallos Paz-Soldán, ed., *Confederación Perú-Boliviana. Volumen I: Estado Nor Peruano-Estado Sud Peruano-Bolivia (1835–1839)*, vol. 9 of *Archivo Diplomático Peruano*, 9 vols. (Lima: Ministerio de Relaciones Exteriores, 1972), pp. 17–19.

11. Paul Gootenberg, *Between Silver and Guano: Commercial Policy and the State in Postindependence Peru* (Princeton: Princeton University Press, 1989), pp. 21–33; Bonilla, *Gran Bretaña*, 5:76–77; Burr, *By Reason or Force*, pp. 30–31, 36–37.

12. Nolan, "Diplomatic and Commercial Relations," pp. 76, 109–110, 255–258.

13. W. M. Mathew, "The Imperialism of Free Trade: Peru, 1820–70," *Economic History Review* 2, 21 (December 1968): 566–567; Gootenberg, *Between Silver and Guano*, pp. 18–21.

14. Ortiz de Zevallos, *Confederación Perú-Boliviana. Volumen I*, pp. 67–71; Alcides Arguedas, *Historia de Bolivia*, 5 vols. (La Paz: Librería Editorial "Juventud," 1981), 2:141–161.

15. Alberto Ulloa Sotomayor, *Posición internacional del Perú* (Lima: Imprenta Torres Aguirre, 1941), pp. 255–259.

16. Francisco A. Encina, *Resumen de la Historia de Chile*, 2d ed., 3 vols. (Santiago: Empresa Editora Zig-Zag, 1956), 2:895–900.

17. Gootenberg, *Between Silver and Guano*, pp. 38–46.

18. Modesto Basadre y Chocano, *Diez años de historia política del Perú (1834–1844)* (Lima: Editorial Huascarán, 1953), pp. 45–46.

19. Burr, *By Reason or Force*, pp. 39–40; Encina, *Resumen*, pp. 901–903; Parkerson, "Sub-Regional Integration," pp. 212–214.

20. Parkerson, "Sub-Regional Integration," pp. 223–228; Crespo, *Santa Cruz*, pp. 265–267; Basadre y Chocano, *Diez años*, p. 56.

21. Carlos Ortiz de Zevallos Paz-Soldán, ed., *Confederación Perú-Boliviana. Volumen II: Ecuador (1835–1839)*, vol. 9 of *Archivo Diplomático Peruano*, 9 vols. (Lima: Ministerio de Relaciones Exteriores, 1974), p. 163; Basadre y Chocano, *Diez años*, p. 53.

22. Burr, *By Reason or Force*, pp. 49–51; Basadre, *Historia*, 2:151.

23. Encina, *Resumen*, pp. 922–925; Basadre y Chocano, *Diez años*, p. 60.

24. Clemente Basile, *Una Guerra poca conocida*, 2 vols. (Buenos Aires: Círculo Militar, 1943), 2:146, 164–166, 192–194.

25. Burr, *By Reason or Force*, pp. 51–52; Roberto Querejazu Calvo, *Bolivia y los ingleses, 1825–1948* (Cochabamba: Editorial "Los Amigos del Libro," 1973), pp. 191, 241.

26. Parkerson, "Sub-Regional Integration," pp. 291–307; Basadre, *Historia*, 2:156.

27. Basadre y Chocano, *Diez años*, pp. 67–71; Burr, *By Reason or Force*, pp. 53–54.

28. Basadre, *Historia*, 2:161–163.

29. Parkerson, "Sub-Regional Integration," pp. 326–329; Basadre y Chocano, *Diez años*, p. 73.

30. Crespo, *Santa Cruz*, pp. 339, 347–348; Basadre, *Chile, Perú y Bolivia*, pp. 191–192.

31. Basadre y Chocano, *Diez años*, pp. 87–117; Basadre, *Historia*, 2:204.

32. Burr, *By Reason or Force*, pp. 66–68.

33. Pérez Concha, *Ensayo*, 1:109–114; Burr, *By Reason or Force*, pp. 64–66.

34. Arturo García Salazar, *Resumen de historia diplomática del Perú, 1820–1884* (Lima: Talleres Gráficos Sanmartí y Cía, 1928), pp. 112–118; Pérez Concha, *Ensayo*, 1:114–127.

FOUR

End of the Beginning, 1845–1862

The election of Ramón Castilla to the presidency of Peru in April 1845 was a milestone in the development of the foreign policy of Peru. Prior to Castilla's elevation, Peru was a weak, divided nation with vague, limited ambitions. Its foreign policy oscillated between the ineffectual and the nonexistent because the fundamental requirements for an effective foreign policy were not in place. Under Castilla, Peru acquired for the first time the degree of internal peace; centralized, efficient state organization; adequate, reliable public funding; and emerging sense of national unity necessary for the articulation and execution of a foreign policy. At the same time, Castilla channeled much of Peru's newly discovered guano wealth toward creation of the foreign policy machinery and professionalism necessary to pursue his international aims and without which the foreign policy itself would have been valueless.

IMPROVED FOREIGN POLICY MACHINERY

Although San Martín had established the Ministry of State and External Relations in August 1821, just six days after the declaration of independence, effective machinery for the conduct of foreign relations did not exist before Castilla became president. From 1821 to 1845 the management of foreign affairs was the purview of a coterie of aristocratic, albeit often highly competent individuals, some of whom had previous experience under the Spanish administration. Peru's approach to foreign relations resembled that of its neighbors: it lacked structure and professionalism. A high priority of the first Castilla administration (1845–1851) was reorganization of the diplomatic and consular services to increase their efficiency and effectiveness. The president was motivated by the past indignities Peru had suffered at the hands of foreign powers, both because Peru did not command respect abroad and because it lacked a vigorous foreign service able to present its case competently to foreign governments.

On June 31, 1846, Castilla signed the draft of legislation, known as decree 90, that reorganized the diplomatic and consular corps and outlined new job classifications, remuneration, and retirement practices. Ratified by the congress in 1853, it was the first diplomatic law worthy of the name in Peru or elsewhere in Latin America, and it eventually became the longest-standing Peruvian diplomatic legislation. Supplemental legislation strengthened the initial organization, notably decree 553, dated December 4, 1856, which detailed the duties of the external relations minister. By this time, the Ministry of External Relations had achieved the basic structure it was to retain until the twentieth century. Castilla used the legislation to expand the number of diplomatic missions abroad and to upgrade the quality of Peruvian diplomats. By 1851 he had reorganized the entire diplomatic corps, improved the professionalism of Peruvian diplomats, and established or upgraded missions in a variety of American and European locations. By 1857 Peru enjoyed abundant diplomatic representation abroad, with missions throughout Latin America, the United States, and Europe. In 1862, the last year of his second term, half of the thirty-six appointed consuls were salaried; only two had been so fifteen years earlier.[1]

DIPLOMACY OF GUANO

Well before the Spanish conquest, native Peruvians had exploited guano deposits in a modest way, but it was not until the 1830s that studies in Europe suggested the importance of the substance as a commercial fertilizer. The so-called guano era began in 1840 when Ramón Castilla, then minister of finance under Gamarra, negotiated the first export contract. Guano was the first major generator of Peruvian capital in the postindependence period, and its exploitation had a tremendous long-term impact on the country's political and economic development. By 1847 guano had become Peru's most important export, and for decades thereafter, guano sales were the government's financial mainstay. Although the income from guano and, later, nitrate sales gave rise to great prosperity, these temporary sources of income proved as much a curse as a blessing for Peru. They encouraged the government to dispense with almost all taxes, except customs, and to develop levels and patterns of expenditure that were unsustainable in more normal times. Due to the debts guaranteed by both products, foreign capital obtained enormous direct influence over the Peruvian economy as well as sporadic indirect influence over the nation's domestic and foreign policies.

On November 10, 1840, Francisco Quiroz, a prominent Peruvian capitalist, in association with several French merchants and the Liverpool firm of William Joseph Myers and Company, negotiated the first guano contract with the Peruvian government. In return for exclusive marketing rights worldwide, the merchants agreed to pay the government 60,000 pesos: 40,000 pesos due immediately, and 10,000 pesos due at the end of both the first and second years of the contract. Of the 40,000 pesos due immediately, the government received 38,500 pesos in the form of depreciated debt certificates from the Lima mint that had been held by one of the French associates, Aquilles Allier. Hence, the initial cash payment received by the Gamarra government was only 1,500 pesos, or approximately 300 pounds sterling. The first guano shipment arrived in England in the spring of 1841, and it was immediately apparent that the product offered potential for enormous profit. Wholesale prices averaged 18 pounds sterling per ton and costs averaged 6 pounds per ton, leaving a profit of 12 pounds sterling per ton. With the volume of 1841 exports estimated at 8,602 tons, the merchants expected to realize profits of roughly 100,000 pounds sterling in the first year, compared with the 300 pounds the Peruvian government had received in cash. Faced with mounting public criticism, the Peruvian government canceled the Quiroz contract on November 27, 1841, on the grounds it was not aware when it granted the contract of the value of guano to Peru. Four months later, the government nationalized the guano deposits.[2]

On December 8, 1841, the Peruvian government signed a second guano contract with the Quiroz group. The new contract ran for only one year and required the merchants to advance the government 287,000 pesos in cash. A third guano contract, dated February 16, 1842, established a corporation composed of the Peruvian government; Quiroz, Allier and Company; the French firm of Puymerol, Poumarrox and Company; and Gibbs, Crawley and Company, the Lima branch of Antony Gibbs and Sons of London. In this contract, the government received an advance totaling 487,000 pesos. The government's demand for these large cash advances was of tremendous consequence because it increased considerably the amount of working capital the guano contractors were obliged to raise. Increasingly large capital requirements put the operation of the guano trade further and further out of the reach of Peruvian entrepreneurs and forced them to turn to England, the chief source of capital in the nineteenth century, for the necessary funds. In 1847 the Peruvian government entered into yet another contract with Gibbs, Crawley and Company and the Montane Company of France, and in 1847–1861, subsequent contracts were made with the Gibbs group.[3]

The details of each guano contract varied considerably, but all of them shared important characteristics. In each, the contractors sought monopoly rights for obvious reasons; the government was willing to grant such rights because they were in conformity with Peruvian tradition and were being granted quite generously in other fields. As to why foreigners were so prominent in the trade, the single most important reason seems to have been that they were the ones best able to provide the government with the large and immediate cash reserves it demanded. This gave foreigners an advantage over their Peruvian rivals, especially as the size of the requisite advances mushroomed. Regarding the relative power within the trade of the contractors and the Peruvian government, evidence suggests that the latter was the stronger, more secure party. Unhappy with the terms of the first contract, the government reshaped the monopoly and nationalized the deposits. By 1842 it had secured for itself the lion's share of any ensuing profits as well as obtained substantial loans in advance of sales without assuming any of the entrepreneurial functions of the trade.

The revenues derived from the sale of guano were of inestimable importance to Peruvian foreign policy in this period. Guano income enabled Castilla to maintain public order. It gave him the means to begin development of a professional army as a disciplined arm of the state. It increased his civilian following by generating thousands of new jobs through public works projects and expansion of the state bureaucracy. It enabled him to consolidate his position among *hacendados* and the new commercial and banking bourgeoisie by granting them virtual immunity from taxation. At a time when governmental expenditures soared to new levels, the internal tax system withered; the government became almost totally dependent on the income from guano and the taxes on foreign trade. It should come as no surprise that the chief objective of Castilla's foreign policy soon became the maintenance of Peruvian sovereignty over the guano deposits. Guano was the irreplaceable source of governmental revenue and thus the key to the successful pursuit of Castilla's foreign and domestic policies.[4]

In default since October 1825, Peru was enabled by its newfound prosperity to commence payment on the national debt. On January 31, 1849, a representative of the Peruvian government, Joaquín José de Osma, and a committee of British bondholders signed an agreement in London that resolved the debts to British investors outstanding since the independence era. The Peruvian government recognized its total foreign debt as 3,776,000 pounds sterling, of which 1,816,000 pounds represented the capital and 1,960,000 pounds three-fourths of the unpaid interest. New bonds were issued to represent the capital and interest, with the Peruvian government agreeing not to buy up the bonds at low market prices, as it had done in the past. Thanks largely to guano revenues, the government was able to service its sterling issues without interruption until 1876. This put Peru in exclusive company: the governments of Chile and Brazil as well as the Province of Buenos Aires were the only other defaulters in the early national period that continued to fulfill their obligations with regularity after clearing up their original defaults.[5]

PROMOTION OF CONTINENTAL SOLIDARITY

During his first administration, President Castilla pursued an alliance with Bolivia that would insure its participation in Peruvian plans for greater hemispheric cooperation. This policy was undermined by many of the same issues that had disturbed Andean relations for the previous two decades. After the conclusion of the 1842 Treaty of Acora, there remained in place a

Bolivian decree, dated February 1842, that put a 20 percent duty on Peruvian agricultural and manufactured goods entering Bolivia. It further included a duty of 25 percent or more on alcoholic beverages. In other areas, commerce between the two states continued to be defined by the 1840 treaty. When the Bolivian government increased its duties in 1844, the Castilla administration retaliated by establishing new or augmented duties on Bolivian imports. At the same time, a clause in the new Peruvian decree indicated that the Castilla administration was willing to rebate Peruvian duties to the same extent as agreed to by the Bolivian government.

Political intrigue and mercantile conflict kept tensions between Peru and Bolivia at a high level, and by 1847 both sides were mobilizing troops and moving them toward the border. Armed conflict was averted when the Bolivian government, faced with popular opposition to war and a congress that refused to authorize military action, proposed a resumption of talks aimed at a new commercial treaty. On November 3, 1847, representatives of Bolivia and Peru met in Arequipa, where they signed a comprehensive treaty of peace and commerce. The signatories agreed to an arbitration of the Bolivian debt to Peru as well as a commission to fix their limits on the basis of natural frontiers. The Bolivian government also agreed to stop the flow of weak money, so-called because its silver content was less than its face value, into southern Peru. Each side agreed to lower or eliminate duties on goods imported from the other as well as goods transshipped to third parties. The Treaty of Arequipa was amended by both parties, and a second treaty was negotiated in Sucre in 1848. In the Sucre agreement, the article relating to limits was couched in general terms but gave clear precedence to colonial titles over natural boundaries. The 1849 treaty also clarified the right of the Peruvian government to charge duties on goods in transit from the port of Arica to Bolivia.[6]

The treaties of Arequipa and Sucre led to temporarily improved mercantile relations between Peru and Bolivia, spawning a series of minor settlements covering commerce and duties at a variety of locations. Unfortunately, the treaties proved to be the last agreements of peace and commerce to be concluded by the two states for well over a decade. Contraband between Peru and Bolivia continued to flourish, and the Bolivian government failed to live up to its treaty obligations concerning the issuance of weak money. In December 1850 and January 1851 armed bands of Bolivians entered Peru, which gave rise to a February 1851 Peruvian decree demanding indemnification for damages arising from such incursions. In his March 1851 congressional message, President Castilla rightly highlighted Bolivia as a potential trouble spot for Peru.[7]

As with Bolivia, the objectives of Peruvian foreign policy toward Ecuador mirrored Castilla's broad concern for enhanced continental solidarity. The Peruvian government sought an alliance with Ecuador that would establish the bases for collaboration of the two states against foreign aggression and provide a mechanism to resolve their troublesome border dispute. Regarding the latter, the Peruvian goal remained Ecuadorian recognition of its title to the provinces of Tumbes, Jaén and Maynas. As part of this broader strategy, the Castilla administration also hoped to secure the tranquility of Peru's northern frontier, thereby eliminating the danger of an Ecuador-Bolivia encirclement, a constant concern of Peruvian diplomacy.

Castilla's Ecuadorian policy was soon put to a practical test. In June 1845 Guayaquil liberals exiled dictator Juan José Flores, the first president of Ecuador and its virtual ruler since independence. Flores proceeded to Europe, where he plotted with European governments, especially Spain, for establishment of a monarchy in Ecuador. Even though the overall motives of Flores remain unclear and may have been simply the reestablishment of himself in Ecuador, his collusion with the Spanish government raised the specter of a wider expedition aimed at reestablishing the Spanish monarchy in Latin America. The Castilla administration rightly viewed the activities of Flores as a potential threat to the security and independence of Peru, especially since the Spanish government had not yet recognized Peruvian independence.[8]

Reacting immediately, the Castilla government joined other Latin American states in sending protest notes to the British and Spanish governments. On November 9, 1846, it asked Bolivia, Chile, and Ecuador to join it in opposing external intervention in the Americas. Two days later, it directed to all the governments in the hemisphere, including the United States, a circular that decried Spanish policy and invited the recipients to a congress in Lima. On the military front, the Castilla administration secured Ecuadorian and Colombian agreement to oppose the Flores expedition by force of arms and sent military supplies to Guayaquil. In December 1846 Castilla unsuccessfully approached the US government with a proposal to buy two warships. The threat posed by Flores eventually collapsed after Great Britain detained the expedition's ships and a change in government occurred in Spain. Nevertheless, the diplomatic campaign mounted by the Peruvian government, combined with its willingess to oppose the expedition with a combination of economic reprisals and joint military operations, was impressive. Although inclusion of the US government in Peruvian circulars and negotiations tacitly invoked the Monroe Doctrine, it was Peruvian diplomacy, not the US government, that effectively mobilized opinion in Europe and the Americas against the Flores expedition and thus contributed to its failure.[9]

The international conference proposed in November 1846 by the Castilla administration was installed in Lima on December 11, 1847; after twenty-one sessions, it closed on March 1, 1848. The delegates sought to guarantee the independence and territorial integrity of the participating states, to mold them into a league of nations capable of resisting aggression, and to codify a uniform body of international law applicable to all the states in the hemisphere. The Flores expedition provided a pretext for the meeting, but the gathering marked an effort by the Castilla administration to continue the work begun at the 1826 Panama Conference. For much of the next two decades, the Peruvian government continued to provide leadership in working toward greater continental cooperation and unity.

The delegates to the Lima Conference signed four treaties, the most important of which was a treaty of union and confederation. Its stated purpose was to sustain the sovereignty and independence of the signatories, to maintain their territorial integrity, and to support one another against outrage or offense. The treaty loosely provided for mutual aid in the event of external attack, regular meetings, and the peaceful resolution of disputes. The delegates also signed a consular convention, a treaty of commerce and navigation, and a postal convention. Peru sponsored the consular convention because the Castilla administration hoped to restrict, in an international agreement, the power of consular agents as part of its overall strategy to reduce foreign claims. The convention outlined the functions, rights, and obligations of consular agents. Denied diplomatic status, they were provided the fundamental immunities and guarantees necessary to their work but otherwise placed under the jurisdiction of local laws and courts. The treaty of commerce and navigation strove to protect and develop the trade of the signatories. New Granada's eventual ratification of the consular convention marked the only one of the four pacts ever to be ratified by any government.[10]

CLAIMS, TRADE, AND DEVELOPMENT

On March 17, 1841, the United States and Peru agreed to a convention that resolved all outstanding claims from the independence era. The agreement, as amended by the Peruvian congress, provided for the payment of $300,000 in ten equal annual installments beginning January 1, 1846. From the beginning, the Peruvian government experienced difficulty in meeting this obligation, and a pattern of delayed payments, coupled with mutual antagonism, developed over the next decade. In 1849 US claimants sought unsuccessfully to credit revenues from guano sales in the United States to the debt owed them by the Peruvian government. Given the importance of guano to its treasury, the Peruvian government viewed any attempt to link claims to guano as potentially dangerous and accordingly vigorously opposed this effort.[11]

The US government focused on the resolution of existing claims; the Castilla administration was more interested in establishing new principles to govern the recognition and resolution of future claims. President Castilla sought to protect the rights of both foreigners and the Peruvian government by insuring that legitimate claims were first treated by the appropriate

Peruvian authorities. In line with this policy, Castilla decreed on April 17, 1846, that the government would entertain diplomatic claims only in cases where Peruvian courts had denied or retarded justice. The decree's underlying principle was that judgments pronounced by national courts were valid and final. When virtually all the diplomatic missions in Lima protested this decree, the foreign minister responded in a note that argued that the decree conformed with the principles of both Peruvian and international law. At the same time, the government began arguing that claims could not be pressed by consular agents, only by fully empowered diplomatic representatives.[12]

On July 26, 1851, Peru and the United States finally concluded the first treaty of friendship, commerce, and navigation to regulate their commercial intercourse for any significant period of time. The 1851 treaty embodied the most-favored-nation principle, but it left the signatories free to set duties and otherwise regulate their mutual commerce. In recognition of Peru's turbulent past, the terms of the treaty protected the citizens of both states from detention and from forced loans or contributions. It also prohibited the confiscation or use of their vessels or merchandise for public purposes without advance payment. In effect for almost twelve years, the 1851 treaty marked the beginning of improved commercial relations between the signatories.

The Castilla administration, together with that of General José Rufino Echenique, took important steps to open the Amazon Basin to trade and settlement. Old trails were repaired and new ones built, and steamers were ordered for the fluvial highways that laced the region. Two large vessels, commissioned the *Morona* and *Pastasa,* were built to operate on the Amazon itself, and two smaller boats, the *Putumayo* and *Napo,* were designed to explore the tributaries. Military posts in the eastern lowlands were reinforced, and the government increased public services and supported the activities of missionaries in the region. In 1857 the littoral province of Loreto was created, its capital Moyobamba; in 1861, Loreto was upgraded to department status.

The legal basis for Peruvian territorial claims in the Amazon Basin centered on the applicability of treaties negotiated by the governments of Spain and Portugal in the eighteenth century. In January 1750 Spain and Portugal had agreed to a set of general principles to be applied in the delimitation of their respective territories. In conformity with these principles, a boundary line was drawn from the Guaporé River down the Madeira River and ended on the eastern bank of the Javary River. The Peruvian government based its claim to the region on this boundary line. The 1750 treaty was superseded by a preliminary agreement concluded at San Ildefonso in 1777 that generally adopted the 1750 boundary. In 1801 Spain and Portugal went to war; the subsequent peace treaty contained no formal provision for the reinstatement of the 1750 or 1777 treaties or for restoration of the *status quo ante bellum.* The Brazilian government argued that the 1801 war invalidated the Treaty of San Ildefonso, and although Peru and Brazil concluded a treaty in 1841 that accepted the principle of *uti possidetis* to fix their boundary, the treaty went unratified.[13]

Representatives of the US government had expressed interest in opening the Amazon as early as the late 1840s, but official interest was first manifest in May 1850 when the secretary of state asked that a vessel be dispatched to explore the area. Real or potential commercial advantage was the primary motive behind the expedition; however, selected officials also saw the Amazon Basin as a possible site either to resettle southern slaves or to gain land grants for southern planters. The expedition left Lima in May 1851, two months before the 1851 commercial treaty granted the United States full use of the Peruvian portion of the Amazon on a most-favored-nation basis.[14]

Viewing the 1851 Peru-United States pact as a threat to its interests, the Brazilian government largely nullified its stipulations in a subsequent treaty with Peru. The 1851 Herrera–Da Ponte Ribeyro convention provided that navigation on the Amazon River system belonged exclusively to the states owning its banks. Although it was the Brazilian government that initiated the negotiations, Bartolomé Herrera, Echenique's minister of justice and part-time foreign minister, strongly desired an agreement with Brazil. Given Peru's diplomatic problems with its neighbors to the north and south, he believed it imperative for Peru to maintain an amicable relationship with Brazil. Ideology was also a factor; Herrera was an admirer of Brazil's monarchical system. The 1851 agreement between Peru and Brazil was also a treaty of commerce and navigation in that it provided for free commerce in the region and prohibited the slave trade. It also outlined a boundary line and provided for a mixed commission to fix the frontier based on the principle of *uti possidetis*.[15]

After 1851 US diplomats continued their efforts to open the Amazon Basin. Peru and Brazil worked to limit those efforts, largely out of fear that US commerce would dominate the region. US Chargé d'Affaires Clay later used the July 1851 commercial treaty to persuade Peruvian Foreign Minister José Manuel Tirado to issue a decree, dated April 15, 1853, declaring Nauta and Loreto ports of entry, with privileges extended to all countries with whom Peru had a most-favored-nation treaty. Allegedly under Clay's influence, Tirado also issued a circular to Brazil, Ecuador, New Granada, and Venezuela in July 1853 asking them to enter into a conference on the opening of the Amazon. In November 1853 Echenique replaced Tirado with Gregorio Paz-Soldán, and a change in Peruvian policy occurred. On January 4, 1854, the Echenique administration granted Brazilian subjects exclusive rights on the Amazon. The US government was then informed that the July 1851 pact applied only to coastal trade, not to interior rivers. On October 22, 1858, the Castilla administration renewed the 1851 fluvial agreement with Brazil in a convention that recognized the principle that navigation of the Amazon belonged exclusively to the riparian states. The opening of the

Amazon was not guaranteed until Brazil issued a decree on December 7, 1866, that stated that nine months later the Amazon River would become free and open to the merchant ships of all nations. Isolated, the Peruvian government followed the Brazilian example on December 17, 1868, when it declared the navigation of its interior rivers open to all nations.[16]

In addition to the Amazon Basin, immigration was a secondary development concern of the Castilla administration. In the middle of the nineteenth century, Peru was not short of population, but it did lack an adequate labor force, especially in the coastal areas. To address this deficiency, the Peruvian congress on November 17, 1849, passed a general immigration law. Intended to attract Occidentals as well as Orientals, its principal effect was to introduce Chinese into Peru. For this reason, it became generally known as the Chinese Law. One of the reasons China was targeted as a labor source was the assumption that economic conditions in the country of origin had to be worse than those in Peru for immigrants to be attracted in the desired numbers. Chinese immigration was thought to offer the additional advantage of presenting little likelihood of future diplomatic problems, an assumption that proved false. The 1849 law granted anyone introducing no fewer than fifty foreign colonists of either sex between the ages of ten and forty years a payment of thirty pesos per person. The first group of Chinese landed in Peru in October 1849, one month before the law was passed; some 90,000 Chinese came before the trade finally ended in 1874. Based on incomplete data, around 90 percent worked on plantations, with a goodly number later helping to construct railroads. Only a few worked on the guano islands, but the inhumane working conditions there made them a recurrent source of international concern. The defects of the trade arose from the fact that most of the Peruvians involved were businessmen looking for a profit. Multiple abuses and sharp criticism eventually forced the Peruvian government to take action; in 1853–1854, it issued a series of decrees designed to better the living and working conditions of Chinese immigrants. When conditions did not improve, the government in 1856 abrogated the 1849 law and temporarily prohibited the trade.[17]

LIMITED CONTINUITY UNDER ECHENIQUE

Ramón Castilla served as chief executive for two nonconsecutive terms, over twelve years. He was the longest-serving military president; only one civilian, Augusto B. Leguía, was president of Peru for a longer period of time. Inaugurated in April 1851, General Echenique served the intervening term. Personal relations between Castilla and Echenique were not good, but Castilla thought Echenique was the best choice of available candidates. Castilla's reservations proved justified, for Echenique's inept diplomacy soon made Peru a center of intrigue against its neighbors, threatening Castilla's policy of continental solidarity. Surrounded by arch-conservatives, many of whom had monarchical leanings, Echenique first challenged the liberal governments of Ecuador and New Granada, and later almost went to war with Bolivia. With the exception of selected regional policies and a few minor events, the remainder of the Echenique administration's foreign policy reflected the principles laid down by Castilla and thus is incorporated into a discussion of the latter.

When Juan José Flores, now resident in Lima, once again moved to overthrow the Ecuadorian government, the Echenique administration reversed the policy of its predecessor and assisted him with an ill-disguised secrecy reminiscent of the assistance extended to Chile's former President Freire fifteen years earlier. The conservative Echenique's approach was dictated by his alarm over the liberal policies of the incumbent Ecuadorian resident, José María Urbina. The Peruvian president hoped Flores would oust General Urbina and then proceed to New Granada and overturn its newly installed liberal government. Echenique's plan backfired when Flores was defeated in 1852, and the Ecuadorian liberals strengthened their grip on power. Determined to stop Flores, the governments of Ecuador, New Granada, and Venezuela had meanwhile come to the brink of war with Peru. The Chilean government had also declared that it was willing to go to war to protect the independence of a sister republic. At the same time, Chile was prepared to offer mediation if the Flores expedition failed and Ecuador and New Granada still threatened to invade Peru.[18]

During the Flores affair, New Granada, allied with Ecuador, had obtained congressional approval to wage war on any country supporting Flores. In response, the Echenique administration sent Santiago Távara to Bogotá, where on October 20, 1852, he negotiated two protocols, in which he agreed to the cancellation of independence-era debts and the proscription of Flores from Peruvian territory. Although the Távara protocols were never ratified, the governments of Peru and Ecuador reached a wider agreement five months later. In the Tirado-Moncayo convention, dated March 16, 1853, the Echenique government agreed to refuse Flores entrance to Peru, place under Chilean arbitration the captured ships and belongings of the expedition, remove from its frontiers Ecuadorians opposed to the present government in Quito, and generally curtail bellicose preparations against Ecuador in Peruvian territory. President Echenique approved the convention, which ratified the principle of nonintervention, but it was never submitted to the Peruvian congress for formal ratification.[19]

Throughout this period, the Peruvian government followed a guano policy designed to maintain the monopoly while extracting maximum profits from the resource. In modern parlance, it was not a user-friendly approach, and there was periodic interest in Europe and the United States in breaking the monopoly. Soon after the product was introduced in England, for example, British farmers began pressuring their government to seek cheaper guano prices. In this context, it is not surprising that British interests questioned the legality of Peruvian claims to the Lobos Islands off Lambayeque once guano deposits were discovered there in the early 1850s. The Lobos deposits offered an opportunity for British interests to break the Peruvian monopoly on the product; nonetheless, the response of the British government was clear and unequivocal. As the colonial secretary remarked in May 1852, the islands were doubtfully Peruvian, but they were clearly not British. In June 1852 the foreign secretary added that the government's policy was to promote the search for undiscovered guano deposits as opposed to protecting merchants breaking into the monopoly system. At no time did the British government seriously advocate the use of force to break the Peruvian monopoly.[20]

The policy of the US government was neither as clear nor as unequivocal. Controversy arose in 1852 when aging and ailing Secretary of State Daniel Webster was duped into supporting the arguments of New York businessmen that no government had a rightful claim to the Lobos Islands. In June 1852 Webster wrote to the businessmen that the US government was unaware that the islands had been occupied by Peru or Spain. He added that the United States would protect citizens visiting the islands to collect guano. Chargé d'Affaires Clay was quickly caught in the middle of the dispute, for he believed the islands belonged to Peru and had conveyed his arguments in a long dispatch to Washington prior to learning of Webster's position. President Millard Fillmore, who had initialed a draft of Webster's June letter, also concluded the United States had no rightful claim to the islands. Nevertheless, his administration pursued an opportunistic policy that sought to pry guano concessions from Peru in return for recognition of Peruvian sovereignty over the islands.[21]

The Lobos Islands controversy was eventually resolved in Washington on November 17, 1852, in an agreement signed by Secretary of State Edward Everett and the Peruvian minister to the United States, Juan Ignacio de Osma. In return for US recognition of Peru's title to the Lobos Islands as well as other guano islands off the coast of Peru, the Echenique administration agreed to pay above-market freight rates for guano carried by US vessels that had sailed for Peru from June 5 to August 25 with properly endorsed contracts. In addition, the Peruvian government agreed to buy the guano equipment that the same vessels had acquired in expectation of being able to load guano at the islands on their own account. The Everett–De Osma treaty was a major diplomatic success for the Echenique administration, the only one it enjoyed in its short, turbulent tenure. The terms of the agreement fell far short of what the Fillmore administration had been demanding, which amounted to the breakdown of the consignment system. By officially recognizing Peruvian sovereignty over the islands, the US government effectively underwrote the Peruvian monopoly on guano, a monopoly that had become virtually the single source of revenue for the Peruvian government.[22]

As the Echenique government was resolving the Lobos Islands dispute, a crisis with Bolivia again clouded the diplomatic horizon. Under the terms of the 1847 Treaty of Arequipa and the 1848 Treaty of Sucre, the Bolivian government had agreed to check the flow of weak money into Peru. When Bolivia failed to cease emitting underweight currency, diplomatic relations between Peru and Bolivia deteriorated into another trade war that involved the interdiction of frontiers, restricted commerce, reprisals, and ultimatums. After Peru seized the Bolivian port of Cobija and broke diplomatic relations with Bolivia, war seemed imminent. An outbreak of hostilities was prevented only by domestic disturbances in Bolivia and a civil war in Peru. Domingo Elías rose in revolt against Echenique at the end of 1853; Ramón Castilla, criticizing several Echenique policies including his support of Flores and the deterioration in relations with Bolivia, joined the rebellion in early 1854. The yearlong civil war ended on January 5, 1855, with the defeat of Echenique at the battle of La Palma. Castilla was named head of a provisional government, and in July was reelected president of Peru. The foreign policy pursued by the second Castilla administration was largely a continuation of the principles and programs followed from 1845 to 1851.[23]

ECUADOR AND THE
SEARCH FOR COLLECTIVE SECURITY

After 1855 Castilla continued to see the movement for continental solidarity as the optimum means for Peru and its neighbors to safeguard their national sovereignty in the face of real or fancied threats of hegemony from the United States and Europe. When Tennessee-born William Walker seized power in Nicaragua, President Castilla shared the apprehensions of many Latin American statesmen that Walker's actions might herald a new era of US expansionism. Peruvian diplomats were instructed to support the diplomatic representatives of the deposed Nicaraguan regime in any way possible, including financial assistance. The Peruvian representative in Washington was also instructed to protest US diplomatic recognition of the government installed by Walker. The Department of State's response that it had recognized the Walker-backed government because it was the only one in existence in Nicaragua was no more satisfactory to the Castilla administration than it was to several other Latin American governments that filed similar protests.[24]

In response to a Chilean request for guarantees against another invasion by Juan José Flores, the Castilla administration proposed a treaty of defensive and offensive alliance that would provide for a union of Latin American nations for their common defense. A Chilean counterproposal, emphasizing the promotion of commercial and cultural relations and a mutual guarantee of independence, formed the basis for a treaty concluded in Santiago on September 15, 1856. Signed by representatives of Peru, Chile, and Ecuador, the 1856 Continental Treaty incorporated many principles that the Peruvian government had long advocated, including the territorial integrity of member states and nonintervention. On the other hand, there was nothing in the body of the treaty that constituted a union of governments. Although the pact created a congress of plenipotentiaries to act as a consultative body, it did not grant the congress important powers, and it did not include an obligation for common action. Article II was controversial in that it guaranteed freedom of navigation on the interior rivers of the signatories by vessels of the contracting states and thus was contrary to the terms of Peru's 1851 fluvial convention with Brazil. Article XIX addressed Castilla's interest in outlawing war but represented a step backward from the 1848 treaty of union and confederation. The new agreement did not outlaw war but, rather, stated only that the member states would not declare war without first exhausting all peaceful forms of solution. The Continental Treaty was complemented by a treaty of alliance and confederation that was concluded in Washington, D.C., on November 9, 1856. The second agreement focused on guarantees of the independence, sovereignty, and territorial integrity of the signatories. It also provided for a congress of plenipotentiaries but stated explicitly that the body would not assume the prerogatives of member states related to sovereignty and independence.[25]

The Castilla administration actively pursued ratification of the Continental Treaty and, at the same time, led other signatories in pursuing wider support for the pact. In December 1856, Castilla dispatched his minister of justice, Pedro Gálvez, on a diplomatic mission to Central America, where he obtained the adherence of Guatemala, Costa Rica, Nicaragua, and El Salvador. Peruvian diplomatic efforts to garner support for the Continental Treaty stretched from 1856 to 1862, but none of the signatories, including the Peruvian government itself, ever ratified the treaty. Critics in Peru worried about the powers of the congress of plenipotentiaries and whether or not the treaty contained the basis for an alliance. In the final analysis, however, it was the details of the treaty rather than its broad principles that caused the Peruvian congress to reject it. Articles deemed unacceptable included those relating to freedom of navigation, extradition, customs, and legal proceedings. Outside Peru, the nations of the hemisphere proved unprepared for the level of commitment and cooperation encompassed in the 1856 agreements.[26]

From the outset of Castilla's second term, Peruvian ties with Ecuador ranged from unsettled to acrimonious. Diplomatic relations broken in 1855 were finally reestablished after Ecuador adhered to the Continental Treaty, and in August 1857 Juan Celestino Cavero, the newly appointed Peruvian minister to Ecuador, arrived in Quito. One month later, the Ecuadorian government ceded land claimed by Peru in the Amazon area of Canelos to

English creditors in payment for Gran Colombian debts assumed by President Flores in 1837. At least twice previously, the Ecuadorian government had attempted to settle debt issues by transferring part of its territory, but this was the first time it had attempted to transfer title over land also claimed by Peru. The Castilla administration protested this action in an exchange of diplomatic correspondence running into mid-1858. In the course of these talks, Cavero embarked on a tactless, belligerent campaign against Ecuador that was contrary to his instructions and detrimental to his mission. On at least one occasion, he was formally reprimanded by Peruvian Minister of Foreign Affairs Ortiz de Zevallos for his actions, and eventually, he was withdrawn at the request of the Ecuadorian government.[27]

In October 1858 the Peruvian government authorized war with Ecuador if diplomatic mediation proved unsuccessful and ordered a naval blockade of the Ecuadorian coast. A preliminary agreement was reached on August 21, 1859, but with failure to come to a permanent settlement, a Peruvian force commanded by President Castilla invaded Ecuador in November 1859. Surprisingly, no armed encounter took place, for the Peruvian army could find no Ecuadorian force to engage. Instead, it encountered a plethora of mutually hostile Ecuadorian factions controlling different regions of the country. Faced with a fluid political and military situation, Castilla signed a treaty with Guillermo Franco, the Ecuadorian caudillo ruling Guayaquil, and sailed for home.[28]

The Treaty of Mapasingue, dated January 25, 1860, ended the Peruvian invasion of Ecuador and reestablished diplomatic relations between the two states. In the treaty, the Franco regime agreed to nullify the cession of Amazonian lands to English creditors and to accept provisionally Peru's claim to the disputed territories on the basis of *uti possidetis* and the *cédula* of 1802. At the same time, the Guayaquil government reserved the right to present, within two years, new documents in support of its claim to Quijos and Canelos; if it failed to present documents that annulled Peru's right of ownership, it lost all its rights and a mixed commission would fix the border based on Peruvian pretensions. The treaty did not involve an immediate transfer of territory and thus was consistent with Castilla's long-articulated principles on the surrender or transfer of territory in Latin America. On the other hand, it set the stage for a boundary settlement in line with Peru's long-term aspirations. Still, the Treaty of Mapasingue proved a pyrrhic victory. Gabriel García Moreno defeated Guillermo Franco in 1861, established a unified government in Ecuador, and declared the 1860 treaty null and void.[29]

At the very end of Castilla's second term, a final confrontation with Ecuador occurred over the issue of collective security. In 1861 Ecuadorian President García Moreno made proposals to the governments of both Spain and France to establish a protectorate over Ecuador. When the Ecuadorian government failed to respond to a Peruvian request for an explanation of these proposals, the Castilla administration issued a circular to the foreign ministries of Latin America calling for an alliance to safeguard Ecuadorian sovereignty and independence. Castilla appeared ready to fight to prevent the imposition of a protectorate to the north, but diplomacy combined with European disinterest eventually defeated García Moreno's monarchical pretensions.

CONTINUED EMPHASIS ON NATIONAL INTEGRITY

Ramón Castilla entered the presidency determined to assert Peru's ability to defend itself against external pressure, especially from the United States and Europe. In his first term, he made considerable progress toward reducing the number of claims lodged and in resolving through the Peruvian court system those that did arise. His emphasis on claims policy continued after 1855, but the growing interrelationship of claims, the guano trade, and other commercial issues complicated policy in this area. New problems arose under Echenique when US sailors loading guano in the Chincha Islands were assaulted by armed Peruvians; the resultant claims were not resolved until March 1857. In the interim, official Peruvian concern intensified as US involvement in the guano trade increased. In 1854 North American interests pursued a guano concession in the Galapagos Islands, and in 1856 the US Congress offered to annex and protect any previously unclaimed guano island discovered by a US citizen. Meanwhile, commercial relations between the two states deteriorated after Peru's 1854 treaty with Brazil closed the Amazon to US vessels and thus overrode the most-favored-nation clause in their 1851 commercial pact. In 1858 claims and guano were again joined when two American ships, the *Georgiana* and the *Lizzie Thompson,* loading guano during the latter days of the Vivanco revolution, were seized and confiscated by government forces.[30]

Unable to obtain satisfaction for these claims, the United States broke diplomatic relations with Peru in October 1860 and did not renew them for over a year. In December 1862 the two governments signed a claims convention related to the 1858 seizures that designated the king of Belgium as an arbitrator. Peru concluded additional claims agreements with the United States in 1863 and 1868. The 1868 convention provided for the definitive settlement of all claims arising before June 4, 1869, the ratification date of the agreements. In 1870 the commission established by the 1868 agreement concluded its labors and ended the early period of claims controversy. President Castilla's dogged determination to bring order and reason to the question of claims had finally borne fruit.[31]

At the beginning of Castilla's second term, diplomatic relations with Bolivia promised to improve; however, long-term problems hampered significant progress in this area. On September 22, 1855, Castilla decreed that both the commerce between the two Andean republics and the passage of Bolivian goods through Peruvian territory would be regulated by an 1852 accord. This policy reflected Castilla's intent to renounce his predecessor's acts, and the Bolivian government responded positively in October 1855, when it accorded special facilities to Peruvian commerce. At the same time, issues of commerce and weak money continued to hamstring relations between the two states, especially after Bolivian President José María Linares moved to abolish former President Belzu's protectionist policies to encourage increased foreign investment. The departure from Tacna of an abortive expedition of Bolivian dissidents, backed by Peruvian money and recruits, whose objective was the overthrow of the Linares regime, only worsened the situation. Finally, on November 21, 1860, the Peruvian congress authorized war with Bolivia, an act not formally invalidated until October 1862.[32]

In 1861–1862 the Castilla administration resolutely pursued Bolivian collaboration to enhance both hemispheric solidarity and continental defense. With the installation of the moderate government of José María de Acha, diplomatic relations again promised to improve, but once more a series of border episodes inflamed old passions. In the end, President Castilla left office without reaching a conclusive agreement for cooperation or unity with the one state with which Peru had the most in common and should have had the closest diplomatic ties. On the other hand, his initiatives did contribute to the Treaty of Limits, Peace and Friendship signed in Lima on November 5, 1863, a treaty whose significance was best measured by the twenty-five years of bad relations that preceded it. In the treaty, the Bolivian government again agreed to stop issuing weak money, and both governments agreed to monetary policies based on similar principles and conditions. The 1863 treaty was followed in 1864 by a commerce and customs agreement that sought to reduce a burgeoning trade in contraband by opening and expanding commerce between Peru and Bolivia. In return for tariff concessions, the Peruvian government agreed to credit Bolivia annually with a fixed amount of pesos.[33]

POLYNESIAN LABOR TRADE

As the supply of internal capital increased and the Civil War in the United States opened new opportunities for the sale of Peruvian cotton, *hacendados* clamored for reinstatement of the immigration law suspended in 1856. Cheap Asian labor promised both to overcome the chronic shortage in the labor supply and to enable plantation owners to maintain the current wage rate. The alternative was to increase wages to a level sufficient to induce Peruvians to migrate from the sierra to the coast, an expensive option that would have had the longer-term advantage of gradually increasing the national labor force. The congress passed a new immigration law on January 15, 1861, but it was vetoed by Castilla on the grounds it was an unsatisfactory means to deal with the present labor shortage. After the congress overrode the veto, a new law permitting introduction of so-called Asiatic colonists was promulgated in March 1861. A much larger number of Chinese immigrated to Peru in the 1861–1874 period than in the 1849–1856 era. This was due to the growing needs of Peruvian planters and the enthusiasm the Balta administration showed for public works programs.[34]

The subject of immigration was of concern to the second Castilla administration because it led to a short-lived, highly controversial trade in Polynesian immigrants. The Polynesian labor trade began almost by accident when the Peruvian ship *Adelante* stopped in 1861 at an atoll in the Northern Cook Islands to investigate the commercial possibilities of its lagoon and ended up recruiting more than 250 islanders to work in Peru. Before the trade was abolished in April 1863, eighteen ships had landed a total of 2,116 recruits, many of them boarded through coercion, with twelve recruiting vessels still at sea. On Easter Island alone, over 1,400 individuals, an estimated 34 percent of the island's population, were brought to Peru.[35]

Foreign governments with interests in the Pacific began to express concern about the Polynesian labor trade as soon as the *Adelante* returned with the first group of immigrants. The recruitment methods and transportation practices of the trade generated a growing storm of international protest over the next eighteen months, condemning it on legal, moral, and humanitarian grounds. Convinced the Polynesian immigration scheme was an economic failure and that its continuation was damaging Peruvian credibility and international standing, the Peruvian government terminated the trade in the spring of 1863. Evidence of the widespread condemnation was a declaration issued on May 13, 1863, by the diplomatic and consular corps resident in Lima. Deploring the abuses committed in the Polynesian Islands by the labor expeditions, resident diplomats expressed satisfaction with the measures taken by the Peruvian government to prohibit the trade.[36]

When Ramón Castilla left office in 1862, he had influenced the formulation and execution of Peruvian foreign policy for a longer period of time than any other chief executive in the nineteenth century. Before 1845 Peru was a weak, divided country, in which domestic concerns and events largely dictated external relations. Under Castilla, it experienced for the first time an administration that outlined a foreign policy at the beginning of its term and then worked to achieve its objectives. Under his tutelage, Peruvian foreign policy became increasingly comprehensive and coherent, and the Peruvian government assumed a leadership role in continental affairs. Equally important, he improved the structure of the Ministry of Foreign Affairs and increased the professionalism of the Peruvian diplomatic corps, which made it better able to support a wider range of foreign policy goals more effectively. A broad diplomatic effort like that which supported the 1856

Continental Treaty had simply been beyond the scope of the state's capabilities only twenty years earlier.

Castilla's foreign policy was founded on the principles of continental solidarity, nonintervention, and national integrity. Peruvian observers have especially emphasized his devotion to continental solidarity, and his commitment to that ideal was certainly explicit throughout the period. Enjoying a military career that began before independence, Castilla was also devoted to the preservation of national integrity; where the two principles clashed, the latter often won out. In the process, it was the principle of nonintervention that most often suffered. Castilla found it easier to oppose the intervention of the United States or Europe in the Americas than to refrain from a similar policy toward Ecuador and Bolivia. His ongoing difficulty in reconciling these three, sometimes contradictory, principles reached its apogee during the 1859 invasion of Ecuador. In the context of the principle of national integrity, the Castilla administrations devoted considerable time and energy to the delimitation of Peru's frontiers. Every major treaty signed by Peru with its neighbors in this era included some reference to boundaries. Nevertheless, the subject proved as intractable as before and no permanent success was achieved. Peru's borders would not be finally fixed for a century after Castilla took office.

NOTES

1. Rosa Garibaldi de Mendoza, "Peru and the Policy of Hemispheric Defense under Ramón Castilla, 1845–62" (Ph.D. diss., Temple University, 1979), pp. 61–84; Perú, Ministerio de Relaciones Exteriores, *Memoria del Relaciones Exteriores (1847)* (Lima: various publishers, various years), p. 40.

2. W. M. Mathew, "Foreign Contractors and the Peruvian Government at the Outset of the Guano Trade," *Hispanic American Historical Review* 52, 4 (November 1972): 602–605; John Peter Olinger, "Dreyfus Freres, Guano and Peruvian Government Finance: 1869–1880. A Chapter in Economic Imperialism" (Ph.D. diss., State University of New York at Binghamton, 1973), pp. 7–8.

3. Jonathan V. Levin, *The Export Economies: Their Pattern of Development in Historical Perspective* (Cambridge: Harvard University Press, 1960), pp. 52–61; Basadre, *Historia,* 3:155–156.

4. Ruben Vargas Ugarte, *Ramón Castilla* (Buenos Aires: Imprenta López, 1962), pp. 120–136; Miguel A. Martínez, *La Vida Heróica del Liberator, Gran Mariscal Don Ramón Castilla,* 2d ed. (Lima: Imprenta Santa María, 1954), pp. 113–142; Shane J. Hunt, *Growth and Guano in Nineteenth Century Peru,* Woodrow Wilson School Discussion Paper 34 (Princeton: Princeton University, February 1973), pp. 71–72.

5. W. M. Mathew, "The First Anglo-Peruvian Debt and Its Settlement, 1822–49," *Journal of Latin American Studies* 2, 1 (May 1970): 81; Basadre, *Historia,* 3:177–178.

6. Mendoza, "Peru," pp. 28, 127–132.

7. Vargas Ugarte, *Ramón Castilla,* p. 141.

8. Ralph W. Haskins, "Juan José Flores and the Proposed Expedition

Against Ecuador, 1846–1847," *Hispanic American Historical Review* 27, 3 (August 1947): 467–470; Mark J. Van Aken, *King of the Night: Juan José Flores and Ecuador, 1824–1864* (Berkeley: University of California Press, 1989), pp. 157–182.

9. Alberto Ulloa Sotomayor, *Congresos Americanos de Lima*, 2 vols. (Lima: Imprenta Torres Aguirre, 1938), 1:166; Pérez Concha, *Ensayo*, 1:89–117; Van Aken, *King*, pp. 225–233.

10. Oscar Barrenechea y Raygada, *Congresos y conferencias internacionales celebrados en Lima, 1847–1894* (Buenos Aires: Peuser, 1947), pp. 27–28; Francisco Cuevas Cancino, *Del congreso de Panamá a la conferencia de Caracas* (Caracas: Oficina Central de Información, 1976), pp. 222–228.

11. Nolan, "Diplomatic and Commercial Relations," pp. 121–124, 150–151; Basadre, *Historia*, 3:132–133.

12. Mendoza, "Peru," pp. 85–111.

13. John Bassett Moore, *Brazil and Peru Boundary Question* (New York: Knickerbocker Press, 1904), pp. 4–6.

14. Percy Alvin Martin, "The Influence of the United States on the Opening of the Amazon to the World's Commerce," *Hispanic American Historical Review* 1, 2 (May 1918): 148–149.

15. Javier Pérez de Cuéllar, "Relaciones del Perú con el Brasil en el Siglo XX," in *Visión del Perú en el siglo XX*, ed. José Pareja Paz Soldán, 2 vols. (Lima: Ediciones Librería Studium, 1962), 1:76–77.

16. Moore, *Brazil and Peru*, pp. 18–21.

17. Watt Stewart, *Chinese Bondage in Peru: A History of the Chinese Coolie in Peru, 1849–1874* (Durham: Duke University Press, 1951), pp. 12–23; Randall, *Comparative Economic History*, pp. 87–88.

18. José Rufino Echenique, *Memorias para la historia del Perú (1808–1878)*, 2 vols. (Lima: Editorial Huascarán, 1952), 1:171–173; Burr, *By Reason or Force*, pp. 81–83.

19. Basadre, *Historia*, 3:342–347.

20. Mathew, "Imperialism of Free Trade," pp. 569–577; Basadre, *Historia*, 3:342.

21. Nolan, "Diplomatic and Commercial Relations," pp. 155–164.

22. Basadre, *Historia*, 3:341.

23. Vargas Ugarte, *Ramón Castilla*, pp. 152–154; Pérez del Castillo, *Bolivia*, pp. 206–208.

24. Pedro Ugarteche, *El Perú en la vida internacional Americana, 1826–1879* (Lima: Imprenta "Garcilaso," 1927), pp. 18–19.

25. Gustave A. Nuermberger, "The Continental Treaties of 1856: An American Union 'Exclusive of the United States,'" *Hispanic American Historical Review* 20, 1 (March 1940): 39–54. Copies of the Continental Treaty and the 1856 treaty of alliance and confederation can be found in Yepes, *Del congreso de Panamá*, 1:241–254.

26. Ulloa, *Congresos Americanos*, 1:xciii–xcvi.

27. García Salazar, *Resumen*, pp. 134–135; Pérez Concha, *Ensayo*, 1:152–158, 169–175.

28. Basadre, *Historia*, 4:239–245.

29. Vargas Ugarte, *Ramón Castilla*, pp. 187–188; Basadre, *Historia*, 4:247–255; Pérez Concha, *Ensayo*, 1:175–181.

30. Nolan, "Diplomatic and Commercial Relations," pp. 177–187.

31. Louis Clinton Nolan, "The Relations of the United States and Peru with Respect to Claims, 1822–1870," *Hispanic American Historical Review* 17, 1 (February 1937): 39–63.

32. Fredrick B. Pike, *The United States and the Andean Republics: Peru, Bolivia, and Ecuador* (Cambridge: Harvard University Press, 1977), pp. 125–126; Basadre, *Historia,* 4:283–285.

33. Mendoza, "Peru," pp. 143–144. A copy of the 1863 treaty can be found in Perú, Ministerio de Relaciones Exteriores, *Tratados, Convenciones y Acuerdos vigentes entre el Perú y otros Estados,* 2 vols. (Lima: Imprenta Torres Aguirre, 1936), 1:55–63.

34. H. E. Maude, *Slavers in Paradise: The Peruvian Slave Trade in Polynesia, 1862–1864* (Stanford: Stanford University Press, 1981), p. 2; Randall, *Comparative Economic History,* pp. 89–92.

35. Maude, *Slavers in Paradise,* pp. 5–11, 20, 135–138.

36. Ibid., pp. 92–105, 147–149; Basadre, *Historia,* 5:175.

FIVE

Rivalry in the Pacific, 1862–1872

The decade of the 1860s offered Peruvian diplomacy a unique opportunity for enhanced regional status and wider continental leadership. The Castilla administrations had for the first time articulated a coherent, comprehensive foreign policy founded on the principles of continental solidarity, nonintervention, and national integrity. They had also helped develop the machinery necessary for the pursuit of a more effective foreign policy by improving the structure and organization of the Peruvian diplomatic corps. In their aftermath, the clear challenge presented successor regimes was to advance and build upon these achievements in a fashion that advanced the external interests of Peru. Faced with this opportunity, all of the presidential administrations that governed Peru in the decade after Castilla pursued similar foreign policy objectives but with only a limited degree of success. Short-term hemispheric solidarity did thwart a Spanish intervention in Latin American affairs and preserve national integrity. At the same time, it highlighted the severe fiscal limitations under which the Peruvian state was operating. Postwar economic policies further restricted the capabilities of the Peruvian state to pursue a successful foreign policy. Most of the decade was a story of politics and diplomacy, but it was the growing economic crisis at the end of the period that proved decisive in subsequent postmortems on what should have been a period to consolidate the gains of Castilla.

SPANISH THREAT TO NATIONAL INTEGRITY

In the four decades after independence, Peru's diplomatic relations with Spain were never amicable. Spanish involvement in Latin American politics, often in concert with other European powers, added to the tensions that characterized this relationship. The Spanish government made feeble attempts to invade Mexico and Central America in 1829 and 1832, and the French government occupied Vera Cruz in 1838 to force Mexico to pay alleged debts. France also blockaded Buenos Aires in 1838–1840, and again five years later, when it joined British forces to discipline Argentine President Juan Manuel de Rosas. Finally, the Flores expedition in the early years of the first Castilla administration raised the specter of a broader intervention aimed at reestablishing the Spanish monarchy in Latin America. Although the real intent of such events remains debatable, ongoing European intervention in the domestic affairs of the Latin American republics fostered Peruvian insecurity, especially because the Spanish government had never formally recognized Peruvian independence.

In the early 1860s the Spanish government again intervened in the Americas. In Santo Domingo, Spain supported a political faction seeking reincorporation with the Spanish empire. In Mexico, it joined England and France in a military intervention intended to force payment of debts. There was little evidence to suggest either action presaged a campaign of general recolonization, but the Spanish interventions in Santo Domingo and Mexico, coupled with European involvement elsewhere in the Americas, were viewed in Peru as a serious threat to the basic principles of its foreign policy. Greatly alarmed, the Castilla administration launched a diplomatic campaign aimed at developing a united opposition to Spanish aggression. In circulars issued in the fall of 1861, the Peruvian government protested Spain's reannexation of Santo Domingo and opposed the joint European intervention in Mexico. It was thus the first American state to take concrete action in opposition to both transgressions.[1]

Concerned with the growing tide of anti-Spanish sentiment that was sweeping Latin America, Madrid responded by dispatching a scientific expedition to the eastern Pacific region that also served as a show of naval force. The confidential instructions given to Rear Admiral Luis Hernández Pinzón, commander of the squadron, stressed that Spain would tolerate no violence against its nationals in South America. Special reference was made to Peru and the fact that its relations with Spain had not been cordial. Pinzón was instructed to emphasize that Spanish policy was one of moderation but firmness. The Spanish government would not tolerate prejudicial acts against Spaniards living in Peru or defamatory remarks against the Spanish state, such as had recently appeared in the Peruvian press. Pinzón's instructions reflected a strong sense of the honor and pride that heavily influenced later Spanish policies.[2]

The Spanish expedition departed Cádiz in August 1862, and after stops in Brazil, Uruguay, and Argentina, it reached Chile in March 1863. In the course of its visit, Pinzón received a letter from José Merino Ballesteros, the recently appointed Spanish vice consul to Peru. On the day he had presented his credentials to the Peruvian government, Ballesteros issued a statement that contained derogatory remarks about a Ramón Castilla speech. In response to this indiscretion, the Peruvian government refused to accredit him on the grounds his presence in Peru would increase tension between the two states. In a note to Pinzón, Ballesteros spoke of the hostile attitude toward Spain that existed in Peru. The contents of the note infuriated the Spanish rear admiral and prompted him to criticize Peru in public statements made in Chile.[3]

The Spanish squadron arrived off Callao on July 10, 1863; an official welcome was extended, but the fleet soon departed, in part to avoid participation in forthcoming Peruvian independence day celebrations. Peru's diplomatic relations with Spain steadily deteriorated over the next nine months, a central event being the so-called Talambo affair. In 1860 a number of Spanish families had immigrated to Peru to work as agricultural laborers on the Talambo estate in the province of Chiclayo. On August 4, 1863, minor grievances over contract violations at Talambo developed into a major incident in which one Spanish laborer was killed and four others were injured. A Peruvian national also died from injuries sustained in the melee. In line with Castilla's approach to foreign claims, the Peruvian government attempted to resolve the issue through the court system. Legal proceedings were begun immediately but progressed slowly in accordance with prevailing legal procedures. The Spanish government found the ensuing delays unacceptable and demanded the Pezet administration intervene in the case and expedite its resolution.[4]

As the Talambo affair unfolded, Eusebio de Salazar y Mazarredo, a former member of the Spanish Chamber of Deputies, happened to be traveling in Peru studying local economic and political conditions. On his return voyage to Spain, he met in Acapulco with Rear Admiral Pinzón to present his observations on recent events in Peru. He also solicited Pinzón's cooperation in what developed into a Spanish occupation of the Chincha Islands off Pisco. Shortly after returning to Spain, Salazar y Mazarredo was appointed resident minister to Bolivia and special commissioner to Peru, and instructed to obtain the satisfaction, in terms of Peruvian treatment of Spanish nationals, due Spain. At the same time, both his public and confidential instructions directed him to seek a peaceful resolution to the dispute.[5]

When Salazar y Mazarredo presented his credentials to Peruvian Foreign Minister Juan Antonio Ribeyro on March 30, 1864, the Peruvian government informed him it could not accept him in the capacity of a special commissioner. Reminiscent of the arbitrary powers of the royal commissioners during the colonial government of Peru, his proposed title aroused fears in Peru that Spain was not disposed to recognize Peruvian independence. On April 1, 1864, Ribeyro directed a polite note to Salazar y Mazarredo that indicated the willingness of the Peruvian government to accept him as an official representative of Spain as long as he adopted a different title, such as envoy extraordinary or resident minister. Ribeyro emphasized that the Peruvian government did not reject the Spanish emissary or raise any objection to Salazar personally; it found only his title objectionable. Salazar y Mazarredo responded to Ribeyro in an arrogant note, dated April 12, 1864, that distorted both the spirit and content of the latter's communication. The response also contained an extensive and arbitrary review of Spanish-Peruvian relations that expressed biased, prejudicial viewpoints on the rejection of Ballesteros and the Talambo affair. With no apparent interest in the Peruvian reply, Salazar y Mazarredo departed Lima the same day to rendezvous in the Pacific with Pinzón.[6]

On April 14, 1864, a Spanish naval force, led by Rear Admiral Pinzón and Special Commissioner Salazar y Mazarredo, overpowered the Peruvian garrison stationed on the Chincha Islands, occupied the islands, and seized the Peruvian naval vessel *Iquique*. In a joint statement issued on the same day, Pinzón and Salazar y Mazarredo argued that it was the hostile course of Peru that had forced them to take this drastic action. Announcing they would continue to service Peru's foreign debt obligations, they added that they would set aside a portion of guano profits as Spanish recompense for past Peruvian policies. The Spanish squadron appeared determined to occupy the islands and hold them hostage until it gained redress for Spanish claims.[7]

In seizing the Chincha Islands, Salazar y Mazarredo exceeded both the spirit and letter of his instructions. Before leaving Madrid, he had been told to obtain the satisfaction due Spain but to do so, if at all possible, through a peaceful resolution of the dispute. A later set of confidential instructions, which Salazar y Mazarredo had not shown Pinzón, explicitly declared their mission to be one of peace in which force should be used only as a last resort. In a June 1864 letter to his government, Pinzón acknowledged that he had only recently seen these confidential instructions and expressed regret that his recent actions were not in line with government policy. Although the Spanish government emphasized two weeks later that its naval expedition did not have orders to seize the Chincha Islands, it quickly concluded that it could not now back down without losing face. Consequently, Pinzón and Salazar y Mazarredo soon received new instructions that demanded both a Peruvian apology to the Spanish government and restitution to the Talambo victims as prior conditions to the return of the islands.[8]

The Spanish seizure of the Chincha Islands put the Pezet government in a quandary because a central objective of Peruvian foreign policy since the outset of the first Castilla administration had been the maintenance of Peruvian sovereignty over the guano islands. In the intervening years, guano had become the irreplaceable source of government revenue and thus the keystone to the successful pursuit of foreign and domestic policy. Unclear as to Spain's exact motives and too weak politically and militarily to confront the Spanish government decisively, the initial response of the Pezet government was hesitant. On April 16, 1864, Foreign Minister Ribeyro directed a protest to the Spanish rear admiral that affirmed Peruvian sovereignty over the islands and expressed doubt that the Spanish government approved of the seizure. On the same day, Ribeyro circulated a note to the diplomatic corps in Lima that informed them of the incident.[9]

On May 2, 1864, the Lima-based diplomatic representatives of Bolivia, Chile, France, and the United States launched a mediation effort, to which

Ribeyro responded favorably. He welcomed their assistance as long as the Talambo affair was not discussed and Peru did not have to negotiate with Salazar y Mazarredo. He also established the return of the Chincha Islands, a Spanish salute of the Peruvian flag, and the return of the Peruvian vessel *Iquique* as preconditions for the opening of talks. Once these demands were met, Ribeyro was prepared to exchange envoys and begin negotiations. When the Peruvian terms were communicated to Pinzón and Salazar y Mazarredo, they agreed to return the *Iquique* immediately but refused to salute the Peruvian flag or to withdraw from the islands. Denying rumors that Spain desired to reestablish the monarchy in South America, Pinzón proposed a mixed commission to address the claims of Spanish nationals in Peru. When the mediators reported back to Ribeyro, they were shocked at the cold reception they received. The Pezet government refused to accept the return of the *Iquique* because Pinzón had rejected its other demands. This decision put the diplomats in the embarrassing position of having to return the vessel to Spanish custody. By the middle of June 1864, the Peruvian position had hardened further, with Ribeyro indicating that his government now wished to settle without sending an envoy to Madrid.[10]

Although the Pezet administration hoped Spain would adopt a more conciliatory position, the negotiating stance of the latter also hardened in the summer of 1864. On June 21 Salazar y Mazarredo submitted to his government a long, distorted report of the Chincha affair and subsequent events. Based on this document, the Spanish government issued a circular in June that argued that Spain had a right to send a diplomatic representative to Peru and the latter had no right to refuse him. Before Peru could recover the Chincha Islands, Spain demanded that Peru declare itself unaware of alleged criminal acts against Salazar y Mazarredo and receive a Spanish envoy with instructions to obtain justice for the Talambo crimes. The introduction of the question of alleged official or unofficial harassment of Salazar y Mazarredo further complicated negotiations because the charge was both contentious and directly related to issues of personal pride and national honor.[11]

The belligerent attitude of the Peruvian government intensified in the fall of 1864. In a series of circulars to the Peruvian diplomatic corps, the new foreign minister, Toribio Pacheco, protested the June declarations of Spain, especially their support for the accusations of Salazar y Mazarredo. In one such communication, the Peruvian minister of foreign affairs described Salazar y Mazarredo's charges of mistreatment as a national insult more grave than either the occupation of the Chincha Islands or the siezure of the warship *Iquique*. On September 9, 1864, the Peruvian congress authorized the Pezet government to go to war if Spain refused to evacuate the islands and salute the Peruvian flag.

In February 1863 the United States had offered to mediate the dispute, but Spain rejected the proposal because it preferred a bilateral solution. When Washington repeated its offer in the summer of 1864, Madrid again declined, arguing that Spanish public opinion would view outside intervention as an unacceptable insult to Spanish pride. At the same time, Secretary of State William H. Seward suggested Peru send a special agent to Spain authorized to negotiate once Spanish forces had withdrawn and Peruvian property was restored. In July 1864 a Peruvian envoy sailed for Europe, reaching London in August, but he never proceeded to Madrid. President Pezet refused to accredit any diplomatic representatives to Spain for the purpose of negotiating a settlement before the Spanish government had retracted its charges and returned the Chincha Islands.[12]

Despite the unilateral approach of the US government, Great Britain regarded the Spanish intervention as a European as well as a Latin American question. The British government favored a policy of concerted diplomatic action, and in October 1864 proposed a joint mediation with France. The exact motivations for their unsuccessful mediation have remained unclear, but both governments were undoubtedly worried about the economic consequences of the Spanish intervention. Great Britain was concerned the dispute would damage its extensive commercial relations with Chile; France was concerned about the economic impact of the Spanish blockade.[13]

SEARCH FOR CONTINENTAL SOLIDARITY

As early as 1861, the Castilla government had called for a new inter-American conference. The threat posed by the Spanish intervention caused the Pezet administration to renew the invitation in January 1864. Although Peruvians later depicted the Second Lima Conference primarily as a reflection of Peru's long-term commitment to continental unity, the delegates also assembled to challenge Spanish policy in the Americas. Before the conference formally opened on November 14, 1864, selected delegates met with Rear Admiral Pinzón to emphasize their view that the occupation of the Chincha Islands threatened all American states. They asked him to evacuate the islands and return them to Peru. Pinzón rejected their petition on the grounds he was awaiting new instructions from his government. In the meantime, he maintained that he was bound by the bases for settlement contained in the June 24, 1864, circular. When the delegates repeated their demands to Pinzón's successor, Admiral José Manuel Pareja, he responded that the dispute was a bilateral one that did not involve the other American states. Pareja added that the Spanish government, in a circular dated November 8, 1864, had outlined three preconditions for a Spanish withdrawal from the islands. Spain must receive satisfaction for the offenses to Salazar y Mazarredo; Peru must accept a special commissioner; and Peru must dispatch a plenipotentiary to Spain. Thereafter, the delegates to the conference discontinued their mediation efforts and turned to the planned agenda. Subsequently, many of them publicly criticized what one described as Peru's vacillating diplomacy.[14]

The Second Lima Conference had no impact on the Spanish intervention, but its work toward the goal of increased continental solidarity was noteworthy. In an effort to advance the process initiated at Panama in 1826 and continued in Lima in 1847, much of the dialogue centered on creation of an international organization of American states. The need for such a body was generally accepted, but opinions varied as to its optimum form. The governments of Colombia, Ecuador, and Venezuela supported a compulsory confederation that would deemphasize national sovereignty and delegate both defensive and peacemaking powers to a powerful congress similar to the one envisioned at the First Lima Congress. In turn, the Chilean government argued convincingly for a voluntary arrangement that would emphasize the merits of unrestricted national sovereignty. Chile pressed for creation of a governing body that would serve largely as a clearinghouse for the drafting of multilateral assistance and arbitration treaties. Signatories to the treaties would then be free to interpret their applicability in any given situation.[15]

The terms of the Treaty of Union and Defensive Alliance and the Treaty on the Conservation of Peace, both signed on January 23, 1865, signaled the triumph of the voluntary approach. The participating states agreed to consider cooperation against a common external threat, but they viewed themselves primarily as sovereign entities in a global system of power politics. The conference delegates also agreed to a postal treaty and a treaty of commerce and navigation. All four treaties were later given the same searching reception that Latin American governments had accorded the 1856 Continental Treaty. Once again, the existing level of political and economic development in Latin America proved unprepared for the envisioned degree of hemispheric cooperation. Of the four pacts, only the postal treaty was ever ratified, and that by the Colombian government alone. In this sense, the deliberations of the Second Lima Conference marked a watershed in Latin American thought, for they represented the final attempt by the Latin American republics to achieve cooperation on the basis of confederation. Thereafter, the search for enhanced continental solidarity entered a new phase in which Peru and its neighbors sought wider cooperation in matters of common interest but not at the expense of national sovereignty.[16]

ABORTIVE ATTEMPTS AT SETTLEMENT

As the Second Lima Conference concluded, a variety of factors combined to soften Peru's policy toward Spain. First of all, the Peruvian armed forces remained too weak to challenge the Spanish navy, especially after the Spanish government had replaced Pinzón with Pareja and reinforced its Pacific fleet with three frigates. Various attempts at mediation, including the intervention by the delegates to the inter-American conference, had not produced a settlement. Spain's November 8, 1864, statement, while disavowing any view of conquest or domination in the Americas, made clear Spanish determination to obtain what it termed redress for repeated and manifest injuries. Further, Pezet's indecisive handling of the Spanish intervention was contributing to the growing domestic criticism of his administration.

On December 24, 1864, Pezet asked General Manuel Ignacio de Vivanco to negotiate a settlement with Admiral Pareja. One month later, Vivanco announced a settlement that both embodied a surrender of virtually all Peruvian claims and was much more severe than Pinzón's original demands. Spain agreed to withdraw from the Chincha Islands but not under the terms Peru had been demanding. Vivanco agreed to accredit a minister to Spain but this obligation was not likewise binding on the Spanish government. As a replacement for Salazar y Mazarredo, he agreed to accept another special commissioner empowered to investigate the Talambo affair. He also agreed to conclude in the Spanish capital a treaty of peace, friendship, navigation, and commerce in a manner specified by the Spanish government. As part of the price for peace, Vivanco also recognized debts allegedly owed Spanish subjects as the result of the war of independence, long a contentious subject between the two states. Finally, he agreed to pay Spain an indemnification of 3 million gold pesos to compensate it for expenses incurred during the intervention. The Vivanco-Pareja treaty compromised Peruvian interests in the dispute and was justly condemned in Peru. Peruvian nationalists viewed it as an affront to national honor, especially its acknowledgment that Spain was the aggrieved party and should be indemnified. Unwilling to approve the treaty, the Peruvian congress adjourned without voting on ratification. In a difficult situation, President Pezet finally issued a decree of approval dated February 2, 1865.[17]

Encouraged by the opposition to the settlement, Colonel Mariano Ignacio Prado, prefect of the Department of Arequipa, rose in revolt at the end of the month. The uprising quickly spread to other parts of the country as other elements took up the struggle. General Pedro Diez Canseco, second vice president in the Pezet administration, joined the rebels in June; and Pezet was eventually overthrown in early November 1865. The Diez Canseco government was recognized by the Lima diplomatic corps on November 8, but it was soon forced out of office. At the end of November, Colonel Prado accepted the title Supreme Provisional Chief of the Republic and assumed the duties of chief executive. Prado's elevation marked a decisive point in Peruvian policy toward the Spanish intervention, for he detested the Spanish and refused to compromise with them.

With its domestic support deteriorating, the Pezet administration had moved quickly to comply with the terms of the 1865 Vivanco-Pareja treaty. Peruvian authorities took control of the Chincha Islands on February 3,

1865, and on March 4 the Peruvian government paid Spain the 3-million-peso indemnity. The Pezet administration also sent Domingo Valle Riestra to Madrid as an envoy extraordinary and minister plenipotentiary with instructions to conclude the treaty of peace and friendship called for in the agreement. In July 1865 Ignacio Albistur arrived in Lima as the new special commissioner from Spain. After presenting his credentials and being received in that capacity, he informed the Pezet administration that his government, desirous of improving relations with Peru, had also named him envoy extraordinary and minister plenipotentiary. With the fall of the Pezet government, Albistur was ignored by both the Diez Canseco and Prado administrations and eventually departed Peru on December 21, 1865.[18]

Although a tenuous peace had been secured, the Spanish squadron did not leave the Pacific region, and its continuing presence afforded new opportunities for conflict. In early February 1865, for example, rioting broke out in Lima between Spanish sailors on shore leave and Peruvian citizens. Because indiscretions were committed on both sides, the resulting hostilities further complicated diplomatic relations. Admiral Pareja also felt compelled to chastise Chile for alleged hostile acts, and this was another reason the Spanish fleet continued its Pacific operations. In May 1865 the Spanish minister to Chile handed the Chilean Foreign Office a list of complaints that included public insults to the Spanish flag, a Chilean circular protesting the Chincha Islands seizure, and the closure of Chilean ports to the Spanish fleet during the conflict with Peru. The Spanish government informed Chile that it would not be satisfied until it had received a denial of intended misconduct, a twenty-one-gun salute that would be returned by a similar Spanish salute, and a faithful and exact fulfillment of their treaty of peace and recognition, especially the commercial provisions. Although the Chilean government responded in a conciliatory fashion, it found the Spanish terms totally unacceptable, and after Admiral Pareja delivered a new ultimatum, Chile declared war on Spain. The early days of the war did not go well for Spain, and after Chile captured the Spanish vessel *Covadonga,* Pareja committed suicide at the end of November 1865.[19]

CONTINENTAL SOLIDARITY
THWARTS SPANISH INTERVENTION

Once Chile had declared war on Spain, it moved to bring its Andean neighbors into the fray. Where the Pezet government had resisted such overtures, one of the first acts of the Prado administration was to conclude a treaty of offensive and defensive alliance with Chile. The Ecuadorian government adhered to the treaty at the end of January 1866, and Bolivia joined later in the spring to form the Quadruple Alliance. Peru and Chile were unsuccessful in attempts to persuade Argentina, Uruguay, and Paraguay to adhere to the treaty, but it was understood that Colombia and possibly Venezuela would join if the conflict was prolonged.

On January 13, 1866, the Peruvian government joined Chile in declaring war on Spain; three days later, Foreign Minister Pacheco issued a manifesto that detailed the reasons. He argued that the Vivanco-Pareja treaty was not binding on the Prado administration because it had not been ratified by the Peruvian congress. More to the point, he contended that the congress would not have ratified the treaty, even if it had been placed before it, because the treaty was contrary to the national will and violated national dignity. In consequence, the Prado administration recalled its envoy to Madrid and withdrew Peruvian recognition of Special Commissioner Albistur. The Peruvian government repeated the above arguments in a circular to friendly governments dated January 20, 1866. In a show of hemispheric solidarity, the Prado administration also argued in both statements that a major reason for its declaration of war was Spain's ongoing policy of threat and intimidation toward Chile.[20]

On December 2, 1865, Great Britain and France proposed a new peace formula in which the Chilean government would acknowledge it had intended no insult to Spanish honor and request peaceful relations. In turn, Spain would disavow any intent to acquire territory in Latin America and state its desire for friendly relations with Chile. The Spanish government quickly accepted without alterations the joint good offices tendered. Its attitude was influenced by growing criticism in Europe, concern that Latin American support for Chile was increasing, and domestic sentiment desirous of a settlement. The Chilean government, on the other hand, soon rejected the terms of the Franco-British mediation. While being careful not to reject the offer of good offices, Chile responded that it was no longer in a position to negotiate a separate peace with Spain because it was now tied to Peru by a treaty of alliance. In turn, the Peruvian government rejected the Anglo-French proposal on the grounds that the process did not consider the interests of Peru. Concerned that Chile might conclude a separate peace with Spain, the Prado administration viewed the position of the Chilean government toward the joint proposal as an unequivocal rejection. The British and French governments saw the Chilean response in the same light and later withdrew their offer of good offices.[21]

The Peruvian government believed that the United States would intervene on its behalf, and this false hope determined its reaction to the Anglo-French mediation. Prior to official recognition by the United States, the Prado government had sent Secretary of State Seward a copy of the Peru-Chile alliance together with a statement of the motives that caused Peru to declare war on Spain. The manifesto discussed the Spanish occupation of the Chincha Islands, the 3-million-peso indemnity levied against Peru, the principle of revindication advanced by Spanish representatives, and the Spanish blockade of Chilean ports. At the same time, the Prado administration invited the United States to join the Peru-Chile alliance, one of the first of few explicit invitations for direct US intervention in Andean affairs. Determined to address the Spanish intervention within the framework of the Monroe Doctrine, the United States reaffirmed its neutral policy in late February 1866, and it did not officially recognize the Prado government until three months later.[22]

After welcoming Franco-British good offices in late 1865, Spain hardened its negotiating position again in early 1866. In part, this was due to the public outcry that occurred in Spain when the Chilean capture of the *Covadonga* and the suicide of Pareja became public knowledge. In late March the new Spanish commander, Admiral Casto Mendez Núñez, delivered a comprehensive proposal to the Chilean government. If Chile would acknowledge no prior intent to insult Spain and return the *Covadonga* and other prizes, the Spanish government would reaffirm their ancient friendship and declare that it had no desire for conquest or exclusive influence in the Americas. As proof of this, Spain would return all prizes in its possession and all prisoners of war. After this exchange, the Spanish commander would ask Chile to salute the Spanish squadron with a twenty-one-gun salute. Spain would then reciprocate with an identical salute. Upon completion of the above formalities, the Spanish commander would proceed to Santiago in the capacity of envoy extraordinary and minister plenipotentiary to negotiate a permanent resolution of the dispute. The Chilean government promptly answered that it could not respond to the Mendez Núñez proposal without prior consultations with its Peruvian ally, and that such talks could not occur before the expiry of a March 27 deadline. In an effort to force a settlement, the Spanish squadron bombarded Valparaiso on March 31, 1866. To emphasize that the city was largely undefended, Chilean armed forces held their fire throughout the attack.[23]

After the bombardment, the Spanish squadron lifted its blockade and sailed north into Peruvian waters. Arriving off Callao on April 25, 1866, Mendez Núñez declared a blockade. On April 26 he issued a manifesto. The document reviewed Spanish-Peruvian relations since January 1865, complained of various affronts to Spanish honor, and indicated that his government had directed him to punish Peru for its actions. To this end, he indicated that he would attack Callao and its fortifications after four days. On May 2, 1866, the Spanish squadron bombarded the port, causing considerable damage. In contrast to the Chileans, the Peruvians had prepared for the battle and were able to inflict some damage on the Spanish fleet, although not as much as Peruvian publicists subsequently asserted. In any case, the battle proved a major political victory for the Prado government because it solidified the Peruvian people in their opposition to Spanish policy. After the battle, public opinion in Peru was increasingly united in opposition to a compromise settlement with Spain.[24]

The attack on Callao was a decisive event in the Spanish intervention.

At the conclusion of the bombardment, the Spanish commander, ignoring the damage done to his fleet, simply declared victory over Peru and sailed for home. When news of the bombardment reached Madrid, the Spanish government attempted to turn events to its advantage by quickly announcing the end of the expedition. Under increasing domestic political pressure, Madrid now hoped to terminate the entire affair as soon as possible. Of course, the major stumbling block remained the question of how best to achieve this result. Spain had thought the bombardments would increase its prestige and respect in Peru and Chile; the opposite occurred—the use of violence intensified nationalist feelings in both countries. The governments of Peru and Chile prepared for additional fighting as they continued to press their neighbors to join an anti-Spain alliance.

FRESH ATTEMPTS AT SETTLEMENT

On the evening of October 6, 1866, Secretary of State Seward met with the Peruvian minister to Washington, Federico L. Barreda, in a session that led to a US offer of mediation. Barreda stated that the allies were aware of the difficulties involved in continuing the war, but as their resources increased, they were better able to put pressure on Spain. He also observed that the war had aroused patriotism and exerted a unifying influence on Peru. In short, he felt the combination of the Spanish intervention and the resulting Pacific coast alliance promised to produce political and social results of considerable national and regional value. In what was a generally accurate assessment of political sentiment at the time, Barreda concluded that the existing state of public opinion made it impossible for the allies to agree to peace terms that were not highly honorable and that did not crystallize in some fashion the principle of continental solidarity.[25]

The reaction of the Peruvian government to Seward's subsequent offer of good offices demonstrated the veracity of Barreda's observations. Inclined initially to reject the US proposal because of the extent to which the Spanish threat was unifying Peru, the Prado administration later informed Barreda that it was disposed to accept the offer. On December 20, 1866, the United States issued a circular to all the belligerents inviting them to an April 1867 peace conference in Washington. Under the terms of the proposed mediation, the United States would provide the nonvoting presiding officer, and all participants would agree to ratify any agreement reached. If an agreement proved impossible, the United States would be empowered to appoint another government to arbitrate the dispute. Once all of the belligerents had accepted the terms of the mediation, an armistice was to go immediately into effect.[26]

Within a month, the Spanish government had accepted in principle the mediation, reserving the right to modify the details of the proposal. In the event no settlement was reached, Madrid wanted restrictions on the person or state to be selected as arbitrator. By March 1867 all of the belligerents except Peru had accepted the US invitation. The Prado administration favored the US approach over earlier Franco-British good offices; nevertheless, due to domestic political considerations, it was inclined to reject all of them. The Peruvian government thus continued to make positive comments about the US approach but refused officially to accept or reject it. The policy was disconcerting to Barreda, who rightly complained that it undermined his diplomacy and weakened his credibility in Washington.

In the end, the Peruvian government did not have to take the lead in rejecting the US approach; the Chilean government on April 17, 1867, accepted the proposal with reservations, which amounted to a rejection, and thus torpedoed the peace conference. Chilean opposition to the plan focused on the provision that the United States, in case of disagreement, would name an arbitrator whose decision would be binding. Chile asked for a clarification of this point as well as a clear statement from Spain, prior to the opening of the conference, that it regretted the bombardment of Valparaiso. The Chilean government also claimed the right at the peace talks to brand Spain the aggressor, but wanted prior agreement that its seizure of the *Covadonga* would not be discussed. Finally, Chile wanted to discuss claims against Spain that had accumulated over the years and grown in number as a result of the war. When Spain refused to attend a conference under these conditions, Chile's formal rejection, drawn up in concert with its allies, reached Washington on June 4, 1867.[27]

On August 3, 1867, the Peruvian government also formally rejected the US offer of mediation, citing two principal reasons. First, Peru felt bound to act in concert with its allies. Second, on June 13, 1867, the Peruvian congress had directed the executive branch to continue the war with Spain until it was ordered to do otherwise. The legislation specifically prohibited the government from initiating negotiations aimed at ending the war or signing treaties, preliminary or otherwise, without prior instructions from the congress. Officially, the US mediation ended in failure because of the arbitration provision. Unofficially, it failed because Peru and its allies were simply not ready to end the war.

On March 27, 1868, Secretary of State Seward revived the US mediation in a circular that again suggested a conference in Washington. President Balta informally approved the Seward proposal in September 1868, but it was not until the end of December 1869 that he finally authorized the Peruvian envoy in Washington to represent Peru at the proposed negotiations. When the peace conference eventually convened, it accomplished little beyond freeing the allies to negotiate separately with Spain. The Peruvian government accepted an armistice with Spain on April 11, 1871, and after the breakdown of the conference, it appeared that Peru and Spain might quickly conclude a peace treaty. On August 22, 1872, matters had progressed to the point that the Peruvian government formally accepted a US offer to mediate talks leading to a separate peace. At the same time, it suggested a date be fixed for official meetings with the Spanish government. In fact, Manuel Freyre, the Peruvian minister to the United States, had already been in unofficial contact with his Spanish counterpart in Washington on at least two occasions. Nevertheless, the Balta administration eventually proved unable to pursue a policy so out of keeping with the spirit of the alliance with which Peru had so long acted in harmony. On September 26, 1872, Freyre informed the US government that Peru had decided to suspend all further proceedings. Peru became the first ally to sign a treaty of peace and friendship with Spain, but it did not do so until April 14, 1879.[28]

DETERIORATION IN
RELATIONS WITH CHILE AND BOLIVIA

As the war with Spain ended, Peruvian diplomatic relations with Chile began to cool. Problems first surfaced in early 1867 when the allies argued over a collective response to the US mediation proposal. In an effort to improve commercial relations, Peru and Chile signed a treaty of friendship, commerce, and navigation on September 13, 1867, but the pact was not ratified. With the return of the Peruvian squadron from Chilean waters and the dissolution of the Quadruple Alliance, other events combined to cast a shadow over Peru-Chile relations. At the end of 1867, the Chilean government withdrew its minister to Peru, Marcial Martínez, a strong advocate of good relations between the two states. In 1868 the overthrow of the Prado government further damaged relations, for the administration was very popular in Chile. President Prado had championed the reaction against the Pezet government as well as opposition to the Vivanco-Pareja treaty. The issue of Pacific coast hegemony remained at the center of the renewed competition between Peru and Chile. The end of the Spanish intervention left Peru in a military position superior to Chile's in terms of naval power and defensive installations. At the same time, the war inflicted enormous damage on the Peruvian economy, and Lima subsequently lacked the resources necessary to maintain the temporary military advantage it enjoyed. In this sense, the war helped clarify for Chile the relative military strengths of both Peru and Bolivia. It also made clear to the Chilean government the need to dominate Peruvian naval power and highlighted the relative weakness of the Bolivian army.

The Peruvian government fully recognized the wider implications of Chilean policy, and it attempted to compete with as well as thwart Chilean naval expansion. During the war, Great Britain had impounded two corvettes being constructed for Chile as well as two Spanish frigates. Following a joint Chile-Spain petition for their release in February 1868, the Peruvian government protested to Chile the sailing of the corvettes on the grounds their departure violated the spirit of the Quadruple Alliance. When this protest was ignored, the Balta administration proceeded with a reorganization of the Peruvian army and created a military college and a naval school for training both commissioned and noncommissioned officers. His administration subsequently negotiated for the purchase of additional warships, but the president died before the deal was consummated.[29]

With conclusion of the Spanish intervention, Peruvian relations with Bolivia also deteriorated. After six years of harsh, incompetent rule, domestic opposition to the Melgarejo administration was considerable. In 1870 Bolivian exiles crossed from Peru into Bolivia to coalesce that opposition and overthrow the government. Melgarejo's reaction was swift and savage, and the resultant campaign of terror along the Peruvian frontier threatened war with Peru. Tension relaxed only after Peru concentrated troops along the border and the Melgarejo government assured Peru of its pacific intent. In a March 1870 protocol, Bolivia agreed to pay damages to Peruvians living near the border and to return any Peruvian nationals sequestered in the Bolivian army. Later in the year, Peru and Bolivia signed a new treaty of commerce and tariffs that included a most-favored-nation clause. Approved by the Peruvian congress on October 31, 1872, it was sanctioned by the Peruvian government in late 1876. Unfortunately, the Bolivian government rejected the pact on October 5, 1876, and it was allowed to lapse.[30]

RENEWED EMPHASIS ON
NATIONAL INTEGRITY AND NONINTERVENTION

In 1851 representatives of Peru and Brazil had signed the Herrera–Da Ponte Ribeyro convention, which outlined a boundary line and provided for a mixed commission to fix their shared frontier, based on the principle of *uti possidetis*. Over the next fifteen years, the mixed commission made little progress and both governments played down the importance of the 1851 agreement. At the same time, the Peruvian government increased its territorial claims in a manner that suggested a return to the terms of the 1777 Treaty of San Ildefonso. In 1863, for example, the Peruvian government urged Brazil to fix the boundary along an east-to-west line drawn from the left bank of the Javary River. This marked a rejection of the principle of possession embodied in the 1851 treaty and a return to the treaty of 1777. To support its pretensions, the Peruvian government after 1864 actively explored its Amazon tributaries, and in 1867 appointed a commission to establish the course of important rivers as well as the location of other geographically significant positions.[31]

Peruvian policy in the Amazon Basin was later undermined by a treaty of amity, limits, navigation, commerce, and extradition agreed to by Bolivia and Brazil on March 27, 1867. The so-called Muñoz-Netto convention, like the

1851 treaty between Peru and Brazil, accepted actual possession as the basis for the demarcation of the frontier, drawing a boundary from the source of the Madeira River, formed by the confluence of the Mamore and Beni rivers, to the Javary River. As soon as the Peruvian government learned of this agreement, it delivered a strong protest note to the Bolivian government. On December 20, 1867, Peruvian Foreign Minister José Antonio Barrenechea informed Bolivia that the latter was ceding to Brazil land over which it had no legal title. Adding that Peru would not allow the 1867 treaty to compromise its territorial rights, Barrenechea insisted upon observance of the 1851 Peru-Brazil treaty as reinforced by an 1858 fluvial agreement between the two states. Replying in February 1868, Bolivian Minister of Foreign Affairs Donato Muñoz assured Barrenechea that Bolivia would fully respect Peruvian rights. Concurrently, he took the opportunity to remind his Peruvian colleague that the 1851 treaty stipulated that only the left bank of the Javary was Peruvian; the right bank was Brazilian. According to the Bolivian foreign minister, this feature effectively excluded Peru from any legitimate interest in the territory in question.[32]

After 1867 the Peruvian government continued its efforts to explore and develop the Amazon region. In 1868 and again in 1874, Peru suggested a tripartite conference with Bolivia and Brazil to discuss Amazonian frontiers. Both proposals betrayed a Peruvian intent to revert to the 1777 treaty, and for that reason, the Brazilian government understandably rejected them. Meanwhile, the mixed commission provided for in the 1851 treaty made sporadic progress toward marking the border. On February 11, 1874, Peru and Brazil signed a new convention covering territory on the Putumayo River, a pact that the Colombian government officially protested on the grounds that Colombia itself claimed some of the territory covered in the agreement. Finally, on September 29, 1876, Peru and Brazil concluded an additional settlement regulating navigation on the Putumayo.[33]

In September 1870 Peru and the United States replaced the 1851 commercial treaty with a treaty of friendship, commerce, and navigation. The 1870 agreement differed from its predecessor in several key aspects. The most important one was an article that stated that diplomatic intervention in support of claims could not occur until the claimant had exhausted all possible legal procedures in the country in which the claim was made. This proviso, coupled with the article in the 1868 claims convention that provided for resolution of all claims made before June 4, 1869, raised US-Peruvian relations in this vexing area to a more positive level. In the process, it vindicated Castilla's determination to use claims policy as a means to project national sovereignty and preserve national integrity. Thereafter, the claims relationship between Peru and the United States continued to improve. This was due in large part to the fact that claims were fewer in number because domestic revolts, the source of most claims, became less frequent. In addition, the character of claims changed as they increasingly involved contracts as opposed to damages. The Peruvian government handled new claims with firmness, energy, and tact. In the process, Lima continued to insist that the overriding principle in the resolution of all claims was that foreigners should submit to the same laws as Peruvian citizens.[34]

ECONOMIC CONSEQUENCES
OF THE SPANISH INTERVENTION

Economically, the war with Spain was disastrous for Peru. In the face of a serious external threat, the government squandered its limited financial resources on stores and armaments. At the same time, the internal tension that arose in part from the prolonged conflict increased the level of government expenditure required to maintain public order. At one point in 1865, three separate regiments, led respectively by Pezet, Diez Canseco, and Prado, were competing for scarce national resources. In addition, the Spanish occupation of the Chincha Islands deprived the Peruvian government of substantial guano revenues, its major source of income, for a prolonged period of time. A measure of the economic impact of the war was the need for the Peruvian government, after negotiating an offshore loan in 1862, to resume borrowing in 1865. In 1867 the Peruvian congress passed a law prohibiting the government from signing new guano consignment agreements. A fiscal commission was also named to investigate alleged irregularities in the consignment of guano, but an insurrection in 1868 annulled its enabling act before it could take action.

During the Balta administration in particular, the government adopted radically new economic policies that had very important long-term consequences for foreign policy. Under the direction of Balta's second minister of the treasury, Nicolás de Piérola, the government negotiated huge foreign loans guaranteed by the nation's guano reserves. In the process, it reversed a policy dating back to Castilla, who had been very sensitive to foreign powers gaining control over guano resources. Ending the guano concessions to native capitalists, the Balta administration contracted directly with the French firm of Dreyfus and Company for the sale of the commodity. In exchange, Dreyfus and Company agreed to make large advances to the Peruvian government. By directly controlling guano sales, Piérola believed the government would derive greater revenues. Through more centralized planning, he argued, it could employ its augmented funds to accelerate national development.[35]

Dated July 5, 1869, the Dreyfus contract provided for the sale of 2 million tons of guano with a corresponding advance of funds. It ended the consignment system in that it involved the sale of a fixed quantity of guano at the source to a foreign firm. The agreed price of 60 soles per ton for most of the guano delivered was more favorable to Peru than that previously received from consignees. In addition, the French corporation agreed to advance 2.4 million soles to the Peruvian government, to make monthly advances of 700,000 soles for a stated period of time, and to assume the obligation of servicing the Peruvian external debt. All of these disbursements carried an annual interest of 5 percent until their liquidation, with the funds credited to a government account one year after the guano was shipped from Peru. As long as the contract remained in effect, Dreyfus and Company had an exclusive franchise for the sale of guano in Europe and served as financial agents for Peru in France.[36]

In addition to the financial gains resulting from higher returns on guano sales together with lower interest rates, the Dreyfus contract offered other advantages to the Peruvian government. The Dreyfus house assumed all government debts to the consignment contractors as well as the service of the bonded foreign debt. Once the consignees were repaid, the yearly subsidies appeared sufficient to cover budget deficits; consequently, there was no anticipated need for short-term loans. The arrangement also relaxed the stranglehold the domestic consignees had on the Peruvian treasury, and it helped reveal the extent of their political influence at the highest levels of the nation. In short, the Dreyfus contract provided the government with an opportunity to put its finances in order, and in that light was a real benefit. If the government had pursued a sound program of tax reform and maintained its expenses at 1869 levels, the regular income provided by the contract should have been adequate for its needs.

On the other hand, the contract gave Dreyfus unprecedented power over the Peruvian economy because it marked the first time one company had gained control over the entire European guano market. By controlling the guano trade and making large advances to the Peruvian government, the syndicate Dreyfus immediately formed with two Parisian banks largely regulated the flow of European capital to Peru from 1869 to 1876. The Dreyfus house began the metamorphosis from buyer of guano to banker for the Peruvian government with its involvement in an 1870 government loan for 12 million pounds sterling. In 1872 it also attempted to float for the government a loan of 36.8 million pounds sterling, but it was undersubscribed. In this sense, the power that Dreyfus and Company soon displayed in dealing with both the consignees and the government largely derived not from its role as businessman or banker but from its role as a critical intermediary between the Peruvian government and overseas finance houses.[37]

The Dreyfus contract was a promising financial arrangement that could have allowed Peru to regain a measure of economic stability if its advantages had not been nullified by a poor selection of development projects. The Balta administration poured all its energies, borrowed money, and dwindling guano resources into the construction of railways, which, while unique engineering triumphs, were not profitable enterprises. Railroad construction was not even a budget item in 1867, but it was consuming some 57 percent of total expenditures by 1872. Debt obligations became overwhelming as the service of the new loans raised in 1870 and 1872 quickly absorbed the monthly stipend from Dreyfus and Company, payments originally intended to be the principal support for the ordinary functions of government. The Balta administration continued its reckless borrowing even after Piérola resigned in July 1871. By 1872 Balta had saddled Peru with a foreign debt of some 49 million pounds sterling, approximately ten times the amount owed when he assumed office four years earlier.[38]

Peruvian foreign policy in the 1860s passed through a period of relative quiet before the storm. Although the government was involved in a prolonged dispute with Spain, its diplomatic efforts focused on the familiar concerns of enhanced continental solidarity, nonintervention, and the preservation of national integrity. Little that was new or lasting was accomplished, but the stage was set for some very important policy changes in the coming decade. The all-important rivalry with Chile, temporarily set aside during the Spanish intervention, resumed with a new intensity that eventually led to armed conflict. Equally important, the Peruvian government continued to follow highly suspect economic and financial practices that increasingly limited its freedom of maneuver. Weakened by the Spanish intervention, postwar Peruvian economic policies eventually allowed Chile to redress the military balance in the region. On a more positive note, the successful conclusion to the conflict with Spain confirmed Peruvian statehood while fostering Peruvian nationalism, and with it a growing sense of national identity.

NOTES

1. Emilio Luna Vegas, *Perú y Chile en 5 siglos* (Lima: Talleres Gráficos de la Librería Editorial "Minerva," 1982), pp. 179–180; Roberto Querejazu Calvo, *Guano, Salitre, Sangre: Historia de la Guerra del Pacífico* (La Paz: Editorial Los Amigos del Libro, 1979), p. 45.

2. William Columbus Davis, *The Last Conquistadores: The Spanish Intervention in Peru and Chile, 1863–1866* (Athens: University of Georgia Press, 1950), pp. 21–24; James W. Cortada, "Conflict Diplomacy: United States–Spanish Relations, 1855–1868" (Ph.D. diss., Florida State University, 1973), pp. 386–387.

3. Luna Vegas, *Perú y Chile*, pp. 180–181.

4. García Salazar, *Resumen*, p. 144.

5. Alberto Wagner de Reyna, *Las Relaciones Diplomáticas entre el Perú y Chile durante el Conflicto con España (1864–1866)* (Lima: Ediciones del Sol, 1963), p. 12.

6. Enrique Chirinos Soto, *Historia de la república: 1821-Peru-1982*, 2d ed. (Lima: Editorial "Minerva," 1982), p. 232; Basadre, *Historia*, 5:210–214.

7. Henry E. Dobyns and Paul L. Doughty, *Peru: A Cultural History* (New York: Oxford University Press, 1976), p. 179.

8. Davis, *Last Conquistadores*, pp. 51–54; Cortada, "Conflict Diplomacy," pp. 387–388.

9. Clements R. Markham, *A History of Peru* (Chicago: Charles H. Sergel & Company, 1892), pp. 357–358; Chirinos Soto, *Historia*, pp. 235.

10. *El Comercio* (Lima), May 11, 1864; Wagner de Reyna, *Relaciones Diplomáticas*, pp. 32–42.

11. Basadre, *Historia*, 5:224–225, 231–232; Davis, *Last Conquistadores*, pp. 93–105.

12. Cortada, "Conflict Diplomacy," pp. 389–391.

13. Joséph Smith, *Illusions of Conflict: Anglo-American Diplomacy Toward Latin America, 1865–1896* (Pittsburgh: University of Pittsburgh Press, 1979), pp. 53–54.

14. Robert W. Frazer, "The Role of the Lima Congress, 1864–1865, in the Development of Pan-Americanism," *Hispanic American Historical Review* 29, 3 (August 1949): 321–322.

15. *El Peruano* (Lima), January 20, 1864; Ulloa *Posición*, p. 368; Ugarteche, *Perú*, pp. 28–30.

16. Copies of the treaties can be found in Ulloa, *Congresos Americanos*, 1:547–557.

17. García Salazar, *Resumen*, pp. 149–150; Pérez del Castillo, *Bolivia*, pp. 229–231; Markham, *History of Peru*, p. 358.

18. Cortada, "Conflict Diplomacy," p. 392.

19. Luis Galdames, *A History of Chile*, ed. and trans. Isaac Joslin Cox (Chapel Hill: University of North Carolina Press, 1941), p. 308; Burr, *By Reason or Force*, p. 97.

20. García Salazar, *Resumen*, p. 151; Basadre, *Historia*, 5:308–309; Chirinos Soto, *Historia*, pp. 242–243.

21. Wagner de Reyna, *Relaciones Diplomáticas*, pp. 219–221; Smith, *Illusions of Conflict*, pp. 51–53.

22. Pike, *United States*, pp. 126–127; Nolan, "Diplomatic and Commercial Relations," pp. 301–303.

23. Cortada, "Conflict Diplomacy," pp. 410–411; Markham, *History of Peru*, pp. 361–362.

24. Basadre, *Historia*, 5:316, 334–335; Chirinos Soto, *Historia*, pp. 244–248.

25. Nolan, "Diplomatic and Commercial Relations," p. 318.

26. Wagner de Reyna, *Relaciones Diplomáticas*, pp. 226–244.

27. Cortada, "Conflict Diplomacy," pp. 422–425; Nolan, "Diplomatic and Commercial Relations," p. 324.

28. García Salazar, *Resumen*, p. 153; Nolan, "Diplomatic and Commercial Relations," pp. 332–334.

29. Víctor Villanueva, *El militarismo en el Perú* (Lima: Empresa Gráfica T. Scheuch, 1962), pp. 23–25; Víctor Villanueva, *Cien Años del Ejército Peruano: Frustraciones y Cambios* (Lima: Editorial Juan Mejía Baca, 1972), pp. 16–19.

30. Juán Pablo Gómez, *Vida, Pasión y Muerte de General Mariano Melgarejo* (La Paz: Ediciones Puerta del Sol, 1980), pp. 93–100; Basadre, *Historia*, 6:94–95, 242–243.

31. Frederic William Ganzert, "The Boundary Controversy in the Upper Amazon Between Brazil, Bolivia, and Peru, 1903–1909," *Hispanic American Historical Review* 14, 4 (November 1934): 430–431.

32. Jorge Escobari Cusicanqui, *Historia Diplomática de Bolivia*, 4th ed., 2

vols. (Lima: Industrial Gráfica, 1982), 2:306–307; J. Valerie Fifer, *Bolivia: Land, Location, and Politics Since 1825* (Cambridge: Cambridge University Press, 1972), pp. 101–102; García Salazar, *Resumen*, pp. 153–154.

33. Moore, *Brazil and Peru*, pp. 18–21; Basadre, *Historia*, 7:95–96.

34. Nolan, "Diplomatic and Commercial Relations," pp. i–iv, 210–215, 253; Evaristo San Cristóval, *Manuel Pardo y Lavalle: Su vida y su obra* (Lima: Librería e Imprenta Gil, 1945), pp. 97–101; Basadre, *Historia*, 6:248–250.

35. William H. Wynne, *State Insolvency and Foreign Bondholders: Selected Histories of Governmental Foreign Bond Defaults and Debt Readjustments*, 2 vols. (New Haven: Yale University Press, 1951), 2:113–114; Heraclio Bonilla, *Guano y Burguesía en el Perú* (Lima: Instituto de Estudios Peruanos, 1974), pp. 75–76.

36. Alberto Ulloa Sotomayor, *Don Nicolás de Piérola: Una época de la historia del Perú*, 2d ed. (Lima: Imprenta Editorial "Minerva," 1981), pp. 136–137; Bonilla, *Guano*, pp. 77–84.

37. Olinger, "Dreyfus Freres," pp. 2, 73, 84; Bonilla, *Guano*, pp. 92–93, 100–101.

38. Charles A. McQueen, *Peruvian Public Finance* (Washington, D.C.: Government Printing Office, 1926), pp. 6–7.

SIX

Road to War, 1872–1879

The 1860s were largely a decade lost in the sense of advancing long-term Peruvian foreign policy objectives. The quixotic behavior of the Spanish scientific expedition fully exposed the vulnerabilities of Peruvian power. Although the Spanish intervention did produce a temporary alliance of Andean republics, the volatile nature of the coalition, coupled with the meager results of the Second Lima Conference, highlighted the limited prospects for broader hemispheric unity. In the coming decade, Peru would have a fresh opportunity to put its political and economic house in order and to regain the regional leadership and sense of direction achieved under Castilla.

Faced with rapidly changing political and economic conditions, the foreign policy of Peru, as reflected in the policies of the Partido Civil, the most influential political movement at the time, exemplified both the strengths and weaknesses of the body politic. Because the guano resource was all but depleted, the Peruvian government desperately searched for new ways to reduce government expenditures and raise public sector revenues. At the same time, it tried to restrain and contain an increasingly aggressive southern neighbor intent on putting sufficient military power in place to achieve its goal of regional hegemony. The conflicting claims of the competing parties in the Atacama Desert remained at the center of the resulting imbroglio as the governments of Bolivia, Chile, and Peru all looked to its nitrate deposits to supplement government revenues. Given the prevailing climate of distrust and discontent, the diplomacy related to increased immigration in general and the traffic in Chinese laborers in particular simply added another element of discord. Fortunately, it also led to the opening of both Peruvian and Latin American diplomatic relations with the Far East.

GROWING ECONOMIC CRISIS

With the end of the guano era in sight, the Peruvian government in 1872 was facing a severe economic and financial crisis. Newly elected President Pardo emphasized to the congress the gravity of the situation: Peru faced, in a word, bankruptcy. The current economic plight was the product of economic policies and practices originating in the Castilla years, but the Balta administration received most of the blame. The previous government had squandered vast sums upon public works, allowed ordinary domestic expenditures to exceed revenues, and incurred large deficits with the guano contractors. The external debt had reached a level that required total guano revenues simply to service it, and there was also a large internal debt and a serious budget deficit. With all guano income earmarked for the foreign debt, the remaining revenues amounted to only half the projected budget. The government deficit was out of control, and default appeared inevitable.[1]

President Pardo told the congress that he proposed to expand ordinary revenues to bridge the gap between domestic income and expenditures. To achieve this result, he outlined several concrete measures that included administrative decentralization, an increase in customs duties, and an export duty on nitrate. He argued that increased direct taxation, given the poverty and isolation of the masses, was out of the question. Like Balta and Castilla before him, Pardo refused to meet the economic needs of Peru by turning to a broad program of taxation designed to capture some of the internal capital available. The new export duty on nitrate was the most promising of his proposals. It was a curious feature of the international economy that Peru initially possessed a near monopoly on the two major natural nitrogenous fertilizers, guano and nitrate of soda. Pardo's decisive approach to Peru's economic difficulties offered some grounds for optimism. On the other hand, many observers, especially foreign sources, remained skeptical that his remedies would do anything more than postpone a serious crisis in the nation's financial affairs.[2]

The Pardo administration was committed to ending the Dreyfus contact, but its most pressing need was cash to keep the government running. The Dreyfus company was the only immediate source of funds. Accordingly, the Peruvian government in October 1872 negotiated an agreement that provided for a year's extension of the monthly subsidy of 700,000 soles on terms more favorable than Dreyfus had previously received. Additional contracts were negotiated in March 1873 and April 1874. The October 1872 contract temporarily solidified the political position of Dreyfus and Company, but the firm's relations with the Pardo government deteriorated rapidly. Pardo was never lenient toward the Dreyfus house, and as contractual disputes developed, his administration dealt severely with the contractor. The final years of the April 1874 contract, which set the terminal date of the Dreyfus concession at October 31, 1876, were turbulent. Guano sales failed to improve and the foreign debt escalated. One set of statistics attests to the seriousness of the situation. In 1869 guano sales had amounted to over 4 million pounds sterling and service on the foreign debt came to 1 million pounds. In 1875 guano sales were 2.6 million pounds and service on the foreign debt was 2.57 million pounds. In this milieu, Dreyfus was chiefly interested in liquidating the syndicate and collecting the debt owed by Peru. Understandably, the Pardo government was more interested in finding a company to assume the Dreyfus position.[3]

In May 1875 the Peruvian government opened negotiations in Europe for a new guano contract; an agreement was concluded in June 1876 with a British corporation organized by the London firm of Raphael and Sons and called the Peruvian Guano Company. The so-called Raphael contract provided for the sale by the Peruvian Guano Company of 1.9 million tons of guano at 12 pounds 10 shillings sterling per ton. After a fixed charge for expenses, the company was to pay the Peruvian government 700,000 pounds sterling annually in monthly installments, with the remainder, after payments to Dreyfus, going to the bondholders. At the time, many Peruvians believed the Raphael contract was a better deal for Peru than the Dreyfus contract; nonetheless, the results were most disappointing. Unlike the monopoly-holding sales agents of earlier contracts, the Peruvian Guano Company had to compete with another guano seller as the Dreyfus house was trying to dispose of its large stock of unsold guano. The competition drove the price down and reduced the volume of Guano Company sales. Equally serious was the growing competition from nitrates, a newly popular source of fertilizer that was just beginning to be exploited in Peru. Finally, what had once seemed inexhaustible mountains of guano were nearing depletion, and what remained was of a lower grade, which compounded the price problem.[4]

After independence, Peru exported increasing amounts of nitrates. As quantities increased and prices improved, the government began to view the nitrate resource as a partial solution to its financial difficulties. The first step toward nationalization of the industry occurred in 1873 when the congress approved formation of a government monopoly to purchase nitrate from local producers for resale in Europe. Originating in the Peruvian congress, the monopoly was appropriate at the time because the internal financial situation and the current budget deficit dictated a search for new revenues. It later became impractical, when falling prices made it impossible to guarantee returns to producers. Realizing that the deepening financial crisis called for a more radical solution, the Pardo administration in 1875 nationalized a large part of the nation's nitrate reserves. Through nationalization, the government hoped the industry could be regulated to provide a more regular and predictable source of income.[5]

The 1875 nationalization of nitrates had important international repercussions: it antagonized the Chilean and European capitalists who dominated much of the industry in southern Peru. These dispossessed owners remained intent on regaining their properties, and various European associations were organized for that purpose. One of the objectives of such organizations was to remove the province of Tarapacá from the Peruvian monopoly, and the former owners proved willing to lend their support to Chile for this purpose. Disaffected stockholders also lobbied against the

Peruvian purchase of European armaments at the same time that they were assisting Chile to obtain military supplies. Aided by such support, Chile grew stronger militarily while the relative military might of both Peru and Bolivia declined.[6]

Peru's financial and economic crises, viewed in the context of guano and nitrate policies, came to a head at the end of 1875. On December 18, 1875, the Peruvian minister to France announced what he described as a momentary interruption in the punctuality with which Peru had always held its engagements relative to the foreign debt. Peru defaulted on a public debt of some 32 million pounds sterling after having serviced its sterling issues without interruption since 1849. In justifying the default, the Pardo administration pointed to decreasing guano sales, the annual service requirements of the foreign debt, and the outstanding debt to Dreyfus. Optimistically, the government argued that the situation was not hopeless and that Peru could honor its obligations with the proper guano contract. In the interim, the government announced it would continue to export guano in an effort to generate the revenues necessary to cover lapsed payments.

FOREIGN AND DOMESTIC POLICY

The economic and financial policies of the Pardo administration had a decisive impact on key elements of both foreign and defense policy. To a degree, Civilismo could be accurately characterized as a businessman's approach to government. The emphasis was on cutting costs and generating revenue in an effort to promote broader, faster economic development. In the prevailing atmosphere, military preparedness was accorded a low priority. Whereas in 1870 the army had numbered 12,000 men, in 1875 the nominal strength was only 4,500 men, consisting of three battalions of infantry, three regiments of artillery, and two brigades of cavalry. Although Pardo did reestablish the national guard, military spending in real numbers dropped due to the reduction in the number of regular troops. At the same time, officers' salaries were increased 25 percent in an effort to retain their loyalty, and technical skills were emphasized through improved training and the establishment of both a military college and a naval school. Economy also proved to be the keystone of naval policy under Pardo. After his administration canceled contracts for new warships, Peru lost the naval superiority it had enjoyed since the 1850s. In an era when air power was nonexistent and the mobility of ground forces was extremely limited, control of the sea was strategically crucial to the conduct of war on the west coast of South America. The Pardo administration knew the Chilean government was purchasing superior war vessels, but it refused to take the steps necessary to maintain its naval superiority.[7]

A variety of influential Peruvians, civilians as well as soldiers, were concerned with Pardo's attempts to economize on military preparedness. His approach seemed particularly rash after nationalization of the nitrate deposits had offended the powerful foreign capitalists who controlled much of the nitrate industry in southern Peru. Pardo believed that conclusion of an alliance with Argentina, together with an offensive-defensive pact with Bolivia, would provide Peru with adequate protection against the threat of Chilean military action. Critics of the government's military and foreign policies argued that Argentina as a potential ally and Bolivia as an actual ally were insufficient. They recalled with approval Castilla's admonition that when Chile purchased one warship Peru should purchase two.

Although the Pardo administration weakened Peru's military might, it strengthened the nation's diplomatic machinery. In August 1872 Pardo authorized creation of a number of consultative commissions, including one at the Ministry of Foreign Affairs. The idea for such a body had surfaced as early as November 1868, when the minister of foreign relations, José Antonio Barrenechea, had submitted a reorganization and reform plan to the congress that included formation of a consultative committee to advise the minister. In a broader perspective, Pardo's action was a natural extension of Castilla's efforts to enhance the foreign policy machinery of the state. The first Consultative Commission of Foreign Relations was named on August 31, 1872, and a second was named in June 1886 during the Cáceres administration. The commission was composed of past foreign ministers, congressional experts on foreign policy, former diplomats, and eminent scholars and international lawyers.[8]

RENEWED INTEREST IN IMMIGRATION

With the expansion of public works and construction of railways under Balta, Peruvian *hacendados* again faced a growing labor shortage. Appealing to the government for assistance, they requested 2 million soles to import Chinese laborers. The Pardo administration was less favorably disposed toward the *hacendados* than Balta, but it responded at the end of 1872 by forming the European Immigration Society. As the name implied, the objectives of the society were limited to encouraging and facilitating the immigration of Europeans. The administration allocated only 100,000 soles annually for its use; nevertheless, the program proved a relative success, for more Europeans settled in Peru during Pardo's term than in any other comparable period. Italians constituted the largest number of European immigrants to Peru in the second half of the nineteenth century. They assimilated well and made a lasting contribution to Peruvian economic development. One of the reasons so many Italians settled in Peru was that the Peruvian government had a large *ad honorem* diplomatic representation in Italy, especially in cities that carried on trade with Peru or sent emigrants.[9]

A major reason for the renewed interest in European immigration was that the year 1868 marked the beginning of the end for the coolie trade initiated in 1849. In January 1868 the vessel *Cayaltí* weighed anchor at Callao loaded with Chinese coolies bound for Peruvian coastal plantations. Somewhere along the coast, the Chinese revolted, seized the ship, and sailed for home. The vessel finally reached Japan in August 1868, and there a dispute over the legal rights of the owners, crew, and coolies focused attention on the more regrettable aspects of the trade. In November 1868 the governor of Macao suspended the emigration of Chinese to Peru through Macao, but the trade was quietly resumed the following year. In early 1870 the British governor of Hong Kong declined to recognize César A. del Río as Peruvian consul to Hong Kong on the grounds he was thought to have engaged in the Macao labor traffic. In April 1873 the British government refused to allow any ship so engaged to anchor in Hong Kong waters or to secure supplies in the colony. As the Foreign Office explained to Pedro Gálvez, the Peruvian minister in London, there was no doubt that deplorable abuses had taken place in the Chinese emigration from Macao and that the Chinese had also been maltreated at their destinations. Although the British government accepted the fact that Peru had shown goodwill in treating abuses, there seemed to be no effective system in place to prevent them from continuing to occur.[10]

The heightened international concern for the traffic in Chinese laborers forced the Peruvian government to alter its approach to the trade. In an 1870 report to the congress, the Peruvian minister of foreign affairs informed lawmakers that local commissions would be appointed to investigate the conditions of Chinese laborers on Peruvian *haciendas*. Declaring that immigration would be better handled if it came direct from the Chinese mainland instead of from colonies on the China coast, he then recommended that the congress authorize dispatch of an emissary to China for the purpose of establishing diplomatic relations and entering into an agreement on emigration. In the meantime, the Peruvian government asked the United States to authorize its diplomatic agents in China and Japan to act temporarily for Peru.[11]

GARCIA Y GARCIA MISSION

In late 1872 the Pardo administration dispatched Captain Aurelio García y García on a prolonged diplomatic mission to Japan and China. In instructions dated December 3, 1872, he was directed to conclude treaties with Japan and China that included extraterritorial and most-favored-nation clauses. In addition, the agreements were to provide for freedom of citizens of each of the contracting states to emigrate to the territory of the other. The right of the signatories to establish consulates was to be observed, and for harmonization of Chinese emigration to Peru, it was hoped that China would send an agent to Peru. García y García was authorized to appoint provisional consuls where he thought it necessary, and if he decided a permanent mission was required in either Japan or China, he was authorized to appoint Juan Federico Elmore, a member of his delegation, as chargé d'affaires *ad interim* and consul general. García y García's instructions were excellent in that they gave him ample powers and left him a wide field for initiative.[12]

The Peruvian mission arrived in Japan on February 27, 1873, and the emperor received Captain García y García less than one week later. Preliminary negotiations focused on an earlier controversy involving the *María Luz,* a ship of Peruvian registry whose captain had been charged with mistreating Chinese coolies. By early summer, Peru and Japan had agreed to arbitration of the dispute; Russia subsequently was chosen as the arbitrator. They also agreed to the immediate sale of the *María Luz,* with the costs of its care being paid immediately and the remainder of the proceeds being held by the Japanese government until conclusion of the arbitration. The delegates then turned to negotiation of a treaty of friendship, commerce, and navigation, which was successfully concluded on August 21, 1873. This was Peru's first treaty with an Asian state, and Japan's first treaty with a Latin American nation. It was ratified by the Peruvian congress on September 5, 1874; ratifications were exchanged on May 17, 1875.[13]

In the 1873 treaty, the governments of Peru and Japan pledged peace, friendship, and the mutual protection of persons and property. Key articles established the right to appoint diplomatic and consular representatives, and recognized most-favored-nation treatment and freedom of movement in the signatory states. Extraterritorial jurisdiction was not formally granted by Japan, but a similar result was achieved when Peruvians were granted every privilege, immunity, jurisdiction, and advantage extended other nationals of other states. Japanese dedication to treaty revision, an intent introduced in the preamble, was reiterated in a later article that stated that when Japan's treaties with other foreign powers were revised, Japan and Peru would also conclude a new treaty. As provided for in his instructions, García y García deemed a consular organization to be required in Japan; consequently, he appointed a consul general before continuing to China.[14]

The treaty of 1873 proved most notable for its resolution of a peculiar and negative problem, namely the *María Luz* affair, as opposed to being the starting point for wider, more positive relations. For the next fifteen years, there was little meaningful contact between Peru and Japan. Peruvian efforts to promote trade were unproductive, largely because neither state offered something the other needed. Japan had no interest in guano, Peru's major export, and Peru had minimal demand for the silk, tea, and rice of Japan. In addition, there was little ship movement between the two states. Peru's tiny merchant marine seldom made transpacific voyages, and the small but growing Japanese merchant marine largely confined itself to the sea lanes in the Northern Hemisphere. When a Japanese vessel first called at a Peruvian port in May 1883, little importance was attached to the event. The Japanese government did not move to revise the 1873 treaty until 1889.

Upon concluding the 1873 treaty with Japan, the García y García mission traveled to China, arriving in Tientsin, some eighty miles from Peking, on October 23, 1873. The delegation found public opinion to be extremely hostile, for Peru was considered one of the worst offenders in the very offensive trade in coolies. Captain García y García presented to his Chinese counterpart seven points, which represented what he described as the elevated designs of the Peruvian government. Rejecting the Chinese demand that all coolies be returned to China before a treaty was signed, he agreed to oblige the employers of those laborers, at the end of their contracts, to return them to China, provided they wished to return and the contracts so stated. In addition, he accepted early termination of the contracts if the laborers desired it, and he also agreed to indemnify employers for the costs of such terminations. Most important, he emphasized that the Peruvian government desired only Chinese immigrants who arrived in Peru of their own free and spontaneous will. García y García closed with a request that the Chinese government accredit an agent or agents to Peru to watch over the interests of its nationals.[15]

On June 26, 1874, the representatives of Peru and China signed a treaty of friendship, commerce, and navigation. It provided for the mutual protection of the citizens and subjects of the signatories and for the exchange of diplomatic and consular agents. It also recognized an inalienable right to change one's homeland, thus providing for free and voluntary emigration. China granted Peru a slightly modified form of extraterritoriality. If the Peruvian consul, in a case involving a Chinese and a Peruvian, could not make a satisfactory settlement, he was obliged to seek the assistance of the appropriate Chinese authorities. The treaty also embodied mutual most-favored-nation treatment as to shipping and mercantile rights. It included an emigration convention that provided for a Chinese commission to visit Peru to establish a fuller understanding of the circumstances of laborers living there. The Peruvian government further agreed to oblige employers of Chinese laborers to return them to China at the end of their contracts, provided they wished to return and their contracts so stipulated. If they desired to return but there was no contractual provision for return passage, the Peruvian government agreed to repatriate them at public expense. Both the Treaty of Tientsin and the emigration convention were approved by the Peruvian congress on October 6, 1874; ratifications were exchanged the following year.[16]

The Tientsin agreements did not kill the coolie traffic to Peru; it had died at the end of 1873, when Portugal closed Macao to the trade. On the other hand, the terms of the treaty, in particular the proviso that emigration was now permitted only on a free and voluntary basis, tended to insure the trade would not soon be reopened, at least as far as Peru was concerned. Otherwise, the Peruvian government came out relatively well in the negotiations. China failed to obtain its key bargaining point, that all coolies be repatriated before a treaty was negotiated, but García y García largely realized the seven points outlined in his November 1873 memorandum. After the 1874 agreements were ratified, Juan Federico Elmore remained in China for some months as a Peruvian agent. Upon his return to Lima, he was appointed Peru's first resident minister to China, setting sail for the Far East on May 20, 1878. The first Chinese minister to Peru did not arrive in Lima until late 1883. As in the case of the 1873 treaty with Japan, the 1874 pacts with China were noteworthy, not because they signaled the beginning of a new era in political or commercial relations but because they ended a vexing problem of long standing.

TREATY OF MUTUAL BENEFITS

While the García y García mission was working to normalize relations in the Far East, diplomatic events of a far greater significance were unfolding closer to home. In 1860 Peru owned a 235-mile-long strip of the nitrate-rich Atacama Desert, which included the coastal provinces of Tacna, Arica, and Tarapacá. Bolivia claimed the next 240 miles, which ran from its Loa River boundary with Peru south to the 25th parallel. Bolivia's southern boundary was contested by Chile, and the discovery of vast new mineral deposits in the Mejillones region of the disputed territory brought the controversy to a head in the early 1860s. Feelings ran so high that the Bolivian assembly, meeting in Oruro on June 5, 1863, authorized the chief executive to declare war if a peaceful settlement to the dispute could not be found. Seizing on a moment of anti-Spanish solidarity, Bolivia and Chile later negotiated a treaty in 1866, often referred to as the Treaty of Mutual Benefits, which placed their boundary in the Atacama Desert at the 24th parallel. In the zone between the 23d and 25th parallels, Chilean and Bolivian businesses were assured equal rights, and the two governments agreed to split equally tax revenues realized from the production and sale of mineral resources. The agreement also called for the Bolivian government to open the bay and port of Mejillones and to establish a customs house there.[17]

It was a generous settlement for Chile. Fixing the frontier at the 24th parallel advanced early Chilean claims by some three degrees. The condominium provision also favored Chile. In effect, the Chilean government would receive half the customs due from minerals exported between the 23d and 24th parallels, and the Bolivian government was to receive the same consideration between the 24th and 25th parallels. These terms were advantageous for Chile because the richest mineral deposits were located north of the 24th parallel. Equally important, the terms of the treaty encouraged efficient, aggressive Chilean business interests to exploit the region. The Chileans soon poured in large quantities of capital, managerial and technical skill, and hardworking labor. In short order, they created in the Atacama Desert a mining-industrial complex that was vastly superior to anything the Bolivians could have hoped to achieve in the foreseeable future.

In the course of the 1866 negotiations, the Chilean government offered to help Bolivia appropriate the Peruvian provinces of Tacna and Arica. In return, the Bolivian government was to renounce its claim to the territory between the coastal settlements of Paposo and Mejillones or even as far north as the Loa River. Although Bolivia declined the offer, its terms were an accurate reflection of Chilean ambitions in the littoral. The proposal also marked a resurgence of the old argument that Arica was the natural Pacific port for Bolivia, an idea that had been discussed as early as the independence era. The Arica-for-Bolivia doctrine ran throughout the subsequent Tacna-Arica controversy.[18]

Differing interpretations of the 1866 treaty soon complicated relations between Bolivia and Chile. Because the document did not specify by name the individual items from which Chile was to derive half the fiscal revenues under the condominium provision, the Bolivian government tried to restrict their number, with predictably acrimonious results. In an effort to avoid sharing customs receipts, the Bolivian government also sought to export minerals extracted from the shared zone through the northern port of Cobija. Another controversy centered on Bolivia's contention that Caracoles, an immensely valuable silver deposit discovered in 1870, did not lie within the zone of condominium. In early 1871 the new Bolivian government of General Agustín Morales pressed Chile to renegotiate the objectionable provisions of the 1866 treaty. Encouraged by both Peru and Argentina, Bolivia and Chile signed the Lindsay-Corral protocol on December 5, 1872. The new agreement was intended to clarify issues related to condominium rights, international boundaries, and joint regulations affecting both mineral deposits and customs houses. It smoothed matters temporarily but ignored the deeper issues at the foundation of the rivalries in the Atacama Desert.[19]

PERU-BOLIVIA DEFENSIVE ALLIANCE

In the course of the Bolivia-Chile negotiations, Peru and Bolivia were simultaneously discussing terms for a defensive alliance. On November 8, 1872, the Bolivian assembly authorized the government to negotiate and ratify an alliance with Peru without submitting it to the legislature for approval. On November 19, 1872, the Peruvian cabinet agreed to support Bolivia in opposing Chilean demands that Peru considered unjust and threatening to the independence of Bolivia. Negotiations began almost immediately, and on February 6, 1873, Peru and Bolivia concluded a treaty of defensive alliance. The treaty guaranteed the independence, sovereignty, and territorial integrity of the signatories. Its key provisions related to when and how it might be invoked. The signatories were to ally if a third party sought to deprive one of them of its territory, form of government, or sovereignty. It gave the party appealed to rather than the party allegedly aggrieved the right to decide if the treaty should be invoked. At the same time, it called for the conciliatory settlement of all disputes, with arbitration highlighted as an often successful approach. An additional article stipulated that the treaty should remain secret as long as the contracting parties, by common accord, agreed its publication was unnecessary.[20]

The 1873 treaty was widely discussed yet poorly understood. On the surface, it appeared to be a defensive treaty of mutual assistance. Peruvians were virtually unanimous in the opinion that there was nothing in the treaty that could justifiably alarm a neighboring state. Chilean scholars and polemicists, on the other hand, argued strongly that its language did not agree with the actions of the signatories, which suggested it was really an offensive instrument directed at Chile. Immediate efforts on the part of Peru and Bolivia to make Argentina a party to the agreement were soon at the center of the controversy over whether the pact was an offensive or defensive instrument. In an attempt to take advantage of an Argentine boundary dispute with Chile, Aníbal de la Torre, the Peruvian minister to Argentina, opened negotiations in early 1873. During the talks, the Peruvian diplomat planned to represent both Peru and Bolivia, but he never received the necessary authorization from La Paz. Consequently, the talks were complicated by the ongoing need to consult the Bolivian government. The Argentine government expressed interest in adhering to the 1873 pact but insisted on two preconditions. First, the Bolivian government must settle its boundary dispute with Argentina; second, a Bolivian rupture of relations with Chile could not be considered a *casus foederis* for the alliance. The Bolivians accepted the first proposal but rejected the second.[21]

The Pardo administration was eager to secure Argentine adherence to the 1873 treaty before Chile could take delivery of the ironclads it had on order, warships that threatened to cancel Peru's diminishing naval advantage. Realizing the danger to its position, the Chilean government ordered the *Almirante Cochrane,* the ironclad nearest completion, to put to sea before it was properly fitted out. At this point, the Peruvian government lost the initiative in the diplomatic arena because Chile was increasingly in possession of the military means necessary to impose its own conditions. The Pardo administration did not abandon its efforts to win Argentina to the alliance, but negotiations in Buenos Aires soon became largely a holding action, eventually collapsing in the summer of 1874.[22]

Brazilian interests also complicated the negotiations with Argentina. Argentina and Brazil were regional rivals, and war between the two had been narrowly averted as recently as 1872, when Brazil violated the terms of the

Treaty of Triple Alliance by making a separate peace with Paraguay. With tension between Argentina and Brazil continuing, the Argentine negotiations with Peru and Bolivia provided some basis for a new understanding between Chile and Brazil, a prospect that concerned the government in Buenos Aires. Chile and Brazil did not conclude a formal entente, but the mere prospect of one increased Argentine hesitancy to adhere to the Peru-Bolivia alliance. At the same time, the Pardo administration had begun to fear that the inclusion of Argentina in the alliance might also compromise Peruvian relations with Brazil and endanger its expanding Amazon interests.[23]

TREATY OF SUCRE

Because the 1872 Lindsay-Corral protocol did not resolve the problems between Bolivia and Chile, the two parties reopened discussions in the fall of 1873. After a year of difficult negotiations, an agreement was signed in August 1874 that replaced the 1866 treaty. Known as the Treaty of Sucre, it recognized the 24th parallel as the boundary between Bolivia and Chile, and except for retention of its claim to 50 percent of the region's guano deposits, Chile relinquished its former rights of condominium. Although these provisions were distinctly favorable to Bolivia, Chile did receive a twenty-five-year guarantee against tax increases on Chilean commercial interests and their exported products. In that regard, the Bolivian government had already negotiated a new contract with the Antofagasta Nitrate and Railroad Company that stated no additional taxes would be levied for a period of fifteen years, beginning January 1, 1874. In the Treaty of Sucre, Bolivia also agreed to establish Mejillones and Antofagasta as permanent ports on the Bolivian littoral. The treaty, as amended by a complementary treaty in 1875, abrogated in its entirety the August 10, 1866, agreement.[24]

The Treaty of Sucre temporarily eased regional tensions by creating a false sense of security in Peru and Bolivia. It also strengthened Chile's relative power position because it largely neutralized the Peru-Bolivia alliance and thus eliminated a potential challenge to Chilean diplomacy. The Chilean position was soon enhanced further by new developments. When the ironclad *Valparaíso* joined the *Almirante Cochrane* in January 1875, the Chilean navy achieved parity with, if not supremacy over, that of Peru. In addition, it became increasingly obvious that Peruvian public finances were in wretched shape. Promulgation of the 1874 treaty also encouraged a new commercial invasion of the Atacama Desert by Chilean interests. The Antofagasta Nitrate and Railroad Company, owned jointly by English and Chilean capital, formed the nucleus for the expansion; but other Chilean concerns were actively involved. Moreover, the well-financed, efficient, and aggressive mining and industrial interests of Chile did not restrict their operations to the Bolivian littoral but expanded into Tarapacá. By the end of the 1870s, foreign interests, European as well as Chilean, had acquired almost half of the productive capacity of the Tarapacá nitrate fields.

As it struggled with regional concerns, the Pardo administration also continued to participate actively in the international movement aimed at extending the rule of international law in the Americas. On December 11, 1875, Peru issued an invitation to the American states to attend an inter-American congress of jurists in Lima. The official objective of the meeting was to unify the principles of private international law applicable to the Americas. The United States and Brazil declined to participate, but the governments of Argentina, Bolivia, Chile, Colombia, Cuba, Ecuador, Guatemala, Honduras, and Venezuela accepted the invitation. The congress formally opened on December 9, 1877, and labored until March 1, 1880, when the War of the Pacific interrupted the proceedings. It produced a treaty regulating international private law, dated November 9, 1878, and a treaty on extradition, dated May 27, 1879. The Peruvian congress quickly approved the former, but the latter was never ratified. Delegates to the congress also concluded covenants covering mercantile societies and bills of exchange. With the Peruvian government joining its neighbors in placing greater reliance on international law, the Lima Conference of Jurists signaled a further abandonment of attempts at hemispheric union.[25]

DIPLOMACY OF THE PRADO GOVERNMENT

At the end of Manuel Pardo's term of office, the Civilistas controlled both houses of the congress, but the party was deeply split over the issue of an 1876 presidential candidate. None of the likely choices had the unanimous support of party leaders. In an increasingly difficult situation, Pardo threw his support behind General Mariano Ignacio Prado. Due to the uninterrupted turmoil that had marred Pardo's administration and the well-known fact that Pierola continued his subversive efforts, Peru's first civilian president concluded that only a military man could hope to maintain order over the next four years. Pardo and Prado had worked well together when Pardo served as a minister during the Prado dictatorship, and because the general enjoyed great popularity, Pardo, perhaps with an eye on the 1880 elections, decided to support him. General Prado easily won the election and took office on August 2, 1876.

Initially, the Prado government pursued a conciliatory policy toward Chile. A diplomatic mission was dispatched to Santiago in search of compromise, and on December 27, 1876, a treaty of friendship, commerce, and navigation was signed. At the same time, the diplomatic overtures of the Prado administration lacked direction and commitment and were thus unsuccessful in creating a regional climate conducive to peace. In large part, this was because the government was unable to overcome its concern that

Bolivia, if divested of its alliance with Peru, might come to terms with Chile and join the latter in despoiling the Peruvian province of Tarapacá. The Prado administration was well aware that the Chilean government had approached Bolivia on previous occasions with just such a scheme, and Peru feared that, in different circumstances, its ally might be tempted to accept.

Under these conditions, the Prado administration frittered away opportunities to secure Argentine adherence to the 1873 treaty, and the government in Buenos Aires remained neutral. Of course, Argentine neutrality was not entirely the result of Peruvian diplomacy because the Argentine government continued to fear that a pact with Peru and Bolivia might precipitate an alliance between Chile and Brazil. In addition, the foreign minister of Chile, Adolfo Ibáñez y Gutierrez, had concluded that the unreliable caudillos ruling Bolivia made the 1874 Treaty of Sucre a dead letter. In the belief that war with Peru was likely if not inevitable, he focused Chilean diplomatic efforts on resolution of the Patagonian question with Argentina. On December 6, 1878, representatives of Chile and Argentina signed a pact, known as the Fierro-Sarratea treaty, that provided for an elaborate series of steps, culminating in arbitration, to determine ownership of the disputed Patagonian territory. The terms generated opposition in both Chile and Argentina, and the treaty was replaced in June 1879 by a new settlement that provided for a more direct resolution of the dispute. The two agreements, especially the one concluded in 1878, epitomized a lost opportunity for Peru to secure an ally who might have either prevented the War of the Pacific or modified its outcome.[26]

TEN-CENTAVO TAX

Suffering from Melgarejo's financial mismanagement and currency debasement as well as the effects of the worldwide depression, the Bolivian economy was in a parlous state when Hilarión Grosole Daza took office in 1876. Unfortunately, the municipal authorities in Antofagasta, Bolivia's main nitrate port, soon needed additional funds to repair the damage caused by the earthquake and tidal wave that struck the Bolivian coast in May 1877. Desperately searching for revenues to prop up his government, Daza pledged to exploit the nation's desert wealth. When the city council of Antofagasta asked the Bolivian government for permission to levy a tax of ten centavos per hundredweight on all nitrates exported by the Antofagasta Nitrate and Railroad Company, the Daza administration, on February 14, 1878, authorized the tax. At the time, not one member of the city council was Bolivian; and over 80 percent of the population of Antofagasta was Chilean, with less than 10 percent being Bolivian. The new tax, which was to supersede all other taxes, was in reality only slightly higher than the rate the company had been previously paying. Although the ten-centavo tax obviously conflicted with the terms of the 1874 treaty with Chile, the official stand of the Antofagasta government, a position supported by the Daza administration, was that the new assessment was an internal affair that did not affect Chile.[27]

The Daza government did not think Chile would respond aggressively to the new tax, but its judgment proved faulty; the Chilean government was strongly opposed. In Chilean eyes, the ten-centavo tax voided the compromise reached in 1872–1874, when Chile recognized the 24th parallel in return for Bolivia's pledge to renounce new taxes for twenty-five years. Over the next twelve months, numerous proposals and counterproposals were made. The Bolivian government was willing to submit the issue to arbitration or to allow it to be settled in the courts; however, the Chilean government remained adamant, refusing to accept any solution short of cancellation of the proposed tax. Thoroughly frustrated by the attitude of both Chile and the foreign concessionaires in the littoral, President Daza ordered enforcement of the tax law with retroactive collection to February 18, 1878. In December 1878 the Antofagasta Nitrate and Railroad Company was directed to pay the taxes due under the law. When George Hicks, the company's English manager, refused, an embargo was placed on the company and an order went out for his arrest. In response to the tax and the subsequent arrest of Hicks, the Chilean government continued to negotiate while posting the vessel *Blanco Encalada* in front of Antofagasta.[28]

President Daza's next step was poorly conceived if he retained any hope of preventing war. In what was viewed in Bolivia as an effort to eliminate the cause of the trouble, the Daza administration canceled the Antofagasta company's concession and proposed to sell its assets at public auction. In the process, Daza forwarded to the prefect of Antofagasta, together with the cancellation order, a letter that outlined the 1873 treaty with Peru and detailed Bolivia's position on the dispute. Addressing the question of why he did not believe Chile would resort to force over the issue, the Bolivian president emphasized that Chile, in its dispute with Argentina, had displayed weakness and a lack of resolution. According to Daza, the Bolivian cancellation of the Antofagasta company's contract was intended to demonstrate to Chile that right was on the side of Bolivia, which was determined to exploit the resources of the coastal region in its own best interests. Daza also informed the prefect that Serapio Reyes Ortiz, the new Bolivian minister to Peru, would soon travel to Lima to confirm Peruvian support for the 1873 treaty.[29]

Daza's letter to the prefect was intercepted by Chilean authorities, who demanded it be rescinded; if not, a Chilean occupation of the Bolivian littoral would follow. When the Daza administration set February 14, 1879, as the date for the sale of Antofagasta company assets, the Chilean government responded by ordering Colonel Emilio Sotomayor, commandant of its military college, to prepare for an occupation of the Bolivian littoral to the 23d parallel. Informed of this decision, Pedro Nolasco Videla, the Chilean representative to Bolivia, returned home immediately. After the *Cochrane* and

O'Higgins joined the *Blanco Encalada* in the Bay of Antofagasta, several hundred Chilean troops landed on February 14, 1879, and occupied the port. Chilean troops also seized Mejillones and the silver mines at Caracoles, and after Bolivia reinforced its army and moved to activate the 1873 treaty with Peru, they occupied Cobija and Tocopilla. The Calama Oasis was also seized to prevent Bolivia from moving troops to the coast from the interior.[30]

PERUVIAN RESPONSE

The Chilean occupation of the Bolivian littoral found the Peruvian government woefully unprepared for war. Most of its warships were in drydock or badly in need of repairs and army units were scattered throughout the country. The general lack of military preparedness was aggravated by ongoing financial difficulties and the high level of political unrest that had obtained since 1876. In a difficult situation, the Prado administration adopted a two-pronged strategy. On the one hand, it accelerated preparations for war by speeding up repairs on its ships and moving some troops south toward Iquique. José Francisco Canevaro, a Peruvian agent in Europe, was also hurriedly dispatched to Rome in a belated effort to buy ironclads. At the same time, the Peruvian government endeavored to avoid hostilities by urging Bolivia and Chile to find a peaceful settlement. When Serapio Reyes Ortiz arrived in Lima on February 16, 1879, he was told that the Peruvian government considered the 1873 treaty null and void. Officials of the Prado administration argued that the 1873 treaty was no longer active because Bolivia had concluded its 1874 treaty with Chile without first notifying Peru, as it was required to do under the terms of the 1873 agreement. As Peru worked to forestall an outbreak of general hostilities, it continued its efforts to derail the Serapio Reyes Ortiz mission by refusing to discuss the 1873 treaty.[31]

At the end of February 1879, President Prado sent the historian and diplomat José Antonio de Lavalle to Santiago as head of a mission entrusted to find a formula for maintaining peace. Few in Lima expected the Lavalle mission to succeed, but it offered the secondary benefit of giving Peru additional time to prepare for war. As feared, Lavalle quickly ran into trouble in Chile. Afraid the 1873 treaty would jeopardize the success of the mediation, Pedro Irigoyen, the foreign minister of Peru, instructed Lavalle to admit to its existence only if pressed and then to emphasize that it did not call for automatic Peruvian intervention in support of Bolivia. The Chilean government of Anfbal Pinto received Lavalle courteously but then proceeded to unmask him. Within days, the Chilean government was raising embarrassing inquiries about the existence of a military alliance between Peru and Bolivia. Of course, Lavalle knew the terms of the treaty because he had received a copy before leaving Lima. And he had participated in a meeting with Reyes Ortiz where it had been the only topic discussed. In a difficult position, Lavalle replied unconvincingly that to his knowledge no such treaty existed. The issue of the secret treaty eroded Lavalle's credibility and supported charges in the Chilean press that his mission was little more than a ploy to give Peru time to rearm.[32]

Once Chilean forces had occupied the entire Bolivian littoral, the position of the Chilean government hardened. When Lavalle proposed a Chilean evacuation in return for Bolivian suspension of the ten-centavo tax, the Chilean government responded that the existing state of Chilean public opinion made withdrawal impossible. Chilean policy then took a new direction as it turned the clock back to 1866, reopening the question of which country really owned the territory Chile had recently occupied. Chilean authorities told Lavalle that Chile had earlier agreed to recognize Bolivian sovereignty over the territory only if Bolivia met certain conditions; because it had failed to fulfill those conditions, Chile was now free to reclaim its territory. Chile eventually rejected the terms of the Lavalle mediation, but did so in a conciliatory mood that encouraged Lavalle to hope for an eventual solution. Events in Bolivia and Peru soon dashed those hopes.[33]

When Bolivia declared war on March 14, 1879, the Chilean government demanded from Peru a declaration of neutrality, together with a categorical denial of the existence of a Peru-Bolivia alliance. Under extreme diplomatic pressure, the Prado administration was compelled to explain the terms of the alliance to Chilean officials, arguing it was a purely defensive treaty that was not directed against Chile. The Prado government also emphasized that the terms of the treaty, one article of which left each signatory free to decide whether a given case required its active support on behalf of the other, left Peru free to mediate in good faith. Chile at once demanded that Peru abrogate the alliance, cease its preparations for war, and issue a declaration of neutrality. Afraid that Bolivia might quickly settle with Chile and join the latter in despoiling Peruvian nitrate deposits in Tarapacá, the Prado administration adamantly refused to disavow the 1873 treaty. Convinced that further negotiations would be pointless, on April 5, 1879, Chile declared war on both Peru and Bolivia.[34]

As the antagonists resorted to arms, the central role in the dispute played by nitrates clarified. In a circular to the Santiago diplomatic corps, the Chilean government accused Peru of fomenting the dispute between Bolivia and Chile to eliminate competition for the Peruvian nitrate monopoly. Although persuasive evidence linking Peru to either the ten-centavo tax or Bolivia's decision to confiscate Chilean holdings in Antofagasta never surfaced, it must be recognized that Peruvian interests had deep-seated economic and political reasons for going to war. At the end of the 1870s, the Peruvian government had a near-monopoly on the nitrate trade, and Bolivia's 1878 tax supported its position. In turn, the consolidation of Chilean control over Antofagasta promised ruinous competition for Peru. Peruvians also remained concerned that Bolivia, if left alone, might ally with Chile and despoil Peruvian nitrate fields in Tarapacá. On the other hand, the Chilean government looked to Peruvian nitrates to indemnify itself for the expense of the war. Continuing its efforts to detach Bolivia from Peru, Santiago hoped to trade Bolivian incorporation of the Peruvian provinces of Tacna and Arica for Chilean sovereignty over the littoral between the 23d and 24th parallels as well as the coastal region north of the Loa River. This Chilean policy of Peruvian dismemberment, which first surfaced in 1866, marked a radical change from Chile's general insistence since 1835 on the status quo along the Pacific coast of South America.[35]

Both the Pardo and the Prado administrations tried unsuccessfully to ensure the security of Peru and compensate for reduced military strength by entering into treaties and alliances with neighboring states. These pacts assumed bilateral and multilateral forms as Lima sought to strengthen the role of international law in regional affairs. To increase the effectiveness of Peruvian diplomacy and decrease military involvement in public affairs, the Pardo government also enhanced the professionalism of its diplomatic service. Economically, the Pardo and Prado governments promoted a mixed economic system that combined the unchecked economic individualism of the past with a measure of central planning and supervision. Endeavoring to move the state away from an excessive reliance on foreign loans and investments, they restructured the marketing of guano and nationalized the nitrate industry. In the process, the continuing Peruvian need for labor led to new efforts at European immigration as well as treaties with China and Japan. In the end, the new economic policies were only marginally successful and later contributed to the Peruvian defeat in the War of the Pacific. Unable to put its political and economic house in order, the Peruvian government drifted toward war. Unprepared to fight, it proved incapable of formulating either a diplomatic strategy or a military policy that developed viable alternatives.

NOTES

1. Robert G. Greenhill and Rory M. Miller, "The Peruvian Government and the Nitrate Trade, 1873–1879," *Journal of Latin American Studies* 5, 1 (May 1973): 108–110.

2. McQueen, *Peruvian Public Finance*, p. 39.

3. Jorge Basadre, *Sultanismo, corrupción, y dependencia en el Perú republicano* (Lima: Editorial Milla Batres, 1979), pp. 84–86.

4. Carlos Miró Quesada Laos, *Autopsia de los Partidos Políticos* (Lima: Ediciones "Páginas Peruanas," 1961), pp. 81–82.

5. Greenhill and Miller, "Peruvian Government," pp. 128–129.

6. William S. Coker, "The War of the Ten Centavos: The Geographic,

Economic, and Political Causes of the War of the Pacific," *Southern Quarterly* 7 (1969): 125–126; V. G. Kiernan, "Foreign Interests in the War of the Pacific," *Hispanic American Historical Review* 35, 1 (February 1955): 14–36.

7. Víctor Villanueva, *Ejército Peruano: del caudillaje anárquico al militarismo reformista* (Lima: Librería Editorial Juan Mejía Baca, 1973), p. 104; Edgardo Mercado Jarrín, *Política y Estrategia en la Guerra de Chile* (Lima: n.p., 1979), pp. 31–32.

8. Pedro Ugarteche, *La Comisión Consultiva de Relaciones Exteriores del Perú* (Lima: Imprenta Torres Aguirre, 1948), pp. 1–15.

9. Janet Evelyn Worrall, "Italian Immigration to Peru: 1860–1914" (Ph.D. diss., Indiana University, 1972), pp. 35–44.

10. Stewart, *Chinese Bondage*, pp. 141–150.

11. C. Harvey Gardiner, *The Japanese and Peru, 1873–1973* (Albuquerque: University of New Mexico Press, 1975), pp. 1–6.

12. Margarita Guerra Martiniere, "Los grupos y las tensiones sociales en el Perú de 1879," in *En Torno a la Guerra del Pacífico*, ed. Percy Cayo Córdoba et al. (Lima: Pontificia Universidad Católica del Perú Fondo Editorial, 1983), pp. 92–97.

13. Basadre, *Historia*, 7:108. Announced in June 1875, the Russian award largely favored the Japanese government.

14. Gardiner, *Japanese and Peru*, p. 16.

15. Stewart, *Chinese Bondage*, pp. 175–176, 189–190.

16. Basadre, *Historia*, 7:109–110.

17. Eudoro Galindo Quiroga, *Litoral Andino: Retrospección y Perspectivas en Torno al Problema Marítimo* (La Paz: Editorial Los Amigos del Libro, 1977), p. 42; Querejazu Calvo, *Guano*, pp. 60–63.

18. Escobari Cusicanqui, *Historia Diplomática*, 1:128–129.

19. Brian Loveman, *Chile: The Legacy of Hispanic Capitalism* (New York: Oxford University Press, 1979), pp. 157–158.

20. Richard Snyder Phillips, Jr., "Bolivia in the War of the Pacific, 1879–1884" (Ph.D. diss., University of Virginia, 1973), pp. 35–36. A copy of the 1873 treaty can be found in Fernando Lecaros Villavisencio, *La Guerra con Chile en sus Documentos*, 3d ed. (Lima: Ediciones Rikchay, 1983), pp. 17–20.

21. Francisco A. Encina, *Las Relaciones Entre Chile y Bolivia (1841–1963)* (Santiago: Editorial Nascimento, 1963), pp. 100–107; García Salazar, *Resumen*, pp. 167–169.

22. Kenneth Ward Crosby, "The Diplomacy of the United States in Relation to the War of the Pacific, 1879–1884" (Ph.D. diss., George Washington University, 1949), pp. 24–25.

23. Burr, *By Reason or Force*, pp. 126–130.

24. Coker, "War of the Ten Centavos," pp. 123–124.

25. Copies of the treaty of private international law and the treaty of extradition can be found in Ulloa, *Congresos Americanos*, 2:343, 383.

26. William F. Sater, *Chile and the War of the Pacific* (Lincoln: University of Nebraska Press, 1986), pp. 8–9; Burr, *By Reason or Force*, pp. 134–145; Basadre, *Historia*, 8:55–56.

27. Luis Peñaloza Cordero, *Nueva Historia Económica de Bolivia: La Guerra del Pacífico* (La Paz: Editorial Los Amigos del Libro, 1984), pp. 171–173.

28. Roberto Querejazu Calvo, *La Guerra del Pacífico* (La Paz: Editorial Los Amigos del Libro, 1983), pp. 52–53.

29. Luis Ortega, "Nitrates, Chilean Entrepreneurs and the Origins of the War of the Pacific," *Journal of Latin American Studies* 16, 2 (November 1984): 356–362.

30. Querejazu Calvo, *La Guerra*, pp. 58–70.

31. Phillips, "Bolivia," pp. 77–78.

32. Basadre, *Historia*, 8:47–48.

33. García Salazar, *Resumen*, pp. 184–185.

34. Sater, *Chile*, pp. 11–12; Pike, *Modern History*, p. 142.

35. Thomas F. O'Brien, Jr., "Chilean Elites and Foreign Investors: Chilean Nitrate Policy, 1880–1882," *Journal of Latin American Studies* 11, 1 (May 1979): 101–121; Jaime Daniel Rivera Palomino, *Geopolítica y Geoeconomía de la Guerra del Pacífico* (Ayacucho: Universidad Nacional de San Cristóbal de Huamanga, 1980), p. 55.

War of the Pacific, 1879–1885

After Chile occupied the Atacama Desert and Peru refused to disavow the 1873 treaty with Bolivia, the die was cast and war became unavoidable. The resounding success of Chile in the War of the Pacific later obscured, both in and out of Peru, the fact that a Chilean victory at the outset was far from certain. Few remembered the early months of the war, when Chileans lived in fear of the Peruvian navy and of being crushed between the Peru-Bolivia hammer and the Argentine anvil. Collectively, Peru and Bolivia could draw on approximately twice as many citizens as Chile, although the population of the latter tended to be more homogeneous, educated, and motivated. The Chilean populace was also endowed with a sense of national identity almost totally lacking in the ill-equipped, poorly trained soldiery of Bolivia and Peru. On the other hand, many Chileans offered only lackluster support at the beginning of the war, and internal political strife complicated the Chilean war effort, as it did that of Peru and Bolivia. If Chile had an initial advantage, it came from its military strategy as opposed to the size or composition of its military forces. Recognizing the need to control the sea, the Chilean government had doggedly pursued a naval buildup over the previous decade.

Although the outcome of the war was thus in doubt, it was clear from the beginning that in the spring of 1879, Peru was embarking, largely unprepared, on an adventure with enormous potential repercussions. Four years later when a peace was concluded that left Chile in control of the Atacama Desert, almost every aspect of Peruvian socioeconomic and political life had been affected. In particular, the conflict modified the objectives and priorities of foreign policy as well as the government's determination to put in place the machinery necessary for its successful pursuit.

ALLIANCE DIPLOMACY

In the spring of 1879, Peru and Bolivia concluded two protocols designed to coordinate the allied war effort. In the first, dated April 15, Bolivia agreed to contribute 12,000 men and Peru 8,000 plus its navy. Bolivia also agreed to reimburse Peru for its war-related costs by allowing Peru to retain 50 percent of Bolivian customs revenues at Arica and Mollendo and 50 percent of all receipts from nitrate exports. In addition, Bolivia promised to lend Peru 100,000 soles interest free. If the allies won the war and Chile paid an indemnity, Bolivia's financial obligations to Peru would be forgiven. The terms of the protocol obviously favored Peru, and Bolivia agreed to them initially because its options were extremely limited. At the same time, the Bolivian government assumed the allies would win the war and Chile would be forced pay for everything. Unhappy with the terms of the April protocol, Bolivia soon pressed Peru for a new agreement. On May 7, 1879, the allies signed a new accord in which Peru agreed to extend a loan to Bolivia. If the presidents of Peru and Bolivia were in the war theater at the same time, the agreement provided that the president of the nation where the fighting was taking place would be designated commander in chief of the allied armies. In his absence, the president of the other allied state would automatically assume this role. President Prado soon proceeded to Tacna to take command of the allied army.[1]

The Peruvian government's willingness to renegotiate the April 15 protocol and Prado's decision to go to Tacna were influenced by ongoing Chilean attempts to detach Bolivia from Peru. In April 1879 President Daza received two Chilean overtures urging him to cooperate with the Chilean government in despoiling the Peruvian littoral. On May 29 the Chilean government formally proposed to Bolivia an agreement in which Bolivia would grant Chile possession of the littoral to 23 degrees south latitude in return for Chilean assistance in helping Bolivia seize from Peru enough territory to readjust its boundary and secure an easy means of communication with the Pacific. In support of this proposal, the Chilean government agreed not to make peace with Peru until the latter had signed a peace with Bolivia.[2]

Chilean ambitions were fueled by a naval victory off Iquique on May 21, 1879. Although the Peruvian navy drew first blood, sinking the Chilean corvette *Esmeralda,* it proved a pyrrhic victory, for Peru lost the ironclad *Independencia* when it struck a reef during the engagement. The loss of the *Independencia* tilted the balance of naval power toward Chile because the *Huáscar* was now the only Peruvian warship capable of challenging the *Blanco Encalada* and the *Almirante Cochrane,* Chile's two ironclads. In the aftermath of its victory at Iquique, Chile again sought to induce the Bolivian government to change sides. A friendly Bolivia, compensated for the loss of its littoral by the incorporation of the Peruvian provinces of Tacna and Arica, would provide a buffer on Chile's northern frontier and the security the Chilean government deemed necessary against Peru. Chile's logic appeared persuasive, but the Daza administration quickly rejected the proposal, which it feared would perpetuate instability on the west coast of South America. At the same time, Daza did not hesitate to use the Chilean offer to extract additional concessions from Peru. On June 15, 1879, the allies signed a third protocol in which each country agreed to pay 50 percent of the war's expenses.[3]

As might be expected, European interest in the war was considerable. By 1879 guano and nitrates had become very important to the world's economies, and the conflict threatened to disrupt trade in both commodities. Nitrates were used in the manufacture of explosives crucial to expanding European arsenals, and both nitrates and guano were desirable fertilizers for the exhausted fields of Europe. In addition, Peruvian nitrate bonds were widely held in Europe, especially in France, Holland, and Italy; creditors in those countries were very concerned that events did not impact negatively on the value of Peruvian guarantees. British financial interests centered on Chile, where the largest commercial houses were English. In support of their investments, British financiers and businessmen openly supported Chile before and during the war, occasionally pressing the Foreign Office to take a more active role.

The high level of foreign investment in Chile in general and in the nitrate industry in particular later spawned a foreign-conspiracy thesis that argued that European governments had influenced events during the war to Peru's disadvantage. The attempt to place the regional conflict in a wider context was laudable, but no evidence has surfaced to substantiate claims of either collective influence or collective intervention. At the same time, the British government was not inclined to pressure Chile to forgo its gains. After Chile occupied both Bolivian and Peruvian territory, any status-quo peace favored Chile; that was how British policy was interpreted in Peru and Bolivia. The British government also condoned efforts by British creditors to seek Chilean recognition of their claims on Peruvian resources. The Peruvian government adamantly opposed the conclusion of such an agreement despite Britain's argument that it implied no recognition of Chilean territorial gains.[4]

In part because of their mutual antipathy for Peru, Chile and Ecuador shared a long tradition of friendship. For this reason, the Chilean government sent Joaquín Godoy to Ecuador in March 1879 to negotiate Ecuadorian assistance against the Peru-Bolivia alliance. Godoy was instructed to suggest to the Quito government that the time was ripe for Ecuador to resolve its ancient boundary dispute with Peru by occupying the disputed territory. In the event Ecuador rejected this proposal, Godoy was told to negotiate an offensive and defensive alliance with the Ecuadorian government. Godoy found public sentiment in Quito favorable to Chile but failed to obtain the support of the Ecuadorian government. The administration of José Ignacio Veintimilla elected to remain neutral, promising only that Ecuador would not assist Peru.[5]

A few weeks later, Ecuador undertook a mediation of the dispute. Former President José María Urbina arrived in Santiago in late June 1879 after stopping at Arica to confer with the presidents of Peru and Bolivia. The allies told the Ecuadorian envoy that they would agree to a cessation of hostilities and arbitration of the dispute if the *status quo ante bellum* was restored and maintained pending arbitration. On these grounds, the Ecuadorian mission stood little chance of success. With the destruction of the *Independencia,* Chile had dealt a decisive blow, and a strong prowar element now demanded the government prosecute the war with even greater energy. Therefore, it was not surprising when the Chilean foreign minister rejected a withdrawal of Chilean forces and insisted the status quo was the only acceptable basis for negotiations.[6]

The failure of early mediation efforts by Ecuador and others did not dampen regional enthusiasm for a peaceful settlement. In June 1879 the Colombian congress adopted a resolution that asked the president to send a special minister to the belligerent countries to offer mediation. The Colombian initiative was motivated by the government's efforts to reconcile Peruvian desires to transship arms via the Isthmus of Panama with Chilean complaints that the practice compromised Colombian neutrality. In July 1879 a Colombian envoy traveled first to Peru and then to Chile, but the Colombian mediation was no more successful than its predecessors. The Peruvian government refused to be the first to accept the Colombian proposal because it was Chile that had initiated hostilities; the Chilean government was interested only in discussing the neutrality issue. Around the same time, Peru and Bolivia also declined a Brazilian offer of assistance because they preferred mediation by the US government.[7]

At the outset of the war, official Peruvian circles were very sympathetic toward the United States, which they viewed as a friendly power. This attitude was reciprocated to a limited degree by members of the Rutherford B. Hayes administration; however, there were strict limits to the extent to which the United States was willing to become involved in the dispute. Throughout 1879 Secretary of State William Evarts insisted that the belligerents observe neutral rights, and his subsequent efforts to mediate the dispute were largely motivated by a concern that the conflict would prove injurious to neutral commerce and property. Evarts was willing to support mediation, especially if it was requested by all parties, but he insisted on a strict policy of nonintervention. Deeply rooted in US foreign policy, this traditional approach was clung to by the secretary of state when a more active stance could have contributed meaningfully to an early resolution of the dispute.[8]

Although the Prado administration refused to recognize it, the central direction of US policy was clear as early as the summer of 1879. After Peru rejected an April offer of mediation by Great Britain, the German and British governments in June proposed to the United States a joint mediation. Evarts quickly rejected their offers on the grounds it was too early to proceed with a joint effort by neutral states. He expressed concern that any such effort might convey an impression of dictation or coercion in disparagement of belligerent rights. When the British government again raised the issue in the fall of 1879, Evarts's reply was noncommittal. He answered that his ministers to the belligerent states were giving attention to the desire of the United States to offer its good offices at a propitious moment. The policy outlined by Evarts closely resembled the policy of the United States during the Spanish intervention, and the Peruvian government should have conceded the limited degree to which the United States was willing to support the allied cause.[9]

ALLIED MILITARY DEFEATS

As diplomats in and out of the region struggled to find a peace formula, the second and decisive phase of the conflict was fought at sea. From the beginning, it was evident to all parties that the war was essentially a maritime conflict. Neither side could win without command of the sea. Once Chile controlled the sea, all Peru could realistically hope to do was to delay the day of reckoning. Because control of the sea would insure victory, Chilean strategy called for an early blockade of Peruvian ports as a prelude to the establishment of naval supremacy. Chile initiated its naval campaign on April 5, 1879, when it blockaded the port of Iquique. By the end of the year, it had widened its embargo to a number of Peruvian ports, including Arica, Huanillos, and Pisagua. In January 1880 Chile extended the blockade northward to Ilo and Mollendo, finally reaching Callao on April 10, 1880. Callao remained under blockade until January 21, 1881, when it was opened to commerce under very restrictive conditions.[10]

The Chilean blockade of Iquique resulted in an inconsequential naval engagement, termed the battle of Chipana or Loa. Thereafter, the naval forces of Peru and Chile were locked for six months in a bitter struggle for naval supremacy. The loss of the *Independencia* was an important event, but it was the battle of Angamos on October 8, 1879, that finally established Chilean naval superiority. In the first real test of ironclads at sea, the Peruvian *Huáscar* was ambushed and captured after its captain and most of his senior officers had been killed. The loss of the *Huáscar* left Chile the undisputed master of the seas, and from this perspective, it was ironic that Peruvian naval power finally came to depend on a single ship. With the battle of Angamos, the naval phase of the war ended, and in effect the war was over. Chile had won undisputed control of the sea together with the greater mobility and flexibility offered by sea transport. Seizing the initiative, Chilean troops landed at Pisagua on October 28, 1879, and began their inexorable march north along the coast. Peruvian forces won a tactical victory at Tarapacá in November 1879, but it had no effect on the deteriorating strategic picture. The Chileans occupied Tacna in May 1880 and Arica in June 1880. By the beginning of 1881, Chilean forces had reached the outskirts of Lima.

The loss of the *Huáscar* and the occupation of Tarapacá prompted President Prado to take an inexplicable action. On November 26, 1879, he handed over command of Tacna and Arica to Admiral Lizardo Montero and returned to Lima. He then abandoned his post and traveled to Europe in search of loans with which to purchase ironclads. Prado sailed secretly from Peru on December 18, 1879; four days later, his government was overthrown by Nicolás de Piérola. On December 28, 1879, *El Comercio* published a letter from Prado in which he justified his actions by arguing that Vice President La Puerta could handle his duties in Peru. Prado contended that his first responsibility was to secure the military equipment needed by Peru and to negotiate stopgap agreements with Peru's guano and nitrate creditors to keep them from backing Chile in the war. In a series of newspaper interviews and letters to Peruvian politicians, Prado later developed similar arguments to justify his decision. No evidence surfaced to suggest that Prado's decision was motivated by other than sincere, patriotic concerns and convictions, but his departure was a fateful political decision.

Named chief of state on December 23, 1879, Piérola inherited a grim economic situation. Business conditions were chaotic, and by the end of the year, commerce was almost dead. With large external debts, the Peruvian government found its creditors reluctant, especially after Chile achieved naval supremacy and occupied Tarapacá, to lend more money. To make matters worse, the Peruvian Guano Company would no longer honor Peruvian drafts. One of the first acts of the Piérola administration was to sign a new guano sales agreement with Dreyfus and Company in which Peru recognized its outstanding obligations and agreed to liquidate them through the sale of guano. Unfortunately, Chilean occupation of the guano beds frustrated implementation of the new contract. Announcing that it would administer the guano deposits, the Chilean government in January 1880 indicated it was also willing to make arrangements with the bondholders to settle their claims. On February 9, 1882, the Chilean government ordered the sale of 1 million tons of guano, with net proceeds to be divided equally between the Chilean government and the bondholders.

The allied defeats at Tacna and Arica exposed many of the political and military shortcomings of the alliance. President Piérola did not trust Admiral Montero, a holdover from the Prado administration, because he feared Montero might build an independent power base in southern Peru. In part due to this concern, Piérola sent only one ship from Lima to Arica between February 25, 1880, and May 26, 1880, and it carried only ordinary shoes and a few guns. Due to the Chilean occupation of Moquegua, supply by land was no longer possible unless the goods were transshipped the long and difficult route via Bolivia. The allies were not uniformly armed, which compounded logistical problems, and they were mostly in open positions because their inexperienced leadership had not ordered them to dig trenches. Chilean artillery wreaked havoc on these exposed, compact bodies of troops. Finally, the allies suffered morale problems and a defeatist attitude. The Chilean troops had become accustomed to winning;

most allied forces, no matter how brave, knew only defeat.

Although the Bolivian government refused to sue for peace, the battle of Tacna had the practical effect of taking Bolivia out of the war. It remained allied to Peru because the Campero administration believed that was the honorable thing to do, but the Bolivian army did not again fight after its defeat at Tacna. The Bolivian government lacked the money, men, and weapons to fight effectively; moreover, it was virtually impossible to transport its army to any place in Peru where it could be of practical assistance. Struggling to keep their alliance active, representatives of Peru and Bolivia met in Lima on June 11, 1880, to sign two confederation agreements. The first protocol established a federal government with an executive, a bicameral legislature, and a judicial branch. Under the terms of the agreement, the departments of each country would become states and would retain a large degree of autonomy. The second protocol consisted of enabling legislation. In the temporary executive, the president of Peru would act as president of the union and that of Bolivia as vice president. The second protocol also created a twenty-man senate to write a constitution and provided for mixed commissions to set the public debt and establish state boundaries.[11]

The Peru-Bolivia confederation was stillborn. Although there was support for the idea in Peru, the council of state decided the issue was too important for it alone to approve. Consequently, it suggested a plebiscite be held so that each Peruvian citizen could express his opinion. Given the existing state of political chaos, that was as far as the union movement progressed in Peru. The issue was more complicated in Bolivia, but the outcome was the same. President Campero paid lip service to the idea, but there was little evidence to suggest he actively supported it. Opinion in the Bolivian congress was badly split; some departments favored the idea, and others threatened to secede if the confederation was adopted. In the end, the Bolivian national committee also concluded that the issue was too important for it alone to decide. Again, the suggested plebiscite was never held. An ill-conceived war measure, the 1880 Peru-Bolivia confederation floundered on national rivalries and was probably doomed from the day of its conception.

In the second half of 1880, diplomatic relations between Peru and Bolivia deteriorated. After Chilean forces captured Arica, they opened the port to Bolivian commerce, a move strongly opposed by the Peruvian government. In response to a Peruvian protest, the Bolivian government temporarily halted commerce through Arica, but faced with a growing scarcity of goods, it soon rescinded the interdiction, rejecting the inevitable Peruvian protest. The Peruvian government retaliated by placing prohibitive duties on Bolivian goods transiting Peruvian territory and by seizing goods for nonpayment of duties, a move that almost ruptured the alliance. In a compromise settlement, Bolivia agreed to pay a 5 percent duty on all goods passing to and from Arica. As the year closed, Bolivia pledged anew its loyalty to Peru. Six months later, representatives of Peru and Bolivia signed a commercial treaty that called for free trade between them until they were united in a confederation.[12]

SEARCH FOR PEACE

In the spring of 1880, several European powers, intent on protecting the investments of their nationals and restless with the hesitant peace efforts of the United States, again offered mediation. The basis of the mediation proposed by the governments of Britain, France, and Italy combined the cession of Tarapacá to Chile with Chilean withdrawal to the Camarones River. The Chilean government was inclined to accept European mediation on these terms, but Peru and Bolivia continue to prefer the good offices of the United States. For once, allied policy con-verged with that of Washington. The renewed possibility of European intervention prompted a US diplomatic initiative in the summer of 1880 that led to a peace conference off Arica in the fall. Held on board the US warship *Lackawanna,* the Conference of Arica consisted of three formal sessions conducted in late October 1880. Unilaterally sponsored by the United States, the three belligerents were reluctant participants. The Piérola administration, supported by the Bolivian government, continued to favor arbitration by the US government. Peru attended only out of deference to the latter, hoping a failure of the talks might lead to more aggressive US involvement. The Chilean government, on the other hand, was winning the war and feared US intervention might rob it of the fruits of victory. Convened under inauspicious signs, the Conference of Arica was not surprisingly a total failure—which only highlighted the ineptitude of US diplomacy. In terms of the War of the Pacific, the conference was noteworthy only because it accented the inflexible, divergent positions maintained by Peru and Chile, positions that made peaceful resolution of the dispute virtually impossible.

In the aftermath of the Arica talks, the Chilean government renewed its military campaign with vigor. Callao was captured on December 6, 1880; after bitter fighting around Lima, the Peruvian capital fell on January 16, 1881. During the skirmishing, Piérola escaped to the mountains, whence he issued a statement on January 20, 1881, that strongly condemned Chilean policy and thus effectively closed the door to further negotiations. Without money or arms, Piérola's obduracy only prolonged the war and compounded its adverse effects on the Peruvian nation. In May 1881 Piérola traveled to Bolivia in an effort to formulate a new campaign strategy. The Peruvian delegation proposed that Bolivia attack the littoral at Antofagasta and Tarapacá while the Peruvian army advanced on Tacna and Arica. This combined attack would draw Chilean forces from Lima, which could then be occupied by Peruvian guerrillas. Needless to say, it was far too late in the war for Peru and Bolivia to execute such a complex joint action, and its mere contemplation was an indication that the Piérola government did not recognize the severe limits now placed on its political and military options.[13]

With Piérola in the mountains, the Chilean government had no one in Lima with whom to negotiate. Consequently, it authorized an assembly of prominent Peruvians to meet outside Lima in February 1881 to form a provisional government. The assembly revived the 1860 constitution and persuaded Francisco García Calderón, a prominent Civilista, to act as chief executive. The García Calderón administration was recognized by the US government in June 1881. The following month, it convened in the town of Magdalena a quorum of the 1879 congress that had functioned until Piérola seized power. The Magdalena congress agreed to recognize the provisional government until proper elections could select a successor. García Calderón was proclaimed president; Admiral Lizardo Montero, first vice president; and General Andres Avelino Cáceres, who had earlier fled to the Andés and initiated a guerrilla campaign against the Chilean army of occupation, second vice president. García Calderón then tried to bring Cáceres into the government, offering him control of the central provinces and continued command of his army; however, the latter refused, arguing only he could govern Peru.[14]

On August 4, 1881, a Chilean plenipotentiary informed García Calderón that Santiago remained determined to occupy the Peruvian provinces of Tacna, Arica, and Tarapacá. In subsequent discussions, García Calderón's negotiating flexibility was severely limited by a congressional decision that prevented him from agreeing to terms based on a permanent alienation of Peruvian territory. In a very difficult situation, it was little wonder that many Peruvians, including some in the García Calderón administration, continued to hope the United States would offer to arbitrate the dispute. In turn, the Chilean government remained opposed to US intervention; to forestall the possibility, it abolished the García Calderón government at the end of September 1881.[15]

One week later, a revolt broke out in southern Peru when army units based in Arequipa pronounced against Piérola. After the rebellion gained strength in Puno and Ayacucho, Admiral Montero also declared against Piérola, as did Cáceres. In the meantime, the Chilean government had arrested García Calderón and other members of his administration and incarcerated them in Santiago. Admiral Montero, who had wisely remained outside the zone of Chilean control, assumed the duties of chief executive in mid-November 1881. Over the next eighteen months, internal rivalry and external pressure combined to hamper the Peruvian war effort. The Chilean government, as well as others interested in peace, were faced with a mélange of political forces and policies that made progress toward a durable settlement impossible.

By 1882 diplomatic relations between Peru and Bolivia were also showing the effects of a war that was into its third year. While assuring Peru of its loyalty to the alliance, the Bolivian government delayed recognition of the administrations of first García Calderón and then Montero. In an effort to improve the situation, Juan C. Carrillo, the Bolivian minister to Peru, met in the spring of 1882 with a number of Peruvians, including Minister of Foreign Affairs Mariano Alvarez. The Bolivian government instructed Carrillo to say that it was obvious that a truce was necessary and that the allies should sit down and agree to a common course of action. Carrillo found some sentiment for a truce in Peru, but it was largely because Peruvians felt an armistice offered the allies a better chance than a formal settlement to regain lost territory. Foreign Minister Alvarez emphasized that the war involved all the Americas, not just the belligerents, and that Peru would never cede territory to Chile. The Peruvian foreign minister naively added that he believed Chile would be the ultimate loser because it could not resist the condemnation of the continent and the world. When Alvarez indicated that Peru had negotiations pending with the US government, Carrillo responded that Bolivia had no confidence in the United States. The conference ended on this sour but highly relevant note. The failure of the Carrillo mission frayed Peru-Bolivia relations, and in September 1882, the Bolivian government invited Admiral Montero to La Paz to prop up the alliance. In the course of a short visit, the Bolivian government agreed to send 2,000 men to Arequipa, but as was often the case, it promised more than it could deliver. The Bolivian troops never left the vicinity of La Paz.[16]

DIPLOMACY OF THE UNITED STATES

With the inauguration in March 1881 of the Garfield administration, US foreign policy reversed course. Largely viewing the war as a case of Chilean aggression backed by British economic interests, James G. Blaine, the new secretary of state, abandoned the impartial policy of his predecessor and replaced it with one openly favorable to Peru and Bolivia. Motivated in part by a desire to advance the commercial interests of the United States, Blaine attempted to find a solution that involved neither European intervention nor territorial cession. Although these objectives were not radically different from those of Secretary of State Evarts, Chilean military operations had subsequently transformed the political situation on the Pacific coast. As a result, Blaine's new policy was now decidedly partisan in the sense that any opposition to the status quo was favorable to the allies. In authorizing the diplomatic recognition of the García Calderón government, Blaine put the moral support of the United States squarely behind the Peruvian government, which made the latter even less disposed to come to terms with Chile.[17]

In May 1881 Blaine also elected to send new envoys to Peru and Chile. General Stephen A. Hurlbut was appointed to the post in Lima; General

Judson A. Kilpatrick was assigned to the legation in Santiago. Blaine retained Charles Adams as minister to Bolivia, largely because no one else was interested in the post. The instructions to Hurlbut and Kilpatrick contained a clear statement of Blaine's peace policy. Hurlbut was told to do all he could to encourage Peru to accept any reasonable condition or limitation necessary to secure peace. Blaine did not deny that a cession of territory might ultimately be necessary, but he hoped it would not become a precondition for negotiations. He added that the Garfield administration did not deem the time opportune to mediate, but if the Peruvian government could work out a program of concessions that had a good prospect of satisfying Chile, the United States would tender its good offices. Blaine's instructions to Kilpatrick were of a similar nature: to urge moderation on Chile. The United States did not presume to judge whether or not an annexation of territory would prove necessary but felt forced territorial change should be avoided whenever possible.[18]

Both Hurlbut and Kilpatrick quickly adopted partisan positions in favor of the countries to which they were posted. The resulting intrigue did much to distort US policy and delay a peace settlement. In particular, Hurlbut made a number of diplomatic blunders that contributed to the growing friction between the United States and Peru. In the belief he had been commissioned to support the García Calderón administration, Hurlbut let everyone in Peru know that he, and by inference his government, was solidly behind the president. In a confidential memorandum to the Chilean naval commander, Hurlbut also emphasized that his government did not recognize war for territorial aggrandizement. Personally opposed to a cession of territory, Hurlbut gave the false impression that the Garfield administration was ready to intervene actively on behalf of Peru. His final diplomatic transgression was his independent negotiation of an agreement with the García Calderón government that would have allowed the United States to establish a coaling station and naval base at Chimbote. When Secretary of State Blaine learned of the Chimbote agreement, he ordered all discussions to stop and informed Hurlbut and Kilpatrick that he was sending a special mission to Peru and Chile to resolve matters relative to peace.[19]

Willian Henry Trescot, a former assistant secretary of state and a man of much diplomatic experience, was appointed to head the special mission. He was told to inquire why the Chilean government appeared to be obstructing the formation of a Peruvian government. Chile's arrest of García Calderón, after Washington had recognized and dealt with his government, was seen by Blaine and others in the Garfield administration as an offensive action, if not a calculated insult. Trescot arrived in Lima on December 22, 1881, and reached Santiago on January 7, 1882. The Trescot mission received a warm welcome in Peru, where he was surprised to find many Peruvians calmly awaiting the results of the long-anticipated US intervention, assuming the outcome would be a peace advantageous to Peru. On the other hand, Chilean public opinion was generally hostile to the mission because the public feared the United States would support the exaggerated expectations of the Peruvians.[20]

After extensive negotiations with the Chilean minister of foreign relations, José Manuel Balmaceda, Trescot signed an agreement, termed the Protocol of Viña del Mar, on February 11, 1882, whose terms were much more comprehensive and punitive than Chile had proposed at the Conference of Arica. In return for Chilean assurances that the arrest of García Calderón was not intended to offend the United States or any other neutral power, Trescot assured Balmaceda that the United States was not contemplating armed intervention in the dispute and would offer mediation only if the belligerents so desired. The Chilean representative responded that Chile would welcome the good offices of the United States as long as the latter accepted several peace conditions. These included the cession to Chile of Tarapacá and the Chilean occupation of Tacna and Arica for ten years, after which Peru must pay Chile $20 million or cede the provinces. If Arica was eventually returned to Peru, it was to remain permanently unfortified. The Chilean government also expected to occupy the Lobos Islands until they failed to produce guano. In the interim, the net proceeds of the guano taken from the islands as well as from the mines being worked in Tarapacá would be divided equally between Chile and the creditors of Peru.[21]

The Trescot mission, together with the Protocol of Viña del Mar, highlighted the limited extent to which US diplomacy could restrain the severity of Chilean peace terms. It also drew attention to Bolivia's isolation from the peace process as the negotiations centered on Peru and Chile, with Bolivia reportedly mentioned only once. Otherwise, Trescot's mission was of no long-term consequence because his conversations with Balmaceda had been overtaken by events outside Chile. With the assassination of President Garfield, the presidency passed to Vice President Chester A. Arthur; Secretary of State Blaine was replaced by Frederick T. Frelinghuysen. As soon as he took office in December 1881, Frelinghuysen challenged in nearly every detail Blaine's Latin American policy, especially his approach to the War of the Pacific. In January 1882 he cabled Trescot, instructing him to extend friendly offices impartially to both Peru and Chile, avoiding any issue that might cause offense and exerting, if possible, a pacific influence. Frelinghuysen added that the García Calderón affair and what he termed its "surroundings" would be dealt with in Washington. Detailed written instructions were dispatched within the week, completely nullifying the instructions Blaine had given Trescot. Frelinghuysen also directed US envoys in the belligerent states to confine their activities to impartial mediation attempts without seeking to dictate peace terms.[22]

Although Trescot saw no need to stay on in Chile, he remained at Frelinghuysen's request until the second half of March, when he sailed for Peru without calling on Balmaceda. Arriving in Lima on March 28, 1882, Trescot did not see General Hurlbut because the latter had died quite suddenly the preceding day. Believing the prestige of the United States would be enhanced by a call on Admiral Montero, Trescot made the long and difficult journey to his seat of government in the Andes. With Montero, Trescot reviewed the terms of the Protocol of Viña del Mar as well as a confidential modification offered by Balmaceda on March 18, 1882, in which Chile, instead of occupying Tacna and Arica for ten years, would simply purchase the two provinces outright. Montero rejected the terms of the protocol and refused to consider the confidential offer, stating that the Peruvian congress had forbidden the executive to agree to a cession of territory. Returning to Lima, Trescot in his final dispatch to Frelinghuysen emphasized that no peace negotiations could succeed as long as the position of the United States remained unclear. If Washington intended to intervene effectively to prevent the disintegration of Peru, the time to do so was now. If it did not intend to intervene, it was even more urgent that it make clear both to Peru and Chile the exact limits of US policy. Trescot concluded that the current policy of the United States was an embarrassment to all parties concerned and should be terminated as soon as possible.[23]

With the conclusion of Trescot's mission, Frelinghuysen initiated a new diplomatic effort to terminate the war. Assuming Peru would have to relinquish some territory, Frelinghuysen instructed Cornelius A. Logan, the newly appointed minister to Chile, to secure for the Peruvian government as large a part of the occupied territories as possible together with the maximum monetary indemnity for whatever territory Chile retained. In pressing these views, the US envoy was instructed to encourage the Chilean government to moderate its demands but was also instructed to be careful not to assume a threatening attitude. Arriving in Chile in September 1882, Logan was well received by the Chilean government. After a series of consultations between Logan and Luis Aldunate, the Chilean foreign minister, Chile modified slightly its demands in the Protocol of Viña del Mar and offered a new opportunity for a peace settlement. The central elements of Chile's revised terms were the annexation of Tarapacá as a war indemnity, the purchase of Tacna and Arica for the sum of $10 million, and control of Peruvian guano deposits until current contracts ran out. In the process, the Chilean government conceded its earlier demand that Peru pay an indemnity of $20 million or cede Tacna and Arica.[24]

Logan was instructed to negotiate with Admiral Montero; however, because García Calderón was under custody in Logan's hotel, he presented the Chilean conditions to him. The two men engaged in extensive discussions, but no progress was made. The Chilean government maintained its demands and the Peruvian representative insisted on his own conditions. Willing to consider the loss of Tarapacá and the guano on the Lobos Islands, García Calderón believed they should be considered full payment of the war indemnity. As part of the settlement, he argued, Chile should also assume the outstanding claims against Peruvian guano deposits. He would not consider the sale of Tacna and Arica and pressed for a formal six-months' armistice to give the Peruvian congress time to consider a settlement. In an effort to reconcile their differences, Logan presented a number of compromise proposals, none of which bore fruit. Meanwhile, García Calderón became increasingly disenchanted with the US envoy because his insistence that Peru would have to cede territory to get a peace agreement seemed to favor Chile.[25]

Attempting to break the deadlock, Logan wrote Admiral Montero in Arequipa asking for a declaration of support for García Calderón if the latter signed a treaty surrendering Tarapacá and granting the sale of Tacna and Arica. Time was of the essence, Logan urged, because the revised Chilean terms were not a standing offer. If they were not accepted soon, Chile might again demand Tacna and Arica without payment of the $10 million indemnity. As for US policy, Logan indicated that Washington continued to prefer a settlement without cession of territory, but he told Montero that Chile did not share that opinion and that it was useless to pursue the matter. After Montero visited La Paz to reaffirm Peru-Bolivia solidarity, he sent an ambiguous reply to Logan that simply stated that García Calderón, as head of the Peruvian government, was free to enter into whatever negotiations he saw fit. If he did reach an agreement, Montero added, he hoped García Calderón would be freed pending its ratification to direct affairs in Arequipa.[26]

Logan's note to Montero formally ended a defunct peace mission. In a long letter written almost a year later, García Calderón set the tone for Peruvian judgments of the Logan intervention. He criticized the US envoy for his activities as a mediator, denounced him for being importunate, and challenged his veracity on a number of occasions. Embittered by the lack of progress, García Calderón did not do justice to Logan. Although Logan may have been overzealous in pursuit of a settlement, his reports do not indicate he was partisan in support of Chile. At a time when the hopes of many Peruvians were wholly unrealistic, Logan helped negotiate the best combination of terms offered Peru since the Conference of Arica. In any case, Logan's letter to Montero marked a watershed in Peruvian relations with the United States. His suggestion that Peru trade Tacna and Arica for a Chilean cash payment created a storm of protest in Peru and helped convince many Peruvians that Washington was not going to intervene on their behalf. President Arthur reinforced this feeling when he declared on December 4, 1882, that US policy toward Peru and Chile had failed because only armed intervention could prevent Chile from annexing a part of Peruvian territory.[27]

On April 22, 1883, Admiral Montero sent a bitter message to the Peruvian congress in which he reached the sad conclusion that the US government would do little more in support of Peru and Bolivia. With a hint of sarcasm, he asked the representatives present to judge for themselves the gratitude that Peru owed the United States for its prolonged intervention on Peru's behalf. In July 1883 a Peruvian congress under Montero assembled at Arequipa and requested European good offices to bring about a peaceful settlement. The problem with the Arequipa initiative was that there was nothing left to mediate. Chile had won the war when it seized Lima; it now commanded, compared to Peru and Bolivia, almost unlimited resources. Santiago controlled all of the guano and nitrate deposits on the Pacific littoral, and it had been exploiting those resources since it occupied the territory. Recognizing that the European states needed both guano and nitrates, the Chilean government saw to it that they got them, and in a more efficient manner than before. The British government gave the Peruvian proposal for European mediation little chance for success, and in the end, the Foreign Office did not even deign to respond to it.[28]

PEACE SETTLEMENTS

On August 31, 1881, General Miguel Iglesias, who had participated in the defense of Lima and was captured after the battle of Chorrillos, issued the so-called Manifesto of Montán, which recognized that peace must be made on the basis of a surrender of territory. The following month, he called for a congress to meet in northern Peru to form a new government. Meeting in late December 1882, the Assembly of the North, mostly composed of the general's family and friends, elected Iglesias president of the republic and authorized him to seek peace with Chile. The determination of García Calderón not to negotiate with Chile on Chilean terms, coupled with Iglesias's desertion from the García Calderón ranks, encouraged the Chilean government to view the general as a possible alternative to the García Calderón–Montero government. Cornelius Logan encouraged this process when he advised Washington that he believed US recognition of the Iglesias government would hasten peace.[29]

Chile formally recognized the Iglesias government on October 18, 1883. Two days later, representatives of Chile and Peru signed the Treaty of Ancón, which reestablished peace between the two states. In the agreement, Peru ceded Tarapacá to Chile, a move that precluded Bolivia's regaining its littoral because Chile could not be expected to give Bolivia territory that would separate Tarapacá from the rest of Chile. Chile would occupy Tacna and Arica for ten years from the date of ratification, after which a plebiscite would determine whether the area would remain a part of Chile or revert to Peru. Unfortunately, the terms of the plebiscite were not detailed, an omission that contributed to abortive efforts, stretching over four decades, to conduct it. As agreed earlier, the winner of the plebiscite was to pay the loser 10 million Chilean pesos or the equivalent in Peruvian soles. Seven of the remaining eleven articles of the treaty dealt with guano or nitrates, a clear reflection of the underlying issues of the War of the Pacific. The Lobos Islands were to remain in Chilean hands until 1 million tons of guano had been extracted, whereupon they would be returned to Peru. The net proceeds from the sale of this guano were to be divided in equal parts between the Chilean government and the Peruvian creditors whose claims were guaranteed by a lien on the guano. The treaty further stipulated that commercial relations between Peru and Chile would be maintained on the same footing as before the war. A supplementary protocol addressed the operation and compensation of the Chilean army of occupation.[30]

Widely condemned in Peru, the terms of the Treaty of Ancón greatly benefited Chile. The victor took as spoils the single most important source of Peruvian and Bolivian wealth—the mineral-rich Atacama Desert. Even though this desert wealth would prove to be an important factor in future Chilean socioeconomic and political development, ratification of the treaty was not secured without some difficulty in Chile. The most formidable obstacle was the attitude of foreign governments, whose citizens feared they might lose the money they had invested in Peruvian guano and nitrate loans. Bondholders specifically rejected a treaty provision that they receive in payment only 50 percent of the net proceeds from the sale of guano when they felt they had been secured by a full mortgage. Bondholder rights were further restricted by a treaty clause in which Chile recognized the special rights of Peruvian creditors only in the case of existing guano deposits. The proceeds from guano beds discovered after the treaty was signed would belong exclusively to Chile. Although the question of bondholder claims remained unsettled for years, it was not enough to block ratification of the Treaty of Ancón. Peru ratified the treaty on March 10, 1884, and ratifications were exchanged on March 28, 1884.

On April 4, 1884, Chile and Bolivia signed a truce agreement that provided for Chilean occupation of the Bolivian littoral, pending conclusion of a treaty of peace. The Bolivian government refused to sign a formal peace treaty before it had received compensation for its territorial losses in the form of a seaport on the Pacific Ocean. In turn, Chile refused to address Bolivian desires until the plebiscite on Tacna and Arica was held. For decades to come, Peruvian insistence on regaining Tacna and Arica and Bolivian determination to have an outlet to the Pacific aggravated regional tensions in South America. The 1884 truce also provided for the mutual return of sequestered Chilean and Bolivian property, and Bolivia agreed to pay Chile an indemnity for war-related damages. A three-member commission, consisting of a Bolivian, a Chilean, and a neutral party, was established to resolve disputes over the indemnity payment. Finally, commercial relations were restored on the basis of free trade between the two states. The conclusion of a formal peace treaty between Bolivia and Chile took another twenty years.

AFTERMATH OF WAR

In Peru, the power of the Iglesias administration grew steadily during the summer and early fall of 1883, with the Chilean government extending active, ongoing support. Following conclusion of the Treaty of Ancón, the Chileans evacuated Lima, and Iglesias entered the city in late October. Three days later, Montero's forces mutinied rather than face a Chilean force advancing on Arequipa, and Montero was forced into exile in Argentina. On December 3, 1883, the Bolivian government formally recognized the Iglesias government when it accepted the credentials of the newly appointed Peruvian minister to Bolivia, Enrique Bustamante y Salazar. On January 13, 1884, Iglesias called for congressional elections. A congress convened in March 1884 to ratify the Treaty of Ancón and proclaim Iglesias provisional president. The United States, followed by Germany and others, finally recognized the Iglesias administration in late April 1884. The new government proved to be fragile; Iglesias was eventually outmaneuvered by General Cáceres and forced into retirement in 1885.

The War of the Pacific revealed deep rifts within the Peruvian ruling class as well as between the various social classes and ethnic groups in Peru. Not surprisingly, Peru's low level of national integration and nascent national identity contributed to its defeat. The often-repeated story of the *serranos* who thought the war was a struggle between two obscure caudillos, General Chile and Don Nicolás or Don Miguel, was a bittersweet illustration of the lack of national integration. The Indian majority had little feeling for the country and even less sympathy for the white minority that ran it. In a profoundly divided society, the war effort often took second place to a simultaneous and much more significant internal struggle between the various classes and political patronages of Peru. As the Chilean army marched northward along the coast, for example, it was greeted enthusiastically by Chinese laborers, who seized the opportunity to sack the estates of their patrons. Elsewhere, Chinese shopkeepers themselves were the victims of pogroms by Indians and mestizos from the defeated Peruvian army. The period from December 1879 to February 1881, in particular, marked peaks in the intensity of ethnic violence, with all racial groups involved in uprisings.[31]

After 1883 the preoccupation with strengthening national integration had a decisive impact on the political and ideological development of the country, including its foreign policy. Articulate, politically aware Peruvians concluded it was necessary to integrate disparate geographical and economic regions. Their objective was to incorporate the selva and sierra economies with the dynamic, capitalist coastal economy and fuse the three cultures into some form of *mestizo* entity. The question of how to turn Peru into a nation-state was of special interest to middle-class intellectuals, a concern that lasted well into the twentieth century. Men like José Carlos Mariátegui and Haya de la Torre pursued a new understanding of Peruvian reality; in the process, they roamed the world searching for solutions to Peruvian problems.[32]

Ironically, the disastrous defeat at the hands of the Chilean armed forces actually enhanced respect for Peruvian military personnel and institutions. A widespread conviction developed that the war had been lost behind the lines and not on the fighting front. Betrayed by a lack of military preparedness and ever more sensitive to the dangers inherent in unresolved frontier questions, Peruvians emerged from the war determined to develop and maintain a powerful military machine. In this context, the question of political and national integration, especially as it related to the development of an effective fighting force, became a special preoccupation of the armed forces.

Peru's defeat in the War of the Pacific also prompted Peruvians to turn a self-proclaimed inferiority complex into a vital ingredient of their myth-fantasy of nationalism. With most Peruvian heroes celebrated for their defeats, Peruvians turned self-deprecation and an acerbic disparagement of national accomplishments into a nationwide pastime. Scholars later attempted to put what amounted to a national inferiority complex into a wider context by relating it to the fatalism of the Peruvian Indian population. Peru's distinctive brand of nationalism enhanced existing attitudes of fatalistic resignation and thus contributed to the preservation of the Indian subculture in a state of docile dependence. It also isolated Peruvian nationalism, both in content and exposition, from that found elsewhere in Latin America.[33]

Socially as well as politically, the war was a disastrous defeat for the ruling oligarchy of Peru. The Chilean authorities exiled or imprisoned scores of prominent Peruvians while occupying the provinces that were the source of much of their wealth. The collapse of the prevailing social structure significantly altered the social stratification of the country as the wealth of the oligarchy decreased and the pauperism of the lower classes increased enormously. When the Chilean forces withdrew after the conclusion of the Treaty of Ancón, they removed a key element of social control: they were then the only force capable of containing a peasant mobilization, without creating an alternative to what they had earlier supplanted. Hence, the Peruvian oligarchy after 1883 devoted much of its energy to the reimposition of social control over the Indian population. This reassertion of oligarchical control was of considerable importance to the foreign policy of Peru because it influenced both its formulation and execution well into the twentieth century.[34]

The economic consequences of the war were disastrous for Peru. Reinforcing the fiscal crisis that began in the early 1870s, the conflict increased government expenditures and resulted in the loss of the territory containing the foreign exchange–earning guano and nitrate deposits. The cost of the war, including the 1 million pesos a month Peru paid the Chilean occupation forces, devastated the national economic structure. Burdened with a foreign debt of staggering proportions, peace brought little relief. The Chilean occupation of the Lobos Islands, as well as the nitrate provinces, seriously handicapped Peru's ability to reschedule its debts and get back on its feet. At the same time, Chile increased its export of nitrates, which depressed the worldwide price of guano from Peruvian deposits other than the

Lobos Islands. Most significant, the devastation of the national economy created conditions in which only foreign capital could provide the economic resources necessary for national reconstruction. When the Peruvian oligarchy again rose to economic preeminence at the end of the century, more often than not it was co-opted by foreign economic interests into partnership roles.[35]

Attempts by the United States to control the course of the war and influence the conditions upon which peace was established ended in failure. In the process, Washington lost prestige and gained enmity in both Chile and Peru. The diplomacy of the United States was inconsistent and ineffective, and its legacy was a feeling of antagonism in Peru. With good reason, Peruvians complained that the United States had encouraged Peru to resist Chile militarily in an attempt to prevent the latter from acquiring Peruvian territory, and then let Peru down in the negotiations. The publicity generated by the open diplomacy of the United States only made its failures more resounding.

Peru's inept, vacillating diplomacy, combined with the financial mismanagement that began during the Castilla administrations, the loss of naval supremacy under Pardo, and the ongoing political turmoil resulting from Civilista-Piérolista feuds, made a Chilean victory in the War of the Pacific virtually inevitable. The Chilean armed forces struck with cold, professional efficiency, and although isolated feats of military valor challenged the inexorable flow of events and offered Peruvians an occasional glimmer of hope, once Chile gained control of the sea, nothing could prevent its land forces from crushing those of Peru and Bolivia. The Treaty of Ancón, with its heavy indemnities, was a punitive pact, guaranteed to retard the improvement of regional relations. The provisions related to the final disposition of Tacna and Arica were especially unfortunate because they constituted an open sore that poisoned hemispheric relations for decades to come. The war, together with its inconclusive peace, thus marked both the end of an era in Peru's socioeconomic and political history and a new beginning. Out of the misery and devastation, a new nation emerged with a broader, stronger, more mature foreign policy.

NOTES

1. Basadre, *Historia*, 8:53–55; Escobari Cusicanqui, *Historia Diplomática*, 1:133–137.
2. Rivera Palomino, *Geopolítica y Geoeconomía*, p. 27; Querejazu Calvo, *La Guerra*, pp. 109–110.
3. Phillips, "Bolivia," pp. 111–120.
4. Heraclio Bonilla, "The War of the Pacific and the National and Colonial Problem in Peru," *Past and Present* 81 (November 1978): 95–96; Kiernan,

"Foreign Interests," pp. 14–36.

5. L. A. Wright, "A Study of the Conflict Between the Republics of Peru and Ecuador," *Geographical Journal* 48 (December 1941): 268; Burr, *By Reason or Force*, pp. 146–147.

6. Herbert Millington, *American Diplomacy and the War of the Pacific* (New York: Columbia University Press, 1948), pp. 57–58.

7. John Phillip Soder, Jr., "The Impact of the Tacna-Arica Dispute on the Pan-American Movement" (Ph.D. diss., Georgetown University, 1970), pp. 65–70.

8. Robert Edwards McNicoll, "Peruvian-American Relations in the Era of the Civilist Party" (Ph.D. diss., Duke University, 1937), p. 78; Millington, *American Diplomacy*, pp. 34–38 and 53–54.

9. Millington, *American Diplomacy*, pp. 54–56.

10. Donald E. Worcester, "Naval Strategy in the War of the Pacific," *Journal of Inter-American Studies* 5, 1 (January 1963): 31–37.

11. Escobari Cusicanqui, *Historia Diplomática*, 2:32.

12. Phillips, "Bolivia," pp. 205, 215–216.

13. Luna Vegas, *Perú y Chile*, pp. 393–424.

14. Basadre, *Historia*, 8:328–331.

15. Miró Quesada, *Autopsia*, pp. 147–148; Basadre, *Historia*, 8:338–348; Crosby, "Diplomacy," pp. 130–137.

16. Phillips, "Bolivia," pp. 267–271; Querejazu Calvo, *Guano*, pp. 666–668; Burr, *By Reason or Force*, pp. 155–156.

17. Dale William Peterson, "The Diplomatic and Commercial Relations Between the United States and Peru from 1883 to 1918" (Ph.D. diss., University of Minnesota, 1969), pp. 9–10.

18. Alice Felt Tyler, *The Foreign Policy of James G. Blaine* (Minneapolis: University of Minnesota Press, 1927), pp. 112–119.

19. Bonilla, *Un siglo*, pp. 164–165.

20. Crosby, "Diplomacy," pp. 187–188.

21. Sater, *Chile*, p. 213.

22. Millington, *American Diplomacy*, p. 122.

23. Oscar Espinosa Moraga, *Bolivia y el mar, 1810–1964* (Santiago: Editorial Nascimento, 1965), pp. 239–241; McNicoll, "Peruvian-American Relations," pp. 126–127.

24. Crosby, "Diplomacy," pp. 259–266.

25. Basadre, *Historia*, 8:399–400.

26. Crosby, "Diplomacy," pp. 269–270.

27. García Salazar, *Resumen*, pp. 207–210; Millington, *American Diplomacy*, pp. 132–133.

28. Basadre, *Historia*, 8:415–416.

29. Miró Quesada, *Autopsia*, p. 154.

30. Copies of the Treaty of Ancón and the supplementary protocol can be found in Perú, *Tratados, Convenciones y Acuerdos*, 1:165–168.

31. Cotler, *Clases*, p. 118; Luna Vegas, *Perú y Chile*, pp. 559–563; Bonilla, "War of the Pacific," pp. 106–114.

32. David P. Werlich, *Peru: A Short History* (Carbondale and Edwardsville: Southern Illinois University Press, 1978), pp. 141–143; Cotler, *Clases*, pp. 120–121.

33. Fredrick B. Pike, *Spanish America, 1900–1970: Tradition and Social Innovation* (London: Thames and Hudson, 1973), pp. 105–106.

34. Howard Laurence Karno, "Augusto B. Leguía: The Oligarchy and the Modernization of Peru, 1870–1930" (Ph.D. diss., University of California, Los

Angeles, 1970), pp. 43–44; Bonilla, "War of the Pacific," pp. 99–118.

35. Randall, *Comparative Economic History*, pp. 124–126; Joslin, *Century of Banking*, pp. 94–95; Cotler, *Clases*, pp. 131–132.

EIGHT

Postwar Reconstruction and Regeneration, 1885–1908

In the immediate postwar period, Peruvian diplomacy concentrated on the complete recovery of the two Peruvian provinces that remained in Chilean hands at the end of the war. The Treaty of Ancón called for a plebiscite after ten years of Chilean occupation to determine whether Tacna and Arica would remain a part of Chile or revert to Peru. Nevertheless, the ten-year period lapsed and no plebiscite was held because the disputants could not agree on the terms for its execution. Determined to retain at least a part of the occupied territories, the Chilean government proposed a variety of other solutions while initiating a policy of Chileanization designed to insure it would win any plebiscite later conducted in either Tacna or Arica.

At the same time, the Peruvian government made some progress in resolving its complicated, often interrelated boundary disputes with Bolivia, Brazil, Colombia, and Ecuador. In the Espinosa-Bonifaz convention, Peru and Ecuador agreed to submit their dispute in the Oriente to arbitration by the king of Spain, a procedure that promised a satisfactory resolution. Peru and Colombia later agreed to papal arbitration of their dispute subject to the outcome of the Peru-Ecuador arbitration. Finally, diplomatic relations between Peru and the United States, soured by the amateurish diplomacy of the latter during the War of the Pacific, showed signs of improvement by the turn of the century. As the economic and political influence of the United States increased in Peru as well as elsewhere in Latin America, Lima again looked to Washington for support in its dispute with Chile.

GRACE CONTRACT

The most urgent task facing the administration of General Andrés Avelino Cáceres, who was inaugurated as the president of Peru in June 1886, was generation of funds for a bankrupt country. The exact level of public debt was unknown but considerable. The external debt had been in default since 1876, there had been no national budget since 1879, and national revenues were uncertain. The extensive, expensive network of railroads had never provided the expected stimulus to mining, industry, and agriculture, and after its completion, it was only a minor source of employment. The profits from guano sales, earlier a major source of revenue, had declined precipitously due to a drop in both supply and demand. In addition, the Treaty of Ancón guaranteed the Chilean government a percentage of guano revenues for an extended period of time. Finally, the nitrate lands that earlier had provided both a source of profits and a guarantee for foreign loans had been ceded to Chile.

At the end of the war, Michael P. Grace, a North American entrepreneur, expressed an interest in Peru's unfinished railways; and in the process of following up on that interest he initiated negotiations that eventually led to a controversial resolution of the Peruvian debt problem. In 1888 the Earl of Donoughmore, a member of the London committee of bondholders, traveled with Grace to Lima to conclude a comprehensive debt settlement. The resultant agreement, signed on October 25, 1888, and termed the Aspíllaga-Donoughmore Contract, passed into history as the Grace Contract in recognition of the instrumental role played by Grace in its negotiation. In the contract, the bondholders relieved the Peruvian government of its responsibilities for foreign debts resulting from the loans of 1869, 1870, and 1872. In return, the government turned over to the bondholders 769 miles of state railways for 66 years. The government also gave the bondholders the exclusive right to export 3 million tons of guano and granted them an annuity of 80,000 English pounds (later reduced to 60,000 English pounds) for 33 years. The bondholders also received a grant of 500,000 hectares for colonization and a franchise for steamer operations on Lake Titicaca. The bondholders were allowed to import railroad and guano equipment duty free, but they were required to repair the railways received within two years and to construct new ones at designated locations on a specified timetable.[1]

Many Peruvian politicians and intellectuals were bitterly opposed to the Grace Contract, and Cáceres convened four extraordinary sessions of the congress and resorted to extralegal pressure before it was finally ratified in October 1889. On January 8, 1890, representatives of Peru and Chile signed the Castellón-Elías protocol, which addressed Chilean concerns about the Grace Contract. In the agreement, Chile ceded to Peru practically all of the guano deposits in Tarapacá with the understanding that Peru would turn them over to the bondholders. In return, the bondholders were to cancel the outstanding bonds on the Dreyfus loans and recognize that the Chilean government was responsible for the Peruvian debt only to the extent stipulated in the Treaty of Ancón. Chilean concessions in the Castellón-Elías protocol satisfied the bondholder committee; and in April 1890 the bondholders formed the Peruvian Corporation, which undertook the rights and obligations of the Grace Contract.[2]

The Grace Contract, because it mortgaged to foreigners both the nation's most valued resource and its greatest technological accomplishment, struck a serious blow to national pride. It was widely criticized in Peru. On the other hand, the country needed to settle its pending foreign debts, obtain foreign capital, and develop its infrastructure. The agreement addressed positively all of these requirements. The contract liquidated the spending orgy of the 1870s, and to a very real extent marked the start of Peru's postwar economic recovery. Although Peru was forced once again to look abroad for resolution of its external debts, the final agreement was not a refunding measure as in the past but a terminal settlement that released Peru fully and absolutely from all responsibility for the bonds issued from 1869 to 1872. The Grace Contract cannot be viewed as a charitable act on the part of foreign capitalists; the Cáceres administration struck an acceptable bargain that was beneficial to Peru, and very likely the best that could be expected under the circumstances.

ABORTIVE ATTEMPTS TO HOLD A PLEBISCITE

As Peru was negotiating the Grace Contract, a newly elected Chilean government initiated a radical shift in its policy on the Tacna and Arica issue that would periodically bedevil Peru for the next forty years. Under José Manuel Balmaceda, the Chilean government sought to gain permanent sovereignty over both provinces, not for the ultimate benefit of Bolivia but to make them an integral part of Chile. In support of this policy, the Balmaceda administration argued that possession of Tacna and Arica would facilitate the defense of Tarapacá in the event Peru attempted to reestablish itself there. In conjunction with this new policy, the Balmaceda government encouraged Bolivia to cede its littoral to Chile in return for some form of compensation other than all or part of Tacna and Arica.[3]

In 1888 the Chilean government offered Peru 10 million Chilean pesos for the permanent cession of Tacna and Arica. The Peruvian government, supported by the British government, refused to consider this offer. Two years later, after the French minister to Chile had complained that French creditors were not receiving the satisfaction Peru provided British creditors, the Balmaceda administration again approached the Peruvian government on the sale of Tacna and Arica. In 1890 Chile increased its earlier offer by 4 million pesos, with the understanding that the additional money would be used by Peru to meet the demands of its French creditors. The Peruvian government quickly rejected Chile's new proposal, making clear its intention to accept no modifications to the plebiscite provision of the Treaty of Ancón. Frustrated in purchase attempts, President Balmaceda reportedly told the Peruvian minister in Santiago that his government would now be forced to undertake the Chileanization of Tacna and Arica to insure a victory in the plebiscite.[4]

In August 1892 Peruvian Foreign Minister Eugenio Larrabure y Unánue invited the Chilean government to confer on possible bases for a protocol governing the plebiscite on Tacna and Arica. One month later, he proposed a totally new solution: Peru would regain Tacna and Arica in exchange for commercial privileges highly beneficial to Chilean shipping and commerce. The Peruvian foreign minister also offered to assist in resolving the Bolivian problem by allotting two-thirds of Arica's customs receipts to La Paz and constructing railways to improve Bolivian communications to the outside world. The Chilean government quickly rejected this innovative proposal, deploring Peru's attempt to link the mutual benefits of a free-trade policy with the controversial question of Tacna and Arica. In its reply, Chile emphasized that it was not interested in any solution that eliminated the possibility of its acquiring the two provinces.[5]

Although significant, the 1892 proposal was only one facet of a broader Peruvian strategy designed to regain control of Tacna and Arica. Despite growing efforts at Chileanization, the population of the two provinces remained predominantly Peruvian, and the Peruvian government was convinced that any fairly conducted plebiscite would go in its favor. Consequently, it focused its diplomatic efforts on securing the plebiscite provided for in the Treaty of Ancón. The key elements of the Peruvian position were that the plebiscite should not be held under Chilean auspices, and only natives of the provinces or residents of more than two years should have the right to vote. Negotiations dragged on throughout 1893, with debate focused on the issues of who would be allowed to vote and who would supervise any election held. On January 26, 1894, a general agreement was finally signed in Lima that provided for a plebiscite under the conditions of reciprocity deemed necessary by both governments to achieve an honest election. In addition to the monetary consolation stipulated in the Treaty of Ancón, Chile could rectify its boundary by moving north to Vitor if it lost the plebiscite, and Peru could extend its boundary southward to Chero if it were the loser. This aspect of the 1894 agreement was a positive one, for it meant neither country could win or lose the whole territory. It marked one of the few examples of serious compromise in the history of the dispute.[6]

At this point, domestic politics in Chile and Peru combined to frustrate what might have been a workable solution. A change in the Chilean government was followed shortly thereafter by the death of Peruvian President Morales Bermúdez. The delay caused by these two events thwarted serious discussions until after the ten-year occupation period provided for in the Treaty of Ancón had passed and a new diplomatic climate had developed. In March 1894 the Peruvian minister to Chile learned that the new government in Santiago had disavowed the January 1894 agreement and was requesting fresh negotiations. The call for reciprocity in the 1894 agreement implied equality between Peru and Chile, and the new Chilean government refused to give Peru equal representation on the plebiscite supervisory board. Negotiations continued after 1894, but little progress was made. The Chilean government pressed for a four-year postponement of the plebiscite or an outright cession of Tacna and Arica, but Peru refused to entertain either proposal. Chile then proposed a new plan in which the two provinces would be divided into three zones with only the middle zone affected by the plebiscite. Lima rejected this compromise because it still hoped the plebiscite provision would allow it to regain the entire occupied territory.[7]

On May 18, 1895, after several months of negotiations, Chile and Bolivia signed three related agreements. The first was a treaty of peace in which Bolivia, in exchange for Chile's assumption of certain Bolivian financial obligations, recognized Chilean sovereignty over its former littoral and over a section of the Puna de Atacama, which, although under Chilean occupation, had been ceded by Bolivia to Argentina. The second was a treaty of commerce that combined a reciprocal trade agreement with mutual guarantees for the protection of nationals. It also included provisions for railroad construction. The third, and by far the most important to Peruvian foreign policy, was a secret commitment on the part of Chile to transfer Tacna and Arica to Bolivia if it acquired the provinces through a plebiscite or direct negotiations. If Chile were unable to acquire them, it agreed to transfer to Bolivia sovereignty over the zone from the Cove of Vitor to the Valley of Camarones, an area in the southern part of the province of Arica and thus not then legally owned by Chile. In two subsequent agreements, dated December 9, 1895, and April 30, 1896, representatives of Chile and Bolivia agreed that the three treaties concluded on May 18, 1895, constituted an integral and indivisible accord. Chile also agreed with Bolivia that the cession of the Bolivian littoral to Chile would be void if Chile did not deliver Tacna and Arica or at least the zone and port provided for in the treaty of transfer. In a vigorous protest to both signatories, the Peruvian government indicated that it would never renounce its intention to regain Tacna and Arica and vowed not to cede any part of its territory to Bolivia, Chile, or a third country.[8]

CLAIMS TALKS WITH THE UNITED STATES

As earlier discussed, US diplomacy during the War of the Pacific generated considerable animosity in Peru. Shortly after his arrival in June 1885, Charles Buck, the new US minister to Peru, commented on the hostility many Peruvians openly expressed toward the United States. Unfortunately, the diplomacy of Buck did little to improve relations between the two states. When he moved to resolve claims arising from the War of the Pacific, in particular the Peruvian seizure of the railways, the Cáceres administration, chronically short of money, adopted what Buck considered to be delaying tactics. At one point, he lost his patience completely and suggested that the US government seize the customs house at Callao to force the Peruvian government to respond in cash to US claims. The formation of a commission to arbitrate the question of US claims was a more sensible Buck proposal, but for a variety of reasons, the Cáceres administration procrastinated, placing a low priority on claims resolution.[9]

On the other hand, the Peruvian government was willing to enter into a treaty of friendship, navigation, and commerce with the United States as long as the latter did not insist that a claims commission be part of the accord. Treaty negotiations were initiated in early 1887, and an agreement was signed on August 31 of the same year. On the issue of claims, the Peruvian congress made its position abundantly clear when it approved all of the articles of the proposed treaty except the one providing for a claims commission. Once the US Senate had also approved the treaty with the claims commission article omitted, ratifications were exchanged on October 1, 1888.[10]

In 1889 the Harrison administration reopened negotiations concerning a coaling station at Chimbote in the belief that naval bases along the west coast of South America would facilitate commercial expansion in the region. The 1889 talks floundered when Washington demanded exclusive territorial jurisdiction to include the right to fly the US flag over the property. In turn, the Peruvian government desired a US guarantee of Peruvian territorial integrity, something the Harrison administration felt the US Congress would not accept. Negotiations eventually broke off at the end of the year after Secretary of State Blaine concluded that an upcoming Pan American Conference in Washington made it an inopportune time to press for territorial concessions in South America. Thereafter, the idea of a US naval facility at Chimbote was an occasional subject of discussion; however, significant negotiations did not occur until the beginning of the next century, when the building of an isthmian canal became a lively prospect.[11]

TERRITORIAL DISPUTE WITH ECUADOR

With Peru preoccupied with the Tacna and Arica issue, the Ecuadorian government in 1887 again tried to cancel foreign debts by granting land concessions in a section of the Oriente also claimed by Peru. As a result, the two governments opened new negotiations that led on August 1, 1887, to the Espinosa-Bonifaz convention. Under its terms, the signatories agreed to submit their territorial dispute to arbitration by the king of Spain. The convention provided for an arbitration so complete that even the points in contention were left to the arbiter with no principles for their definition specified. Ecuadorian critics of the convention later argued it was null and void because the open-ended procedure offered no securities for the weaker party. The agreement also provided for direct negotiations to continue concurrently with the arbitral process; if the former were successful, their results would be brought to the knowledge of the arbitrator. The arbitration would then be terminated or limited to unresolved points.[12]

Both Ecuador and Peru had more faith in direct negotiations than in the Spanish arbitration, and serious talks aimed at a comprehensive settlement were immediately opened. The Tacna and Arica issue influenced the Peruvian approach because Lima hoped to remove the difficulties inherent in its dispute with Ecuador in order to concentrate on recovery of the lost provinces. The bilateral talks led to the 1890 García-Herrera treaty, which granted Ecuador extensive concessions in the Oriente, including access to the Marañon River from the Santiago River to the Pastaza River. Because the Peruvian government had long opposed making Ecuador an Amazonian power, the terms of the treaty marked a high-water mark of compromise for Peru. Faced with a very favorable settlement, the Ecuadorian congress quickly approved the pact on July 19, 1890. The congress of Peru conditionally approved the treaty in October 1891, but refused to grant final approval until several modifications were made. The changes demanded would have given Peru a larger share of the disputed territory while restricting Ecuador's Marañon River access to the mouth of the Santiago River. In 1893 the Peruvian congress reconsidered the terms of the García-Herrera treaty but continued to insist on either treaty modifications or full arbitration by the king of Spain. Ecuador refused to accept the modifications demanded by Peru, and on July 25, 1894, the Ecuadorian congress retired its approval of the García-Herrera treaty.[13]

After Colombia protested that the terms of the García-Herrera treaty violated its territorial rights, the signatories agreed to broaden the 1887 arbitral convention to include the Bogotá government. The Tripartite Additional Arbitration Convention, dated December 15, 1894, provided both for Colombian adherence to the arbitration provisions of the 1887 Espinosa-Bonifaz convention and for an arbitral decision based on legal title as well as equity and convenience. Ecuador signed the 1894 convention, but the Ecuadorian congress later rejected it out of fear that a tripartite settlement could lead to Peru and Colombia's dividing the Oriente between them. Ecuadorian concerns proved well-founded; its neighbors subsequently partitioned the Oriente, with little consideration given to Ecuadorian claims. When it became clear that Ecuador would not ratify the 1894 convention, the Peruvian congress, on January 29, 1904, revoked its approval, which cleared the way for a resumption of Spanish arbitration. In the intervening years, a variety of Peruvian nationals, in particular Colonel Pedro Portillo, prefect of Loreto from 1901 to 1904, traveled widely in the Oriente in an effort to buttress Peru's de facto claims to the region. As both sides probed the disputed territory, sectional tensions rose and fell in a most unpredictable pattern.[14]

FIRST PAN-AMERICAN CONFERENCE

As the Peruvian government worked to resolve its regional disputes, the United States issued an invitation in 1888 for the Latin American states to attend an inter-American conference in Washington, D.C. Peru eventually accepted the invitation, although it temporarily delayed its official response in an effort to get the Tacna and Arica issue on the conference agenda. The invitation to the conference called on the delegates to discuss a variety of specific subjects, most of which involved trade and customs. In this sense, the conference reflected the interests of US businessmen who were beginning to recognize Latin American trade and investment opportunities. The conference invitation also called for adoption of an arbitration procedure, an objective that highlighted US interest in using the inter-American system as an instrument to promote international stability through refined peacekeeping procedures. Finally, Washington saw the inter-American system as a convenient structure to gather the Latin American states under US leadership. With these considerations in mind, the First Pan-American Conference marked a significant shift in the rationale for the inter-American system. From a largely idealistic foundation, the inter-American movement was tilting toward a more pragmatic, utilitarian one, increasingly dominated by the United States.[15]

Delegates to the Washington conference discussed a variety of issues, including a customs union and the International Bureau of American Republics; however, the arbitration question was the subject that elicited most interest because it touched upon a variety of national rivalries. Secretary of State Blaine was the leading spirit behind the arbitration project, and soon after the conference opened, the US government informally submitted a draft arbitration treaty. The Chilean government, although not alone in questioning the US proposal, was at the forefront in opposition to obligatory arbitration. The Chilean delegation readily accepted the principle of arbitration, but with the Tacna and Arica dispute in mind, it concluded that Chile could not accept the principle as unconditional and obligatory, especially because it might be applied to pending disputes. In turn, the Peruvian government, in concert with Argentina and other supporters, tried to exploit the arbitration issue to bring the question of Tacna and Arica before the conference. The conference also addressed a related report that recommended adoption of a resolution condemning the right of conquest. Again, the Chilean delegation found itself in a delicate position, although widespread delegate concern with the report minimized Chilean embarrassment. In the end, the anticonquest resolution was tied to the arbitration agreement, and with the latter, it was adopted but not ratified.[16]

MILITARY REFORM UNDER PIEROLA

In 1890 the Civilistas were unable to confront the military successfully, and Colonel Remigio Morales Bermúdez handily won the presidential election. After Bermúdez died peacefully in office in April 1894 the presidency passed temporarily to the second vice president, Colonel Justiniano Borgoño. In July 1894, General Cáceres was elected head of state and inaugurated with wide-ranging powers. Facing another four years out of power, the Civilistas turned to their bête noire, Nicolás de Piérola, who had recently escaped prison and taken refuge in Chile. Assured of Civilista support, Piérola returned to Peru to lead a revolution against Cáceres. The reconciliation of the Civilistas with Piérola, the Democratic chieftain, marked an important postwar step toward the political reconstruction of Peru. It ended a feud that had divided Peru since the Balta era, contributed to its defeat in the War of the Pacific, and fueled the political instability that followed the Treaty of Ancón. After months of heavy fighting, Cáceres resigned in March 1895, and a provisional government, headed by the Civilista Manuel Candamo, temporarily governed the nation. Running unopposed in the July 1895 presidential elections, Piérola took office on September 8, 1895.

Military reform was one of the most pressing and troublesome problems facing Peru at the end of the nineteenth century. Opposed to military dictatorships, Peru's civilian governments acknowledged the need to maintain an armed force capable of defending the nation. The Piérola administration sought to increase the scientific and technical knowledge of the armed forces, and to instill in them a greater sense of professional pride. Piérola contracted a French military training mission in 1896, established the Escuela Militar in Chorrillos to train officers, instituted obligatory military service, and regulated salaries, promotions, and the system of military justice. In the process, he increased civilian control over an increasingly professional armed force, a goal that had eluded the Civilistas under Pardo. Piérola's military reforms were continued and expanded by his successors. A law governing military conscription came into effect on July 12, 1900, and on November 22, 1901, a new law established a more equitable system for military promotions. The contract for the French military mission was renewed in 1902 and again in 1905. The Pardo government acquired the transport *Iquitos* in 1905; the following year it contracted for the construction in England of two cruisers, the *Almirante Grau* and the *Coronel Bolognesi,* both of which entered service in 1907. As the Tacna and Arica dispute dragged on, successive Peruvian governments demonstrated their determination to develop and maintain a military arm adequate to support the nation's foreign policy.[17]

The efforts to reform and rebuild the Peruvian armed forces were facilitated by the economic growth that occurred in Peru at the end of the nineteenth century. Two conditions previously lacking promoted revitalization of the economy. First, Piérola's second administration was a time of peace and political stability free of foreign wars and generally free of domestic uprisings. Second, the governing coalition shared a socioeconomic philosophy that encouraged the government to promote economic development. The Piérola administration created a ministry of development, established a national society of industries, and enacted a variety of laws that contributed to the modernization of Peru. After 1895 the government revised the tax structure, reformed tax collection procedures, created new credit institutions, resumed service on the foreign debt, and improved the nation's foreign credit rating. Due to these and other measures, the Peruvian economy entered its second cycle of export-led growth and was well on its way to recovery by the turn of the century.[18]

IMPROVING RELATIONS WITH THE UNITED STATES

The recovery of economic and political stability under Piérola contributed to a restoration of US economic influence in Peru. Another favorable circumstance was the development by US businessmen of an increasingly active interest in Latin America in the wake of the 1893 depression. Entrepreneurs in the United States reasoned that expanded foreign trade and increased investment abroad would contribute to economic recovery at home. The friction that developed between the Peruvian Corporation and the Peruvian government was a third factor that paved the way for a recovery of US economic influence. In this period, the most significant US investments occurred in the mining sector, principally in the Cerro de Pasco region, and they took place at the expense of the Peruvian Corporation and the Grace interests associated with it.[19]

With the recovery of US economic influence in Peru, Washington's diplomatic and political influence also increased. The overall improvement in relations was boosted by a convergence of regional interests. In the two decades after 1890, a central objective of US foreign policy was the maintenance of peace and stability along the west coast of South America. Achievement of this objective was threatened, at least potentially, by Chile, which had emerged by 1900 as the dominant power in the region. Washington policymakers worried that another conflict on the scale of the War of the Pacific could lead to renewed European intervention in South America. From this perspective, a key to maintaining regional peace and stability was the effective employment of US influence to prevent Chile from taking advantage of its weaker neighbors. The Peruvian government attempted to capitalize on such concerns by sporadically urging US intervention in Peruvian territorial disputes, especially the Tacna and Arica issue.[20]

Unwilling to force its good offices on Chile, Washington continued to explore alternate means to maintain the balance of power in South America.

As a result, when Peruvian Vice President Isaac Alzamora revived the question of a US-controlled coaling station at Chimbote, the Roosevelt administration expressed interest. In a 1902 memorandum, Alzamora called for a reciprocity treaty between Peru and the United States. The Peruvian government was willing to lease the port of Chimbote to the United States for ninety-nine years in return for a guarantee of Peruvian territorial integrity and support for the Peruvian position on Tacna and Arica. Alzamora's memorandum also called for a reduction in the US tariff on Peruvian sugar exports, the donation of US warships to Peru, admission to the US Navy of Peruvian naval personnel for instruction and training, and a loan sufficient to improve the port of Callao and pay off the Tacna and Arica indemnity. Once again, the Peruvian government was prepared to grant the United States a coaling station at Chimbote, but the asking price was high.[21]

Additional discussions were held on the question of a naval station at Chimbote, but the issue was largely dormant by 1904 because too many political factors arose to complicate the scheme. A segment of the Peruvian public was vocally opposed to the arrangement; consequently, the López de Romaña administration preferred to leave the lease decision to its successor. President López de Romaña also objected to Alzamora's involvement in the scheme due to the latter's ties to a group of US-Peruvian speculators with interests in the coalfields near Chimbote. In the United States, the State Department was totally opposed to a guarantee of Peruvian territorial integrity because it had decided that the US sphere of influence in the Caribbean should not be extended to South America. Finally, the US Navy expressed growing concern as to the resources required to develop the Chimbote site.

CHILE STRENGTHENS ITS DIPLOMATIC POSITION

As the Peruvian government courted Washington's diplomatic support, it continued to search for a bilateral solution to the Tacna and Arica dispute. In 1898, four years after the plebiscite had been scheduled to take place, Peru and Chile reopened negotiations. The intransigence of Peru and Bolivia, coupled with a renewal of the Chile-Argentina boundary dispute, prompted the Chilean government to seek a new understanding. At the time, Peru appeared to enjoy a relatively strong negotiating position. In addition to the political advantage gained from Chilean apprehension over its dispute with Argentina, the Piérola administration, because of a salt monopoly instituted in 1896, was well placed financially to promise a large settlement. As its negotiator, Peru dispatched to Santiago Guillermo E. Billinghurst, first vice president of Peru and a close friend of Piérola. Billinghurst had many well-placed friends in official Chilean circles and seemed ideally suited to conduct the mission. He was instructed to take advantage of Chilean difficulties with Argentina to negotiate the best possible solution to the Tacna and Arica dispute.[22]

The Billinghurst–La Torre protocol, dated April 9, 1898, provided for a plebiscite in Tacna and Arica with the queen regent of Spain to decide voter eligibility. The elections were to be conducted by a three-man board consisting of a Peruvian, a Chilean, and a neutral member designated by the Spanish arbitrator. The terms of the agreement were probably the optimum that Lima could have negotiated at the time, and in Peru, the protocol was widely considered a triumph for Peruvian diplomacy. On July 13, 1898, the Peruvian congress approved the Billinghurst–La Torre protocol by a wide margin, with both Civilistas and Democrats supporting it. The Chilean Senate also approved the pact, but the Chilean House later rejected it, requesting clarification through new negotiations.[23]

The 1898 negotiations represented the only serious Chilean attempt to hold the plebiscite between 1894 and 1925. The terms of the Billinghurst–La Torre protocol marked a major, albeit temporary, shift in Chilean policy. The Chilean government knew it was unlikely to win a fairly conducted plebiscite; therefore, by agreeing to participate in one, it abandoned the possibility of an early rapprochement with Bolivia in exchange for a more stable and amicable association with Peru. A major factor behind Chile's subsequent rejection of the protocol was a September 1898 agreement between Chile and Argentina to submit their boundary dispute to British arbitration. As the war threat subsided, Chilean opposition grew and the protocol was pigeonholed, pending assurances that the Chilean nitrate monopoly would be protected and perpetuated. Chilean rejection of the Billinghurst–La Torre protocol was significant because it reaffirmed Santiago's determination to retain both Tacna and Arica.[24]

Thereafter, Peruvian diplomatic relations with Chile deteriorated. On November 15, 1900, the Peruvian minister to Chile protested the alleged Chileanization of Tacna and Arica. For several weeks, the protest note went unanswered, and then it was simply acknowledged by the Chilean government. On December 24, 1900, Peru repeated its protest; its note again went unanswered. In March 1901, two weeks after the Chilean lower house buried the Billinghurst–La Torre protocol, Peru broke diplomatic relations with Chile, not restoring them until 1905. This was the first time the Tacna and Arica dispute had resulted in a break in diplomatic relations, and the Peruvian action highlighted the level to which relations between Peru and Chile had degenerated. In 1902 the Chilean government proposed to Peru a final settlement based on an annulment of the Treaty of Ancón. The occupied provinces would be divided, with Chile taking Arica and Peru claiming Tacna. The parties would mutually renounce the $10 million indemnity, and Chile would adhere to the claims provisions of the earlier Bacourt-Errázuriz treaty. When Peru rejected the proposition, Chile moved to strengthen its regional power position. In January 1902 the Chilean government concluded a series of accords with Colombia that were designed to promote a Colombia-

Ecuador-Chile entente. Later in the spring, Argentina agreed not to intervene in the question of the Pacific in return for a Chilean affirmation that it entertained no further thoughts of territorial expansion.[25]

On October 20, 1904, Chile and Bolivia concluded a treaty of peace, friendship, and commerce. In the Bello Codesido–Gutiérrez treaty, Bolivia ceded to Chile in perpetuity the former Bolivian littoral, including the ports of Mejillones, Cobija, Tocopilla, and Antofagasta. In return, Chile guaranteed Bolivia commercial transit rights through Chile, together with facilities at selected Chilean ports, notably Arica and Antofagasta. Chile also agreed to pay Bolivia 300,000 pounds sterling and promised to build a railroad from the port of Arica to La Paz.[26]

Widely criticized in Bolivia, the 1904 treaty was a major diplomatic victory for Chile because it ended a long and troublesome deadlock on essentially Chilean terms. Regarding the Tacna and Arica issue, the treaty tied Bolivian fortunes to those of Chile because Bolivia could now be assured of a long-term commercial outlet at Arica only if Chile secured permanent sovereignty over the occupied provinces. Similarly, Chilean sovereignty over Tacna and Arica would be necessary to insure the favorable demarcation between Bolivia and the two provinces that was promised by Chile in a secret additional agreement to the 1904 treaty. Finally, selected terms of the treaty buttressed Chile's *de jure* and de facto claims to the disputed provinces. Both the treaty provision relating to the demarcation of Tacna and Arica and Chile's commitment to build a railroad through Arica were subsequently used by Chile as evidence it was exercising effective sovereignty over the region.

Taken together, Chile's adjustments with Argentina and Bolivia greatly enhanced its power position vis-à-vis Peru. Chilean diplomacy was strengthened further by a growing entente with Colombia and Ecuador at a time when both states were at odds with Peru over unsettled boundary disputes and various incidents arising from rubber-collection activities in the disputed areas. Cognizant of the shift in the regional balance of power, the Peruvian government in February 1905 strongly protested both Chile's treaty with Bolivia and its exercise of sovereignty over Tacna and Arica. Chile responded that the Treaty of Ancón had in reality ceded the two provinces to Chile. The ten-year Chilean occupation stipulated in the 1883 treaty, it added, was not a strict limitation of time before a plebiscite should be held but only a minimum period over which Chile was to exercise sovereignty. Faced with this novel interpretation, the Pardo administration focused its attention on the 1904 pact. Peru argued that Chile had no right to contract treaties regarding territories not under its exclusive jurisdiction. Peruvian protests intensified after 1906, when Chile undertook to build a railroad from Arica to La Paz despite the fact it was no more than an occupying force in the region through which nearly half the track would run. Nevertheless, the construction work continued, and the railroad was inaugurated in 1913.[27]

TERRITORIAL AGREEMENTS
WITH BOLIVIA, BRAZIL, AND COLOMBIA

After 1883 the Tacna-Arica issue remained Peru's central diplomatic concern, but other regional issues were also on the foreign policy agenda. War debts as well as the perennial problem of boundaries clouded diplomatic relations with Bolivia. In April 1886 Manuel María del Valle, the Peruvian minister to Bolivia, raised the repayment issue, reminding the Bolivian government that it had agreed in June 1879 to pay half of allied war expenses. The Bolivian foreign minister, Juan Crisóstomo Carrillo, responded that his government no longer recognized the obligation because both states had taken equal risks and made joint sacrifices during the war. The Peruvian envoy replied that the debt was a binding obligation with liquidation possible and practical. At the same time, he indicated a willingness to negotiate. Eventually, a compromise was reached in which Bolivia agreed to a total payment of 1 million bolivianos to be paid in 50,000-boliviano increments twice a year over a ten-year period. Shortly thereafter, the Valle-Carrillo agreement was replaced by a new understanding. On October 26, 1886, Peruvian Foreign Minister Ramón Ribeyro and the Bolivian minister to Peru, General Eleodoro Camacho, agreed to forgive Bolivian debt and abandon any pretense of compensation for war costs.[28]

With the successful conclusion of the debt negotiations, Peru-Bolivia relations focused on resolution of boundary issues. These problems were complex because they involved large, ill-defined geographical areas. The Amazonian disputes were further complicated by the involvement of the Brazilian government, which claimed portions of the contested territory. On April 20, 1886, representatives of Peru and Bolivia signed a preliminary treaty of limits that provided for a mixed commission to survey Peru's southern boundary and fix the frontier. Although a complementary protocol provided for the king of Spain to arbitrate disputes arising from the delimitation, border incidents occurred in 1892 and again in 1894–1895. Peru and Bolivia later agreed in the Candamo-Terrazas protocol to Brazilian arbitration of the dispute. The agreement also outlined an alternate means to resolve the dispute without going to arbitration, but settlement by either method proved impossible. In 1896 Bolivia aggravated the issue by creating customs zones in the Purús, Aquiri, Manú, and Madre de Dios regions, all areas claimed by Peru. In the first half of 1897, a diplomatic confrontation between Peru and Bolivia threatened to lead to armed conflict, but protocols signed in May and June temporarily defused the crisis.[29]

On November 21, 1901, Peru and Bolivia concluded a general arbitration treaty that provided for the resolution of present and future disputes based on the principle of *uti possidetis* of 1810. In September 1902 they agreed to proceed with the demarcation of their common boundary from the Chilean border to the west, defined in accordance with Article III of the Treaty of Ancón, as far east as the Nevados de Palomani; the latter description was later modified to read where the eastern limit meets the Suches River. In the 1902 treaty, the signatories also agreed to proceed with a demarcation of the line between the Peruvian provinces of Tacna and Arica and the Bolivian province of Carangas as soon as the former were returned to Peru. Peru and Bolivia further agreed on December 30, 1902, to submit their dispute in the Madre de Dios area to arbitration by the president of Argentina. The bases for the Argentine arbitration were the colonial boundaries of the Audiencia of Chárcas within the Viceroyalty of Buenos Aires and the Viceroyalty of Peru as both existed in 1810.[30]

In 1903 Peru claimed against Brazil a boundary line that extended more than 600 miles due east along the parallel of 6 degrees 50 minutes south latitude from the source of the Javary River to the Madeira River. Peru based its claim on the 1777 Treaty of San Ildefonso; Brazil based its title on its 1851 treaty with Peru as well as its long-term occupation of most of the disputed territory. In 1902 Peru began challenging Brazil's de facto title by systematically establishing outposts in the disputed region. On October 18, 1902, for example, a small detachment of Peruvian troops established a military post and customs house at the mouth of the Amonea River, an effluent of the upper Yuruá River. On June 23, 1903, a similar expedition appeared on the upper Purús River opposite the mouth of the Chandless River. Initially, Brazil limited its response to Peruvian encroachments to verbal requests to withdraw, but when Peru refused to do so, Brazil emphasized in late December 1903 that the current state of affairs risked the maintenance of good relations. In response, Peru reinforced its garrisons on both the Purús and the Yuruá, and armed clashes of an ill-defined nature soon occurred between Peruvian and Brazilian forces.[31]

In the interim, Peru tried to include itself in ongoing Bolivia-Brazil negotiations over ownership of the vast Acre district on the Upper Amazon. In January 1903 Peru made an informal proposal to the Brazilian government for a mixed tribunal to be established by Peru, Bolivia, and Brazil to discuss their boundary disputes. When Brazil rejected this suggestion, Peru formally requested in July 1903 that it be allowed to participate in fresh negotiations about to take place between Bolivia and Brazil. Again, Brazil rejected the Peruvian proposal, arguing that the aims of the three states and the grounds of their claims were different and that the existing state of crisis between Bolivia and Brazil demanded immediate attention. At the same time, the Brazilian government indicated it would not hesitate to submit its dispute with Peru to arbitration if Peru would evacuate the positions in the disputed territory it had occupied after 1902 and produce legal titles in support of its territorial pretensions.[32]

In the 1903 Treaty of Petropolis, Bolivia and Brazil reached a final settlement in which Brazil received some 73,000 square miles of land south of 10 degrees 20 minutes, an area considerably larger than Portugal, Holland, and Belgium combined. In turn, Bolivia received some 2,000 square miles of territory between the Madeira and Abuná rivers, which provided access to the Madeira River. It also received four marshy tracts of land that provided windows toward the Paraguay River. Recognizing the inequity of the territorial exchange, Brazil agreed to pay Bolivia an indemnity of 2 million English pounds and to construct a railroad around the Madeira falls, which would give Bolivia access to the lower Madeira River. Once the terms of the 1903 treaty were known, the Peruvian government protested vehemently that Peruvian rights were jeopardized because the area acquired by Brazil included territory that Peru and Bolivia had agreed in 1902 to submit to Argentine arbitration. In early 1904 Peru dispatched a military expedition to the Acre region, and events on the Peru-Brazil frontier assumed dangerous proportions. Peru proposed that Brazil join it in evacuating the disputed area and neutralizing the entire region, but Brazil, rejecting the proposal, demanded an immediate evacuation by Peru. When Lima ignored its protests, the Brazilian government responded by prohibiting the transit of Peruvian war materials on the Amazon River. A Peruvian protest that the embargo violated the rights of transit granted by Brazil in their 1891 commercial treaty fell on deaf ears.[33]

As the controversy escalated, both governments recognized the dangers inherent in current policies and negotiations were opened in Rio de Janeiro that led to two agreements being signed on July 12, 1904. The first was a *modus vivendi* intended to prevent further conflict in the Yuruá and Purús regions until the signatories reached a definitive settlement through negotiation or some other amicable means. The second established an arbitral tribunal for the purpose of settling Brazilian and Peruvian claims arising from injuries received in the upper Yuruá and the upper Purús after 1902. The July 1904 agreements restored the peace, albeit largely on Brazilian terms, and the Brazilian government soon revoked its prohibition on the Peruvian transit of arms via the Amazon. At the same time, Brazil denounced the 1891 treaty of commerce and navigation, declaring on May 18, 1905, that it was no longer binding.[34]

On May 6, 1904, representatives of Peru and Colombia also signed a treaty that provided for arbitration, based on both legal title and convenience, by the king of Spain. In addition, the signatories concluded a *modus vivendi* that established their respective rights along the Napo and Caquetá rivers. When both pacts were opposed in Colombia, the two governments concluded a new *modus vivendi* in September 1905. It provided for papal arbitration of the Peru-Colombia dispute, subject to the outcome of the Peru-Ecuador arbitration under way before the king of Spain. The terms of the Peru-Colombia treaty would be operative only if the king granted Peru territories also claimed by Colombia. The 1905 agreement further declared that its terms did not modify an Ecuador-Colombia treaty concluded on November 5, 1904. A complementary act, dated September 23, 1905, stated that the 1905 *modus vivendi* did not signify Peruvian acceptance of the legitimacy of a November 1904 Ecuador-Colombia agreement. The Peruvian government was concerned that the latter treaty might exclude from the Spanish arbitration territory over which Peru claimed rights. In a third agreement, signed on July 6, 1906, Peru and Colombia recognized the status quo in the disputed territory until a final solution was reached through the procedure provided for in the September 1905 agreement.[35]

THIRD PAN-AMERICAN CONFERENCE

As the Peruvian government struggled to resolve its regional disputes, it continued to participate in the Pan-American movement. Although the First Pan-American Conference had made no formal provision for subsequent gatherings, Secretary of State John Hay in February 1900 proposed a second conference; and a few months later, the Mexican government agreed to host the meeting. The Peruvian government saw the Second Pan-American Conference as a new opportunity to force Chile to agree to arbitration of the Tacna-Arica dispute; before the sessions began, it issued a circular that argued that Chile appeared determined to retain Tacna and Arica illegally. In support of this charge, the Peruvian government stated that Chile had recently offered to compensate Peru for the loss of Tacna and Arica by assisting it to conquer and divide Bolivia. During the conference, Peru joined other Latin American states in advocating compulsory arbitration of pending and future questions, and the Chilean delegation, backed by Brazil, supported either the limitation of compulsory arbitration to future disputes or voluntary arbitration. In the end, conference delegates accepted a compromise proposal that endorsed the principle of voluntary arbitration as embodied in the 1899 Hague Convention.[36]

In preparations for the Third Pan-American Conference, the arbitration issue was again at center stage. The Peruvian recommendations to the program committee pressed for unrestricted discussion of the issue. To emphasize the importance it placed on arbitration, Peru's note indicated it was withholding its decision to attend the conference until it was informed of the principles and regulations adopted. In addition to the Tacna-Arica dispute, the Peruvian government hoped to apply the principle of compulsory arbitration to its territorial controversy with Brazil. In turn, the Chilean government, supported by Brazil and Ecuador, opposed passage of an obligatory arbitration resolution in any form. In fact, Chile wanted the subject of arbitration left off the agenda completely. Arguing that a discussion of arbitration was unnecessary, Chile emphasized that delegates to the Second Pan-American Conference had earlier agreed to adhere to the principle of voluntary arbitration embodied in the 1899 Hague Convention. In addition, ten delegations to the 1901 conference, including Peru, had signed an agreement providing for compulsory arbitration. The final agenda for the Third Pan-American Conference represented a significant diplomatic victory for the Chilean government because the subject of obligatory arbitration was excluded. For the time being, Chile had succeeded in thwarting a discussion of obligatory arbitration; furthermore, a conference resolution referring the arbitration question to the Second Hague Conference temporarily removed the issue from Pan-American jurisdiction.[37]

In the two decades after the War of the Pacific, the most important influence on Peruvian foreign relations was the growing ascendancy of the United States, both politically and economically, in the affairs of Latin America. In 1889 the first comprehensive international conference of American states met to establish a permanent inter-American organization known as the International Bureau of American Republics. This new body, especially as its activities related to the Caribbean where US imperialism was rampant, was largely dominated by the United States. In South America, only the government of Argentina, the most powerful country in the Southern Hemisphere, seriously contested US leadership. Although the natural sympathies of Peru often lay with Argentina, its ongoing need for development capital and diplomatic support forced Lima to cultivate good relations with Washington. At the same time, regional competition and conflict rather than cooperation and unity remained the prevailing pattern within Latin America. In Peru, great bitterness was felt toward Chile; and the Tacna and Arica question remained a central foreign policy issue. Border disputes flared with Bolivia, Brazil, Colombia, and Ecuador; occasionally, sectional tensions were very high. Many of the disputes involved undemarcated boundaries in the forests of the Amazon Basin, and the boom in natural rubber prices that occurred in the 1890s fueled long smoldering fires of discord. Like its neighbors, Peru continued to find it difficult to safeguard its political and economic interests in remote areas isolated from any vestige of central authority.

NOTES

1. Rory Miller, "The Making of the Grace Contract: British Bondholders and the Peruvian Government, 1885–1890," *Journal of Latin American Studies* 8, 1 (May 1976): 80–85.
2. Wynne, *State Insolvency*, 2:160.
3. Conrado Ríos Gallardo, *Chile y Perú, los pactos de 1929* (Santiago: Editorial Nascimento, 1959), pp. 11–16.
4. Raúl Palacios Rodríguez, *La Chilenización de Tacna y Arica, 1883–1929* (Lima: Editorial Arica, 1974), pp. 53–58.

5. Burr, *By Reason or Force*, p. 201.

6. Ríos Gallardo, *Chile y Perú*, pp. 19–23.

7. McNicoll, "Peruvian-American Relations," pp. 205–206.

8. Querejazu Calvo, *La Guerra*, pp. 137–143.

9. Peterson, "Diplomatic and Commercial Relations," pp. 39–55; *El Comercio* (Lima), January 25, 1887.

10. McNicoll, "Peruvian-American Relations," pp. 156–176.

11. Seward W. Livermore, "American Strategy Diplomacy in the South Pacific, 1890–1914," *Pacific Historical Review* 12 (March 1943): 33–36.

12. Perú, *Memoria (1890)*, pp. 79–80. A copy of the 1887 Espinosa-Bonifaz convention can be found in Perú, *Tratados, Convenciones y Acuerdos*, 1: 271–273.

13. Ulloa, *Posición*, pp. 70–71. A copy of the 1890 García-Herrera Treaty can be found in Zook, *Zarumilla-Marañón*, pp. 295–299.

14. Perú, *Memoria (1896)*, pp. 153–161; Wagner de Reyna, *Los límites*, pp. 77–79; Pérez Concha, *Ensayo*, 1:247–284.

15. Samuel Guy Inman, *Inter-American Conferences, 1826–1954: History and Problems* (Washington, D.C.: University Press, 1965), pp. 33–34.

16. James Brown Scott, ed., *The International Conference of American States, 1889–1928* (New York: Oxford University Press, 1931), p. 44; Cuevas Cancino, *Del congreso de Panamá*, pp. 284–293.

17. Villanueva, *Ejército Peruano*, pp. 124–138.

18. Rosemary Thorp and Geoffrey Bertram, *Peru, 1890–1977: Growth and Policy in an Open Economy* (New York: Columbia University Press, 1978), pp. 4–7, 26.

19. Charles Harper McArver, Jr., "Mining and Diplomacy: United States Interests at Cerro de Pasco, Peru, 1876–1930" (Ph.D. diss., University of North Carolina, 1977), pp. 91–121; Manuel Burga and Alberto Flores Galindo, *Apogeo y crisis de la república aristocrática*, 2d ed. (Lima: Ediciones Rikchay Perú, 1981), pp. 65–80.

20. Peterson, "Diplomatic and Commercial Relations," pp. 119–120, 176–177, 233–234.

21. Livermore, "American Strategy," pp. 37–42.

22. Ulloa, *Don Nicolás*, pp. 366–368.

23. A copy of the 1898 Billinghurst–La Torre protocol can be found in William Jefferson Dennis, *Documentary History of the Tacna-Arica Dispute* (Iowa City: University of Iowa Press, 1927), pp. 228–232.

24. Emilio Bello C., *Anotaciones para la historia de las negociaciones diplomáticas con el Perú y Bolivia, 1900–1904* (Santiago: La Ilustración, 1919), pp. 25–42.

25. Luna Vegas, *Perú y Chile*, pp. 534–535.

26. A copy of the 1904 treaty can be found in Dennis, *Documentary History*, pp. 232–234.

27. Juan Pedro Paz-Soldán, *El canciller Porras y sus doctrinas internacionales* (Lima: Librería e Imprenta Gil, 1920), pp. 43–47.

28. Basadre, *Historia*, 9:283–284.

29. Cano, *Historia*, pp. 73–74.

30. Copies of the 1901 arbitration treaty and the 1902 boundary treaty can be found in Perú, *Tratados, Convenciones y Acuerdos*, 1:69–72, 122–124.

31. Moore, *Brazil and Peru*, pp. 18–29.

32. Perú, *Memoria (1903)*, pp. 117–121; Wagner de Reyna, *Historia diplomática*, 1:64–66.

33. Ganzert, "Boundary Controversy," pp. 441–444.

34. Moore, *Brazil and Peru*, pp. 29–32.

35. Cano, *Historia*, p. 60; Basadre, *Historia*, 12:31–35.

36. A. Curtis Wilgus, "The Second International American Conference at Mexico City," *Hispanic American Historical Review* 11, 1 (February 1931): 32–40.

37. A. Curtis Wilgus, "The Third International American Conference at Rio de Janeiro, 1906," *Hispanic American Historical Review* 12, 4 (November 1932): 443–448.

NINE

Leguía and the Delimitation of Peru, 1908–1930

Inaugurated as president of Peru on September 24, 1908, Augusto B. Leguía strongly supported liberalized social and economic policies at home. In foreign affairs, he emphasized settlement of regional disputes in the belief that Peru's international credit, together with his reputation as a statesman, would rise with their resolution. Between 1908 and 1930, Leguía served as the chief executive of Peru for some fifteen years, or almost three-quarters of the period. In that time, he forged permanent, albeit often controversial, settlements to his nation's territorial disputes with Bolivia, Brazil, Chile, and Colombia. He also aided and abetted a dramatic increase in the role of foreign capital in the Peruvian economy. In the belief that external investment was the key to rapid economic growth, the Leguía administration aggressively recruited foreign capital, technicians, and administrators, particularly from the United States. The resultant threat of Yankee hegemony eventually developed into a recurrent domestic political issue that long outlasted the second Leguía administration.

FOREIGN POLICY OF
THE FIRST LEGUIA ADMINISTRATION

In the general area of foreign affairs, the first Leguía administration accomplished several major achievements. Within a year of Leguía's taking office, solutions were found to both the Brazil and Bolivia boundary disputes. In the latter case, Argentine President José Figueroa Alcorta, in accordance with the 1902 agreement, announced on July 9, 1909, an arbitral decision that awarded three-fifths of the disputed territory to Peru. The Leguía government immediately accepted the award, but in Bolivia, the Ismael Montes administration later rejected it. Bolivian mobs attacked both the Argentine and Peruvian legations, and the Bolivian government moved troops to the Peruvian frontier. Although the Argentine award favored Peru, there were other, equally important, reasons that the Leguía administration was eager to settle with Bolivia. One was the belief that an early settlement would counter Chilean diplomacy as well as invigorate that of Peru. With the Tacna and Arica question still unresolved, Peru accused the Chilean government of falsely encouraging Bolivia to believe that a Chile-Brazil mediation would result in a more favorable settlement. At the same time, the Peruvian government wisely refrained from outright criticism of Brazilian policy despite evidence to suggest that Brazil was cooperating with Chile in an effort to encourage Bolivia to reject the Argentine award.[1]

The above considerations also encouraged the Peruvian government to compromise with Brazil. The 1904 Peru-Brazil agreements had provided for joint technical commissions to explore the upper Yuruá River and the upper Purús River to collect geographical data to facilitate a settlement. But the nature of the terrain made the task difficult, and the time for completion had to be extended. Diplomatic discussions were also prolonged because the Peruvian minister to Brazil took leave and was then replaced. As diplomatic intrigue threatened to complicate the dispute, the Leguía administration seized the initiative, offering Brazil territorial concessions in the upper Acre region in return for neutrality in what it termed the Bolivia-Chile complications. The 1909 Treaty of Limits, Commerce, and Navigation on the Amazon River Basin completed the delimitation of the frontier between Peru and Brazil, as well as established general guidelines to govern commerce and navigation in the region. Based on the principle of *uti possidetis*, the lines drawn by the treaty were heavily influenced by the findings of the joint technical commissions. The treaty conceded to Brazil the land over which it held de facto possession, which constituted the bulk of the territory in dispute. Peru was left with the territories on the upper Yuruá and upper Purús, neutralized in 1904 and populated by Peruvians, as well as a small parcel between the parallel of Catay and the Santa Rosa River. The 1909 treaty completed the Peru-Brazil boundary that the 1851 convention had begun on the Japurá River and ended at the confluence of the Yavarí and Amazon rivers. The boundary was extended to the Acre River and then to a point opposite the Yaverija River where Peruvian territory ended and Bolivia began. Treaty ratifications were exchanged in Rio de Janeiro on April 30, 1910.[2]

The terms of the Peru-Brazil treaty encouraged Bolivia to settle with Peru. On September 17, 1909, the Andean neighbors signed an agreement, known as the Polo–Sánchez Bustamante treaty, that executed the Argentine award and thus fixed Peru's boundary with Bolivia. Although the boundary detailed in the treaty paralleled the line specified in the arbitral award, minor modifications were made to accommodate both natural features and the reciprocal interests of the signatories. On March 30, 1911, following a series of incidents in the Manuripi River region, Peru and Bolivia concluded a complementary protocol that provided for a friendly settlement of the boundary between the mouth of the Heath River and the confluence of the

Yaverija and Acre rivers.[3]

Although the Leguía administration also pressed Ecuador and Colombia for early settlements, little progress was made. The 1887 Spanish arbitration led to a projected award in 1910 that largely accepted Peru's juridical thesis. When the provisions of the award became known in Ecuador, they led to violent demonstrations against Peru in Quito and Guayaquil that produced reprisals in Lima and Callao. As both countries mobilized, the Ecuadorian government suggested direct negotiations in Washington, but Peru refused to consider a solution other than arbitration. War appeared imminent, but a tripartite mediation by Argentina, Brazil, and the United States eventually restored the peace. After Peru and Ecuador agreed to return to a peacetime footing, the king of Spain resolved not to pronounce his award. With the end of the Spanish arbitration, the mediating powers advised Peru and Ecuador to bring the dispute before the Permanent Court of Arbitration at The Hague. The Peruvian government accepted this proposal, but Ecuador continued to insist on direct negotiations.[4]

As the Leguía administration negotiated with Ecuador, it agreed with Colombia, in the 1909 Porras–Tanco Argáez treaty, to arbitrate their dispute if they had not reached a settlement by the time the Peru-Ecuador question was resolved. The 1909 treaty and a complementary convention concluded in 1910 were thought to have ended violence in the region, but such was not the case. After Colombia established a fortified customs post at La Pedrera on the Caquetá River, clashes occurred between Peruvian and Colombian forces, in which a slightly larger Peruvian force succeeded in occupying the Colombian post. In a *modus vivendi* dated July 19, 1911, the Peruvian government agreed to return the Colombian post if Colombia pledged not to augment the garrison or attack Peruvian settlements on the Caquetá and Putumayo rivers. Although the incident was resolved peacefully, the battle of La Pedrera had an electrifying effect on Peruvian public opinion and generated enormous prestige for Oscar R. Benavides, the commander of the Peruvian expeditionary force.[5]

A few days before Leguía was inaugurated, the Chilean minister to Peru, José Miguel Echenique Gandarillos, proposed to lay a wreath in the name of the Chilean government at the crypt honoring Peruvian dead in the War of the Pacific. As soon as the Leguía government was installed, Foreign Minister Melitón Porras rejected the proposal. He argued that any improvement in diplomatic relations must be based on a faithful compliance with the Treaty of Ancón. Diplomatic relations between Peru and Chile steadily deteriorated over the next eighteen months. In a note dated September 30, 1909, Foreign Minister Porras argued that Chile had no right to exercise acts of sovereignty over Tacna and Arica. Chilean Foreign Minister Agustín Edwards responded on November 5 with the now-familiar Chilean argument that the ten-year period fixed by the Treaty of Ancón was only a minimum amount of time in which a plebiscite should be held. In the ensuing months,

Chile expelled Peruvian priests and Peruvian laborers from the occupied provinces and shipped arms to Ecuador for possible use against Peru. Foreign Minister Edwards even suggested that Peru and Chile agree to a Chilean annexation of Tacna and Arica and then hold a *pro forma* plebiscite to give the appearance of a popular vote. On March 18, 1910, the Peruvian government again broke diplomatic relations with Chile. In the note announcing the break, Peru complained of Chilean persecution of Peruvian citizens in the occupied provinces as well as the recent expulsion of Peruvian priests.[6]

In November 1910 the Chilean government sent Paulino Alfonso on a confidential mission to Lima to discuss the possibility of a new understanding. At the time, Peru and Bolivia were again embroiled in troubles that the Leguía government suspected were encouraged and abetted by Chile. The Peruvian government reached a tentative agreement with Alfonso that provided for a division of Tacna and Arica, with precise boundaries and indemnity to be settled later. In the course of the talks, Alfonso also agreed to end Chilean involvement in the Peruvian disputes with Bolivia and Ecuador. Unfortunately, Alfonso had exceeded his instructions in concluding the agreement, and the Chilean government soon disavowed his actions. The Chilean foreign minister subsequently indicated that a division of Tacna and Arica would be acceptable only if the Arica to La Paz railway and the port of Arica remained under Chilean control. No further progress toward a solution to the Tacna and Arica dispute occurred during the first Leguía administration.[7]

On the other hand, diplomatic relations with the United States continued to improve. A treaty of arbitration, signed in Washington on December 5, 1908, provided for submission of legal differences and treaty interpretations to the Permanent Court of Arbitration at The Hague. A naturalization convention, signed on October 15, 1907, but not proclaimed until September 2, 1909, provided that citizens of the United States who had been naturalized in Peru would be considered Peruvian citizens. The first treaty highlighted Peru's continuing support for the principle of arbitration. Although limited in scope and impact, both treaties exemplified the determination of the two countries to develop broader, deeper diplomatic ties.[8]

After 1909 the Peruvian government raised the question of a US naval facility at Chimbote on several different occasions. In 1911 President Leguía offered Washington a package deal that involved the sale of North American submarines to Peru, US acquisition of Chimbote, and a US guarantee of Peruvian territorial integrity. To put the offer in perspective, the Leguía administration had been discussing the purchase of submarines for several months as part of a strategy to court US favor in its disputes with Chile and Ecuador. In Washington, Secretary of State Knox was receptive to the sale because it would bring concrete results to his policy of dollar diplomacy. The State Department referred the Peruvian proposal to the Department of the

Navy, which expressed disinterest because it believed the Panama Canal would provide all the facilities it needed. In April 1912, only a few months before he left office, Leguía made yet another attempt to persuade the United States to acquire Chimbote, offering the port at practically no cost. The Department of State did not respond to Leguía's request, and the 1914 completion of the Panama Canal ruled out, at least from a strategic point of view, any need for the United States to acquire naval facilities in the region.[9]

BILLINGHURST, PARDO, AND WORLD WAR I

The short, tumultuous presidential term of Guillermo E. Billinghurst (1912–1914) focused on domestic concerns, but an abortive attempt to resolve the Tacna and Arica dispute engendered widespread distrust because Billinghurst owned nitrate works in Tarapacá and had close friends in the Chilean government. On November 10, 1912, only six weeks after assuming office, the Billinghurst administration initiated an exchange of cables with the Chilean government that fixed the bases for a plebiscitary agreement. The Huneeus-Valera protocol called for immediate resumption of diplomatic relations, negotiation of a commercial treaty of reciprocity, payment by Chile of an indemnity to Peru, and postponement of the plebiscite until 1933. Voting in the plebiscite would be limited to Peruvians and Chileans able to read and write and either natives or residents in the provinces for at least three years. The plebiscitary process would be conducted by an election board consisting of two Peruvians, two Chileans, and the president of the supreme court of Chile, who would serve as the presiding officer.[10]

President Billinghurst saw the agreement as a means to establish a *modus vivendi* to replace the difficult international situation facing Peru. Concerned with the dangers inherent in confronting Bolivia, Colombia, Ecuador, and Chile simultaneously, Billinghurst argued that Peru's only recourse was to table the Tacna and Arica question while it developed its economic, military, and political capabilities. Eventually, this strategy would enable Peru to contend with Chile on equal terms. Not surprisingly, his critics rejected such arguments, contending Billinghurst was so anxious to reach a settlement that he was willing to cede the Peruvian provinces to Chile in return for the payment of a nominal fee. Peruvian public opinion strongly opposed the Huneeus-Valera protocol, and the Peruvian congress, ignoring the president's pleas, adjourned without taking action. The Chilean government supported the agreement, but after it became obvious that Peru would not ratify, the Chilean congress also failed to act.[11]

President Billinghurst also moved to resolve the disputes with Ecuador and Colombia. In early 1913 he suggested to the Ecuadorian plenipotentiary in Lima what later became known as the "mixed formula" because it consisted of both a direct settlement and limited arbitration. Billinghurst proposed that the dispute be submitted to the Permanent Court of Arbitration at The Hague with the understanding that negotiations would occur at the same time as the arbitral proceedings. The Ecuadorian government accepted the Billinghurst proposal in principle, but it later concentrated on a direct settlement. Long opposed to arbitration of the dispute, Ecuador focused on bilateral negotiations while postponing consideration of arbitration, a procedure contrary to both the spirit and the letter of the Billinghurst proposal. The mixed formula did not bear fruit during Billinghurst's term in office, but it was significant because it was the first time a solution based on both negotiation and arbitration was proposed.[12]

By the end of his first year in office, Billinghurst had alienated powerful sectors of Peruvian society, and the growing opposition united to block his congressional initiatives. Billinghurst's foreign policy, in particular his overture to Chile, was a special source of concern because the 1912 agreement seemed likely to leave both Tacna and Arica in the hands of Chile. Attacking government profligacy, the president slashed the military budget, alienating the armed forces and raising additional questions about his resolve to defend the national patrimony. Matters came to a head in early 1914 when Billinghurst threatened to dissolve the congress, hold new elections, and rewrite the constitution. Isolated from the established political parties, the president turned to the masses for support, threatening to arm them as a counterpoise to the regular army. Concerned with the president's idiosyncrasies, lack of restraint, and inability to brook opposition, a group of conspirators plotted his overthrow, using the army chief of staff and hero of La Pedrera, Colonel Oscar R. Benavides, as their instrument. Following the *golpe,* Benavides was declared provisional president on May 15, 1914.

The outbreak of World War I found the Peruvian government in a difficult financial position. Unfavorable economic circumstances after 1912, in particular falling sugar and rubber prices, were aggravated by the unstable political conditions already discussed. When the war began, its immediate effect was to paralyze trade, which brought about a sharp drop in customs receipts—still the foundation of the Peruvian fiscal system—as well as a decline in revenue from other sources. At the same time, the credit of the government, especially its European credit, practically disappeared. With its most important assets already mortgaged, the Peruvian government was reduced to making frantic efforts in practically every quarter to borrow large or small sums. To meet the crisis, the government resorted to a banking moratorium and the issuance of paper currency backed by gold and short-term securities. The reelection of José Pardo in May 1915 coincided with a noticeable betterment in Peru's financial situation. Renewed demand for raw materials augmented Peruvian exports and added to the confidence generated by Pardo's conservative economic policies.[13]

Although commerce was again flourishing by 1916, World War I permanently modified Peru's historical trade patterns. US exports to Latin

America in general and Peru in particular had been growing since 1900, but they exploded after 1914 when European goods were scarce. A shortage of European shipping, high freight rates, and the risk of German submarines and raiders all contributed to this trade dislocation. Positive factors promoting greater US trade with Peru included the opening of the Panama Canal in 1914, establishment of new steamship lines between New York and South American ports, and creation of a Latin American division within the Bureau of Foreign and Domestic Commerce in Washington. Before the war, Great Britain had dominated trade with Peru, but by 1916, the United States had increased its share of Peruvian exports and imports to over 60 percent. Even though US economic interests were unable to retain these high market shares, they remained at war's end the dominant force in Peruvian trade.[14]

Despite considerable popular sympathy for the Allied cause, President Benavides steered Peru on the more prudent and profitable course of neutrality. At the initiative of the Peruvian government, the Pan-American Union created a special neutrality commission in 1914. At its opening session, Peru proposed establishment of a neutral zone in the Atlantic from the territorial sea to a point equidistant between that limit and the coast of Europe. Although the Pan-American Union took no further action on this proposal, the Pardo administration maintained a neutral stance until October 1917, when it severed diplomatic relations with Germany. The principal event behind this action was the German sinking in February 1917 of a Peruvian merchant ship, the *Lorton,* coupled with the subsequent German refusal to pay compensation. The Pardo government argued the case involved a neutral ship from a neutral state carrying noncontraband goods to a neutral country. Germany countered that the nitrates on board were absolute contraband destined for a belligerent state. Because the vessel could not be conveyed to a German port without endangering the safety of the German submarine in question, the German government concluded that the captain of the submarine was justified in sinking it. The *Lorton* incident precipitated Peru's break with Germany, but it did not result in more aggressive Peruvian action in support of the Allied cause.[15]

Although the Peruvian people generally supported the United States and the Allied cause, there was an additional, more parochial reason for the break in diplomatic relations with Germany. The Tacna and Arica dispute had reached another state of crisis, and by placing Peru firmly on the side of the United States, the Pardo administration hoped to obtain stronger support from Washington. As early as July 1917, President Pardo announced Peru's adherence to the principles of right, justice, and self-determination set forth by President Woodrow Wilson. And in his 1918 presidential message, Pardo stated that Peru could hardly remain indifferent to the principles of morality and international justice proclaimed in firm and elevated terms by the US president. In 1919 the citizens of Lima sent a long cable to President Wilson in which they expressed their conviction that the "Father of Peace" and the

"Priest of Justice" could not oppose imperialism in Europe while condoning the right of conquest in the Americas. As Peruvians enthusiastically greeted Wilson's idealistic statements, the United States hastened to clarify its position on the specific issue of Tacna and Arica. At the end of 1918, Washington informed the Peruvian minister to the United States that it was not inclined to offer a mediation of the dispute and doubted the wisdom of placing the question before the Paris Peace Conference.[16]

FOREIGN POLICY OF THE *ONCENIO*

After living abroad for a number of years, Augusto B. Leguía returned to Peru in February 1919 to campaign for the presidency. His principal opponent, Antero Aspíllaga, was backed by President Pardo; however, by 1919 Civilismo in general and the Pardo government in particular had fallen into disrepute in Peru. Leguía capitalized on the existing dissatisfaction, charging that Aspíllaga, Pardo, and the Civilistas did not understand the social, economic, and political changes sweeping Peru. Portraying himself as a national renovator, Leguía drew political support from diverse sectors of the electorate. His emphasis on social and economic reform attracted the nascent middle sector, largely composed of business and professional people, that was emerging in Peru. In addition, his vague promises of a more vital and equitable society drew support from a variety of political interests ranging from members of the upper class to the newly formed Socialist Party. He was also popular with Peruvian students, who twice elected him to the symbolic post of mentor of the youth.

As for foreign policy issues, Leguía emphasized the Tacna and Arica question, promising to regain not only Tacna and Arica but also Tarapacá. Long interested in Peru's territorial disputes, Leguía hoped to build on his Bolivian and Brazilian settlements by resolving the questions with Ecuador and Colombia, thus completing the delimitation of Peru. In the course of a September 1918 interview with a Colombian journalist, Leguía indicated that he would see his reelection as explicit approval of the policy of American solidarity, which he had followed for years, as well as clear recognition that he had always defended the rights and interests of Peru. Granted this vote of confidence, he promised to direct the foreign policy of his second administration toward honorable solutions to the Tacna and Arica question and the Colombia and Ecuador disputes.[17]

In the May 1919 presidential elections, Leguía won a convincing victory over Aspíllaga. Not waiting for his constitutional installation, President-elect Leguía and his supporters seized the national palace on July 4, 1919, and exiled President Pardo. The official explanation for the *golpe* was that it squelched a plot by Pardo and members of the congress to prevent Leguía from taking office. At the same time, it also enabled Leguía to dissolve a hostile congress and orchestrate the election of one more amenable to his demands. The constitution provided for the election of only one-third of the congress every two years, and because the current congress contained a hostile majority, it was advantageous for Leguía to dissolve that body and reconstitute it with a partisan majority. Leguía's ploy proved successful, the congress after 1919 offered little effective opposition to his policies and programs. Congressmen who dared oppose the president were generally accused of attempted revolution or another fabricated charge and imprisoned or exiled.

In addition to the boundary disputes with Ecuador and Colombia and the recovery of the occupied provinces, Peru after 1919 struggled to expand and deepen its relationship with the United States. Of course, these issues were often entwined, for the Peruvian government and people, for much of the period, anticipated the support and assistance of the United States in resolving the territorial disputes. In part because of these expectations, Washington was aggressively and extensively involved in resolution of the territorial questions, although not always in accordance with Peruvian desires. US foreign policy seldom met Peruvian anticipations, and its failure to do so precipitated or accelerated the growth of major new tenets in Peruvian foreign policy.[18]

The Woodrow Wilson administration quickly recognized the Leguía government, and in 1920 both governments elevated their diplomatic missions to the ambassadorial level. Recognition of the Leguía administration was a departure from Wilson's policy of not recognizing revolutionary governments. Leguía's critics charged that Washington acted posthaste because of Leguía's friendly attitude toward the United States and the potential for US investment in Peru. Thereafter, a convergence of economic interests fostered expansion of US economic activities in Peru. The Leguía government opted for a pattern of export-led growth, the success of which depended on a rapid increase in exports, primarily to the United States. The capital requirements for this growth coincided with those of US bankers, who had funds available to invest abroad. Under these circumstances, North American investors rapidly expanded their Peruvian operations, which increased their economic influence in the country. For the first time, US private capital eclipsed British investments, and US trade also grew significantly.

With the growth in US investment and trade, there was a concomitant increase in US economic and political influence in Peru. From 1919 to 1930, a growing number of North Americans worked in key ministries and departments of the Peruvian government. The close relationship that developed encouraged a number of controversial Peruvian policies, such as declaring July 4 a public holiday in honor of the birthday of the United States and supporting US military intervention in Nicaragua. It was little wonder that critics of Leguía later charged that by 1930 Peru was directed, governed, and supervised by the US Secretary of State. Such judgments were exaggerated, but US interests and responsibilities in Peru undoubtedly expanded after 1919. The change aroused the expectations and support of some Peruvians and the criticism and animosity of others.[19]

LONG ROAD TO SETTLEMENT WITH CHILE

By virtue of having broken diplomatic relations with Germany, Peru was a participant in the Paris Peace Conference, which assembled on January 18, 1919. South American issues were not included on the conference agenda, but the Peruvian government was told it could submit the Tacna and Arica question to the League of Nations as soon as the peace treaty was ratified. The Treaty of Versailles was submitted to the Peruvian national assembly on September 25, 1919, and was unanimously approved on November 17, 1919. With ratification, Peru became a founding member of the League of Nations.

On November 1, 1920, the Peruvian delegation to the League requested that the first League Assembly consider and revise the Treaty of Ancón. The Peruvian note demanded the return of Tacna, Arica, and Tarapacá both because new concepts of international law rejected territorial annexation by force and because the Chilean government had annulled the Treaty of Ancón by systematically violating clauses favorable to Peru. On the same day, the Bolivian government presented a related request to the League that demanded the return of the Bolivian littoral. The Peruvian note indicated that the Leguía administration acknowledged and supported the Bolivian proposal. League action was forestalled when the secretary general informed Peru and Bolivia that their requests had been submitted too late to be considered by the 1920 Assembly. On December 2, 1920, the Leguía administration formally withdrew its request, reserving the right to place the question of Tacna and Arica before the League at a later date.[20]

From 1919 to 1921 the Peruvian government opposed direct negotiations with Chile, preferring action by the League of Nations or arbitration by the United States. During the 1919 election campaign, the Peruvian people had strongly supported Leguía's maximum policy, which demanded the return of Tacna, Arica, and Tarapacá, and the president feared an early agreement to negotiate would erode domestic support. Leguía was also concerned that the Chilean government might prolong negotiations as a means to block a subsequent arbitration of the dispute. For this reason, his administration refused to receive Federico Puga Borne, an elderly and respected former Chilean foreign minister, when he arrived in Lima in August 1920 to open direct negotiations. The abortive Puga Borne mission was Chile's first attempt in ten years to open direct negotiations, and its failure helped convince the Chilean government that arbitration was the only solution acceptable to Peru. The Peruvian government's publication in 1921 of a white paper entitled *Exposición documentada* reinforced this viewpoint. It argued that the terms of the Treaty of Ancón could not be fulfilled and that Tacna, Arica, and Tarapacá should be returned to Peru without either a plebiscite or a monetary payment.[21]

At the end of 1921, the Chilean government of Arturo Alessandri offered a new diplomatic initiative. Chile's proposal, dated December 12, 1921, suggested that Peru and Chile revive the 1912 Huneeus-Valera protocol, which had provided for a plebiscite in 1933. Expressing surprise that Chile considered the 1912 exchange of cables to have executive force, the Peruvian government replied that internal conditions in Tacna and Arica had so changed by 1921 that it was now impossible to hold a plebiscite. Foreign Minister Alberto Salomón then suggested that Peru and Chile jointly submit the issue to arbitration by the US government. Chile's reply, dated December 20, 1921, argued that the 1912 negotiations were more than a simple exchange of cables and concluded by inviting Peru to continue direct negotiations. Salomón later rejected Chile's contention that Article III of the Treaty of Ancón was the only point under discussion and again invited Chile to participate in an impartial arbitration under the auspices of the United States.[22]

Chile's December 1921 initiative was preceded by discussions with the US government that positively influenced a January 1922 invitation by the Harding administration for Peru and Chile to open talks in Washington. Although the United States was willing to consider arbitration if the negotiations failed, it refused to accept the wording of the initial Peruvian acceptance, which suggested the Harding administration had invited Peru to submit the problem to arbitration. Delegations from Peru and Chile negotiated in Washington for two months in the summer of 1922 but were unable to reach a settlement. Deadlocked, they asked President Harding to arbitrate the dispute, and in July 1922 Secretary of State Charles Evans Hughes persuaded them to accept the compromise embodied in the 1922 Protocol and Supplementary Agreement of Washington. The key provisions of the agreement limited arbitration to the unfulfilled provisions of Article III of the Treaty of Ancón. If the president ruled a plebiscite should be held, he was to determine the necessary conditions; if he decided it could not be held, the good offices of the United States would be available to facilitate a settlement.[23]

Although both governments portrayed the Washington protocol as a diplomatic victory, the agreement was widely criticized in Peru and Chile. Motivated in part by domestic political considerations, opposition to the Alessandri administration argued Chile had nothing to gain and everything to lose from abandoning its insistence on a bilateral solution to the dispute. The Chilean Senate finally ratified the pact in November 1922, but Chilean Foreign Minister Ernesto Barros Jarpa was severely censured and eventually forced to resign. In Peru, Leguía's critics roundly criticized the agreement because the designated arbitrator was a politician rather than a judge. Many felt this opened the way for a political as opposed to a legal settlement. The Leguía administration was also criticized because the terms of the protocol constituted abandonment of former policies involving a revision of the Treaty of Ancón, the return of Tacna and Arica because Chile had failed to comply with the 1883 treaty, and the recovery of Tarapacá. On the positive side, the protocol incorporated arbitration by the US government, which was the solution sought by successive Peruvian governments. In addition, the arbitral proceedings provided an excuse for maintaining public order and distracted public attention from Peruvian domestic problems.[24]

Under the terms of the protocol, Peru and Chile were given up to eight months to prepare their legal cases. In the interim, President Harding died and was replaced as arbitrator by Calvin Coolidge. The Peruvian government presented its case in two quarto volumes, with the first containing legal arguments in English and the second consisting of maps, documents, and supporting evidence. The heart of the Peruvian position was spelled out in the introduction, which argued that a plebiscite was not held in 1894 because the Chilean government refused to allow it, and since that time, there had been a change in the circumstances contemplated in the Treaty of Ancón. The Peruvians concluded that Chile's failure to hold a plebiscite, which could be taken as proof that Peru would have been victorious, invalidated the 1883 treaty and called for the automatic return of the occupied provinces to Peru. The Peruvian case was later criticized because the arbitrator was not empowered to rule on these issues but only on the question of whether or not the plebiscite could be held. In contrast, the Chilean case, which also filled two quarto volumes, focused on the issue at hand, concluding that a plebiscite could and should be held. Five months later, Peru and Chile presented counterarguments that added little to their initial presentations. Peru concluded that a plebiscite could not now be held and argued that the only just and equitable solution was to return both provinces to Peru. Chile criticized Peruvian attempts to broaden the scope of the arbitration and again concluded a plebiscite could be held, asking the arbitrator to fix the conditions necessary for its execution.[25]

In the opening section, the Coolidge award, dated March 4, 1925, emphasized that the arbitrator was empowered to rule only on the question of whether or not to hold a plebiscite. Questions like the causes and conduct of the War of the Pacific or the economic effects of the Treaty of Ancón were simply outside the scope of the arbitration. On the issue at hand, the arbitrator ruled there was no reason that a fair plebiscite could not be held or that it should not be held. As to the conditions of the plebiscite, the arbitrator ruled that members of the armed forces, police, and civil servants would not be allowed to vote, but Peruvians born in Tacna and Arica and later expelled would be allowed to return. Striking at Chile's argument that it should be responsible for conducting the plebiscite, the arbitrator established a plebiscitary commission, empowered to rule on questions like registration and ballot counting, to insure a fair election.[26]

The Coolidge award provoked rejoicing in Chile and outrage in Peru. Chileans saw the award as a vindication of Alessandri's policies, and when a *golpe* returned him to power in March 1925, he was accorded a hero's welcome. Peruvians felt the award ignored the justice of their cause, and public reaction was intense. The opposition to Leguía harshly criticized both the decision to go to Washington and the preparation and presentation of Peru's legal case. The US government was also roundly condemned for its alleged inability to understand the moral and juridical theses of Peru. Leguía refused to criticize the award openly, but he allowed Solón Polo, the president of the Peruvian Defense Commission, to object strongly in a memorial to President Coolidge. Polo maintained that the Treaty of Ancón had set a specific limit of ten years for the holding of a plebiscite. He also rejected Coolidge's assertion that the evidence of Chileanization offered by Peru was insufficient to conclude that the essential conditions for a fair plebiscite were unobtainable.[27]

The plebiscitary commission held its first formal meeting on August 5, 1925, and for the next ten months, it struggled to organize and execute a free and honest plebiscite. When this proved impractical, the president of the plebiscitary commission, on June 9, 1926, introduced a motion that resolved that a free and honorable plebiscite was impossible. At the next meeting of the commission, on June 14, 1926, the president criticized the Chilean government for failing to establish and maintain the conditions necessary to conduct the plebiscite envisioned by the Coolidge award. On the same day, the commission, with the Chilean representative abstaining, approved a resolution to terminate the proceedings. The failure to hold a plebiscite was a tremendous diplomatic victory for the Peruvian government, and it fortified Leguía's domestic political position. In his 1926 message to the congress, the president asserted that the termination of plebiscitary proceedings invalidated the Coolidge award and demonstrated the issue could not be resolved without invoking the real rights of Peru. The breakdown in the proceedings also reaffirmed Peru's earlier faith in the power and justice of the United States, although it did not completely eliminate the disillusionment that came from a comparison of Peruvian hopes in 1919 with the realities of 1926. In this regard, the prevailing attitude in Peru was probably best expressed by an editorial in the June 26, 1926, issue of *Variedades,* which advised that Peru should now stand on its own feet and not let itself again be involved with Washington.[28]

The events that led to a final settlement of the Tacna and Arica dispute began on the steamer *Essequibo,* which carried both the Chilean and Peruvian delegations to the Sixth Pan-American Conference in Havana. The cordial relations that developed during the passage continued at the conference and led to an unofficial exchange of ideas once the delegates returned home. Aware that relations were improving, the US government, on July 9, 1928, suggested that Peru and Chile reestablish the diplomatic ties severed in 1910. Weary of the dispute, both sides soon agreed that a negotiated settlement was the only way to break the impasse. The final settlement took eight months to negotiate and was largely the work of President Leguía and the Chilean ambassador to Peru, Emiliano Figueroa Larraín. Nevertheless, Leguía carefully masked his role in the negotiations by insisting that the final terms appear to originate under the good offices of the president of the United States. In so doing, he hoped to avoid responsibility for the settlement by giving the appearance it had been dictated by the US government.

On June 3, 1929, representatives of Peru and Chile signed the Tacna and Arica Treaty and Additional Protocol. The agreement divided the occupied provinces, with Tacna going to Peru and Arica to Chile. In addition, the Chilean government agreed to grant Peru a wharf, customs office, and railway station at Arica Bay, as well as to pay Peru a $6 million indemnity. Peru and Chile agreed to build a monument on the Morro de Arica, to commemorate their improved relations. The most significant proviso of the additional protocol stipulated that neither Peru nor Chile could cede to a third state any of the territories over which they were granted sovereignty in the 1929 treaty without the prior agreement of the other signatory. It also provided that neither signatory could build new international railway lines across those territories without the approval of the other. These provisions later frustrated Bolivian efforts to obtain an outlet to the sea.[29]

The 1929 treaty was well received by a majority of citizens in both Peru and Chile. With the exception of Bolivia, which viewed the settlement with dismay, the remainder of the American republics were also delighted to see the issue finally resolved. The possession of Tacna and Arica had never been economically profitable for Chile, and the conclusion of the dispute freed the Chilean government to pursue a broader leadership role in the Western Hemisphere. In Peru, sporadic student demonstrations against the settlement sparked little support from other political or economic interest groups. For the most part, the Peruvian populace was simply weary of the protracted litigation and disabused by the contrast between the eloquent proclamations of the past and the dull reality of the present. Criticism in Peru stemmed largely from nationalists, who censured Leguía for betraying the public interest and yielding to the dictates of Washington. At the same time, Leguía's distortion of the US role in the settlement helped generate anti-United States feeling as significant numbers of Peruvians blamed Washington for the final solution. Some critics even argued that President Hoover had originated the idea of a division of the provinces and forced Leguía to accept it. In fact, the idea had surfaced as early as 1882 and had been suggested many times thereafter.

CONTROVERSIAL SALOMON-LOZANO TREATY

Although Leguía's first priority was the Tacna and Arica dispute, he was also interested in reaching settlements in the Oriente. The Colombian government, sharing Leguía's hopes, was encouraged by his campaign statements that he intended to finalize Peru's northern boundaries. In 1919 Peru and Colombia opened negotiations aimed at reducing the zone of arbitration through a direct settlement, but no progress was made and the talks were eventually broken off. When the League of Nations refused to consider the Tacna and Arica question, Leguía again turned his attention to the century-old Colombian dispute. In March 1921 an editorial in *Mundial* saluted Fabio Lozano y Torrijos, the Colombian minister to Peru, and opined it was time to terminate the problem between Peru and Colombia. Later in the year, Leguía acknowledged sentiment in both countries favoring a settlement and promised a satisfactory formula would soon be found. About that time, he initiated secret, personal negotiations with Fabio Lozano that led to conclusion of the Treaty of Frontiers and Free Inland Navigation on March 24, 1922.[30]

The 1922 treaty, generally referred to as the Salomón-Lozano treaty, granted Colombia frontage on the Amazon River in return for ceding Peru territory south of the Putumayo River that Colombia had received from Ecuador in 1916. The agreement provided for a mixed commission to mark the boundary and granted the signatories freedom of transit by land as well as the right of navigation on common rivers and their tributaries. Unfortunately, the pact did not contain an adequate compensation clause, and the Peruvians who owned land in the ceded area later charged that they were unable to receive a fair price for their properties. The treaty was also very unpopular with many Peruvian nationalists. Criticism centered on the secret nature of the negotiations, the fact that treaty provisions were kept secret after the treaty was signed, and the inadvisability of Leguía's conducting talks without the assistance of Peru's experts on territorial issues. Critics especially condemned the decision to give Colombia access to the Amazon River through the so-called Leticia Trapezoid, a narrow corridor of land between the Putumayo and Amazon rivers that includes the Amazon port of Leticia.[31]

The 1922 treaty generated considerable public interest, but its terms were not well understood. Debate focused on the decision to give Colombia frontage on the Amazon River when a far more significant consideration was the extent to which the treaty undermined Ecuadorian claims in the Oriente. The territory south of the Putumayo River, ceded by Colombia to Peru, penetrated to the heart of the area disputed by Peru and Ecuador. Its acquisition greatly enhanced the Peruvian government's position in the region vis-à-vis Ecuador. Overnight, Quito found itself confronted by an antagonist where previously it had had an ally. From the San Miguel River eastward, Ecuador was now enclosed on the north, east, and south by

Peruvian territory. In addition to destroying any legal support that the 1916 treaty might have given Ecuadorian claims, the 1922 treaty eliminated the possibility of Colombian support, either military or diplomatic, for Ecuador in its dispute with Peru. After 1922 Ecuador's primary interest was in nullifying the Salomón-Lozano treaty, while Colombia's interest was in confirming its stipulations. Although few Peruvians acknowledged the importance of this new geographical and political reality, the violent reaction in Ecuador to news of the 1922 agreement testified to its strategical importance. The Ecuadorian government justifiably felt betrayed; it had sacrificed territory to Colombia in 1916 because it thought the treaty would make the latter its ally in the dispute with Peru.

The secret nature of the treaty negotiations, coupled with the unpopular character of the main provisions, led many Peruvian nationalists to conclude that the treaty was a product of US pressure. Critics alleged that Washington sacrificed Peru in the negotiations in order to compensate Colombia for its loss of Panama. Because the negotiations were conducted in secret, it has remained difficult to refute such charges conclusively, but no documentation has ever surfaced to substantiate them. On the other hand, the US government clearly pressured Peru to ratify the pact. As early as October 1923, Secretary of State Hughes instructed the US ambassador to Peru to inform Leguía that it would be highly gratifying to the United States if he would arrange for submission of the treaty to the Peruvian congress. Between 1923 and 1928, the US government made no fewer than eight oral or written appeals to the president or foreign minister of Peru urging that some action be taken. This continuous pressure was resented and censured by Peruvians unhappy with the terms of the treaty.[32]

LIMITED PROGRESS ON OTHER ISSUES

In an effort to implement the so-called mixed formula, Peru and Ecuador had agreed in February 1919 to present the boundary line each considered to be its maximum concession. Peru presented its proposal in April 1920, but the Ecuadorian government failed to respond, and negotiations were later interrupted by domestic politics in Ecuador. In late 1921 the Leguía administration again asked for Ecuador's reply to its April 1920 proposal, and Quito suggested that both sides name delegations to negotiate in Washington. Even though the Leguía government later agreed to negotiate if the Harding administration issued an invitation, Peru was not eager to conclude a final settlement in the early years of the *oncenio*. Deeply involved personally in both the Tacna and Arica dispute and the Salomón-Lozano negotiations, Leguía lacked the diplomatic resources to deal simultaneously with Ecuador. In this light, the 1921 attempt to reopen negotiations was apparently a delaying tactic to divert Ecuadorian attention from Peruvian talks with Chile and Colombia. As the Peruvian minister of foreign affairs emphasized in the 1923 *Memoria,* Peru wished to take the Ecuadorian dispute to Washington as soon as the United States concluded the Tacna and Arica negotiation.[33]

Eventually, the talks between Peru and Ecuador led to the conclusion on June 21, 1924, of a formal agreement, the Ponce–Castro Oyanguren protocol. It provided for implementation of the mixed formula once the Tacna and Arica dispute had been resolved. With the prior assent of the US government, the signatories would convene in Washington to negotiate a definitive boundary; where they were unable to agree, they would submit the unresolved segments to the arbitral decision of the United States. The 1924 protocol was a compromise that attempted to reconcile Peruvian insistence on a juridical arbitration with Ecuadorian insistence on an equitable arbitration or direct negotiations. Ambiguous to a fault, the agreement was initially proclaimed a diplomatic victory in both countries; however, it was soon subjected to growing criticism in Ecuador, where detractors focused on its vague, incomplete provisions and the delay in settlement. Nine years passed before talks opened, and in the interim, internal disorder repeatedly compromised Ecuadorian efforts to revise the agreement.[34]

Soon after the Peruvian government signed the Ponce–Castro Oyanguren protocol, a new crisis arose concerning the Salomón-Lozano treaty with Colombia. In November 1924 the Brazilian government presented a memorandum to Peru that made friendly but formal observations that the 1922 treaty dealt in part with territory that Brazil claimed against Peru and had never settled in its dispute with Colombia. The Brazilian government then asked for assurances from Colombia that the 1922 agreement would not affect the validity of the existing Brazilian boundary with Peru. The Brazilian government eventually withdrew its formal observations in a *procès-verbal* signed in Washington on March 4, 1925. The agreement provided for ratification of the 1922 Peru-Colombia treaty and negotiation of a new treaty by Brazil and Colombia that would recognize the Apaporis-Tabatinga line as their common boundary. Because it ended any hope of modifying the 1922 treaty, the 1924 *procès-verbal* was condemned by Leguía's critics, doubly so because it carried the same date as the Coolidge award. Although the settlement was not advantageous for Peru, Leguía was understandably reluctant to reverse his two-year policy of official support for the 1922 treaty. With the US government about to rule on the Tacna and Arica question, he was also reluctant to anger Secretary of State Hughes, who hoped to conclude the *procès-verbal* before he left office. Diplomatic relations between Peru and Brazil were generally favorable for the remainder of the *oncenio*. In 1927 a demarcation commission finally completed the task begun in 1913 of fixing and marking the boundary between Peru and Brazil. Ratifications of a general obligatory arbitration convention between the two states occurred the same year.[35]

After 1924 the Leguía administration repeatedly recommended to the Peruvian congress approval of the 1922 treaty with Colombia, and in November 1927 a congressional commission also recommended its approval. Describing the pact as an example of inter-American harmony, the commission also emphasized that the territory ceded by Peru was of considerable economic and military importance. One month later, the Peruvian congress approved the 1922 treaty by a vote of 102 to 7. The Colombian government had already approved the treaty on October 30, 1925, and the signatories exchanged ratifications in Bogota on March 19, 1928. Once the frontier was marked, the Peruvian government officially ceded the Leticia Trapezoid to Colombia in August 1930. Peru's ratification reflected Leguía's omnipotence as well as the absence of an effective opposition and thus was not an accurate measure of public concern for the Salomón-Lozano treaty. Opposition coalesced around Julio C. Arana, the former rubber king, who argued that Leticia was Peruvian and that the Putumayo River was the only just boundary between Peru and Colombia. Between 1922 and 1927, Arana actively opposed the treaty, and when he denounced it the day after its approval, copies of his manifesto were seized by the police on direct orders from Leguía. Enrique A. Vigil was another powerful Amazonian businessman who opposed the accord. After ratification, he remained one of the main organizers of adverse sentiment, charging the agreement did not take adequate account of Peruvian interests in Leticia.[36]

For Leguía, the end came on the morning of August 5, 1930. Under pressure from a military *golpe,* he renounced the presidency, boarded the cruiser *Almirante Grau,* and sailed for Panama. He was later returned to Peru, and after a prolonged illness, compounded by inadequate medical care, he died in prison on February 6, 1932. Together with a number of other Latin American governments, Leguía's downfall was primarily a product of the world economic depression. The 1929 crash decreased the value of Peruvian exports and stopped the inflow of investment capital from the United States. With budget deficits occurring in every year after 1920, the Leguía government had borrowed heavily and the deteriorating economic situation found it unable to meet its obligations. Although dissatisfaction with territorial settlements was only a secondary reason for Leguía's ouster, they were a significant source of discontent, and their importance should not be minimized. Leguía's territorial settlements, especially the division of Tacna and Arica, alienated large segments of the populace and provoked sharp dissent within the armed forces and other nationalistic circles. Equally important, Leguía's close association with North American interests nurtured the growth of Peruvian nationalism. The current of anti-United States feeling that subsequently developed became a permanent part of the foreign policy environment of Peru.

NOTES

1. Cano, *Historia*, pp. 74–75; Fifer, *Bolivia*, pp. 142–145.
2. A copy of the 1909 treaty can be found in Perú, *Tratados, Convenciones y Acuerdos*, 1:141–145.
3. A copy of the Polo–Sánchez Bustamante treaty can be found in Perú, *Tratados, Convenciones y Acuerdos*, 1:91–93.
4. David H. Zook, Jr., "The Spanish Arbitration of the Ecuador-Peru Dispute," *Americas* 20 (April 1964): 359–375; Ulloa, *Posición*, pp. 179–182; Pérez Concha, *Ensayo*, 1:355–393.
5. Juan Angulo Puente Arnao, *Historia de los límites del Perú* (Lima: Imprenta de la Intendencia General de Guerra, 1927), p. 114; Paquita Benavides de Peña et al., *El Mariscal Benavides: Su Vida y Su Obra*, 2 vols. (Lima: Imprenta Editora Atlántida S.A., 1976), 1:120–162.
6. Karno, "Leguía," pp. 127–144.
7. Soder, "Tacna-Arica Dispute," pp. 309–312.
8. Copies of the 1907 naturalization convention and the 1908 arbitration treaty can be found in US Department of State, *Foreign Relations of the United States* (Washington, D.C.: Government Printing Office, 1909), pp. 498–502.
9. Livermore, "American Strategy," pp. 45–51.
10. Peter Blanchard, "A Populist Precursor: Guillermo Billinghurst," *Journal of Latin American Studies* 9, 2 (November 1977): 251–273; Wagner de Reyna, *Historia diplomática*, 1:139–140.
11. Basadre, *Historia*, 12:238–240; *La Prensa* (Lima), July 24–26, 1913.
12. Francisco Tudela, *The Controversy Between Peru and Ecuador* (Lima: Imprenta Torres Aguirre, 1941), pp. 38–43.
13. L. S. Rowe, *Early Effects of the War upon the Finance, Commerce and Industry of Peru* (New York: Oxford University Press, 1920), pp. 14–43; Bill Albert, *South America and the First World War: The Impact of the War on Brazil, Argentina, Peru and Chile* (Cambridge: Cambridge University Press, 1988), pp. 46–47.
14. David Joslin, *A Century of Banking in Latin America* (London: Oxford University Press, 1963), pp. 216–217; Bonilla, *Un siglo*, pp. 82–98; Albert, *South America and the First World War*, pp. 115–118.
15. Juan Bautista de Laballe, *El Perú y la Gran Guerra* (Lima: Imprenta Americana, 1919), pp. 50–51; José Carlos Martin, *José Pardo y Barreda: El Estadista* (Lima: Compañía de Impresiones y Publicidad, 1948), pp. 101–102.
16. Perú, Presidente, *Mensaje del Presidente de la República (1918)*, 40 vols. (Lima: various publishers, various years), pp. iv–v; Francisco E. Málaga Grenef, *Una carta a Wilson* (Lima: Imprenta Americana, 1919); *El Comercio* (Lima), January 20, 1919.
17. Guillermo Forero Franco, *Entre dos dictaduras*, 2 vols. (Bogotá: "El Gráfico," 1934), 1:82–84; Perú, *Mensaje* (1920), pp. iv–vi.
18. Ronald Bruce St John, "The End of Innocence: Peruvian Foreign Policy and the United States, 1919–1942," *Journal of Latin American Studies* 8, 2 (November 1976): 325–335.
19. Pedro Ugarteche, *La política internacional peruana durante la dictadura de Leguía* (Lima: Imprenta C. A. Castrillon, 1930), pp. 13–14, 20–33; Víctor Andrés Belaúnde, *La realidad nacional* (Paris: "Le Livre Libre," 1931), pp. 221–222, 242–244.
20. José Carrasco, *Bolivia ante la Liga de las Naciones* (Lima: Librería e Imprenta Gil, 1920); Francisco Tudela, *La política internacional y la dictadura de don Augusto Leguía* (Paris: Imprimerie OMNES, 1925), p. 8; *La Prensa* (Lima),

December 13–16, 1920.

21. Perú, Ministerio de Relaciones Exteriores, *Exposición documentada sobre el estado actual del problema del Pacífico* (Lima: Imprenta Torres Aguirre, 1921); Perú, *Memoria (1923)*, pp. 99–100.

22. Perú, *Memoria (1922)*, pp. 37–43, 57–60; Pío Max Medina, *La controversia peruano-chileno*, 2 vols. (Lima: Imprenta Torres Aguirre, 1925), 1:227–236.

23. A copy of the Washington Protocol and Supplementary Agreement can be found in Perú, *Tratados, Convenciones y Acuerdos*, 1:171–173.

24. Belaúnde, *La realidad*, pp. 221–233; Arturo Alessandri, *Recuerdos de Gobierno*, 3 vols. (Santiago: Editorial Nascimento, 1967), 1:140–143.

25. Perú, Ministerio de Relaciones Exteriores, *Arbitration Between Peru and Chile: The Case of Peru in the Matter of the Controversy Arising out of the Question of the Pacific* (Washington, D.C.: n.p., 1923); Chile, Ministerio de Relaciones Exteriores, *Tacna-Arica Arbitration: The Case of the Republic of Chile Submitted to the President of the United States as Arbitrator* (Washington, D.C.: n.p., 1923).

26. United States of America, Executive, *In the Matter of the Arbitration Between the Republic of Chile and the Republic of Peru, With Respect to the Unfulfilled Provisions of the Treaty of Peace of October 20, 1883, Under the Protocol and Supplementary Act Signed at Washington July 20, 1922. Opinion and Award of the Arbitrator* (Washington, D.C.: Government Printing Office, 1925).

27. Alberto Ulloa Sotomayor, *El fallo arbitral del presidente de Estados Unidos de America en la cuestión de Tacna y Arica* (Lima: n.p., 1925), pp. 68–69, 104–105; William Jefferson Dennis, *Tacna and Arica: An Account of the Chile-Peru Boundary Dispute and of the Arbitrations by the United States* (New Haven: Yale University Press, 1931), pp. 213–226.

28. Perú, *Mensaje (1926):* 9–10; "De Jueves A Jueves," *Variedades* 22 (June 26, 1926):3–4; Joe Foster Wilson, "An Evaluation of the Failure of the Tacna-Arica Plebiscitary Commission, 1925–1926" (Ph.D. diss., University of Georgia, 1965); *El Comercio* (Lima), June 25, 1926.

29. A copy of the 1929 treaty and additional protocol can be found in Perú, *Tratados, Convenciones y Acuerdos*, 1:183–187.

30. Forero Franco, *Entre dos dictaduras*, 1:82–84.

31. Perú, *Mensaje (1926)*, p. 5; Manuel A. Capuñay, *Leguía: Vida y obra del constructor del gran Perú* (Lima: Compañia de Impresiones y Publicidad, 1952), pp. 206–219. A copy of the 1922 treaty can be found in Perú, *Tratados, Convenciones y Acuerdos*, 1:251–254.

32. Ronald Bruce St John, "Peruvian Foreign Policy, 1919–1939: The Delimitation of Frontiers" (Ph.D. diss., University of Denver, 1970), pp. 246–247.

33. Perú, Ministerio de Relaciones Exteriores, *Boletín del Ministerio de Relaciones Exteriores (1919)* (Lima: various publishers, various years), no. 61, p. 33; Perú, *Memoria (1923)*, pp. 62–63; Perú, *Mensaje (1922)*, p. 6.

34. A copy of the protocol can be found in Perú, *Tratados, Convenciones y Acuerdos*, 1:278–279.

35. Pedro Ugarteche, *Documentos que acusan (El tratado Salomón-Lozano)* (Lima: Litográfico Tipograficos Estanco Del Tabaco, 1933), pp. 18–29; Basadre, *Historia*, 13:161–162.

36. Julio César Arana, *El protocolo Salomón-Lozano o el Pacto de Límites con Colombia* (Lima: Sanmarti y Compañía, 1927), p. 21.

TEN

New Horizons for the Foreign Policy of Peru, 1930–1962

In the three decades after Leguía, the foreign policy of Peru passed through a short period of consolidation followed by a longer term in which the nation's external affairs expanded in scope and direction. In this broader context, the forceful occupation of Leticia in 1932 proved to be an aberration, after which the terms of the 1922 treaty with Colombia together with other international agreements were generally reaffirmed. In particular, successive Peruvian governments worked to consolidate their diplomatic position in the south with Chile and Bolivia. In the case of Chile, the Peruvian government worked to fulfill the duties and obligations of the 1929 treaty while opposing Chilean negotiations aimed at giving Bolivia land that once belonged to Peru. With Bolivia, Peruvian diplomacy focused on their respective limits on the Copacabana Peninsula, joint use of the waters of Lake Titicaca, and enhanced trade and economic development.

The Peruvian government had announced its withdrawal from the League of Nations in 1939 but immediately joined the United Nations in 1945. An active participant in the new international body, it remained a forceful advocate of regional organizations whenever issues under discussion involved questions of regional peace or security. Reflecting this concern for enhanced regional cooperation, Peru in 1954 joined its Pacific neighbors in announcing that none would unilaterally diminish its claim to exercise sovereignty and jurisdiction over the continental shelf and insular sea to a distance of 200 nautical miles from the coast without prior consultation and agreement. In the eyes of many observers, this growing involvement of Peru in the more controversial aspects of the law of the sea was a natural extension of its longtime interest in territorial issues. The timing of the maritime issue, which was raised by the Bustamante administration in the aftermath of World War II, seemed almost propitious because the 1942 Rio Protocol had appeared to resolve the dispute in the Oriente, the final boundary question remaining from the independence era. The post-Leguía period was also a time in which Peru progressed toward a more mature, if often ambivalent, relationship with the United States. In the process, Peruvian nationalism, which continued to grow in strength and intensity, exerted an increasingly important influence on Peruvian foreign policy.

FOREIGN POLICY ISSUES IN
THE 1931 ELECTION CAMPAIGN

In a manifesto to the nation issued from Arequipa on August 22, 1930, Luis M. Sánchez Cerro had critiqued the evils of the *oncenio,* outlined what his regime hoped to accomplish, and called on the Peruvian armed forces to support his revolution. His goals centered on wider individual freedoms and increased economic prosperity. In terms of foreign policy, Sánchez Cerro made no mention of great personal or public dissatisfaction with Leguía's handling of the territorial problems with Chile, Colombia, or Ecuador. More to the point, he did not assign those issues an important place in the foreign policy of post-Leguía Peru. In fact, the only international question addressed by the manifesto was the policy of ceding oil concessions to foreign firms, a practice that Sánchez Cerro condemned. Once Sánchez Cerro had replaced Leguía in office, he remained an ardent nationalist; however, his early financial and investment policies walked a careful line between the demands of radical elements and the interests of the conservative elite. Sánchez Cerro's first administration was one of the most uncertain in the history of the republic. Unable to govern effectively, he announced his resignation on March 1, 1931; six days later, he left Peru for voluntary exile in Europe.[1]

Sánchez Cerro soon returned to Peru to campaign for the October 1931 elections. His political platform called for balanced budgets and sound currency, increased political participation, administrative decentralization, freedom of the press, and agrarian reform. With the United States in mind, the section on foreign affairs pledged to reestablish the international prestige of Peru and to condemn energetically all policies of political, diplomatic, economic, and administrative submission to the dictates of outside powers. It added that Peru must abandon former policies of ceding territory and compromising basic rights, and replace them with an emphasis on maintaining national sovereignty and defending the security of the country. The platform suggested that a Sánchez Cerro government would be a determined opponent in any negotiations with Ecuador, but it did not presage an intent to reopen the territorial questions with Chile and Colombia. Overall, Sánchez Cerro's platform was nationalistic in tone and content, but it did not augur a policy of expansionism or territorial reclamation.[2]

Víctor Raúl Haya de la Torre, who had founded the American Popular Revolutionary Alliance (APRA) in 1924, also returned to Peru in 1931 to run in the presidential elections. His early statements suggested the presidential campaign would be marked by sharply contrasting ideologies, but he soon tempered the Aprista position, especially its anti-imperialism and nationalization planks. Instead, Haya focused on a so-called minimum reform program for Peru that balanced foreign and domestic economic interests to establish a total and harmonious economy. On the issue of territorial settlements, he pledged to resolve both the pending boundary controversy with Ecuador and the problem in the Oriente created by the 1922 treaty with Colombia. The general direction of APRA's campaign rhetoric placed the movement to the left of the Revolutionary Union Party; nonetheless, the differences between the two parties were more of degree than of kind.[3]

The 1931 presidential campaign was a two-man race between Sánchez Cerro and Haya de la Torre. Backed by an effectively organized and well-financed campaign, Sánchez Cerro gained widespread support from the lower classes, the armed forces, the conservative coastal oligarchy, and right-wing nationalists. The Aprista program had a worker–middle-class orientation; and from the outset, Haya focused his efforts on the newly emergent middle sectors that Leguía had proved a potent source of political and economic power. Although Haya was never able to match the visibility and public recognition of Sánchez Cerro, he drew significant support from his home base in northern Peru as well as from the Lima-Callao area. The results of the 1931 presidential election were hotly contested, but a consensus later emerged that Sánchez Cerro won a basically honest election by a substantial margin. Unfortunately, his election failed to restore calm to the Peruvian political scene. On the contrary, his second administration was racked by growing political instability and profound economic crisis.[4]

LETICIA AFFAIR

On September 1, 1932, the Sánchez Cerro government received a telegram from Jesús Ugarte, the prefect in Iquitos, that stated that Peruvian filibusterers had seized Leticia, the only village of any importance in the trapezoid-shaped territory ceded by Leguía to Colombia in the 1922 treaty. Accomplished without bloodshed, the occupation of Leticia was the product of joint military and civilian planning; later charges of government premeditation and orchestration of the incident proved unfounded. Both nationalistic considerations and economic grievances motivated the filibusterers. Their number included employees of Enrique Vigil, a strong critic of the 1922 pact, who argued the Colombian government had failed to pay adequate compensation for his properties in the ceded territory. No Peruvian soldiers on active service participated in the raid, but members of the Peruvian armed forces stationed in Loreto quickly supported the seizure. On September 4, 1932, General Isauro Calderón, head of a newly formed junta in Iquitos, informed the Peruvian government that his forces intended to protect all Peruvian citizens in the area. In the communication, Calderón concluded that the Sánchez Cerro government should request revision of the 1922 treaty or at least a plebiscite to determine whether the inhabitants of the area wished to be a part of Colombia.[5]

The seizure of Leticia, followed by immediate civilian and military support for the rebels in Loreto, placed the Sánchez Cerro administration in a difficult position. It was locked into a mortal confrontation with APRA; hence, failure to support the filibusterers would threaten additional domestic unrest, which could lead to the overthrow of the government. Facing a conundrum, Sánchez Cerro informed the Colombian minister to Peru that Leticia had been seized by procommunist agitators who were enemies of the Peruvian government. He promised that his administration would join the Colombian government in efforts to subdue them. Sincere at the outset, Sánchez Cerro's position changed radically once the strength of Loretian backing for the filibusterers became clear and political support for a renegotiation of the 1922 treaty surfaced elsewhere in Peru. Within two weeks, José Matías Manzanilla, a former Peruvian foreign minister who was reappointed at the end of 1932, told the US ambassador to Peru that the Peruvian government could no longer consider withdrawing from Leticia because Peruvian public opinion overwhelmingly supported the seizure. When Manzanilla asked if the US government would influence Colombia to receive proposals for a revision of the 1922 treaty, the US ambassador refused on the grounds that reopening any boundary issue after force had been used threatened to throw the world into chaos. Thereafter, Washington continued to oppose the occupation of Leticia; its policy on this issue increased the existing ill will between the United States and Peru.[6]

The Leticia dispute dragged on for almost two years, and in that time, Colombia and Peru developed extensive arguments in support of their respective diplomatic positions. The Colombian government insisted that it was entitled to restore public order over territory that the 1922 treaty clearly recognized as Colombian. Although it did not rule out future discussions on territorial transfer, it refused to participate in such talks before it had restored Colombian sovereignty over the Leticia Trapezoid. Regarding the Peruvian complaint that the treaty had not been fulfilled because Peru was unable to occupy the Sucumbios Triangle, Bogota responded that Peru's inability to occupy this isolated piece of ground was no fault of Colombia's.[7]

In the absence of strong legal arguments, the Sánchez Cerro administration resorted to a variety of historical, political, and moral justifications. Stating that the filibusterers were motivated by irrepressible patriotic aspirations, the Peruvian government argued that it could not abandon in good conscience such patriotic citizens to the uncertainty of the Colombian forces dispatched to restore order. Accepting the validity of the 1922 treaty, Peru still refused to evacuate its forces before the frontier was modified. In support of this seemingly contradictory position, it emphasized that the treaty had been negotiated in secret by the dictator Leguía and that the Peruvians living in the area had never been given an opportunity to voice their determination. In the end, the Peruvian position proved indefensible, for Lima was never able to develop a convincing argument for treaty revision that did not also involve declaring the 1922 treaty null and void. Unable to resolve its dilemma, Peru continued to recognize the validity of the treaty while at the same time demanding its revision.[8]

As the two governments amplified their respective positions, a variety of avenues to settlement were explored, including the good offices of the United States, negotiations through the Permanent Commission of Inter-American Conciliation, and mediation by Brazil. None of these efforts produced a settlement, and tension mounted as a Colombian expeditionary force under orders to reoccupy Leticia steamed slowly up the Amazon River. The flotilla reached Colombian waters around February 12, 1933, and two days later, it attacked and occupied a Peruvian post at Tarapacá, a point some eighty kilometers from the nearest Peruvian territory. On February 15, 1933, the Colombian government announced that it was breaking diplomatic relations with Peru, an act that precipitated the sacking of the Colombian legation in Lima. About the same time, the Peruvian government asked the League of Nations to prohibit the use of force. In response to this request, the Leticia issue was placed on the agenda of the League Council, and a committee of three was appointed to study the dispute. On February 25, 1933, the committee submitted a plan for settlement that involved the inter-nationalization of Leticia and the replacement of Peruvian troops by a mixed international force that would include Colombian troops. The Colombian government quickly accepted the plan, but the Sánchez Cerro government rejected the withdrawal of Peruvian forces. Peru countered with a request that the dispute be submitted to arbitration, but Colombia rejected this new proposal.[9]

Throughout the spring of 1933, the League of Nations continued its search for a peaceful settlement acceptable to both sides. The Colombian capture on March 26, 1933, of a Peruvian force at Gueppí, a Peruvian outpost located on the southern bank of the Putumayo River over 300 miles west of the Leticia Trapezoid, made its task more difficult. Meanwhile, the Colombian government continued to win the struggle for international support. By March 1933 it was apparent that the Peruvian oligarchy, motivated in part by the threat of new taxes to finance the war effort, wanted to replace Sánchez Cerro or at least circumscribe his power. It preferred a more moderate alternative with a class background and loyalties more in concert with its own. The appointment of General Benavides in April 1933 to the post of commander in chief of the armed forces was a sign its power was growing. Another indication was Peru's acceptance of an April 7 League of Nations proposal that would have led to a quick settlement had Colombia also adopted it. In the end, it was an assassin's bullet and not the League that removed the seemingly insurmountable obstacle to a settlement. On April 30, 1933, President Sánchez Cerro was mortally wounded as he left a military review at Lima's Santa Beatriz racetrack.

CONTINUITY AND CHANGE UNDER BENAVIDES

On the day of Sánchez Cerro's assassination, the Peruvian cabinet declared a state of siege, suspended all constitutional guarantees, and asked the congress to elect a new president to complete Sánchez Cerro's term. In the ensuing election, an overwhelming majority elevated General Benavides to the office of chief executive. Although his election violated the 1933 constitution, which declared members of the armed forces on active duty ineligible for the presidency, Benavides's position as commander in chief was the major reason for his election. With the Peruvian political scene in a state of considerable uncertainty, legislators placed a high priority on maximum guarantees of order and security. Pledging to end the conflict with Colombia, Benavides formed a cabinet of concord and peace and reconstituted the Consultative Commission of Foreign Relations, which had ceased to function after the López de Romaña administration.

When General Benavides assumed the presidency, Peruvian filibusterers remained in control of Leticia, but Colombian forces had captured both Tarapacá and Gueppí. They were also threatening the village of Leticia as well as the port of Iquitos. During the *oncenio*, Benavides had been a harsh critic of the Salomón-Lozano treaty; nonetheless, he did not believe the Leticia dispute merited a war with Colombia and soon adopted a more conciliatory policy. Meeting with Alfonso López, an old friend who was also the head of the Liberal Party in Colombia and a candidate for the Colombian presidency, Benavides accepted a league proposal made on May 10, 1933, for a mixed commission appointed by the League to occupy Leticia in the name of Colombia. Once the commission was in place, Peru and Colombia agreed to open negotiations in Rio de Janeiro covering all outstanding problems, including an examination of legitimate Peruvian interests. On June 23, 1933, the commission received Leticia from the occupying Peruvians and hoisted both the Colombian flag and the standard of the League of Nations. In a concession to Peruvian nationalism, the Peruvian flag was not lowered; instead, the flagpole was detached and carried to Peruvian territory with the flag still flying. Although this device reportedly pleased many Peruvians, the general terms of the armistice were criticized by Peruvian nationalists, who argued that Peru's position throughout the dispute had been too formal and legalistic.[10]

In October 1933 the Rio negotiations opened under the mediatory auspices of Afranio de Melo Franco, a former foreign minister of Brazil. During the talks, the Peruvian delegation made two separate proposals that effectively divided the conference into two distinct stages. Initially, Peru hoped to regain at least the lower part of the Leticia Trapezoid by granting Colombia territorial compensations on the upper Putumayo River. When Colombia rejected the principle of territorial exchange, the Peruvian delegation countered with a proposal that the dispute be submitted to arbitration. The Colombian government then suggested that the issue be presented to the Permanent Court of International Justice at The Hague. Peru rejected this proposal on the grounds that an international court was inadequate to resolve the problem. Deadlocked, the negotiations entered a second stage, in which Peru pursued a formula that retained the possibility of a subsequent modification of the frontier. The Peruvian delegation also sought guarantees for Peruvian traffic and commerce on those portions of the Amazon and Putumayo rivers controlled by Colombia. Peru and Colombia finally agreed to a compromise proposal suggested by Melo Franco in late April 1934.[11]

In the final settlement, dated May 24, 1934, the Peruvian government expressed regret for the occupation of Leticia, and both countries agreed to renew diplomatic relations. Provisional arrangements were established for frontier police, freedom of navigation, and customs on the fluvial territories between the signatories; a mixed commission was created to develop these arrangements in detail. Finally, the governments of Peru and Colombia agreed that the Salomón-Lozano treaty could not be altered except by mutual consent or decision of an international tribunal.[12]

Throughout Peru, the Rio agreement was greeted warmly. In Lima, a large parade was organized to acclaim a settlement that had dissipated the war clouds gathering over the Amazon. Even in the Department of Loreto, where the Leticia Trapezoid was returned to Colombia without incident, the pact received a generally favorable reception. Endeavoring to put a positive face on an obvious diplomatic defeat, right-wing nationalists portrayed the agreement as a minor diplomatic victory that ended the conflict but retained the possibility of a future modification to the 1922 treaty. Officially, the Benavides administration accepted the Rio settlement as a contribution to Latin American unity and friendship. In reality, diplomatic, political, military, and economic considerations made it impossible for the Peruvian delegation to leave Rio de Janeiro without a settlement; therefore, it eventually accepted the best available terms.[13]

The Rio settlement largely vindicated the Colombian position, and it received a generally sympathetic response in Bogotá even though ratification was delayed when the question became a political issue. Ratification became even more problematic when Fabio Lozano Torrijos, a signatory to the Salomón-Lozano treaty, joined the opposition on the grounds that selected provisions of the 1934 settlement could eventually lead to a modification of the 1922 pact. After considerable debate, the settlement was finally approved by both houses of the Colombian congress, and ratifications were exchanged on September 27, 1935. For the remainder of the decade, the governments of Peru and Colombia enjoyed largely cordial relations. In 1936 President Alfonso López was the guest in Lima of President Benavides, and in the same year, the two governments concluded new agreements promoting intellectual and cultural exchanges. In June 1938 the mixed commission installed in 1934 to reach agreement on questions like free navigation, customs regulations, and frontier transit finished its work and disbanded.[14]

Upon conclusion of the Leticia affair, the Benavides administration turned its attention to the dispute with Ecuador. When the Peruvian filibusterers occupied Leticia, the Ecuadorian government had declared itself neutral in the dispute. At the same time, it maintained that its rights were involved in the affair and stated that it was and would be an Amazonian nation. Meant to be conciliatory, Ecuador's statement shocked a Peruvian public that had generally forgotten that Ecuador still claimed large tracts of the Oriente. At Quito's urging, the Sánchez Cerro government in April 1933 agreed to open bilateral talks that would be separate but parallel to Peruvian negotiations with Colombia. The agreement also recognized Ecuador as an interested observer in the latter talks. The Benavides government later opposed an Ecuadorian presence at Rio on the grounds that Ecuadorian participation in any form was contrary to the territorial interests of Peru. Assuring Ecuador that the Rio talks would not go beyond the terms of the Salomón-Lozano treaty, the Benavides administration invited Quito to open negotiations in Lima in accordance with the terms of the 1924 Ponce–Castro Oyanguren protocol. Believing Washington would support its claims, Ecuador reluctantly accepted the Peruvian proposal, and in April 1934 a series of desultory talks opened in Lima. Unable to find common ground, the negotiations broke down completely in August 1935, with Ecuador withdrawing its delegation in November. For the next eighteen months, the two governments argued over the nature of the dispute and the form future proceedings should take. Finally, on July 6, 1936, they agreed to take the dispute to Washington for a *de jure* arbitration, during which both states would maintain their existing territorial positions.[15]

The Washington conference lasted two long years and, more than anything else, proved a test of patience and an exercise in futility. Both the sessions and the proposals were long, repetitious, boring, and unproductive. From the beginning, the Ecuadorian delegation insisted that the central issues were territorial because they involved ownership of large areas of the Oriente north of the Tumbes, Huancabamba, and Marañón rivers. Later, Ecuador proposed a complete juridical arbitration of the dispute. Although the proposal suggested a shift in its attitude toward arbitration, it was largely an attempt to precipitate a Solomon-like judgment by the US government. In contrast, the opening statement of the Peruvian delegation emphasized that the dispute was not one of organic sovereignty but, rather, one of frontiers. According to Peru, the issue at hand was the exact location of the boundary line between the three Peruvian provinces of Tumbes, Jaén, and Maynas and adjacent Ecuadorian territories. When the conference ended, Peruvian Foreign Minister Carlos Concha explained that it was impossible for Peru to continue because Ecuador's proposal for total arbitration was outside the spirit and letter of the 1924 protocol, a pact that had contemplated only an eventual and partial arbitration by the president of the United States. Concha added that the only legitimate areas for discussion remained the exact limits separating Tumbes, Jaén, and Maynas from Ecuador.[16]

After the Washington conference, the Benavides administration refused to budge from its insistence on simple, direct negotiations in Lima. In October 1938 the Peruvian government rejected an Ecuadorian proposal for a five-power mediation of the dispute and restated its preference for bilateral diplomatic action. When the Eighth Inter-American Conference opened in Lima later in the year, Benavides expressed an interest in resolving the dispute but repeated Peru's preference for direct negotiations. In particular, the Peruvian government refused to consider the Ecuadorian proposal for a total arbitration by the president of the United States. This approach involved the introduction of a third party to the dispute, a step Lima had long been reluctant to take. Peruvians remembered with distaste the 1925 Coolidge award and remained concerned that arbitration by the United States might ignore strict legal rights and result in an equitable solution to the dispute.[17]

As it negotiated with its neighbor to the north, the Benavides government worked to solidify its diplomatic position in the south. On November 21, 1933, Peru and Chile agreed to erect a symbolic monument on the Morro de Arica to commemorate their friendship. Four months later, they concluded two additional agreements. A treaty for the liquidation of obligations called for Chile to give the city of Tacna 2.5 million Chilean pesos in building materials to fulfill the requirements in the 1929 settlement related to the creation of port facilities at Arica Bay. This agreement was very unpopular in Peru, especially in the Department of Tacna, and the Benavides government later withdrew it from congressional consideration. A treaty of commerce, known as the Polo–Rivas Vicuña treaty, regulated the flow of goods between Peru and Chile. Slightly modified by the Concha-Subercaseaux protocol, dated February 2, 1935, ratifications for the 1934 commercial treaty were exchanged on November 25, 1935.[18]

In 1932 Peru had concluded with Bolivia a pact known as the Concha-Gutierrez protocol that fixed their respective limits on the Copacabana Peninsula. For much of the remainder of the decade, diplomatic relations between the two states revolved around the Chaco War. When fighting broke out in June 1932 between Bolivia and Paraguay, the Peruvian government agreed to work with its neighbors for peace in the hemisphere. In May 1933 Peru declared itself neutral in the dispute, and in June 1935 it joined other South American states in signing a protocol that adopted both a cease-fire and a procedure for final settlement. For the next three years, the Peruvian government supported the search for peace; however, it played only a minor role in the peace treaty concluded in July 1938. In the meantime, an Aprista delegation approached the Bolivian government with an offer to support Bolivian efforts to obtain the port of Arica in return for assistance in overthrowing the Benavides regime. Motivated by ideological compatibility and the belief that an Aprista government would help Bolivia obtain Arica from Chile, President Toro responded in August 1936 with an offer of arms and ammunition. Aware of the plot, the Benavides government acted quickly to forestall Bolivian support. In September 1936 Peru and Bolivia signed a nonaggression pact that prohibited intervention in the internal or external affairs of the signatories. In the treaty, the Bolivian government traded a guarantee of free transit of goods for a declaration that it had no political or territorial problems with Peru.[19]

Throughout the 1930s, the Benavides administration remained concerned about unsolicited US participation in Peruvian affairs. There were practical reasons for this concern, as evidenced by US government support in 1930 for the Cerro de Pasco Mining Company after labor unrest had forced the company to cease operations. On the other hand, the economic policies pursued by Peru during the depression years, policies that increased the nation's dependence on the United States, were determined by the Peruvian government and not by Washington. For example, the Benavides administration after 1933 placed a high priority on the restoration of Peru's badly shattered credit, especially in the United States. In this context, it was misleading to picture the mounting dependence of Peru on the United States as solely or even largely the consequence of the latter's pursuit of national interests. On the contrary, the US government stood ready to abandon many of the practices that had given past offense to Peru and other Latin American states. It was increasingly circumspect in entering into boundary-dispute diplomacy and came to welcome, as in the case of the Leticia dispute, League of Nations involvement in such thankless tasks. Toward the end of the decade, Washington modified the laws governing the purchase of foreign sugar and assigned Peru a higher import quota, a move welcomed in Lima. At the same time, the United States began to commit public funds through the Export-Import Bank to Latin American development. By the outbreak of World War II, significant changes were occurring in both the political and economic relationships of the United States and Peru although the extent and direction of these changes were not fully recognized by either state.[20]

Change of a very different kind took place in the Peruvian relationship with Japan, an association of considerable symbolic importance because Peru had been the first Latin American government to establish diplomatic relations with Japan. Leguía's critics had considered his administration pro-Japanese, and the relative economic well-being of Japanese-Peruvians in the deepening economic malaise of the 1930s made their position doubly precarious. As a result, a number of unpleasant incidents occurred at the out-set of the decade in which Japanese-Peruvians were roughly handled and their property damaged. With the occupation of Leticia, the situation reversed itself, for many Peruvians saw parallels in the intransigent policies of the League of Nations and the United States toward both Manchuria and Leticia. Diplomatic relations further improved with the Peruvian purchase of Japanese arms; but after the death of Sánchez Cerro, the Benavides administration adopted a strongly anti-Japanese policy. On October 5, 1934, Peru denounced the 1924 treaty of friendship, commerce, and navigation because of its unfavorable trade balance with Japan. After imposing import quotas on Japanese cotton cloth and cotton articles in 1935, the Benavides administration later moved to restrict Japanese immigration and business activity. When Peru broke diplomatic relations with Japan in January 1942, the Manuel Prado administration froze Japanese funds and deported Japanese-Peruvians to internment camps in the United States. A dozen Latin American states participated in the deportation program, but Peru was the most enthusiastic; it accounted for 83 percent of the deportees from Latin America.[21]

WORLD WAR II AND ITS AFTERMATH

For the official candidate in the 1939 presidential elections, President Benavides selected Manuel Prado, a socially prominent banker and the son of a former president. Opposed by José Quesada Larrea, a weak and ineffective campaigner, Prado triumphed handily in elections that were not a model of the democratic process. Although the Apristas denied a pact with Prado, events prior to the election suggested that APRA had agreed not to oppose his election in return for a promise to legalize the party. After the election, Prado's tolerant attitude toward the Apristas was encouraged by the metamorphosis that APRA ideology underwent in the 1940s. Before World War II, Haya had begun to court the US government as well as influential North American citizens to encourage their intervention on APRA's behalf. During the war years, Aprista cooperation with the United States increased as APRA backed Prado's policy of support for the Allies in general and the United States in particular. The old diatribes against Yankee imperialism stopped, and the Good Neighbor Policy of the Roosevelt administration was praised. Most remarkable, APRA toned down its attacks on the capitalist system to the point that many party pronouncements resembled statements made by Leguía in the 1920s.

World War II dominated the foreign policy of the first Prado administration. Where General Benavides had been cool toward the United States and displayed some affinity with the fascist regimes in Spain and Italy, Prado was a Francophile and a firm supporter of the Allied cause. After the United States entered the conflict in 1941, Prado broke diplomatic relations with the Axis powers and affirmed Peru's adherence to the Atlantic Charter. Although Peru did not declare war for another three years, the Peruvian government remained a strong supporter of the Allied war effort. Militarily, the Prado administration allowed the United States to build an airfield at Talara to defend the Panama Canal, cooperated with the US navy to patrol the area south of that waterway, and replaced an Italian air mission with one from the United States. Politically, it seized the assets of Axis nationals, cooperated with US intelligence agencies in the internment of Axis agents, and deported Japanese-Peruvians to the United States. Economically, Peru concluded a loan agreement with the United States, adopted a policy of price stabilization, and cooperated with Washington to develop Peruvian deposits of strategic materials.[22]

During Prado's first term, the single event of major diplomatic significance other than the war was a brief conflict with Ecuador. From 1940 to 1941, border incidents along the unmarked jungle frontier increased as both Peru and Ecuador asserted their territorial claims in the disputed region. Ecuadorian probes, returned in kind by Peruvian units, were accompanied by an aggressive press campaign in Quito that charged that Peru was preparing for war. As the political situation deteriorated, the governments of Argentina, Brazil, and the United States offered their good offices in an effort to prevent a wider conflict. Although the Peruvian government accepted the offer, it was with the understanding that Peru intended to retain Tumbes, Jaén, and Maynas. Willing to employ good offices to reduce the possibility of war, the Prado administration remained determined to act decisively in the Ecuadorian crisis. With both the War of the Pacific and the abortive Leticia affair in mind, civilian and military leaders alike strongly supported government preparations for a possible military solution to the dispute.[23]

Hostilities opened in early July 1941 in the Zarumilla sector, with both sides claiming the other fired the first shot. The conflict spread quickly as Ecuador launched new attacks in the eastern sector along the Tigre and Pastaza rivers. After intense fighting in several areas, Peruvian forces blocked the Ecuadorian advance and successfully counterattacked. Peru's swift and overwhelming defeat of the Ecuadorian army was the result of the military reorganization it had undergone during the Benavides administration, as well as the vast superiority of forces it achieved in the main theater north of Tumbes. In contrast, the Ecuadorian army, which was largely unprepared for war, suffered from a lack of war materiel as well as limited civilian support for the war effort. By the end of July, Peru had advanced some 65 kilometers and occupied 1,000 square kilometers of the disputed territory.[24]

With the outbreak of hostilities, the governments of Argentina, Brazil, and the United States, later joined by Chile, worked to organize a peaceful settlement. Their efforts were rewarded on October 2, 1941, when representatives of Peru and Ecuador signed an armistice at Talara. Peace negotiations held in Rio de Janeiro in early 1942 produced a protocol of peace, friendship, and boundaries, which provided a procedure for settlement. Peru agreed to withdraw its forces to a designated area within fifteen days, after which technical experts would mark the boundary outlined in the agreement. Under the terms of the settlement, Argentina, Brazil, Chile, and the United States agreed to guarantee both the protocol and its execution. On February 26, 1942, the Peruvian congress unanimously approved the Rio

Protocol, and ratifications were exchanged on April 1, 1943. The mixed Ecuador-Peru demarcation commission was installed in Puerto Bolívar on June 1, 1942; the border was soon marked in the west, but the demarcation of the Oriente was never completed. The Rio Protocol was a major diplomatic victory for Peru because it confirmed Peruvian ownership of most of the disputed territory. In Ecuador, the settlement was widely condemned, and subsequent Ecuadorian governments continued to assert that Ecuador had been and would remain an Amazonian state.[25]

World War II had caused severe economic problems for Peru, and there was little improvement in the immediate postwar period. Elected in 1945, President José Luis Bustamante y Rivero inherited both a shortage of consumer goods and a troublesome inflationary spiral, and his economic problems were further compounded by the sharp decline in exports and the rapid increase in imports that occurred at the end of the war. Forced to choose between a major devaluation and the imposition of exchange controls, the Bustamante administration chose the latter. Unfortunately, the control mechanisms adopted to maintain the exchange rate failed to check the mounting inflation, and the entire program had to be abandoned in 1948. In an attempt to improve the overall economic situation, Bustamante concluded a controversial agreement with the International Petroleum Company (IPC), a subsidiary of Standard Oil of New Jersey, which allowed it to explore for oil in the Sechura Desert, an area in northern Peru set aside as a national reserve. Within days of the new agreement, every political group in Peru as well as both major Lima newspapers had entered the fray in defense of the national interest. Economic nationalists and domestic capitalists anxious to exploit Peru's petroleum resources vehemently denounced the Sechura Contract as a treasonous surrender of the national patrimony. Warmly supporting the agreement, Aprista leaders argued the arrangement was consistent with the party's anti-imperialist ideology, which encouraged foreign investment as long as it was under strict government supervision. Both APRA and Bustamante further emphasized that the contract covered exploration only and that the exploitation of any new petroleum deposits would necessitate separate contracts. With wholehearted APRA support, the agreement was approved by the Chamber of Deputies in June 1946, but the upper house later rejected the measure.[26]

In the aftermath of the Leticia affair, the Peruvian government had taken little interest in the activities of the League of Nations. On April 8, 1939, it announced its intention to withdraw at the conclusion of the requisite two-year waiting period. Expressing a profound belief in international justice and solidarity, the Peruvian government based its decision on the inability of the League to achieve the high ideals for which it was founded. At the same time, Peru expressed a desire to continue participating in the technical functions of the League as well as in the International Labour Organisation and the Permanent Court of International Justice at The Hague. With this background, the Peruvian government approached the 1945 discussions that led to the founding of the United Nations with a cautious optimism tempered by pragmatism. Deeply concerned that any new international body recognize regional jurisdiction in matters of peace and security, the Peruvian delegation at San Francisco was a strong and articulate advocate for the primacy of regional agencies. At the Conference for the Maintenance of Peace and Security in Rio de Janeiro in 1947 and the Ninth Inter-American Conference in Bogotá in 1948, Peru subsequently joined the other American states to develop institutions and procedures for maintaining peace among themselves. Thereafter, the Peruvian government, together with its hemispheric neighbors, preferred the Organization of American States over the United Nations as a forum for the discussion of questions related to regional peace and security.[27]

EXPORT-LED GROWTH AND PERUVIAN NATIONALISM

On October 27, 1948, General Manuel A. Odría, a hero of the 1941 war with Ecuador, launched a revolution that was quickly supported by a variety of military and civilian elements. President Bustamante left the country two days later, and Odría was sworn in as provisional president at the end of the month. Bustamante fell primarily because he was unable to deal successfully with APRA, a political party in the throes of ideological upheaval. After a period of rule by a military junta, Odría was elected president on July 2, 1950. Initially, Odría's regime appeared to revive the traditional alliance between the military and the oligarchy; however, it later proved the beginning of the end for that association. By the 1950s, the oligarchy had become increasingly concerned with the ability of the military to defend oligarchical interests; as an alternative, it pursued an informal alliance with APRA. At the same time, junior military officers, who had begun to question the premises on which the military-oligarchy alliance had been founded, initiated a gradual, prolonged, and contradictory process of ideological transformation within the armed forces.

President Odría ended the Peruvian experiment with interventionist financial and economic policies, and after 1948 Peru became the principal Latin American example of an export-led system with minimal government participation. Cyclical balance-of-payments difficulties were addressed through domestic demand restraint and exchange devaluation while the entry of foreign capital and the repatriation of profits went largely unrestricted. Liberal mining and petroleum legislation was designed to attract new foreign investment, and while its provisions applied to domestic and foreign capital alike, it was primarily the foreign sector that responded. In the 1950s the Peruvian government attracted North American investment at a rate above the Latin American average; followed closely the guidelines of the International

Monetary Fund during the cyclical crisis at the end of the decade; and hastened to dismantle the restrictions on foreign trade and exchange markets imposed during the mid-1940s. It also expanded the industrial sector, but the belated swing toward industrialization did not signal an increased capacity for autonomous development. On the contrary, the Peruvian pattern resembled the rest of Latin America in that industrialization was promoted by multinational firms, depended largely on imported technology and brand names, and distorted local markets. At the same time, the nation's dependence on export performance as the principal source of economic growth remained undiminished, and income distribution became increasingly unequal.[28]

With its friendly attitude toward North American investors, the Odría administration enjoyed strong support in Washington. The Peruvian government was one of the first Latin American governments to sign a treaty of aid and mutual defense with the United States. The Eisenhower administration later decorated Odría, as well as a number of other Latin American dictators, at a time when he was being criticized at home for alleged human rights violations. In the bilateral aid and mutual defense pact concluded in February 1952, Peru received arms and assistance from the United States in return for the sale of strategic minerals and the right to establish military bases in Peru. In addition, the US Department of Defense continued the policy begun during World War II of sponsoring study missions and goodwill visits for Peruvian officers to US military installations.[29]

Many aspects of US policy toward Peru were strongly resented by Peruvian nationalists and thus fostered a revival of the anti-United States sentiment so visible in the 1930s. Another reason for the growth in Peruvian nationalism was that more and more Peruvians were becoming aware of the North American dominance of key sectors of the Peruvian economy. Peruvians were also concerned about the extent to which the sale of Peruvian exports to the United States tied the Peruvian economy to the North American economy in general and the inevitable economic cycles of the latter in particular. Ill will also stemmed from the low prices Peruvian exports commanded in the United States and the mounting threat of US quotas or tariffs on key Peruvian exports. Anti-United States feeling mounted toward the end of the 1950s as falling export earnings, rising inflation, strikes, political unrest, and a decline in the GNP increased political instability in Peru. Regionally, the Odría administration focused on the consolidation of diplomatic settlements reached over the previous three decades. In June 1950 the Bolivian government, which had long been attempting to revive the issue of a Pacific port, proposed to Chile direct negotiations aimed at granting Bolivia a sovereign exit to the Pacific Ocean. Although the Chilean government agreed to discuss the issue, its response raised the question of compensation and emphasized that under the terms of the 1929 treaty it was obliged to consult with Peru. The 1950 negotiations made little progress after this initial exchange of diplomatic correspondence. Many Bolivians opposed a related Chilean scheme that suggested that compensation for a Pacific port take the form of water from the Bolivian *altiplano* for use in the economic development of Tacna and Arica. Popular opposition to a settlement also developed in Chile, especially in the northern part of the country. In Peru, the Odría government, drawing support from a variety of political forces, opposed any negotiations aimed at granting Bolivia territory that had once been part of Peru. In addition, the Peruvian government was adamantly opposed to the Chilean suggestion that the waters of Lake Titicaca be used to compensate Chile for a Bolivian port. The Peruvian government had long considered those waters held in condominium by Peru and Bolivia for their exclusive use.[30]

Three years later, Peru and Bolivia signed a joint declaration, dated July 30, 1955, that covered construction of a railway between Puno and La Paz; the building of roads between Ilo, Moquegua, Desaguadero, and La Paz as well as between Tacna, Charaña, and La Paz; the joint utilization of Lake Titicaca; and the negotiation of a treaty facilitating transit between the two states. Concerning Lake Titicaca, the declaration recognized that Peru and Bolivia enjoyed joint sovereignty over its waters, which could be exploited only with the direct consent of both states. This declaration, consistent with Peru's long-held legal position that riparian states could not change the conditions of water utilization or navigation without prejudicing the rights and conditions of other riparian states, effectively checked Chilean ambitions in the area. On February 19, 1957, Peru and Bolivia concluded an additional convention related to Lake Titicaca, in which they agreed to develop a plan for the common use of its waters. The signatories also agreed to construct a road between Ilo, Moquegua, Desaguadero, Guaqui, and La Paz. Four years later, the development ministers of both states met in Arequipa to adopt measures aimed at increasing commerce between them and improving the services of the port of Matarani.[31]

To the north, José María Velasco Ibarra, a three-time president of Ecuador, initiated in 1960 a critical and destructive campaign for reelection in which he asserted the Rio Protocol could not be executed. Velasco's arguments focused on a geographical flaw in the 1942 agreement. In the Cordillera del Cóndor region, the protocol defined the border as the *divortium aquarum* between the Zamora and Santiago rivers, but aerial surveys subsequently placed the Cenepa River where the watershed was originally thought to be. Once the size and location of the Cenepa River was known, the Ecuadorian government concluded that execution of the protocol in this sector was impossible, and a section some seventy kilometers long went unmarked. In August 1960 the Velasco administration used this discrepancy as justification for declaring the Rio Protocol null and void. One month later, the Ecuadorian foreign minister argued that Peru and Ecuador must return to the terms of the 1829 treaty, which had fixed the Amazon River as their natural boundary. At the same time, he repeated allegations that the Rio Protocol was unjust, imposed by force, and incapable of execution. A few days later, he stood before the General Assembly of the United Nations and again proclaimed the nullity of the protocol. Ecuador's revival of the dispute helped block the opening of the Eleventh Inter-American Conference in Quito in February 1960 because member states were afraid the host country would use the meeting as a forum to discuss its border dispute with Peru.[32]

The final noteworthy aspect of Odría's foreign policy related to Peru's expanding involvement in the growing controversy over the law of the sea. On August 1, 1947, the Bustamante administration had issued a supreme decree that stated its intention to exercise national sovereignty and jurisdiction over the continental shelf and insular seas to a distance of 200 nautical miles from the coast of Peru. The decree explicitly recognized the right of free navigation by ships from all nations, but it made no mention of foreign fishing rights within the zone, an omission that implied that foreign fishing vessels might eventually be banned. Nine months later, the Peruvian government granted the state petroleum enterprise a concession covering oil fields off the northern coast of Peru within the limits specified in the earlier decree. In August 1952 the Odría administration reinforced Bustamante's policy when it joined Chile and Ecuador to proclaim sole sovereignty and jurisdiction over a maritime zone adjacent to the coast of each country and extending not less than 200 nautical miles from the coast. The fishing industry was becoming increasingly important to the Peruvian economy, and as the Peruvian government emphasized at the time, economic factors, especially the control of fishery and mineral resources, were the dominant considerations in its expanded claim. The United States and Great Britain, together with several other developed states with sizeable maritime interests, condemned the claims advanced by Peru, Chile, and Ecuador, and Washington unsuccessfully exercised considerable pressure throughout the 1950s to force a change in Peruvian policy.[33]

In a display of enhanced regional cooperation, Peru, Ecuador, and Chile announced in 1954 that none would unilaterally diminish the 200-mile claim without prior consultation and agreement. They also declared their intention to enforce their claims to sovereignty by all necessary means. When a fishing fleet flying the Panamanian flag tested Peruvian jurisdiction in late 1954, the Peruvian navy seized five of the boats and took them to the Peruvian port of Paita, where they remained until a fine was paid. In January 1955 the first two US fishing vessels were captured and fined, an event that became commonplace in later years. From 1953 to 1956 the Organization of American States sponsored three conferences in an effort to resolve the dispute, and the governments of Peru, Chile, Ecuador, and the United States participated in a quadripartite conference in 1955. The issue was also on the agenda of the Law of the Sea Conferences held in Geneva in 1958 and 1960, but no definitive agreement was reached on either the width of the territorial sea or the maritime zone. Throughout the period, the position of the Peruvian government remained clear: it consistently maintained that new rules of international law, specifically regarding the delimitation of maritime zones, were required to deal with new concepts and new situations.[34]

AMBIVALENT RELATIONS WITH THE UNITED STATES

During the 1956 presidential campaign, General Odría urged the Apristas to support Hernando de Lavalle; nevertheless, two days before the balloting, APRA threw its support behind former President Manuel Prado, who won by a comfortable margin. Fernando Belaúnde Terry, a young architect, was second in the balloting and won over one-third of the votes cast. By the end of the Odría administration, few of the military men who had constituted the core of his October 1948 movement remained his close comrades. In 1956 the armed forces as an institution no longer identified with Odría's traditional views on the role of the military in national affairs. The Prado administration marked the second attempt in the contemporary history of Peru to establish a populist government and was the first administration in which a traditional bourgeois executive enjoyed APRA's support. Over the next six years, APRA pursued a policy of moderation that eventually led to its participation in the 1962 elections. In the process, its association with the Prado administration, known as the *convivencia,* or coexistence, meant it shared the blame for the shortcomings of a government that accomplished little of enduring significance.[35]

Deeply interested in foreign affairs, President Prado hoped to increase Peru's visibility and impact on the international stage. Long an admirer of both Great Britain and France, he was especially anxious to draw closer to Europe, in part to reduce Peru's dependence on the United States. In 1956 he articulated a vague scheme, later known as the Prado Doctrine, that envisaged closer cooperation between Latin America and Europe in common cause against totalitarianism. In turn, Prado's foreign policy toward the United States reflected the animosity that had developed in Peru over the past decade. Fueled from a number of sources, including the rapid influx of North American capital, the disputed maritime zone, and the Eisenhower administration's public support for right-wing, authoritarian regimes, the high level of Peruvian dissatisfaction was dramatically demonstrated during the brief visit of Vice President Richard M. Nixon to Lima in May 1958. Diplomatic relations deteriorated further after the Eisenhower administration imposed import quotas on Peruvian exports of lead and zinc. The quota system enraged Peruvians, and they were only partially mollified when the United States, after the Soviet bloc offered to purchase Peru's surplus lead and zinc along with its excess cotton, later lifted its import restrictions.[36]

On the other hand, the US government continued to be Peru's major source of military aid. From 1956 to 1962 US military assistance to Peru totaled over \$70 million. In addition, Washington promoted civic action projects that resulted in a considerable amount of military aid being channeled to road building and other development projects. These activities were consistent with the evolving ideology of the Peruvian military, but they were only a partial answer to the dilemma the armed forces faced in maintaining increasingly expensive conventional forces while responding to rising social consciousness and popular demands. From this perspective, Peruvians were heartened by the Eisenhower administration's agreement in 1960 to commit public funds to social reform projects in Latin America. Washington's traditional reliance on private enterprise and private investment to promote economic development had never produced the level of prosperity desired in Peru or elsewhere in Latin America.

After 1930 and especially after World War II, both the challenges and opportunities of Peruvian foreign policy expanded enormously. A rapidly shrinking world made it increasingly difficult for Peruvian leaders to draw a clear line between domestic and foreign affairs. Recognizing that modern diplomacy involved far more than the simple defense of the nation's frontiers, they responded by broadening the scope and outlook of their foreign policy. With resolution in 1942 of the last remaining territorial dispute, the Peruvian government resumed the leadership role in continental affairs that it had largely abandoned in the nineteenth century. At the same time, it demonstrated a growing interest in Latin American economic cooperation and development. Peru participated in multilateral conferences and declarations on maritime fishing and mineral resources, and it joined the Latin American Free Trade Association when that body was created with great enthusiasm in early 1960. Dissatisfied for political as well as economic reasons with private sector investment as the sole means to generate economic development and growth, the Peruvian government explored alternative sources for financial and technical assistance, including the United Nations and the Organization of American States. These tentative steps in the direction of a broader, more multilateral approach to foreign affairs paralleled a noticeable decline in the power and prestige of the United States in Peru. Post-Leguía foreign policy was marked by a heightened sense of nationalism in which the Peruvian government repeatedly displayed a determination to resolve international issues on its own terms. An extreme distrust of the motives and policies of the US government lingered in Peru and fed this nascent nationalism as well as colored Peruvian policies toward the United States.

NOTES

1. Luis M. Sánchez Cerro, *Manifesto a la nación* (Lima: La Imprenta Peruana, 1930); Pedro Ugarteche, *Sánchez Cerro: Papeles y Recuerdos de un*

Presidente del Perú, 4 vols. (Lima: Editorial Universitaria, 1969–1970), 2:xxxii–xxxiii, 59–68, 90–94.

2. Luis M. Sánchez Cerro, *Programa de gobierno del comandante Luis M. Sánchez Cerro candidato a la presidencia de la república del Perú* (Lima: n.p., 1931); Carlos Miró Quesada Laos, *Sánchez Cerro y su tiempo* (Buenos Aires: "El Ateneo," 1947), pp. 149–177.

3. Víctor Raúl Haya de la Torre, *El Plan de Aprismo* (Lima: Editorial Libertad, 1931), pp. 1–56; Víctor Villanueva, *El APRA en busca del poder, 1930–1940* (Lima: Editorial Horizonte, 1975), pp. 40–48, 71–78.

4. B. W. Loveday, *Sanchez Cerro and Peruvian Politics, 1930–1933*, Occasional Papers No. 6, Institute of Latin American Studies (Glasgow: University of Glasgow, 1973), pp. 10–17.

5. Humberto Araujo Arana, *Conflicto fronterizo Perú-Colombia Año 1932–1933*, 3 vols. (Lima: Talleres de Litografía Huascarán, 1965), 3:38–39, 47–49.

6. Perú, Ministerio de Relaciones Exteriores, *Correspondencia diplomática con Colombia sobre el incidente de Leticia* (Lima: Tip. de la Escuela de la Guardia Civil y Policía, 1933), pp. 5–6.

7. Colombia, Ministerio de Relaciones Exteriores, *El conflicto de Leticia* (Bogotá: Editorial Minerva, 1934); Colombia, Senado de la República, *Para la historia: El conflicto con el Perú en el parlamento* (Bogotá: Santafe, 1934); Germán Cavelier, *La política internacional de Colombia*, 2d ed., 4 vols. (Bogotá: Editorial Iqueima, 1960), 1:141.

8. Diómedes Arias Schreiber, *Exposición sobre los motivos jurídicos que justifican la revisión del Tratado de Límites celebrado por el Perú y Colombia el 24 de marzo de 1922* (Lima: E. B. y B. Sucesor, 1933), pp. 74–104.

9. Manley O. Hudson, *The Verdict of the League: Colombia and Peru at Leticia* (Boston: World Peace Foundation, 1933), pp. 9–61; Pedro Ugarteche, interview with author, Lima, Peru, April 29, 1968.

10. Ulloa, *Posición*, pp. 193–196.

11. Details of the talks in Rio de Janeiro can be found in St John, "Peruvian Foreign Policy," pp. 410–421.

12. A copy of the 1934 protocol and additional act can be found in Perú, *Tratados, Convenciones y Acuerdos*, 1:255–264.

13. Wagner de Reyna, *Historia diplomática*, 2:225, 229.

14. Perú, *Memoria (1934–1936)*, pp. xxviii–xxxiii; Perú, *Boletín (1936)*, no. 124, p. 296; Colombia, Ministerio de Relaciones Exteriores, *Documentos sobre el protocolo de Rio de Janeiro* (Bogotá: Imprenta Nacional, 1934); Colombia, Senado de la República, *Informe de la comisión de relaciones exteriores del senado, relativo al protocolo de Rio de Janeiro* (Bogotá: Imprenta Nacional, 1935); Alfonso López, *La política internacional* (Bogotá: Imprenta Nacional, 1936), pp. 83–102, 120–122.

15. Perú, *Boletín (1935)*, no. 121, pp. 364–368; Ecuador, Ministerio de Relaciones Exteriores, *Protocolo firmado en Quito por los Excelentisimos Señores Doctor Don N. Clemente Ponce, Ministro de Relaciones Exteriores del Ecuador, y Don Enrique Castro Oyanguren, Enviado Extraordinario y Ministro Plenipotenciario del Perú* (Quito: Talleres Tipográficos Nacionales, 1935); Felipe de la Barra, *Tumbes, Jaén y Maynas* (Lima: Los Talleres Gráficos del Diet, 1961), pp. 45–46; *La Prensa* (Lima), July 8, 1936.

16. Perú, Ministerio de Relaciones Exteriores, *Documentos relativos a la conferencia perú-ecuatoriana de Washington* (Lima: Talleres Gráficos de la Editorial "Lumen," 1938), pp. 25–81; Ecuador, Ministerio de Relaciones Exteriores, *Las negociaciones ecuatoriano-peruanos en Washington setiembre 1936–julio 1937* (Quito: Imprenta del Ministerio de Gobierno, 1937); Ecuador,

Ministerio de Relaciones Exteriores, *Las negociaciones ecuatoriano-peruanos en Washington agosto 1937–octobre 1938* (Quito: Imprenta del Ministerio de Gobierno, 1938).

17. Raúl Porras Barrenechea, *El litigio peru-ecuatoriano ante los principios jurídicos americanos* (Lima: n.p., 1942), pp. 11–12.

18. Perú, *Memoria (1934–1936)*, pp. xxiv–xxv; Perú, *Memoria (1936)*, p. xxxiv. Copies of the treaties can be found in Perú, *Tratados, Convenciones y Acuerdos*, 1:212–224.

19. Perú, *Memoria (1934–1936)*, pp. iv–viii; Perú, *Memoria (1937–1939)*, pp. vii–viii; Ulloa, *Posición*, pp. 277–286, 339.

20. Pike, *United States*, pp. 237–241.

21. Perú, *Memoria (1934–1936)*, pp. lxxi–lxxiii; Alberto Ulloa Sotomayor, *Perú y Japón* (Lima: Imprenta Torres Aguirre, 1943), pp. 8–11; Amelia Morimoto, *Los inmigrantes japonesas en el Perú* (Lima: Taller de Estudios Andinos, 1979), pp. 17–53; Edward N. Barnhart, "Japanese Internees from Peru," *Pacific Historical Review* 31 (May 1963): 169–178.

22. J. M. Ramírez Gastón, *Política, Económica y Financiera, Manuel Prado: Sus Gobiernos de 1939–45 y 1956–62, Apuntes para la Historia Económica* (Lima: Editorial Litográfica "La Confianza," 1969), pp. 7–101; James C. Carey, *Peru and the United States, 1900–1962* (Notre Dame: University of Notre Dame Press, 1964), pp. 102–128.

23. Perú, *Memoria (1940–1941)*, pp. xcv–cxiv; Perú, Ministerio de Relaciones Exteriores, *Exposición del Ministro de Relaciones Exteriores del Perú, Dr. Alfredo Solf y Muro, a las Cancillerías de America* (Lima: n.p., 1941), pp. 3–19.

24. Perú, Ministerio de Guerra, *Biblioteca militar del oficial no. 31: estudio de la cuestión de límites entre el Perú y el Ecuador* (Lima: Imprenta del Ministerio de Guerra, 1961), pp. 71–72.

25. Perú, *Memoria (1941–1942)*, pp. xxxi–lxii. A copy of the 1942 Rio Protocol can be found in Perú, Ministerio de Relaciones Exteriores, *Protocolo Peruano-Ecuatoriano de Paz, Amistad y Límites* (Lima: Tipografía Peruana, 1967), pp. 27–30.

26. José Luis Bustamante y Rivero, *Tres años de lucha por la democracia en el Perú* (Buenos Aires: Artes Gráficas, 1949), pp. 188–245; Rolf Hayn, "Peruvian Exchange Controls: 1945–1948," *Inter-American Economic Affairs* 10, 4 (Spring 1940): 47–70; Cotler, *Clases*, pp. 255–268. After 1913 Standard Oil of New Jersey, which created a new subsidiary called the International Petroleum Company to control its various oil properties in Peru, gradually became the dominant oil producer; by the 1920s it controlled some 80 percent of Peruvian oil production, including the most important oil field in the country, the Lobitos deposit located on the La Brea y Pariñas *hacienda*.

27. Perú, *Memoria (1937–1939)*, pp. lxxxiii–lxxxv; Perú, *Mensaje (1939)*, p. 20; Yepes, Del Congreso de Panamá, 2:81–95, 107–218.

28. Thorp and Bertram, *Peru*, pp. 205–300; Cotler, *Clases*, pp. 272–278.

29. John Leslie Davidson, "The Impact of U.S. Arms Transfer Policies on Relations with Peru: 1945–1978" (Master's thesis, North Texas State University, 1979), pp. 21–24.

30. Luis Fernando Guachalla, *La cuestión portuaria y las negociaciones de 1950* (La Paz: Editorial Los Amigos del Libro, 1976), pp. 34–104.

31. Escobari Cusicanqui, *Historia diplomática*, 2:55–113.

32. José Zarate Lescano, *Reseña histórica del problema limítrofe peruano-ecuatoriano* (Lima: Ministerio de Guerra, 1960), pp. 61–79; *El Comercio* (Quito), September 30, 1960; Enrique Chirinos Soto, *Perú y Ecuador* (Lima: Talleres

Gráficos P. L. Villanueva, 1968), pp. 7–29.

33. Eduardo Ferrero Costa, *El Nuevo Derecho del Mar: El Perú y las 200 Millas* (Lima: Pontificia Universidad Católica del Perú, 1979), pp. 43–89; Barry B.L. Auguste, *The Continental Shelf: The Practice and Policy of the Latin American States with Special Reference to Chile, Ecuador and Peru* (Geneva: Librairie E. Droz, 1960), pp. 13–24, 133–165, 183–192, 297–299.

34. Washington Durán Abarca, *La Soberania y las 200 Millas* (Lima: n.p., 1983), pp. 47–48; Arthur D. Martinez, "The United States–Peruvian Territorial Waters Controversy: Juridical, Political, Economic, and Strategic Considerations" (Ph.D. diss., University of California, Riverside, 1974), pp. 28–37.

35. Jorge Rodriguez Beruff, *Los militares y el poder: Un ensayo sobre la doctrina militar en el Perú, 1948–1968* (Lima: Mosca Azul Editores, 1983), pp. 3–130; Villanueva, *Cien Años del Ejército Peruano*, pp. 133–138.

36. Ding Wu Kuo, "Peru's Foreign Policy; Ends and Means, 1945–1968" (Ph.D. diss., Tulane University, 1969), pp. 43–56; Thomas Scheetz, *Peru and the International Monetary Fund* (Pittsburgh: University of Pittsburgh Press, 1986), pp. 100–105.

ELEVEN

Search for Autonomy, 1962–1991

The three decades after Leguía, themselves a time of considerable change in the scope and direction of the foreign policy of Peru, set the stage for even greater innovation in the contemporary period. After 1962 foreign policy moved in totally new directions, in which it addressed unfamiliar issues, adopted fresh approaches, and consummated new bilateral and multilateral relationships. The government diversified arms transfers, expanded trade links, pursued a leadership role in the Non-Aligned Movement, advocated a radical reorganization of the inter-American economic and political system, and pressed for enhanced subregional economic cooperation.

In this era of considerable change, each presidential administration naturally emphasized different problems and opportunities; however, the central direction of Peruvian foreign policy reflected a continuity that transcended individual interests. In pursuit of heightened Peruvian sovereignty, successive governments from Belaúnde to Fujimori moved to reduce external pressures and imposed conditions, especially from the United States. As Peru searched for greater autonomy, a certain ambiguity continued to characterize its diplomatic relationship with the United States due to the conflicting demands of Peruvian nationalism and the need for US cooperation to achieve many foreign policy goals. In the process, all facets of Peruvian foreign policy were increasingly undermined by the intractable economic problems experienced by the Peruvian government. The circumstances surrounding the latest of the periodic debt crises that have bedeviled Peru since independence were not as unique as many Peruvians argued. Nonetheless, the complexity and severity of those financial problems made it very difficult for the Peruvian government to address effectively the wide variety of issues on its foreign policy agenda.

BELAUNDE AND THE INTERNATIONAL PETROLEUM COMPANY

By the early 1960s, there was widespread disillusionment with the *convivencia* strategy that the Apristas pursued during the Prado administration. As a result, APRA lost its preeminence as a civilian reform movement and became just one of several reform parties, including the Popular Action Party of Fernando Belaúnde Terry, to contest the 1962 elections. Haya de la Torre won those elections in a contest widely considered to be among the most honest in Peruvian history, but he did not capture the requisite one-third plurality necessary for election. Under the circumstances, the constitution stipulated that the Peruvian congress, where APRA held a plurality, should select a president from among the three candidates obtaining the largest number of valid votes. At this point, the civilian reformers of Peru faced a choice between uniting behind a compromise candidate or continuing to fight among themselves and likely precipitating a *golpe* by the armed forces. When they proved unable to reconcile their differences, the Peruvian armed forces mounted an institutional coup d'état that overthrew the Prado administration and nullified the presidential elections.

The reaction of the US government to the military takeover was immediate, although largely unexpected. On the day of the *golpe,* Washington broke diplomatic relations and denounced the overthrow as a setback to the Alliance for Progress. On the following day, the Department of State suspended all but humanitarian aid to Peru. During the 1962 presidential campaign, the US government had informed the Peruvian armed forces that it had no intention of supporting APRA or any other political group in the elections and would not intervene in the Peruvian political process. At the same time, the Kennedy administration emphasized its support for representative democracy and said it would be difficult for it to grant either diplomatic recognition or aid to a military regime that overthrew an anticommunist, democratic government. Even though the US ambassador to Peru aggressively and openly supported Haya de la Torre during the election campaign, the Kennedy administration subsequently depicted its sanctions as an affirmation of its support for democratic government. In this sense, US policy toward Peru in the summer of 1962 was not as new, novel, or guided by principled commitment to democratic development as it was described at the time. The Kennedy administration was equally concerned about the growing nationalist ideology of the Peruvian military and its consequent refusal to acquiesce in prescriptions offered by Washington.[1]

The junta responded to the break in diplomatic relations by solidifying its ties with the US business community in Peru, which reacted positively by affirming its support for the military regime. On the strength of these assurances, together with the junta's general respect for civil liberties and its promise to hold elections in 1963, the Kennedy administration resumed diplomatic relations and reinstated economic assistance programs one month later. US diplomatic recognition was conditioned by reservations regarding the internal political situation in Peru, and military aid was not restored until October 12, 1962. The official Peruvian acknowledgment of the resumption in diplomatic ties stated that the US government was out of place in commenting on the domestic politics of Peru. This attitude of defiance toward external interference received favorable support in the Peruvian press. The entire incident appeared relatively minor at the time, but its impact on future relations between Peru and the United States should not be underestimated. Virtually all Peruvians, especially those affiliated with the military, resented what they viewed as an unacceptable level of US interference in Peruvian internal affairs.[2]

In 1963 Fernando Belaúnde Terry, supported by a heterogenous political base that included middle-sector elements and the armed forces, won the presidency by a narrow margin, but his Popular Action Party failed to win a congressional majority. The military supported Belaúnde because his reformist approach offered the best opportunity to neutralize APRA. At the same time, the armed forces remained uncertain as to whether or not Belaúnde could fulfill the extravagant political expectations he raised. Their concerns proved justified because a major weakness of his government, an administration that promised planning and development, was its technocratic inefficiency. Throughout his presidential term, the gap between expectations and performance dogged Belaúnde. From the outset, the military thus represented a challenge as well as an opening for Belaúnde because the armed forces expected him to generate fundamental change in Peruvian society. If he failed to satisfy these expectations, there remained ambitious, impatient army officers ready to argue that their vision of the country's future took precedence over the strictures of the constitution.

Belaúnde appeared to adhere closely to the Kennedy administration's specifications for democratic, socially progressive political leaders able to carry the torch of the Alliance for Progress. Still, Washington's promise of low-interest loans with easy repayment terms never materialized, and after 1963 a variety of longer-term controversies between Peru and the United States came to a head. As a result, the Peruvian government faced a full or partial suspension of US aid for four of the five years Belaúnde was in office. Although the International Petroleum Company (IPC) had not been a major political issue in either the 1962 or 1963 presidential campaigns, it quickly became one after Belaúnde failed to reach a settlement within a self-imposed ninety-day deadline. In November 1963 the Peruvian congress revoked the 1918 law that authorized the president to submit the issue to arbitration, and renounced the 1922 arbitral award that established the oil fields' tax schedule. Negotiations in 1964 almost produced a settlement that provided for IPC operation of the fields under contract, but in the end, the Belaúnde administration retreated from this formula. As time passed, the IPC issue became progressively inflated in political importance, which made any form of solution increasingly difficult.[3]

Throughout the period, the linkage of US aid to a solution of the IPC issue remained ambivalent because it was never explicitly stated and the intensity of its application varied considerably, depending on the incumbent assistant secretary of state for inter-American affairs. Economic and military aid programs were turned on and off, despite the fact that no provision of US law or principle of US foreign policy required Washington to suspend aid to compel a sovereign government to negotiate an agreement with a private US company. Moreover, there was no evidence that the IPC ever asked the US government to bring explicit pressure on Peru or to take other actions on its behalf. On the other hand, US policy undoubtedly stiffened the negotiating posture of the IPC and thus made resolution of the dispute more difficult. The year 1966 proved to be pivotal for the controversy because it was probably the last one in which Belaúnde could have negotiated a settlement acceptable both to the IPC and to the Peruvian congress and people. Thereafter, congressional opposition, a turbulent domestic political climate, US policies, and unfavorable economic developments progressively undermined Belaúnde's domestic political position.[4]

As the Belaúnde government struggled to implement reform programs, its efforts were increasingly undercut by growing economic problems, many of which were created or accentuated by regime policies. The export-led growth begun under Prado continued during the first three years of the Belaúnde administration, but important characteristics of the economic expansion changed. After 1962 most of the growth in export earnings came from higher international prices, particularly for copper and fish meal, while export volumes increased only marginally. In other words, export income continued to increase from 1963 to 1966 but only because of favorable international prices totally outside the control of Peru. Investment stagnated from 1962 to 1964, with private investment actually dropping in this period. Several factors impacted negatively on both export volumes and investments. These included the prevailing political uncertainty, the reaction of the private sector to Belaúnde's emphasis on land reform and a solution to the IPC issue, a shortage of investment opportunities, and surplus capacity in the manufacturing sector. Given the low level of direct foreign investment and the lack of expansion in export volume, the Belaúnde administration was forced to undertake substantial borrowing from international agencies and commercial banks to finance public works and cover general government expenditures. From 1962 to 1968 the external public debt increased more than fourfold; it would have increased more except that the foreign borrowing capacity of the Peruvian government was increasingly limited by its worsening relations with the United States.[5]

In the mid-1960s, several Latin American states, including Peru, notified the US government that they needed to replace significant amounts of World War II– or Korean War–vintage military equipment. Washington responded by asking each country to draft a five-year plan outlining its future needs. It also informed the countries involved that supersonic aircraft would not be supplied to the region before 1969. At this time, Cuba was the only state in Latin America with supersonic aircraft, and the US government hoped to delay others from reaching that threshold as long as possible. Accepting the position of the United States, most Latin American governments agreed to order subsonic aircraft, but both Peru and Chile insisted on the purchase of supersonic Northrop F-5A/B Freedom Fighters. When the United States remained adamant, the Chilean government responded by buying twenty-one British Hawker Hunter jets and the Belaúnde administration announced the purchase of fourteen Dassault Mirage V fighter-bombers. Shortly thereafter, the Peruvian government also purchased six Canberra light bombers from the United Kingdom. The introduction of Mirage aircraft into South America caused a stir because they were clearly superior to any aircraft then operating in the area.[6]

As the arms issue intensified, the IPC question again came to the forefront of Peruvian domestic politics. On June 26, 1967, the Peruvian congress passed a new law concerning the IPC that voided its title to the oil fields and placed the oil deposits in the national reserve. The measure also authorized the president to expropriate all surface equipment and property. The Peruvian government subsequently registered the subsoil at La Brea y Pariñas as the property of the state, tendered bids from other companies to operate the fields, and made formal findings that the IPC owed Peru more than $144 million in back debts. The 1967 law ended hopes for US aid while making it generally more difficult for Peru to obtain financial support from other external sources. As Peruvian resolve strengthened, major changes in the Peruvian petroleum industry increased pressure on the IPC. Domestic consumption increased, which meant that production was gradually absorbed by the domestic market to the point that Peru lost its status as a petroleum exporter. At the same time, production at La Brea y Pariñas declined, and the IPC lost its monopoly position in the industry as well as its monopoly on refining operations. As these changes occurred, the bargaining power of the IPC diminished while accusations increased that it took large profits out of the country without investing adequately in the development of new fields. Concluding that nationalization was inevitable, the IPC accepted a settlement in 1968 that was much more favorable to the Peruvian government than the earlier version discussed in 1964.[7]

Known as the Act of Talara, the agreement reached on August 13, 1968, consisted of several separate but related agreements. The main provisions called for the transfer of the surface installations and subsoil minerals at La Brea y Pariñas to the Peruvian government in return for cancellation of Peruvian tax claims against the IPC, a ten-year contract for the sale of natural gas to the IPC, a similar six-year contract for the sale of La Brea y Pariñas crude to the IPC refinery at Talara, and new exploration concessions for the IPC elsewhere in Peru. Immediately after the agreement was signed, Carlos Loret de Mola, the disgruntled head of the Peruvian national oil company, the Empresa Petrolera Fiscal (EPF), denounced the agreement as a gigantic fraud that dishonored Peru. Although Loret de Mola opposed the agreement in principle as well as in detail, his criticism centered on the alleged absence of the last page of the settlement, on which the oil sale prices by the EPF to the IPC were supposedly specified. Within a month, the agreement was totally discredited. The existence of page eleven was never confirmed, but the saga of leaked terms, missing pages, and charges of betrayal destroyed the credibility of the Belaúnde government and led to yet another *golpe* by the armed forces.

REVOLUTION IN FOREIGN POLICY

The military coup d'état on October 3, 1968, was the product of a general and prolonged politicization of the Peruvian armed forces. Reformist influences on the military dated back to the 1896 French military mission and included the more recent US military advisory teams as well as the Centro de Altos Estudios Militares (CAEM). Once in power, the Revolutionary Government of the Armed Forces headed by General Juan Velasco Alvarado, the senior Peruvian general, enthusiastically joined the rising chorus of economic nationalism, declaring the end of external dependence to be the fundamental objective of the Peruvian revolution. In other statements, the revolutionary government declared its intention to transform Peru's basic socioeconomic structures, increase the responsiveness of foreign investors to Peruvian needs, and pursue a third road to development that was neither communist nor capitalist. Thereafter, the foreign policy of the Velasco administration emphasized two distinct but related goals. It played on the themes of nationalism and anti-imperialism to generate domestic political support, and it worked to modify Peru's economic relationships with other countries, especially the United States. As Velasco emphasized in mid-1969, the military government's approach to economic cooperation called for elimination of pressures or imposed conditions from abroad.[8]

The Velasco government soon took a number of specific measures designed to assert heightened Peruvian sovereignty. These included the immediate, uncompensated expropriation of the International Petroleum Company; stronger enforcement of the 200-mile thesis on the law of the sea, including an escalation of the seizure of US fishing vessels; creation of state monopolies for the commercialization of minerals and hydrocarbons; and formulation of guidelines to insure Peruvian participation in the profits and management of foreign firms operating in Peru. In addition, the government prohibited new foreign investment in sensitive sectors like banking, insurance, and communications, and it stipulated that foreign mining companies must begin development of mineral concessions or forfeit them. With its neighbors, the Velasco administration promoted subregional economic integration to stimulate industrialization, increase exports, and strengthen the bargaining position of the Andean states vis-à-vis the multinational corporations and developed market economies. Outside the region, the military regime undertook an impressive diplomatic effort to gain support for its opposition to nuclear testing. Numerous antitest protocols were concluded, and in July 1973, the Velasco government broke diplomatic relations with France over this issue.[9]

The revolutionary government also quickly expanded its diplomatic and commercial relations. As Velasco repeatedly emphasized, his administration intended to disregard East-West rivalries and establish contacts with all countries whose markets were open to Peruvian products or whose economic and technical cooperation could be beneficial to national development. Accordingly, the Peruvian government established diplomatic and commercial relations with the Soviet Union, the People's Republic of China, and Cuba, as well as a variety of other socialist states. With China and Cuba, the establishment of diplomatic relations was preceded by the conclusion of commercial accords, which suggests that these states used economic concessions to purchase their diplomatic toehold on the continent. In any case, the initiatives toward the socialist world produced tangible benefits for Peru as they opened new markets for nontraditional exports and new sources of assistance for development projects. They also enabled the Peruvian armed forces to broaden the policy of arms transfer diversification initiated under Belaúnde.

After 1968 the Velasco administration took the lead in demanding a radical reorganization of the inter-American economic and political system. In effect, its policies here constituted a systematic questioning of the entire system and its principal institutions, including the Organization of American States (OAS), the Inter-American Reciprocal Assistance Treaty, and the Inter-American Development Bank. The Peruvian government called for an end to the OAS embargo of Cuba and pushed for creation of a Latin American economic front directed at the United States. It also cosponsored resolutions in the OAS to relocate its seat to Latin America and to modify the OAS charter to include recognition of the right to ideological pluralism in the Western Hemisphere. In response to this latter proposal, the OAS later approved a modified concept calling for a plurality of ideologies. In addition, the Peruvian government called for reorganization of the Inter-American Development Bank to eradicate paternalism, which it largely defined in terms of US control. It also endorsed publicly the Panamanian government's demands for the nationalization of the Panama Canal.[10]

Finally, the Velasco regime radically increased Peruvian participation in the Non-Aligned Movement, especially the Organization of Non-Aligned Countries and the Group of 77. In the process, Peru became a leader in the North-South confrontation. It joined in the call for a new international economic order, a restructuring of the international monetary system, the formation of a cartel of Third World primary producers, and an end to the systematic "economic aggression" of developed states against developing states. Strong verbal support was also extended to national liberation movements as far afield as South Vietnam and Angola. The Peruvian government's new policies in these areas provided the military regime with powerful symbols of Peruvian independence. Such policies were instrumental in reinforcing political support for the Velasco government.[11]

Early policies of the revolutionary government, especially those intended to reduce Peruvian dependency on the United States, served to heighten tension between the two states. After using the IPC scandal as the pretext for its revolution, the military immediately expropriated IPC properties to establish its legitimacy as a nationalist regime. There were solid bases in Peruvian domestic law for the actions of the revolutionary government; nevertheless, in an effort to avoid a major confrontation with the United States, the Velasco administration took a moderate position, arguing that the IPC was a unique case in Peru. Under US law, the Hickenlooper Amendment to the 1962 Foreign Assistance Act required the president to terminate after six months foreign assistance to any government that expropriated US property owned by US nationals or corporations without taking appropriate steps toward compensation. In the ensuing negotiations, the US government took the position that Peru had the legal right to expropriate the IPC but was also obligated under international law to pay effective compensation for the holdings. The threat of sanctions was maintained throughout the negotiating process but never employed.[12]

In the intervening months, the revolutionary government took a more radical stance in the 200-mile-seas-controversy. In February 1969 the Peruvian navy detained the US-flagged *Tuna Clipper* for allegedly fishing in Peruvian waters. The incident occurred soon after the capture of a US military vessel by North Korea and three days after diplomatic and commercial relations with the Soviet Union were established. Therefore, it inflamed relations between the United States and Peru more than would otherwise have been the case. California fishermen demanded enactment of the Pelly Amendment, a provision attached to the 1968 Foreign Military Sales Act that required suspension of military aid to any country that illegally seized US fishing boats. They also proposed curtailment in the purchase of Peruvian fish products. When Washington responded by provisionally invoking the Pelly Amendment, the Velasco administration expelled most of the US military mission to Peru and declared unwelcome a scheduled visit by special presidential envoy Nelson Rockefeller. The migratory schools of tuna did not visit the Peruvian coast from 1970 to 1972, which helped defuse the fishing controversy, but their return in 1973 reopened the dispute. After Peru seized more than a score of US fishing vessels, Washington invoked the Pelly Amendment, which added to the tension between the two states.[13]

Velasco's diplomatic initiatives were both dynamic and innovative, but regime economic policies undermined their success. The key to the military's strategy for breaking dependency was an export-led development model not unlike those pursued in the past. In brief, the military tried to buy room for maneuver by concluding contracts with foreign companies for large projects in the hope it would be possible to borrow against the export income expected to result. The combination of borrowing and future tax revenues could then be used to transform the economy without squeezing the middle sectors. It was a strategy that entailed both high costs and high risks; in the end, its implementation suffered greatly from gross mismanagement and plain bad luck. The expected oil boom failed to materialize; fish-meal production dropped precipitously with the disappearance of anchovies off the coast of Peru; and copper prices collapsed with the end of the international commodity boom. At the same time, the complex and ambitious program developed to control and manage foreign capital put the regime in the difficult position of trying to attract new foreign capital while at the same time exerting greater control over existing foreign investment.[14]

The heavy government borrowing that occurred in 1972–1975 significantly altered both the structure and magnitude of the external public debt. Over the previous two decades, supplier credits had been the single most important source of loans; however, by the mid-1970s foreign banks supplied almost half of all external loans, with foreign governments providing the bulk of the remainder. As a result, foreign loans were relatively more expensive in terms of the interest paid, and repayment was generally due in much shorter periods of time. Consequently, the level of external public debt, after slow growth in the 1960s and 1970s, more than doubled from 1970 to 1973 and more than doubled again from 1973 to 1976. In total, outstanding debt increased fivefold ($1.1 billion to $5.6 billion) from 1970 to 1976. At the same time, payments for interest and amortization of the principal increased from $100 million annually in 1970 to $500 million annually in 1976. This deteriorating economic picture was further aggravated by the military's failure to diversify foreign markets significantly and thereby escape the consequences of the recession that struck the developed market economies in 1974. Important new markets were cultivated, especially in Eastern Europe and the People's Republic of China, but they proved inadequate to offset fully the reduced demand for Peruvian exports in the West. All of these conditions combined to produce a growing economic crisis that was aggravated by Velasco's ill health and led to his replacement in 1975 by General Francisco Morales Bermúdez. Morales later emphasized that government policy would remain the same, but a fundamental disagreement over economic policy was clearly the principal reason for the change in command.[15]

The Morales administration immediately imposed a mild austerity program, but the country's financial condition failed to improve. In mid-1976 the government resorted to more severe measures, including currency devaluations, restrictions on imports, elimination of subsidies for consumer items, wage and price regulation, and substantial budget cuts for social services and development projects. Through such measures, the government hoped to stimulate exports while holding down imports, regain the confidence of Peru's foreign creditors, and stimulate private investment to compensate for the drop-off in public investment. In themselves, the austerity policies were extremely unpopular, and when published reports highlighted the role in their development played by North American banks, a political crisis developed within the military. The specter of neo-imperialism fueled debate within the government over whether or not to default on the external public debt. The crisis sharpened in 1977, when foreign creditors refused to negotiate additional aid without International Monetary Fund (IMF) involvement. By the following year, the external debt of Peru had reached $7.2 billion, an amount equal to 44.4 percent of the Peruvian GNP, and the debt service was consuming 31.3 percent of export earnings. In a very difficult situation, the Morales administration agreed in August 1978 to an IMF standby agreement whose harsh terms included increases in gasoline and fuel prices, a progressive devaluation of the sol, interest-rate hikes, and limited wage and salary adjustments. This austerity package had a devastating impact on lower-income groups in Peru, and severely damaged both the limited popularity of the Morales government and the institutional prestige of the armed forces as a bulwark against dependency. Acceptance of the IMF proposal also highlighted the full extent to which Peru, after over a decade of rule by a military regime determined to reduce its dependency on foreign countries and institutions, remained further than ever from autonomy.[16]

The growing need to appease Peruvian creditors and attract more foreign investment contributed to a gradual reorientation of Peruvian foreign policy in the second half of the decade. Less than a month after taking office, the Morales administration announced a compensation agreement covering the recent nationalization of the Marcona Corporation. Following a 1974 agreement that had resolved earlier investment disputes, this was seen as a clear signal to Washington that Peru wanted to improve diplomatic and commercial relations. At the same time, the new government progressively disassociated Peru from the radical political positions of the Non-Aligned Movement. At the August 1976 Conference of Non-Aligned Countries, Peru announced reservations to several resolutions passed by the conference, including the endorsement of Cuban support for the Angolan government and the description of US control of Puerto Rico as colonialism. As the direction and tone of Peruvian foreign policy moderated, Morales publicly expurgated the term *socialism* from the revolution's vocabulary on the grounds it had a negative connotation that served only to confuse and discourage private investors. With the Carter administration eager to promote a resurgence of democracy in Latin America, these tentative steps were welcomed in Washington, and Peruvian relations with the United States gradually improved in the second half of the decade.[17]

As the Morales government reemphasized its commitment to regional diplomatic ties, territorial disputes again complicated relations with Bolivia, Chile, and Ecuador. In early 1975 the Bolivian government opened negotiations with Chile aimed at obtaining an outlet to the sea. In response to the Bolivian initiative, the Chilean government proposed in December 1975 to exchange a narrow strip of land north of Arica along the Peruvian border for equivalent territorial compensation in the Bolivian *altiplano*. Although it welcomed commencement of negotiations, the Bolivian government eventually rejected the offer on the familiar grounds that Bolivia should not have to make territorial compensations to obtain land seized in an aggressive war. At this point, the Morales administration, alarmed that the talks centered on territory that was originally Peruvian, entered the discussions. Peru suggested a round of talks in Lima aimed at a comprehensive solution to the problem, and when Chile attempted to delay negotiations, the Peruvian foreign ministry introduced a new formula that undercut the earlier Chilean initiative. The Peruvian proposal called for creation of a zone of joint Peru-Bolivia-Chile sovereignty between the Peruvian border and the city of Arica, with Bolivia receiving a corridor feeding into this area. The Peruvian proposal offered the Bolivian government as much as the Chilean proposition, and, at the same time, reintroduced the question of Peruvian rights in the disputed zone. Because it called for trilateral economic development of the territory, it was also consistent with the renewed emphasis of the Peruvian government on Andean cooperation and integration. The initiative brought the negotiations to an abrupt halt because Chile refused to consider it, charging the proposal introduced issues unrelated to the question at hand, infringed on Chilean sovereignty, and threatened modifications to the 1929 treaty.[18]

The revival of the dispute over the Atacama Desert coincided with a deterioration in Peruvian relations with Ecuador. In October 1976 the Ecuadorian ambassador to the United Nations stated that Ecuador's territorial claims in the Amazon Basin were a formidable obstacle to Peruvian goals for enhanced regional economic cooperation. Demanding a renegotiation of the 1942 Rio Protocol, the Ecuadorian diplomat argued that Peruvian occupation of the Oriente blocked Ecuadorian access to the Amazon River network and thereby severely limited Ecuador's participation in any future multilateral development of the region. Diplomatic relations between the two states were strained further the following month when a leading Ecuadorian newspaper accused the Soviet Union of arming Peru for an invasion of northern Chile. The Morales government initiated a modest peace offensive in early 1977, but news of Ecuador's intention to acquire a squadron of sophisticated jet fighters renewed concern in Lima, as did subsequent reports of the mistreatment of Peruvian nationals in Ecuador. The political situation remained generally stable for the rest of the year, but in January 1978 Peruvian and Ecuadorian forces were again involved in minor armed clashes along their Amazon frontier.[19]

At about the same time, the dispute over the Atacama Desert intensified. In March 1978 the Bolivian government, citing Chilean insincerity and inflexibility, broke diplomatic relations with Chile and opted for a confrontationist strategy. In part, Bolivian diplomacy was motivated by the growing isolation of the Chilean government. Chile's record on human rights, coupled with its refusal to cooperate with the United States in a case of suspected political assassination, led to widespread criticism of the Pinochet government. In addition, intensification of the Beagle Channel Islands dispute made Argentina a potential ally for either Peru or Bolivia in a confrontation with Chile. On the other hand, Brazilian diplomacy in the region threatened the creation of a conservative, anti-Peruvian axis linking Brazil, Bolivia, and Chile. Pursuing a rapprochement with Brazil, the Morales government succeeded in turning a long-standing Brazilian proposal for an Amazon integration pact into the multilateral Treaty for Amazonic Cooperation, which was signed on July 3, 1978. The treaty recognized the prior existence of the Andean Group and carefully avoided taking a position on outstanding border disputes. Throughout most of 1978, diplomatic relations between Peru and Chile remained tense, and they deteriorated at the end of the year. The discovery of an extensive Chilean espionage network, coordinated through the Chilean embassy and directed at sensitive Peruvian military installations, later precipitated an open split between the two countries.[20]

During this protracted period of geopolitical tension, the Morales government continued the buildup of military forces begun by Belaúnde and accelerated by Velasco. From 1968 to 1977, per capita GNP rose by only 40 percent, but per capita military expenditure increased by over 82 percent, with most of the expansion in the 1974–1977 era. After 1973 the Soviet Union replaced the United States as Peru's chief arms supplier, and for the first time in a century, Peru achieved military parity with Chile. In early 1974 President Velasco called for a ten-year moratorium on the purchase of offensive arms, but subsequent meetings of the Andean states, including a September 1975 conference in Lima, failed to produce a workable formula for ending the regional arms race. In the meantime, Peruvian interest in Soviet military equipment increased after the United States again briefly suspended military assistance in February 1975. Motivated by institutional interests as well as ongoing regional pressures, the Peruvian armed forces elected to pursue a rapid increase in the procurement of Soviet arms. In the process, they effectively substituted one form of dependency for another because replacement parts and munitions for their Soviet arms were largely available only from the source country.[21]

The formal movement toward enhanced subregional cooperation began during Belaúnde's administration with the 1966 Declaration of Bogotá, which committed Chile, Colombia, Ecuador, Venezuela, and Peru to negotiate an agreement for economic integration. The 1969 Cartagena Agreement, which established the Andean Common Market or Andean Group, was signed by Bolivia, Chile, Colombia, Ecuador, and Peru, and received the enthusiastic support of the Velasco government. The signatories to the Cartagena Agreement, which Venezuela joined in 1973, later developed a number of collective policies consistent with the objectives of the Peruvian government. These policies included a code for the common treatment of foreign capital, industrial programming among member countries, and the eventual establishment of a common external tariff.

Within the guidelines of the Andean Pact, subregional economic integration made some progress in the early years; however, the process encountered major obstacles after 1975. In particular, implementation of provisions for the common treatment of foreign investments proved extremely difficult. Approved in December 1970, Decision 24 created a common regime for the treatment of foreign capital and set a limit in most cases of 14 percent for the profit remittances of new foreign firms. The code also required the transformation of foreign firms to mixed or nation companies if they intended to take advantage of the Andean Group's tariff reductions. Decision 24 also included a safeguard clause that enabled members to suspend its provisions when such action was deemed essential for development goals. In the wake of the September 1973 coup in Chile, the new military government insisted on significant revisions to the Andean investment code that included an increase in the profit remittance limits for foreign firms. Although the Morales government expressed sympathy with the call to permit foreign capital to repatriate a higher percentage of profits, it accepted the decision of the majority when Andean Pact ministers in August 1976 largely rejected the Chilean proposals. After further negotiations, the Chilean government in October 1976 withdrew from the Cartagena Agreement. Because of Chile's geographical location and relatively high level of economic development, its departure represented a major setback for Peruvian goals for subregional economic integration. Moreover, the manner in which the dispute was eventually resolved set an unfortunate precedent for the reconciliation of Andean Group objectives with national development goals.[22]

The prolonged controversy over the treatment of foreign investment also retarded progress toward economic integration in other areas. The agenda for industrial programming, which was of special interest to Peru, was designed to promote the industrial development of the subregion through joint programming. Although some progress was made, the allocation of industrial activities among countries proved very complicated, and the initial allocations were interrupted by Venezuela's tardy agreement to the pact and later by Chile's decision to withdraw. As a result, only three agreements had been concluded by 1980, and all suffered problems of implementation. As for trade liberalization, a variety of economic and political problems hampered early programs, and with the withdrawal of Chile from the Andean Group, the remaining members had to postpone for several years the deadlines for both complete liberalization of intraregional trade and adoption of a common external tariff. Despite these setbacks, the Peruvian government reaped important trade advantages from its participation in the Andean Common Market. By the late 1970s fully 66 percent of Peruvian intraregional exports were manufactures, compared with only 8 percent of its global trade. In addition, the Peruvian economy had begun to participate in intraindustry specialization and trade. Therefore, any breakdown in regional integration threatened to impact negatively on Peruvian industrialization, which apparently had become at least partially dependent on regional markets to maintain economies of scale.[23]

SECOND BELAUNDE ADMINISTRATION

During the 1980 election campaign, both Popular Action and the Apristas emphasized domestic issues and presented similar programs. At the polls, Popular Action won over 45 percent of the presidential vote and almost 48 percent of the congressional seats. Given the prevailing multiparty system, in which fifteen parties had presidential candidates, the results constituted a landslide for Belaúnde. His party won a plurality in twenty-one of Peru's twenty-five departments; APRA carried only three departments in the traditionally solid Aprista north. The election results signaled a significant shift in the Peruvian electorate from both left and right toward the center of the political spectrum. At the time, Belaúnde's promise of gradual change seemed the most realistic approach to voters fearful of violence and losing faith in the efficacy of revolution. It later proved ironic that the Maoist Sendero Luminoso, or Shining Path, guerrilla movement, based in the poor, isolated Department of Ayacucho, chose election day 1980 to launch a "people's war" in Peru. In the first six months of the Belaúnde administration, some 232 acts of terrorism were attributed to the Sendero Luminoso, and the problem worsened as the decade progressed.

Geopolitically, the first foreign policy issue addressed by the Belaúnde government was the border dispute with Ecuador. Diplomatic relations between the two neighbors had been relatively good in the previous two decades due to several positive developments, such as work on the marginal Amazon highway, the Andean Pact, the 200-mile thesis, and joint development projects on the frontier that included the Catamayo-Chira and Puyango-Tumbes irrigation schemes. Relations degenerated in the late 1970s as technical problems hampered advancement of the Puyango-Tumbes scheme and the two states diverged on selected Andean Pact issues. In January 1981 the mounting tension led to skirmishes in and around Paquisha in the Cordillera del Cóndor region from which Peru emerged militarily triumphant. Nevertheless, the terms of the subsequent cease-fire were criticized in Peru because they did not provide for a demarcation of the boundary, refer to the OAS principle of respect for international agreements, or involve the guarantors of the 1942 Rio Protocol. Critics expressed concern that the character of the dispute appeared to be shifting away from the long-term Peruvian focus on respect for international treaties. This concern resurfaced in October 1983, when the Ecuadorian congress again declared the 1942 protocol null and void and reaffirmed Ecuador's territorial rights in the Amazon Basin.[24]

A variety of other geopolitical concerns also preoccupied the Belaúnde government. Peru refused to sign the 1982 United Nations Law of the Sea Convention on the grounds it was a hasty, unconstitutional decision that necessitated further discussion. It also pursued revisions to the fishing agreement concluded with the Soviet Union during the military dictatorship. In 1981 the Peruvian government adhered to the 1959 Antarctic Treaty; and in 1983, the Peruvian National Antarctic Commission and the Peruvian Institute for Antarctic Studies were founded in Lima. Thereafter, the Belaúnde administration strengthened diplomatic efforts in support of a multitude of claims in the region. It even considered establishing a permanent base in Antarctica and proposed making the continent a war-free zone. During the conflict between Argentina and Great Britain over the Malvinas Islands, Belaúnde viewed Argentina's position sympathetically and attempted to mediate a peaceful solution to the dispute. His diplomatic efforts came to naught after a failure in communications resulted in the sinking of the *Belgrano* and a continuation of the fighting. Finally, the Bolivian government in 1983 again raised with Chile the question of a sovereign port on the Pacific Ocean. In response to this overture, the Belaúnde administration articulated the now-familiar policy of insisting, under the terms of the 1929 treaty and its complementary protocol, on Peruvian involvement in any substantive negotiations.[25]

Although the Belaúnde administration reaffirmed the Peruvian commitment to subregional cooperation, its approach to national development goals, especially its choice of a model dependent on the goodwill of the United States and the international financial community, slowed progress toward Andean integration. The economic problems inherited by Belaúnde—which included $9 billion in foreign debt, an IMF standby agreement, acute unemployment, and an economy dependent on the vagaries of commodity export prices—persuaded his government to pursue economic growth under a more open economic system based on tariff reductions and a more liberal policy toward foreign capital. Within a year, Belaúnde announced economic policies that suggested a softening in Peru's commitment to the Andean Group's integrative strategy. He called for modifications in the foreign investment code to encourage more foreign investment and a suspension or liberalization of sectoral industrial programs. Equally important, the Peruvian government lowered tariffs on industrial products, which made progress toward a common external tariff, already years behind schedule, virtually impossible. Finally, the Belaúnde administration opposed the earlier tendency of the Andean Group to take political stands on nonpact issues.[26]

As the Belaúnde administration struggled to reorder Peruvian economic policies, it searched for a more positive relationship with the United States. But the growing ambiguity that characterized US-Peruvian relations, an uncertainty that stemmed from the conflicting demands of Peruvian nationalism and the need for US cooperation to achieve foreign policy goals, left little room for sustained improvement. Economically, the Belaúnde administration clashed with the United States over levels of economic assistance as well as the enforcement by the latter of countervailing duties on Peruvian textiles. Multiple crises also developed over a dispute with Eastern Airlines concerning carrier routes and landing rights. Politically, the terrorist issue in general and the Sendero Luminoso in particular became a source of bilateral tension. As the administration attempted to deal firmly with a movement it rightly viewed as a serious threat to social peace and order, the news media in the United States increasingly focused on the human rights issue. Diplomatically, the Reagan administration could not accept Peruvian support for the Contadora Group, which sought a negotiated solution to the crisis in Central America. In turn, the Peruvian government termed US policy toward the war in the Malvinas both blind and anachronistic, and lambasted the United States for its support of Great Britain. At one point, Belaúnde even suggested ousting the United States from the Organization of American States. Finally, when the United States invaded Grenada, Belaúnde deplored the action and condemned armed intervention and interference in the internal affairs of another country.[27]

In the end, Peru's economic concerns, made worse by natural disasters, the insurgency problem, a growing traffic in narcotics, and bickering within the Popular Action Party, proved more than the Belaúnde administration could accommodate. An inflation rate of around 60 percent in 1980 had spiraled to well over 100 percent by 1983 and was approaching 200 percent, the highest level recorded in Peru to that time, when Belaúnde left office in 1985. At that point, some 60 percent of Peruvian industrial capacity was idle; upwards of two-thirds of the labor force was unemployed or underemployed; real wages had plunged some 40 percent since 1980; and per capita income was down to the level of the mid-1960s. To service the $9 billion in foreign debt and finance huge deficits in trade and budget accounts, the Belaúnde administration eventually borrowed an additional $4 billion. With a substantial debt load in place, the effect of the run-up of international interest rates in 1981–1982, combined with a sizeable drop in the purchasing power of commodity exports, was especially painful for Peru. In a period of sustained turmoil, the one thing most Peruvians agreed upon was that Belaúnde's successor would inherit the worst economic crisis of the century and very likely the worst in Peruvian history.[28]

APRISTA FOREIGN POLICY

Throughout the 1985 election campaign, economic problems remained paramount in the minds of Peruvian voters. With the Popular Action Party unable to improve on its economic record, the presidential race was hotly contested; preelection polls gave Alan García Pérez, the new APRA leader, a commanding lead over the other eight presidential candidates. When the votes were finally counted, APRA won a landslide victory and its first presidency since the founding of the party in 1924. García won over 45 percent of the votes cast and finished better than 2-to-1 ahead of his nearest competitor. In contrast, Popular Action went from 45 percent of the vote in 1980 to 6 percent in 1985. García's triumph was truly national in scope as he polled over 77 percent of the vote in one department, a simple majority in as many as seventeen departments, and at his worst, almost one-third of the votes in the Department of Tacna. The Apristas also captured absolute majorities in both houses of the legislature and thus were in the enviable position of not needing to form a parliamentary coalition with the opposition.

When García assumed office, Peru's external debt approached $14 billion; the Belaúnde administration had made only token interest payments on this obligation in the previous twelve months. Full service on the debt was unthinkable because it would have required almost all of Peru's 1985 export earnings as well as an estimated 133 percent of 1986 earnings. Driven by the need for national development, García attacked the debt issue directly by emphasizing that Peru would pay its obligations but not at the expense of economic growth. The president added that in the coming year Peru would limit interest payments on the public external debt to 10 percent of the nation's export earnings. He also rejected the International Monetary Fund (IMF) as the formal mediator between Peru and its consortium of private lenders. The 10-percent-of-exports policy allowed Peru to increase its net international reserves and to pursue a more independent and nationalistic foreign policy, and few observers were surprised when the policy was later continued.[29]

In addition, the García administration announced complementary measures that included a halt to payments on medium- and long-term private foreign debt and a prohibition for two years on the remission abroad of foreign currency derived from profits, royalties, or other benefits. On August 15, 1986, the IMF declared Peru ineligible for future loans, a move that formalized Peru's isolation from foreign government lenders and commercial banks. The IMF cutoff also hampered Peruvian efforts to obtain new loans from the World Bank, one of its last potential sources of outside credit. Matters worsened in June 1987, when the World Bank, followed by the Inter-

American Development Bank, suspended loan disbursements because Peru was overdue in making payments on outstanding credit.[30]

At home, President García rejected orthodox austerity and chose instead to reactivate the economy through increased consumer spending. The government froze prices on goods and services to slow inflation, granted pay increases to boost real wages, cut taxes to enhance purchasing power, tightened exchange controls to benefit local production, and reduced interest rates. Although García's economic policies worked well at first, his economic program and his personal popularity were later undermined by the poor export performance of the Peruvian economy. As imports grew in tandem with the economy's strong performance, exports failed to keep pace due to a slump in commodity prices. The Peruvian government has traditionally managed its trade deficits through external borrowing; however, this approach was no longer available to the García administration because its policy toward debt repayment had restricted access to foreign credit. Similarly, a July 1987 announcement that the banking system would be nationalized discouraged domestic investment. At the same time, the Peruvian government experienced difficulty in negotiating a common Third World approach to the debt question. By 1988 the Peruvian economy was in deep recession and the inflation rate stood at record levels. In a desperate attempt to shock the economy back to reality, García reversed course and imposed three economic austerity packages between September 1988 and March 1989. By the end of the year, positive results were visible as the rate of inflation slowed, real wages increased, and the level of foreign exchange reserves grew. On the other hand, the foreign debt burden was estimated to be in excess of $23 billion.[31]

The early regional policy of the García administration centered on greater arms control as a means to reduce regional tension and manage the external debt crisis. In November 1985 the Peruvian government presented a regional disarmament proposal that received the support of Bolivia, Chile, and Ecuador among other Latin American states. Thereafter, the governments of Peru and Chile held a series of negotiations aimed at a withdrawal of military forces along their common border. At the same time, they attempted to complete the unfulfilled terms of the 1929 treaty and complementary protocol that obligated Chile to build a dock and other facilities at Arica for the benefit of Peru. After a late November 1985 round of talks, Peru and Chile released a joint communiqué that discussed greater autonomy for the port of Arica as well as the construction by Chile of a symbolic peace monument on the Morro de Arica. Disarmament talks continued over the next three years, but no specific agreements were reached. García's disarmament policy did achieve a minor success in the spring of 1986, when the Peruvian government negotiated a reduction in the planned purchase of French Mirage 2000 fighters from twenty-six planes to twelve plus a ground simulator. In addition, the establishment by the United Nations of the Regional Center for Peace,

Disarmament, and Development in Lima provided a tangible measure of the growing stature of the Peruvian government as a leader in the field of arms control.[32]

The García administration also pursued better relations with Ecuador and Bolivia. Soon after taking office, Foreign Minister Allan Wagner paid an unprecedented visit to Ecuador, where he discussed a variety of issues in an effort to develop a climate of mutual trust and understanding. One result of these talks was resumption of the Puyango-Tumbes irrigation project, which had been halted since the 1981 border clash. Early progress on this question suggested better overall relations were possible, but detailed negotiations on issues involving national security awaited resolution of Ecuadorian demands for access to the Amazon River. The Peruvian foreign minister also traveled to Bolivia, where talks focused on improved commercial relations as well as joint efforts to control the narcotics traffic. Later, President García indicated to Bolivia that his government would accept Chilean cession of a strip of land to Bolivia to provide the latter with access to the sea. This pronouncement marked a significant shift in Peruvian policy because the Morales administration had earlier opposed a deal between Chile and Bolivia that would have provided Bolivia with a Pacific port. In regard to the Andean Group, the García government remained committed to the Aprista ideal of Latin American unity. At the same time, it subscribed to a December 1986 protocol that amended the Andean Pact and weakened subregional unity. Although President García later participated in Andean summit meetings intended in part to rejuvenate the Andean Pact, his administration demonstrated little interest in pursuing the strong initiatives necessary to resolve the growing crises that the Andean Group faced in the second half of the decade. The García administration also supported its maritime neighbors in articulating a 200-mile thesis, and it followed the practice of its predecessor in refusing to sign the 1982 Law of the Sea Convention.[33]

The crisis in Central America, especially as it concerned Nicaragua, was a third policy area emphasized by the García government. During the presidential campaign, García had suggested that Peru might join the Contadora Group; when that later proved impractical, he proposed creation of a group of South American states to support the Contadora Group. His proposal resulted in the creation in August 1985 of the Contadora Support Group, composed of Peru, Argentina, Brazil, and Uruguay. The Peruvian government consistently supported all attempts to end external intervention in Central America and to bring about peace based on a mutually acceptable agreement. In pursuit of these objectives, it openly supported the Nicaraguan position while opposing US aid to the contras as well as any potential military intervention in Nicaragua. Peruvian support for the Nicaraguan government was largely rhetorical, but the García administration emphasized on more than one occasion that it would break diplomatic relations with any government that attacked Nicaragua. When the United States invaded Panama in December 1989, the Peruvian government recalled its ambassador to Washington and denounced what it considered to be an outrage against Latin America.[34]

One of the García government's first acts was to break diplomatic relations with the South African government, and it later established diplomatic ties with the South West African People's Organization (SWAPO). It also participated actively in international conferences aimed at ending apartheid. In June 1986 the foreign minister of Peru was elected president of the UN World Conference on Sanctions against South Africa. In part to publicize its debt policy, the Peruvian government also took a more active role in the Non-Aligned Movement. García attended the 8th Summit of Non-Aligned States in Zimbabwe in September 1986, where the final conference declaration recognized the Peruvian position on external debt. For a time, there was even speculation that García could become the next president of the Non-Aligned Movement, a prospect he did not publicly rule out until late August 1988. On the other hand, the García administration tried to maintain an independent, if not critical, posture toward the socialist countries to avoid being labeled communist. This was one of the reasons the government pursued a closer association with the social democratic groups of Western Europe. Similarly, it was behind the Peruvian decision to host the 17th Congress of the Socialist International in Lima in June 1986. At the same time, the government established full diplomatic relations with North Korea in late 1989, justifying the controversial move on the grounds of increased sovereignty and ideological independence.[35]

The García administration also played an energetic role in a variety of other international organizations. It was an active participant in the Latin American Economic System (SELA), which it viewed as an important forum to generate support for its economic policies. For the 12th SELA Meeting of Foreign Ministers, the group convened in Lima, where it provided measured support for the Peruvian position on foreign debt. Peru was also a founding member of the Andean Reserve Fund (FAR), a five-nation group backed by $0.5 billion in reserves and a lending potential of $4 billion. In addition, the García administration promoted creation of a Latin American monetary fund that would include regional economic powers like Argentina and Brazil. In the OAS, the Peruvian delegation supported charter amendments and proposed creation of the International Organization for Latin America and the Caribbean (OELAC) to serve as a permanent mechanism for regional political consultation. Informal political discussion and networking occurred in a variety of forums. These included the Contadora Group and the Contadora Support Group as well as the newer Group of Eight, which the García administration was instrumental in organizing to increase political interchange and consultation among the Latin American states. Peru also remained active in the UN General Assembly, where its emphasis remained on the issues of foreign debt and reduced arms expenditure.[36]

The activist foreign policy of the García administration left little room for improvement in bilateral relations with the United States. Problems related to the external debt, a civil aviation accord, increased bilateral aid, and protectionist sentiment toward Peruvian imports were carried over from the Belaúnde government. In addition, García's condemnation of US policy in Central America in general and in Nicaragua in particular put him in direct conflict with the Reagan administration. On the debt issue, less than 20 percent of Peruvian obligations were owed to North American banks; nevertheless, the US government feared that other debtor nations, where North American liabilities were considerably larger, might be tempted to adopt García's 10 percent solution. An early controversy with multinational petroleum producers in which the García administration charged they failed to use tax breaks to boost exploration also contributed to the deterioration in relations. Finally, García frequently employed strong language and a confrontational style toward the United States, especially over the issues of external debt and Central American policy. Although his rhetoric often appeared to be designed primarily for internal political consumption, it exacerbated Peruvian relations with Washington. On the other hand, a commercial air agreement in November 1986 ended the dispute that had originated four years earlier, when the Belaúnde administration canceled the previous agreement. The Peruvian government also won occasional praise in Washington for its response to the growing traffic in narcotics, and at the end of the regional drug summit in February 1990, President García commended the US government for displaying a clearer understanding of the social and economic dimensions of the cocaine trade. In this milieu, bilateral relations were strained but probably as good as could be expected.

FOREIGN POLICY OF FUJIMORI

The economic policies of the García administration set the stage for the 1990 presidential campaign. From 1987 to 1989, the gross domestic product of Peru dropped by 28 percent while real wages fell 60 percent. By mid-1990, government expenditures were running three times as large as government revenues, and the annual rate of inflation was in excess of 3,500 percent. At the same time, the level of public debt swelled from $14 billion to $20 billion as the administration proved unable to maintain even the limited repayment schedule of 10 percent of export earnings defiantly proclaimed in 1985. By the end of the decade, the government had defaulted on approximately $2 billion in loans from the IMF and other international lending agencies, which made it one of the leading debtor nations in the world.[37]

Mario Vargas Llosa, the internationally celebrated novelist, was the early front-runner in the 1990 elections. In a campaign focused on the prolonged economic crisis, he prescribed a severe economic shock in the form of orthodox austerity and free market policies intended to reduce the rate of inflation to a manageable 10 percent. Vargas planned to eliminate the budget deficit by ending immediately all government subsidies and by selling the 161 state-owned companies that collectively cost the country $2 billion annually. He also promised to resume payment on the foreign debt. Alberto Keinya Fujimori, a founder of the Cambio '90 movement, eventually emerged as the principal challenger to Vargas. Fujimori also called for an austerity campaign and free market policies. On the other hand, he argued that the shock treatment proposed by Vargas was both too drastic and unnecessary. As an alternative, he proposed the use of development projects to increase supply and restore economic stability without causing a depression. Fujimori did surprisingly well in the April 1990 first round of the elections, and in the June runoff, he garnered almost 57 percent of the ballots compared to only 34 percent for Vargas. Fujimori carried twenty-three of the twenty-four departments in Peru and won 70 percent of the votes in the working-class districts of Lima.[38]

Understandably, the deplorable state of the Peruvian economy was the first priority of the Fujimori administration. In an effort to improve relations with the international financial community, President-elect Fujimori traveled both to Japan and the United States before his inauguration in July 1990. In return for promises to implement an austerity program and resume service on the external debt, an international consortium that included Japan, Spain, and the United States made a preliminary commitment for bridge loans to cover the $2 billion in defaulted debts to the IMF and other multilateral lending agencies. The Peruvians hoped that support from these international institutions might bring Peru relief from its commercial creditors. Less than two weeks after the inauguration, the Fujimori administration announced the first phase of a stern economic stabilization program, dubbed "Fujishock" by Peruvians, that was largely based on policies he had denounced during the election campaign. The key elements of the program included a liberalization of foreign trade policies through elimination of exchange controls, a lifting of restrictions on most imports, and a deep cut in tariff rates. Public-sector companies were directed to raise their prices to levels that would make them profitable, implement a hiring freeze, and furlough all employees hired during the last months of the García administration. Most important, the government overnight ended price controls and subsidies in effect for decades. As a result, Peru experienced its steepest one-day price increase in the twentieth century, and the popularity of Fujimori plummeted among his poorer constituents.[39]

Thereafter, the Fujimori government pursued orthodox economic policies both at home and abroad in an effort to restore the international standing of Peru and allow it to reenter the world economic order. Domestically, the government moved to reduce the rate of inflation, cut back on the bureaucracy, privatize state companies, increase tax revenues, and promote foreign investment. In an effort to liberalize commerce and encourage free competition, it also eliminated tariffs, ended state monopolies, and lifted restrictions on holding foreign currency. Abroad, it resumed interest payments on some international obligations, moved to restore its credit rating, and sought new external sources of funding. In talks with multilateral lending agencies like the World Bank and the Inter-American Development Bank, as well as with a variety of governments including Japan and the United States, Peruvian officials pressed for creation of a support group of creditor nations willing to make fresh loans to lift Peru out of its current crisis. The Peruvian strategy was eventually successful; the governments of Japan and the United States agreed in mid-1991 to a $750 million bridge loan intended to help Peru cancel back payments to international institutions. Once these back payments were normalized, the Fujimori administration hoped to receive the loans, credits, and heavy foreign investments necessary to reactivate the Peruvian economy and rebuild its worn-out infrastructure.[40]

From the beginning, the Fujimori government recognized that the active support of the United States would be a critical element in the success of its strategy to restore the international standing of Peru. As a result, early contacts between the two states focused on the issue of drug production and drug trafficking, the policy area of greatest interest to the Bush administration. This approach highlighted the pragmatism of the Fujimori administration, for Peruvians in and out of government had long been far more concerned with combating guerrilla movements like the Sendero Luminoso than they had been with the drug war. The Cartegena Agreement of February 1990 between the governments of Bolivia, Colombia, Peru, and the United States had emphasized the drug problem and provided substantial new resources to address it. Some of these resources were allocated to Peru before Fujimori took office; others required a specific commitment by the new Peruvian president before they would be made available. Although Fujimori was expected to agree to a substantial infusion of military assistance from the United States to combat the drug problem, he surprised most observers by ultimately choosing not to accept a July 1990 proposal to this effect. Arguing that Peru's problems in general and the drug problem in particular could not be solved by military means alone, the Fujimori administration in January 1991 proposed an alternative approach that addressed the drug issue but emphasized economic as opposed to military solutions. The Peruvian proposal eventually became the basis for the formal umbrella agreement concluded between Peru and the United States in May 1991. While recognizing the importance of the drug question to the United States, this agreement focused on economic concerns, including the Alternative Development Agency, the Enterprise for the Americas Initiative, and the good offices of the United States in international economic organizations. Going beyond simple security concerns to address social, economic, and political issues, the May agreement responded much more fully than the original US proposal to the needs and priorities of Peru and thus represented a substantial diplomatic achievement for the Fujimori administration.[41]

At the same time, the Peruvian government continued to foster its long-term commitment to enhanced regional cooperation and development. In mid-February 1991, Fujimori presided over the opening meeting of the Andean Parliament when it convened its eighth ordinary session in Lima. In May 1991 he joined the presidents of Bolivia, Colombia, Ecuador, and Venezuela for a two-day Andean summit in Caracas. In the so-called Declaration of Caracas, the participants committed to establishment of a free trade zone by January 1992 and a common market by 1995. They also called for a meeting with representatives of the US government to discuss trade, investment, environmental, and drug trafficking issues. Finally, the Andean presidents called for the US Congress to pass a pending bill that would provide trade benefits to their four nations. The bill was designed to encourage Andean agricultural workers to substitute coca production for farm products exportable to the United States under preferential terms. It highlighted the importance the Andean states in general and Peru in particular assigned to a broad approach to the drug war that addressed simultaneously both the issues of drug trafficking and the economic development needs of the rural areas in which coca is grown. This question was at the heart of the dialogue earlier in the spring between Peru and the United States about the most appropriate approach to the drug war.[42]

Over the past three decades, successive Peruvian governments have pushed for greater independence in the conduct of their external affairs. Early on, these efforts produced notable results; but in the latter half of the 1970s, Peru began to lose space for diplomatic maneuver. The government pursued simultaneously a policy of autonomous national development, and the abject failure of regime economic policies undermined its foreign policy objectives. In the aftermath of World War II, well over two decades of largely unin-terrupted growth were followed after 1974 by sixteen years of almost uninterrupted decline. In this latter period, the government lost the momentum needed to solidify the major changes in foreign policy that it had sought as part of its overall development strategy. As a result, Peru entered the 1990s further than ever from the goals of autonomous national development and an independent foreign policy. The Fujimori administration rightly recognized that very little could be done to improve the international posture of Peru until it successfully addressed the serious economic problems it faced. Thereafter, the orthodox policies it initiated could again be supplanted by more dynamic, creative departures.

NOTES

1. John V. Van Cleve, "The Latin American Policy of President Kennedy: A Reexamination: Case: Peru," *Inter-American Economic Affairs* 30, 4 (Spring 1977): 29–44; Arnold Payne, *The Peruvian Coup d'État of 1962: The Overthrow of Manuel Prado* (Washington: Institute for the Comparative Study of Political Systems, 1968), pp. 81–82.

2. Davidson, "Impact," pp. 21–27; Jane S. Jaquette, "The Politics of Development in Peru" (Ph.D. diss., Cornell University, 1971), pp. 90–92.

3. Fernando Belaúnde Terry, interview with author, Denver, Colorado, May 16, 1969; Richard N. Goodwin, "Letter from Peru," *New Yorker* (May 17, 1969), p. 60; Adalberto J. Pinelo, *The Multinational Corporation as a Force in Latin American Politics: A Case Study of the International Petroleum Company in Peru* (New York: Praeger Publishers, 1973), pp. 103–110.

4. Manuel R. Millor, "Algunos Aspectos de la Política Exterior del Nuevo Regimen Peruano," *Foro Internacional* (April/May 1970): 411–412; Julio Cotler, "Political Crisis and Military Populism in Peru," *Studies in Comparative International Development* 6, 5 (1970–1971): 99–100; Charles T. Goodsell, *American Corporations and Peruvian Politics* (Cambridge: Harvard University Press, 1974), pp. 127–130.

5. Francois Bourricaud, *Power and Society in Contemporary Peru* (London: Faber and Faber, 1970), pp. 244–247, 324–327; Pedro-Pablo Kuczynski, *Peruvian Democracy under Economic Stress: An Account of the Belaúnde Administration, 1963–1968* (Princeton: Princeton University Press, 1977), pp. 48–49, 127–135.

6. Víctor Villanueva, interview with author, Lima, Peru, July 14, 1983; Davidson, "Impact," pp. 31–35, 48; Efraín Cobas, *Fuerza Armada, Misiones Militares y Dependencia en el Perú* (Lima: Editorial Horizonte, 1982), pp. 152–159.

7. Fernando Belaúnde Terry, interview with author, Denver, Colorado, May 16, 1969; David Scott Palmer, *Peru: The Authoritarian Tradition* (New York: Praeger Publishers, 1980), pp. 99–100; Kuczynski, *Peruvian Democracy*, pp. 119–122, 260–266.

8. Alfred Stepan, *The State and Society: Peru in Comparative Perspective* (Princeton: Princeton University Press, 1978), pp. 248–256; Víctor Villanueva, *El CAEM y la revolución de la Fuerza Armada* (Lima: IEP Ediciones, 1972), pp. 23–51; Rubén Berríos, "Relaciones Perú-Paises Socialistas: Comercio, asistencia y flujos de tecnología," *Socialismo y Participación*, 22 (June 1983): 55–65.

9. Perú, Ministerio de Relaciones Exteriores, *El Perú y su política exterior* (Lima: Empresa Editora del Diario Oficial "El Peruano," n.d.); Henry Pease García, *El Ocaso del Poder Oligarquico: Lucha política en la escena oficial, 1968–1975*, 3d ed. (Lima: DESCO, 1980), pp. 205–209; Richard Stuart Olson, "Economic Coercion in International Disputes: The United States and Peru in the IPC Expropriation Dispute of 1968–1971," *Journal of Developing Areas* 9, 3 (April 1975): 395–413.

10. Hélan Jaworski C., "Peru: The Military Government's Foreign Policy in Its Two Phases (1968–1980)," in *Latin American Nations in World Politics*, ed. Heraldo Muñoz and Joséph S. Tulchin (Boulder; Colo.: Westview Press, 1984), pp. 207–209.

11. Thomas J. Dodd, "Peru," in *Latin American Foreign Policies: An Analysis*, ed. Harold Eugene Davis et al. (Baltimore: Johns Hopkins University Press, 1975), pp. 372–377; Vazquez Ayllon, "Política," pp. 34–35.

12. Dale B. Furnish, "Peruvian Domestic Law Aspects of the La Brea y Pariñas Controversy," *Kentucky Law Journal* 59 (1970): 351–384; H. Leslie Robinson, "The Hickenlooper Amendment and the IPC," *Pacific Historian* 14 (Spring 1970): 22–51.

13. Cotler, "Political Crisis," pp. 103–104; Alberto Adrianzén, "Estados Unidos frente al proceso peruano," *Cuadernos de Marcha* 1, 4 (November–December 1969): 69.

14. George D.E. Philip, *The Rise and Fall of the Peruvian Military Radicals, 1968–1976* (London: Athlone Press, 1978), pp. 148–149, 155–158; Daniel M. Schydlowsky and Juan J. Wicht, *Anatomía de un Fracaso Económico: Perú, 1968–1978*, 6th ed. (Lima: Universidad del Pacífico, 1982), pp. 97–106; Barbara Stallings, *Banker to the Third World: U.S. Portfolio Investment in Latin America, 1900–1986* (Berkeley: University of California Press, 1987), pp. 290–291.

15. Mario Bazán Gonzáles, *El Sector Externo de la Economía Peruana, 1950–1976* (Lima: Centro de Documentación y Estudios Sociales, 1978), pp. 50–51; Carlos Parodi Zevallos and Frenando González Vigil, *Empresas Transnacionales, estado y burguesía nativa* (Lima: DESCO, 1983), pp. 37–85; Richard J. Collings, "Debt, Dependence, and Default: Is Peru the Wave of the Future?" (Paper delivered at the XIV International Congress of the Latin American Studies Association, New Orleans, Louisiana, March 17–19, 1988), pp. 6–9.

16. Oscar Ugarteche, *Teoría y práctica de la deuda externa en el Perú* (Lima: IEP Ediciones, 1980), pp. 47–48; Scheetz, *Peru*, pp. 121–150; Schydlowsky and Wicht, *Anatomía de un Fracaso Económico*, pp. 97–106.

17. Henry Pease García et al., *Perú, 1968–1980: Cronología política*, 9 vols. (Lima: DESCO, 1974–1982), 5: 2139–2145.

18. Ronald Bruce St John, "Hacia el Mar: Bolivia's Quest for a Pacific Port," *Inter-American Economic Affairs* 31, 3 (Winter 1977): 70–73; Galindo Quiroga, *Litoral Andino*, pp. 93–121.

19. Pease García et al., *Perú*, 5:2249.

20. Stephen M. Gorman, "Present Threats to Peace in South America: The Territorial Dimensions of Conflict," *Inter-American Economic Affairs* 33, 1 (Summer 1979): 51–71; Julio Cotler, *Democracia e integración nacional* (Lima: IEP Ediciones, 1980), pp. 91–92.

21. Hugo Palma, *America Latina: Limitación de armamentos y desarme en la región* (Lima: CEPEI, 1986), pp. 65–73; Davidson, "Impact," pp. 68–81.

22. Ernesto Tironi, "Políticas frente al capital extranjero: La Decisión 24," in *Pacto Andino: Carácter y Perspectivas*, ed. Ernesto Tironi (Lima: IEP Ediciones, 1978) pp. 71–110; Rafael Vargas-Hidalgo, "The Crisis of the Andean Pact: Lessons for Integration among Developing Countries," *Journal of Common Market Studies* 17, 3 (March 1979): 213–226.

23. Jan Ter Wengel, *Allocation of Industry in the Andean Common Market* (Boston: Martinus Nijhoff, 1980), pp. 2–3; Augusto Aninat, "El programa de liberación y el arancel externo común," in *Pacto Andino: Carácter y Perspectivas*, ed. Ernesto Tironi (Lima: IEP Ediciones, 1978), pp. 111–183.

24. Ronald Bruce St John and Stephen M. Gorman, "Challenges to Peruvian Foreign Policy," in *Post-Revolutionary Peru: The Politics of Transformation*, ed. Stephen M. Gorman (Boulder, Colo.: Westview Press, 1982), pp. 188–190; Edgardo Mercado Jarrín, *El conflicto con Ecuador* (Lima: Ediciones Rikchay Perú, 1981), pp. 22–106.

25. US Ambassador to Peru Frank V. Ortiz, interview with author, Lima, Peru, July 11, 1983; Edgardo Mercado Jarrín, "La Antártida: Intereses Geopolíticos," in *El Perú y la Antártida*, ed. Edgardo Mercado Jarrín (Lima: Instituto Peruano de Estudios Geopolíticos y Estratégicos, 1984), pp. 107–146;

Jack Child, *Antarctica and South American Politics: Frozen Lebensraum* (New York: Praeger Publishers, 1988), pp. 156–167.

26. Julio Cotler, interview with author, Lima, Peru, July 15, 1983; William P. Avery, "The Politics of Crisis and Cooperation in the Andean Group," *Journal of Developing Areas* 17, 2 (January 1983): 156–165.

27. Fernando Belaúnde Terry, interview with author, Lima, Peru, July 11, 1983; Ronald Bruce St John, "Peru: Democracy under Siege," *World Today* 40, 7 (July 1984): 305–306; Hélan Jaworski C. "Política exterior de Perú: una interpretación crítica," in *Las Políticas exteriores latinoamericanas frente a la crisis*, ed. Heraldo Muñoz (Buenos Aires: Grupo Editor Latinoamericano/Prospel, 1985), pp. 200–201.

28. Julio Cabrera Moreno, "Un mensaje vacío," *equis X* 9, 401 (August 6–12, 1984): 7; Pedro-Pablo Kuczynski, "Latin American Debt," *Foreign Affairs* 61, 2 (Winter 1982/83): 345; Carol Wise, "Peru's Political Economy, 1980–1987" (Paper delivered at the XIV International Congress of the Latin American Studies Association, New Orleans, Louisiana, March 17–19, 1988), pp. 5–23.

29. Eduardo Ferrero Costa, "Peruvian Foreign Policy: Current Trends, Constraints and Opportunities," *Journal of Interamerican Studies and World Affairs* 29, 2 (Summer 1987): 58–60; Jaworski, "Política exterior," pp. 201–202.

30. David P. Werlich, "Debt, Democracy and Terrorism in Peru," *Current History* 86, 516 (January 1987): 31–32; *Caretas* 900 (April 14, 1986): 16–17.

31. Pedro-Pablo Kuczynski, *Latin American Debt* (Baltimore: Johns Hopkins University Press, 1988), pp. 150–151; Alfred H. Saulniers, "The Peruvian President's Economic Dilemmas," *LASA Forum* 16, 4 (Winter 1986): 15–21; David Scott Palmer, "Peru's Persistent Problems," *Current History* 89, 543 (January 1990): 5–6.

32. Carol Wise, "Alan García, el disarme, Reagan y la guerra de las galaxies," *Quehacer* 39 (February–March 1986): 68–76; Hélan Jaworski C., "La política exterior del Perú 1985: El aprismo a la busqueda del tiempo perdido," in *America latina y el caribe: políticas exteriores para sobrevivir*, ed. Heraldo Muñoz (Buenos Aires: Grupo Editor Latinoamericano/Prospel, 1986), pp. 274–276.

33. Eduardo Ferrero Costa, "200 Millas: Continue el debate," *Caretas* 893 (February 24, 1986): 31, 67; Jaworski, "La política exterior del Perú 1985," pp. 273–277; Ferrero Costa, "Peruvian Foreign Policy," pp. 64–66; "Mar sin derecho," *Caretas* 1045 (February 20, 1989): 23.

34. Ferrero Costa, "Peruvian Foreign Policy," pp. 66–68; *Caretas* 929 (November 11, 1986): 24.

35. Rubén Berríos, "The Search for Independence," *NACLA Report on the Americas* 20, 3 (June 1986): 27–32.

36. Ferrero Costa, "Peruvian Foreign Policy," pp. 73–74; *Caretas* 993 (February 15, 1988): 30.

37. Yves Saint-Geours, "Comment pacifier et reconstruire un Pérou à la dérive?" *Le Monde Diplomatique* (Paris), July 1990; David P. Werlich, "Fujimori and the 'Disaster' in Peru," *Current History* 90, 553 (February 1991): 61–62.

38. *Caretas* 1110 (May 28, 1990): 10–26; Werlich, "Fujimori," pp. 64, 81; *International Herald Tribune* (Hong Kong), June 12, 1990.

39. Alma Guillermoprieto, "Letter from Lima," *New Yorker* (October 29, 1990): 116–117; *Caretas,* 1114 (June 25, 1990): 10–19, 82, 88; James Brooke, "After the Fujishock: Desperation," *International Herald Tribune* (Hong Kong), August 18–19, 1990.

40. Siavosh Ghazi, "Les traitements de choc d'"El Chino,'" *Jeune Afrique* 1566 (January 8, 1991): 42–43; Felipe Ortiz de Zevallos, "New Peruvian Finance Minister's Aim Is True," *Asian Wall Street Journal* (Hong Kong), April 4, 1991;

James Brooke, "Fujimori Charts Free-Market Course for Peru," *International Herald Tribune* (Singapore), May 2, 1991; "Regreso sin Gloria," *Caretas* 1155 (April 15, 1991): 10–14, 89.

41. Eugene Robinson, "Peru Puts Damper on U.S. Drug Effort," *International Herald Tribune* (Singapore), November 6, 1990; Gustavo Gorriti, "Terror in the Andes: The Flight of the Asháninkas," *New York Times Magazine* (December 2, 1990): 40–48, 65–72; Convenio con Problemas," *Caretas* 1160 (May 20, 1991): 16–72; Clifford Krauss, "U.S. to Send Military Advisers to Peru Drug-Producing Front," *International Herald Tribune* (Singapore), August 8, 1991; David Scott Palmer, "United States–Peru Relations in the 1990s: Asymmetry and Its Consequences," in *Latin America and Caribbean Contemporary Record*, vol. 9, *1989–1990*, ed. Eduardo Gamarra and James Malloy (New York: Holmes and Meier, 1992).

42. E. Ferrero Costa, "Parlamento Andino: Nuevos Caminos," *Caretas* 1147 (February 18, 1991): 23, 92; "Andean Nations to Have Free Trade Zone," *Bangkok Post* (Bangkok), May 20, 1991; "Acelerando al Grupo," *Caretas* 1160 (May 20, 1991): 26.

TWELVE

Conclusions

At the outset of the independence era, the economic, social, and political traditions of Peru stemmed from the adaptation of Spanish colonialism to the realities of the New World. The struggle for independence introduced a modicum of change, but it did not result in a substantial transformation of colonial structures. On the contrary, political independence from Spain left intact the fundamental elements of Peruvian society that had developed and crystallized over some 300 years of colonial rule. Peru's socioeconomic structures after 1825 were not fundamentally different from those prior to the battle of Ayacucho, and its colonial character remained intact well into the nineteenth century. For the most part, this meant a hierarchical society with extremely limited opportunities for meaningful political participation and an economy geared to agricultural and mineral export. Eventually, the dominant characteristics of colonial society began to change, but the evolution was slow and painful.

The composition of its society contributed to the political turmoil that emasculated Peru in the two decades after independence with devastating impact on its early external policies. Even though Peru adopted a democratic form of government, the Spanish colonial system had not prepared the citizenry to respond within the framework of a democratic republic. At the same time, the independence movement lacked a clear ideology. Well into the nineteenth century, Peruvians were generally split into liberal and conservative camps, with the central issue of the ongoing ideological debate being the optimum form of government for their nation. This question was of great significance because it encompassed first the monarchy-versus-republic split and then the issue of centralism versus federalism. In the meantime, the nation endured a long period of capricious, chaotic, and destructive rule by a succession of military chiefs. Militarism surfaced before independence was won, and it remained for a prolonged period a prominent feature of Latin American politics in general and Peruvian politics in particular. Similarly, caudillismo had a strong influence on Peruvian foreign policy in the early decades of national life. Peru did not experience its first civilian head of state until 1872, and it did not enjoy protracted periods of civilian rule until the following century. Compared with circumstances

existing in other South American states, the forces of militarism and
caudillismo had a significant, sustained, and largely negative impact on
Peruvian external policy.

In the milieu prevailing in the early decades of independence, the foreign
policy of Peru understandably took a narrow focus that concentrated on
subregional and regional issues. For most of the nineteenth century, its basic
principles could best be summarized as political sovereignty, territorial
integrity, continental solidarity, and economic independence. Like most small
states, Peru remained highly vulnerable to external penetration and
exploitation; consequently, its foreign policy remained closely tied to internal
conditions as well as to questions of national development. Limited national
integration and low levels of consensus contributed to the prevailing level of
domestic instability and had a pernicious influence on Peruvian foreign
policy for decades to come. Regionalism as a political force also contained
the seeds of international conflict; competition with its neighbors enveloped
Peru in repeated controversy. Internationally, initial diplomatic contacts and
concerns generally focused on Europe, especially Great Britain, although they
also encompassed the United States. Elsewhere, the Far East was the only
geographical area of any significance to Peru until recent times, and interest
there was sporadic and concerned almost exclusively with immigration. Often
an emotional issue, repeated attempts to bring workers to Peru highlighted
early on traditionally close ties between external policy and internal economic
development.

As it did in many Latin American states, enhanced continental solidarity
dominated the diplomacy of Peru for much of the nineteenth century. Símon
Bolívar was a strong supporter of the movement, and although his Federation
of the Andes ultimately failed, the conventions concluded at the 1826 Panama
Conference included a treaty of union, league, and confederation. The
conference was the formal beginning of the movement for inter-American
cooperation, and although the meeting did not achieve its objectives, it was
significant that Peru participated in and supported the general direction of the
deliberations. On the other hand, Peruvian diplomacy at Panama drew
attention to the bifurcation of interests and concerns that characterized its
regional policies. In support of interdependence, Peruvian foreign relations
with its sister republics evidenced a feeling of kindred spirit and solidarity, if
not interest in formal union. On the side of independence, increasingly bitter
rivalries with neighbors over economic and territorial issues worked against
any centripetal tendency toward unity. A nascent state of Peruvian
nationalism, combined with the search for a sense of national unity,
preoccupied Peruvians throughout the nineteenth century, which further
complicated the issue. With the demise of the Peru-Bolivia Confederation,
the Peruvian government joined its neighbors in pursuing enhanced regional
cooperation outside the constraints of formal union, league, or confederation.
Although the agreements concluded at the 1847 Lima Conference included a

treaty of union and confederation, the Second Lima Conference in 1864 opted for a voluntary approach to continental union. In so doing, the conference marked a watershed in inter-American relations; it was the last time the American republics seriously pursued greater cooperation on the basis of confederation.

By the end of the century, Peru had joined its neighbors in setting aside the union issue in favor of increased emphasis on international law as a means to regulate regional affairs. The First Pan-American Conference in 1889 signaled a significant shift in the rationale behind the inter-American system. The movement tilted away from the somewhat idealistic aims of regional union and toward more practical, utilitarian objectives in areas like customs, trade, and procedures for the peaceful resolution of disputes. On the latter issue, the Tacna and Arica question dictated Peruvian policy, which advocated the application of compulsory arbitration to both pending and future disputes. The Peruvian government again supported compulsory arbitration at the 1901 Pan-American Conference, but the delegates eventually endorsed the principle of voluntary arbitration embodied in the 1899 Hague Convention. Nevertheless, Peru joined ten other participants at the end of the meeting in signing an agreement providing for compulsory arbitration. Although Peru also pressed for a discussion of obligatory arbitration at the 1909 Pan-American Conference, Chile succeeded in thwarting discussion of the topic. Thereafter, the Peruvian government continued to support the principle of juridical arbitration in public and private forums; nevertheless, its adherence to the principle was often more theoretical than practical.

Outside the region, Peru participated very selectively in multinational organizations and conferences. It joined the League of Nations in 1919 but quickly withdrew from active membership after Geneva refused to consider either the Tacna-Arica question or other issues of interest to the Latin American republics. Later, it joined the United Nations as well as regional bodies like the Organization of American States. The Peruvian government also became a regular participant in UN General Assembly debates and selected other UN activities like the Law of the Sea Conferences. At the same time, it joined the Latin American Free Trade Association, and later became an active participant in the subregional Andean Pact. For many Peruvians, this growing involvement in subregional, regional, and extraregional affairs was welcomed as an opportunity to reduce the overall influence of the United States. At the same time, wider participation in international bodies carried with it new restraints on political and economic autonomy.

Together with the issue of continental solidarity, territorial disputes and border conflicts plagued Peruvian diplomacy throughout the nineteenth century. Peru's fixation upon frontier issues is particularly noteworthy because it delayed development of broader external interests and concerns. The issues stemmed from the failure of Spain to delineate clearly its colonial possessions, as well as from the unsatisfactory resolution of local territorial disputes. They were further complicated by the commercial advantages at stake as the Andean nations quarreled initially over trade routes and seaports and later over guano and nitrate deposits, rubber wealth, and petroleum reserves. Ideological differences frequently intensified such conflicts, as did concern for regional hegemony. Even today, Peruvian foreign policy toward Chile remains heavily influenced by considerations of national power and prestige. Peru's emphasis on these matters differed little from that of its neighbors—most South American states put a high priority on the delineation of postindependence boundaries. Peruvian territorial concerns focused on the Amazon Basin with Ecuador and Colombia, the Eastern March with Brazil, and the Atacama Desert with Bolivia and Chile. In the middle of the twentieth century, the continental shelf and insular sea became a fourth area of geopolitical interest. Most recently, the Peruvian government has viewed the continent of Antarctica, where it has pressed for a wider range of rights and obligations, as a new arena of geopolitical competition.

Often condemned, the final territorial settlements concluded by Peru produced reasonable results that maintained the territorial essence of the republic. The tendency in Peru has been to emphasize ground lost as opposed to ground retained, but the government in reality has negotiated away very little of its patrimony. The Brazilian and Colombian settlements involved the loss of some territory, but it was largely land over which Peru lacked definitive legal or other claims. On the other hand, very little ground was ceded to Bolivia. In the case of Ecuador, Peru retained possession of most of the disputed territory and ended up with much more land than it had been awarded in the abortive 1910 Spanish arbitration. From this perspective, most of the territory lost by Peru has been the result of interstate conflict, in particular the War of the Pacific, as opposed to any alleged or real shortcomings of Peruvian diplomacy.

As for the order of settlement, the first priority of the Peruvian government was Chile, the most politically sensitive of the issues, while Ecuador, the weakest antagonist, was relegated to last place. With Chile firmly in control of Tacna and Arica, Peruvian procrastination only hurt its cause. In the Oriente, on the other hand, it was Peru that had long occupied most of the disputed territory and thus could best afford to delay a settlement. With all of the disputes, the government supported arbitration; however, policy was much more complicated than most Peruvian observers have been willing to acknowledge. In the case of Chile, Peru agreed to a juridical arbitration; but its presentation to the arbitrator stressed extralegal arguments. In the disputes with Colombia and Ecuador, Peru again insisted on a juridical arbitration; but it later employed both legal and extralegal arguments in support of the general principle of *uti possidetis*. When arbitration failed to produce an acceptable settlement, the government finally resorted to personal diplomacy to resolve both disputes.

National economic growth has been an important objective of the Peruvian government since independence and was the last major focus of early Peruvian foreign policy. With few exceptions, Peruvian governments after 1824 embraced a policy of export-led growth. When demand was strong and prices were high, the results of this approach were generally positive. When the reverse occurred, its pursuit highlighted the real constraints that the world economic system placed on national independence. Reliance on export-led growth left the nation highly vulnerable to the vagaries of international economic cycles, with inevitable consequences for the national economy. Cycles of debt, dependence, and default occurred in the 1820s, 1870s, 1930s, and 1980s. Successive Peruvian governments, including most recently the García administration, portrayed each of these periodic debt crises as unique, unfortunate, and unfair, but they formed part of a pattern that began immediately after independence and recurred at fifty-year intervals.

From the beginning, the export-led nature of the Peruvian economy meant that trade policy would have a major influence on foreign policy. Early trade policies were both impulsive and intimately bound to regional rivalries, and they were often a source of conflict and controversy. This was frequently reflected in relations with neighboring Bolivia, Brazil, Chile, and Ecuador as all parties maneuvered aggressively for commercial advantage. Economic policies were equally important to Peruvian links with extracontinental powers like England and the United States. Investment and trade remained central Peruvian concerns throughout the nineteenth century, with claims being a decidedly secondary source of diplomatic interchange. In the twentieth century, the importance of economic, financial, and trade policies to foreign policy took on new dimensions. Successive governments attached a high priority to economic growth, but to achieve this goal, they needed to stay on reasonable terms with the power brokers in the industrialized states because only they could provide the requisite capital. This involved maintaining an acceptable relationship with the international business and financial community. It also required Peru to preserve good relations with the US government to forestall any efforts to deny Peru full access to international lending agencies.

The United States has been involved in Peru from the first days of the republic, but both its early focus and its initial influence were limited. Once Washington had granted diplomatic recognition in 1826, its envoys pressed for payment of the damage claims presented by US citizens. The ensuing controversy, which took five decades to conclude, dominated diplomatic exchange. By the 1840s, the Amazon Basin had become an object of romantic and commercial interest for many North Americans, and it was due in part to pressure from Washington that Brazil and Peru later opened their rivers to the vessels of all nations. The Peruvian guano boom of the mid-nineteenth century also stimulated much international interest and involvement by a variety of governments, including the United States.

During the War of the Pacific, Peru was repeatedly frustrated by US policy because it expected far stronger diplomatic support than Washington proved willing to provide.

Upon conclusion of the 1887 treaty of friendship, navigation, and commerce, Peru's diplomatic relations with the United States steadily improved. In part, the change was based on a more mature understanding by both of their respective strengths and mutual interests in South America. It was also encouraged by growing North American participation in the expanding Peruvian economy. Peruvians both in and out of government continued to look to the United States for support and protection. As Peruvian foreign policy concentrated on boundary disputes, the recovery of Tacna and Arica, and the continuation of economic recovery, successive governments in Lima generally supported the US position on regional and international issues. Although seldom discussed openly, Peruvian policy in this regard was founded on the assumption it would boost US support for local foreign policy questions. Based on experience, it appeared very unrealistic for a subregional power of limited means like Peru to approach the United States, which was rapidly becoming a major world power, on what amounted to a quid-pro-quo basis. Prior to the War of the Pacific, a similar policy had proved disastrous for Peru; in the first decade of the twentieth century, it offered new potential for misunderstanding and disappointment.

In other ways as well, Peruvian foreign policy in the two decades after the War of the Pacific appeared driven by contradictory objectives. Concerned with economic recovery, civilian governments desired a speedy resolution to all territorial issues and boundary disputes, even if the final solutions involved some sacrifice of territory, because active disputes clouded the business climate and threatened to sabotage economic recovery. On the other hand, the same governments, concerned with maximum utilization of national resources, placed a strong emphasis on preserving the national patrimony, especially when disputed areas were thought to contain valuable economic resources. When these two objectives came into direct conflict, government critics argued that the former often exerted more influence on government policy than the latter.

By the beginning of World War I, the Peruvian economy had begun to move out of the sphere of European trade and investment; this process accelerated during the *oncenio*. Throughout the 1920s, the bulk of Peruvian loans were floated in the United States, and by 1929 US financial interests nearly monopolized certain sectors of the economy, such as copper and vanadium mining, petroleum production, and communications. The Leguía administration welcomed growing US economic involvement because it helped turn Peru into a modern capitalist nation. Initially, the Peruvian populace also welcomed increased political and economic involvement by the United States, but by 1930 attitudes were changing, largely because the

United States was again proving unable to fulfill high expectations. March 4, 1925, the date of the Coolidge award and the Brazilian *procès-verbal,* is often cited as a symbolic turning point for Peruvian opinion; those agreements combined to dispel the illusions of most Peruvians as to the power and concerns of the US government.

The level of ideological debate also intensified as the century progressed and increasingly affected both foreign and domestic policies. For the first time, political leaders attempted to construct a political order responsive to the needs and demands of all Peruvians. But as politics grew to be more and more a contest of styles and strategies, there was less and less agreement on the rules of the game and no concept of a loyal opposition. As a result, politics became less the art of compromise and more an internecine war in which little quarter was expected or given. The Aprista movement began a long-term, influential involvement in Peruvian politics that eventually carried it to the presidential palace. Equally important, the armed forces began to explore new approaches to the socioeconomic and political development of the nation, a process that had important repercussions in the more immediate future.

By the early 1960s, the social, economic, military, and political dependence of Peru on the United States had reached a dangerous level, which often led Peruvian leaders to support Washington's political objectives. This circumstance was the result of internal factors, forces, and interests, as well as the pursuit by the United States of its own economic, political, and military objectives. In any case, the position of the United States in Peru was rendered more and more paradoxical. As postwar US foreign policy heightened the awareness of both governments of the complexity of their interests and relations, a growing number of Peruvians increasingly distrusted the United States and resented its extensive presence in significant aspects of Peruvian internal and external affairs. The conflicting demands of postwar nationalism and the need for continued cooperation with the United States to achieve many of Peru's foreign and domestic policy goals contributed to a growing ambiguity in a complex, total relationship.

In turn, the United States saw Peru, as well as the rest of Latin America, as falling within a highly sensitive security zone. For this reason, Peruvian foreign policy, despite Peru's formal sovereignty, was effectively constrained by the bounds of US tolerance. This left the Peruvian government free to follow any policy it desired as long as its actions did not affect the security interests of the United States as defined by Washington. For the first half of this century, Lima successfully accommodated itself to these restrictions; however, in the 1960s, a combination of developments in Peru posed an entirely new challenge for Washington. Peruvian diplomacy took major steps in the direction of geographical diversification, multilateral diplomacy, and ideological pluralism. As part of this reorientation, the security goals of the Peruvian state underwent a thoroughgoing redefinition. Threat perceptions continued to play an important role in the foreign policy process, but a central objective became one of mobilizing external resources for internal economic development. Security considerations were increasingly defined in nonmilitary as well as military terms. More and more, issues like poverty, population growth, food insecurity, and the failure of development efforts lay at the heart of Peruvian security concerns. Hampered by limited resources, Peru, like many smaller nations, relied on legal instruments and moral arguments as well as economic means to maximize its political influence. At the same time, it reordered defense requirements and rethought arms-sourcing policies.

The resultant conflict between Peru and the United States drew attention to the asymmetrical nature of their relationship. Because of its size, power, and location, the United States has long loomed large on the Peruvian horizon. Especially in this century, diplomatic and economic relations with the United States have been a principal concern of every Peruvian government and a matter of interest to almost every Peruvian citizen. Commercially and politically, any move made in Washington or New York could have and often has had a major impact on Peru. Viewed from the opposite direction, of course, the case is quite different. Since independence, Washington has generally viewed Peru as a relatively remote and unimportant country. Relations with Peru have rarely had any significant influence on US foreign or domestic policy, and they have seldom gained the attention of the US public. Consequently, what was good for Peru not only was not necessarily good for the United States, but it often was of no interest to the United States. The failure of Peruvians to understand these differing perspectives has repeatedly led them to expect too much from US policy.

This observation is especially relevant to a discussion of international economic policy. For most of this century, Peru's interest in the United States has been more economic than political or related to security. Peruvian exports and imports were oriented toward North America, and Washington was often an actual or potential source of trade advantage. Moreover, the United States remained Peru's primary source of capital and technology; its government, corporations, and financial institutions played an important intermediary role in obtaining international resources. From this perspective, it is hardly surprising that questions of internal economic growth and development have remained much more important to Peru than international issues like the conflict in Indochina or the cold war. The overriding importance of domestic well-being also helps explain the growing role of government institutions like the central bank and the finance ministry in the external relations of Third World states like Peru.

US influence has grown since the turn of the century, but it has not been the only new external force affecting Peru's foreign policy. International actors other than nation-states have played increasingly important roles. For example, multinational corporations like Cerro de Pasco, W. R. Grace &

Company, and the International Petroleum Company became more and more influential. They intervened directly and indirectly in both internal and external affairs, and regardless of their motives or concerns, their collective actions were deeply resented by the Peruvian people. As a result, the policies of the multinationals contributed directly to the growth of Peruvian nationalism and to the increased politicization of the political system after 1930. With Peruvian public finance moving from crisis to crisis, the International Monetary Fund and the international banking community have also impacted on Peruvian foreign policy. In part because their interventions generally occurred during critical periods, their involvement was also often a source of resentment. More recently, a host of other international bodies, including the United Nations, the Organization of American States, the Andean Pact, and the Non-Aligned Movement, have also played a role in determining the content and emphasis of Peruvian external policies.

Even so, the foreign policy of Peru has remained closely tied to domestic forces, structures, and policies. With violence an integral part of the Peruvian political system, internal conflict has long disrupted external policy—the latter often being largely a reflection of the former. The sustained influence of forces like militarism, caudillismo, and ideology has also been mentioned. As new political movements and forces developed, a growing number of actors participated in the political system and influenced the direction and content of the nation's foreign policy. Peruvian exporters in league with the armed forces generally dictated the central tenets of foreign policy in the nineteenth century; important contemporary domestic actors have included labor federations, new political parties, and the state bureaucracy. The legislature has also played a long-term role, which was first evidenced under Castilla. More recently, Aprista-dominated congresses strongly affected the administrations of first Bustamante and then Belaúnde. All of these domestic forces and organizations continue to bear upon the nation's foreign policy, together with totally new ones like international drug syndicates and insurgent groups like the Sendero Luminoso and the Tupac Amaru Revolutionary Movement.

Critical dialogue and debate in the 1960s, which centered on the external constraints and impositions of international capitalism on Third World states, culminated in what came to be known loosely as dependency theory. In the preceding analysis, the author has deliberately avoided any direct critique of the dependency approach both because it is beyond the limits of this study and because that body of literature, when applied to the Peruvian case, is deceiving on descriptive and explanatory grounds. Since 1824 a wide variety of factors have influenced the external affairs of Peru at different times in a multitude of ways. The external constraints and impositions of international capitalism were one of the forces that shaped foreign policy after independence, but they seldom were the decisive causal force even in periods of maximum influence. Consequently, the concentration of an approach like dependency theory on a single theme, pattern, or system is clearly inadequate to account for the history of Peru's foreign policy or its future direction and emphasis. For this reason, any attempt to convey the content and direction of Peru's foreign policy as a reflection of the capitalist world system appears to be both one-dimensional and misleading.

On the other hand, there is a strong correlation between size and foreign policy capabilities in the Peruvian case. In terms of geographical area, Peru is the largest state on the west coast of South America, and the third-largest state in South America. It is almost twice the size of Chile and a little less than five times the size of Ecuador. It is approximately twice the size of Texas and equal to the combined areas of France, Spain, and the United Kingdom. In terms of population and natural resources, it compares favorably with its neighbors. Guano and nitrates were the dominant exports in the middle of the last century, but considerable agricultural potential later developed, with coffee, cotton, and sugar cane becoming important export crops. Mineral resources include copper, lead, zinc, and silver. The country also produces much iron ore and petroleum, and ranks among the world's leading fishing countries.

Topography, climate, and the lack of certain raw materials have presented formidable obstacles to the effective growth of Peruvian power. The concentration of the population in coastal areas, especially in the megalopolis of Lima-Callao, and the disjunction of the interior by the Andes range and dense forests of the Amazon Basin have inhibited national integration. In addition, large tracts of Peru are covered either by inaccessible, barely habitable jungle or dry, rugged desert. The overall energy situation remains precarious because known petroleum reserves, many of which are located in inhospitable regions, are not adequate to satisfy national needs. In terms of scope and direction, the foreign policy of Peru has focused on regional actors and issues, and its alliance politics have centered on its neighbors as opposed to international powers. Moreover, it has often found it difficult to influence external events, but its own domestic structures have proved sensitive to actions taken by outside centers of decisionmaking authority. In these respects, Peru is a relatively small state whose historical position has generally been as impressive as its geopolitical attributes seem to warrant.

In conclusion, Peruvian foreign policy after 1824 was strongly influenced by a variety of internal and external forces that made it difficult to confront successfully the often conflicting demands of independence and interdependence. In the beginning, the struggle centered on whether Peru would remain a sovereign state or be incorporated into a subregional grouping. Later, it focused on a successful adjustment to the obligations and limitations of enhanced regional interdependence. Most recently, Peru has taken advantage of reduced global bipolarity to expand its social, political, and economic ties, and it has participated actively in a novel attempt at subregional integration. In addition, the government has played an increasingly active role in a wide variety of Third World organizations whose common interests include the creation of an alternative world order that they believe will lead to greater justice, increased participation, and more equality. This wider involvement in the international system, commonly viewed in Peru as an expression of self-determination, has imposed unexpected new constraints on freedom of action. In this sense, it simply marks a new chapter in the prolonged Peruvian struggle to adjust to an ever-changing set of background influences as it seeks to moderate the often incompatible demands of national sovereignty and international solidarity.

Bibliography

GOVERNMENT AND OTHER DOCUMENTS

Chile. Ministerio de Relaciones Exteriores. *La cuestión chileno-peruana.* Santiago: La Penitenciaria, 1919.

Chile. Ministerio de Relaciones Exteriores. *La cuestión chileno-peruana. El debate diplomático de 1918.* Santiago: Imprenta Universitaria, 1919.

Chile. Ministerio de Relaciones Exteriores. *La cuestión de Tacna y Arica: Respuesta del Ministro de Relaciones Exteriores de Chile a las declaraciones de la cancillería peruana.* Oruro: Antonio Alba López, 1919.

Chile. Ministerio de Relaciones Exteriores. *El debate diplomático de 1918.* Santiago: Imprenta Universitaria, 1919.

Chile. Ministerio de Relaciones Exteriores. *Tacna-Arica Arbitration. The Appendix to the Case of the Republic of Chile Submitted to the President of the United States as Arbitrator.* Washington, D.C.: n.p., 1923.

Chile. Ministerio de Relaciones Exteriores. *Tacna-Arica Arbitration: The Appendix to the Counter-Case of the Republic of Chile Submitted to the President of the United States as Arbitrator.* Washington, D.C.: n.p., 1924.

Chile. Ministerio de Relaciones Exteriores. *Tacna-Arica Arbitration: The Case of the Republic of Chile Submitted to the President of the United States as Arbitrator.* Washington, D.C.: n.p., 1923.

Chile. Ministerio de Relaciones Exteriores. *Tacna-Arica Arbitration: The Counter-Case of the Republic of Chile Submitted to the President of the United States as Arbitrator.* Washington, D.C.: n.p., 1923.

Chile. Ministerio de Relaciones Exteriores. *Tacna-Arica Arbitration: Notes on the Peruvian Case and Appendix Submitted with the Counter-Case of the Republic of Chile to the President of the United States as Arbitrator.* Washington, D.C.: n.p., 1924.

Chile. Ministerio de Relaciones Exteriores. *Tacna-Arica fallo arbitral.* Santiago: Imprenta Chile, 1925.

Colombia. Legación España. *Un gran triunfo de Colombia. Documentos publicados por la legación de Colombia en España.* Madrid: Imprenta de Juan Pueyo, 1923.

Colombia. Ministerio de Relaciones Exteriores. *El conflicto de Leticia.* Bogotá: Editorial Minerva, 1934.

Colombia. Ministerio de Relaciones Exteriores. *Documentos sobre el protocolo de Rio de Janeiro*. Bogotá: Imprenta Nacional, 1934.

Colombia. Senado de la República. *Debate del protocolo en el senado. Informe de la comisión de relaciones exteriores y discursos del presidente de la comisión doctor José Joaquin Caicedo Castilla*. Bogotá: Imprenta Nacional, 1936.

Colombia. Senado de la República. *Informe de la comisión de relaciones exteriores del senado, relativo al protocolo de Rio de Janeiro*. Bogotá: Imprenta Nacional, 1935.

Colombia. Senado de la República. *Para la historia. El conflicto con el Perú en el parlamento*. Bogotá: Santafe, 1934.

Colombia. Senado de la República. *La soberanía de Colombia en el Putumayo*. Bogotá: Imprenta Nacional, 1912.

Ecuador. Ministerio de Relaciones Exteriores. *Cuestión de límites con el Perú*. Quito: Imprenta y Encuadernación Nacionales, 1910.

Ecuador. Ministerio de Relaciones Exteriores. *Exposición del Ministerio de Relaciones Exteriores del Ecuador a las cancillerías de América*. 2d ed. Quito: Imprenta del Ministerio de Gobierno, 1941.

Ecuador. Ministerio de Relaciones Exteriores. *El memorándum final del Perú: Contramemorándum de Honorato Vázquez*. Madrid: "Sucesores de Rivadeneyra," 1909.

Ecuador. Ministerio de Relaciones Exteriores. *Memorándum para el Ministerio de Relaciones Exteriores de la República del Ecuador por Honorato Vázquez*. Madrid: "Sucesores de Rivadeneyra," 1907.

Ecuador. Ministerio de Relaciones Exteriores. *Las negociaciones ecuatoriano-peruanos en Washington agosto 1937–octubre 1938*. Quito: Imprenta del Ministerio de Gobierno, 1938.

Ecuador. Ministerio de Relaciones Exteriores. *Las negociaciones ecuatoriano-peruanos en Washington setiembre 1936–julio 1937*. Quito: Imprenta del Ministerio de Gobierno, 1937.

Ecuador. Ministerio de Relaciones Exteriores. *Negociaciones limítrofes ecuatoriano-peruanos. El Ecuador insiste en su proposición de someter el litigio al arbitraje total de derecho, 30 de agosto de 1938*. Quito: Imprenta del Ministerio de Gobierno, 1938.

Ecuador. Ministerio de Relaciones Exteriores. *Protocolo firmado en Quito por los Excelentisimos Señores Doctor Don N. Clemente Ponce, Ministro de Relaciones Exteriores del Ecuador, y Don Enrique Castro Oyanguren, Enviado Extraordinario y Ministro Plenipotenciario del Perú*. Quito: Talleres Tipográficos Nacionales, 1935.

League of Nations. *Treaty Series: Publication of Treaties and International Engagements Registered with the Secretariat of the League of Nations*. 205 vols. Various publishers, various years.

Peru. Cámara de Diputados. *Asambles Nacional de 1919: Discursos oficiales*. Lima: Imprenta Torres Aguirre, 1920.

Peru. Cámara de Diputados. Roberto Mac-Lean y Estenos. *Discursos parlamentarios*. Lima: Librería e Imprenta Gil, 1943.

Peru. Ministerio de Guerra. *Biblioteca militar del oficial no. 31: estudio de la cuestión de límites entre el Perú y el Ecuador*. Lima: Imprenta del Ministerio de Guerra, 1961.

Peru. Ministerio de Relaciones Exteriores. *Alegato del Perú en el arbitraje sobre sus límites con el Ecuador presentado a S. M. el árbitro la reina regente de España por D. José Pardo y Barreda.* Madrid: Imprenta de los hijos de M. G. Hernández, 1905.

Peru. Ministerio de Relaciones Exteriores. *Arbitraje de Tacna y Arica: Documentos de la Comision Especial de Límites.* Vol. 1. Lima: "La Opinión Nacional," 1926.

Peru. Ministerio de Relaciones Exteriores. *Arbitration Between Peru and Chile: Appendix to the Case of Peru in the Matter of the Controversy Arising out of the Question of the Pacific.* Washington, D.C.: n.p., 1923.

Peru. Ministerio de Relaciones Exteriores. *Arbitration Between Peru and Chile: Appendix to the Counter-Case of Peru in the Matter of the Controversy Arising Out of the Question of the Pacific.* Washington, D.C.: n.p., 1924.

Peru. Ministerio de Relaciones Exteriores. *Arbitration Between Peru and Chile: The Case of Peru in the Matter of the Controversy Arising Out of the Question of the Pacific.* Washington, D.C.: n.p., 1923.

Peru. Ministerio de Relaciones Exteriores. *Arbitration Between Peru and Chile: The Counter-Case of Peru in the Matter Arising Out of the Question of the Pacific.* Washington, D.C.: n.p., 1924.

Peru. Ministerio de Relaciones Exteriores. *Arbitration Between Peru and Chile: The Memorial of Peru and the Ruling and Observations of the Arbitrator.* Washington, D.C.: n.p., 1925.

Peru. Ministerio de Relaciones Exteriores. *Boletín del Ministerio de Relaciones Exteriores.* Various publishers, various years.

Peru. Ministerio de Relaciones Exteriores. *Circulares diplomáticas.* Lima: Imprenta Americana, 1919.

Peru. Ministerio de Relaciones Exteriores. *Colección de los tratados, capitulaciones, armisticios y otros actos diplomáticos y políticos celebrado desde la independencia hasta el día. Publicación oficial del ministerio de relaciones exteriores.* 14 vols. Lima: Imprenta del Estado, 1890–1919.

Peru. Ministerio de Relaciones Exteriores. *Conferencia de Washington para el arreglo de la cuestión de límites entre el Perú y el Ecuador. Proposición presentada por la delegación del Perú a la delegación del Ecuador en la sesión del 30 de junio de 1937.* Washington, D.C.: n.p., 1937.

Peru. Ministerio de Relaciones Exteriores. *Conferencia de Washington para la cuestión de límites entre el Perú y el Ecuador. Replica de la delegación peruana a la contraproposición ecuatoriana del 9 de agosto de 1937.* Washington, D.C.: n.p., 1937.

Peru. Ministerio de Relaciones Exteriores. *Correspondencia diplomática con Colombia sobre el incidente de Leticia.* Lima: Tipografías de la Escuela de la Guardia Civil y Policía, 1933.

Peru. Ministerio de Relaciones Exteriores. *La cuestión de límites entre el Perú y el Ecuador.* New York: n.p., 1937.

Peru. Ministerio de Relaciones Exteriores. *Documentos relativos a la conferencia perú-ecuatoriana de Washington.* Lima: Talleres Gráficos de la Editorial "Lumen," 1938.

Peru. Ministerio de Relaciones Exteriores. *Documentos relativos al plebiscito de Tacna y Arica.* 7 vols. Lima: various publishers, 1926–1928.

Peru. Ministerio de Relaciones Exteriores. *Documentos oficiales relativos al problema de Tacna y Arica.* Lima: Talleres Tipográficos de la Prensa, 1925.

Peru. Ministerio de Relaciones Exteriores. *Exposición documentada sobre el estado actual del problema del Pacífico.* Lima: Imprenta Torres Aguirre, 1921.

Peru. Ministerio de Relaciones Exteriores. *Exposición del Ministro de Relaciones Exteriores del Perú, Dr. Alfredo Solf y Muro, a las Cancillerías de América.* Lima: n.p., 1941.

Peru. Ministerio de Relaciones Exteriores. *Memoria del Relaciones Exteriores del Perú.* Lima: various publishers, various years.

Peru. Ministerio de Relaciones Exteriores. *El Perú y su política exterior.* Lima: Empresa Editora del Diario Oficial "El Peruano," n.d.

Peru. Ministerio de Relaciones Exteriores. *El proceso de Tacna y Arica (1925–1927).* Lima: Casa Editora "La Opinión Nacional," 1927.

Peru. Ministerio de Relaciones Exteriores. *Protocolo Peruano-Ecuatoriano de Paz, Amistad y Límites.* Lima: Tipografía Peruana, 1967.

Peru. Ministerio de Relaciones Exteriores. *El protocolo Salomón-Lozano o el pacto de límites con Colombia.* Lima: Sanmarti, 1927.

Peru. Ministerio de Relaciones Exteriores. *The Question of the Boundaries Between Peru and Ecuador: A Historical Outline Covering the Period Since 1910.* Baltimore: Reese Press, 1936.

Peru. Ministerio de Relaciones Exteriores. *The Question of the Boundaries Between Peru and Ecuador: Reply of the Peruvian Delegation to the Ecuadorian Document of August 9.* Baltimore: Reese Press, 1937.

Peru. Ministerio de Relaciones Exteriores. *The Question of the Boundaries Between Peru and Ecuador. Statement of the Peruvian Delegation to the Washington Conference Concerning the Scope of the Boundary Negotiations with Ecuador, in Accordance with the Protocol of the 21st of June, 1924, Within the Historical-Juridical Process of the Controversy.* Baltimore: Reese Press, 1937.

Peru. Ministerio de Relaciones Exteriores. *Réplica a la circular de la cancillería chilena: 12 de enero de 1919.* Lima: Imprenta Americana, 1919.

Peru. Ministerio de Relaciones Exteriores. *Résumé of the Historical-Juridical Proceedings of the Boundary Question Between Peru and Ecuador.* Washington, D.C.: n.p., 1937.

Peru. Ministerio de Relaciones Exteriores. *El tratado Salomón-Lozano y la cuestión de Leticia.* Lima: San Cristóbal, 1932.

Peru. Ministerio de Relaciones Exteriores. *Tratados, Convenciones, y Acuerdos vigentes entre el Perú y otros Estados.* 2 vols. Lima: Imprenta Torres Aguirre, 1936.

Peru. Presidente. *Mensaje del Presidente de la República.* 40 vols. Lima: various publishers, 1900–1946.

United States of America. Department of Commerce. Foreign Broadcast Information Service. *Daily Report: Latin America (FBIS-LAM).* 1978–1989.

United States of America. Department of Commerce. Office of Technical Services. *Joint Publications Research Service (JPRS).* 1980–1989.

United States of America. Department of State. *Foreign Relations of the United States.* Washington, D.C.: Government Printing Office, various years.

United States of America. Executive. *In the Matter of the Arbitration Between the Republic of Chile and the Republic of Peru, With Respect to the Unfulfilled*

Provisions of the Treaty of Peace of October 20, 1883, Under the Protocol and Supplementary Act Signed at Washington July 20, 1922. Opinion and Award of the Arbitrator. Washington, D.C.: Government Printing Office, 1925.

UNPUBLISHED MATERIALS

Ciccarelli, Orazio A. "The Sánchez Cerro Regimes in Peru, 1930–1933." Ph.D. diss., University of Florida, 1969.

Cortada, James W. "Conflict Diplomacy: United States–Spanish Relations, 1855–1868." Ph.D. diss., Florida State University, 1973.

Crosby, Kenneth Ward. "The Diplomacy of the United States in Relation to the War of the Pacific, 1879–1884." Ph.D. diss., George Washington University, 1949.

Davidson, John Leslie. "The Impact of U.S. Arms Transfer Policies on Relations with Peru: 1945–1978." Master's thesis, North Texas State University, 1979.

Flores, Pastoriza. "History of the Boundary Dispute Between Ecuador and Peru." Ph.D. diss., Columbia University, 1921.

Gerlach, Allen. "Civil-Military Relations in Peru: 1914–1945." Ph.D. diss., University of New Mexico, 1973.

Gleason, Daniel Michael. "Ideological Cleavages in Early Republican Peru, 1821–1872." Ph.D. diss., University of Notre Dame, 1974.

Karno, Howard Laurence. "Augusto B. Leguía: The Oligarchy and the Modernization of Peru, 1870–1930." Ph.D. diss., University of California, Los Angeles, 1970.

Kuo, Ding Wu. "Peru's Foreign Policy: Ends and Means, 1945–1968." Ph.D. diss., Tulane University, 1969.

Maiguascha, Juan. "A Reinterpretation of the Guano Age, 1840–1880." Ph.D. diss., Oxford University, 1967.

Martinez, Arthur D. "The United States–Peruvian Territorial Waters Controversy: Juridical, Political, Economic, and Strategic Considerations." Ph.D. diss., University of California, Riverside, 1974.

McArver, Charles Harper, Jr. "Mining and Diplomacy: United States Interests at Cerro de Pasco, Peru, 1876–1930." Ph.D. diss., University of North Carolina, 1977.

McNicoll, Robert Edwards. "Peruvian-American Relations in the Era of the Civilist Party." Ph.D. diss., Duke University, 1937.

Mendoza, Rosa Garibaldi De. "Peru and the Policy of Hemispheric Defense Under Ramón Castilla, 1845–62." Ph.D. diss., Temple University, 1979.

Nolan, Louis Clinton. "The Diplomatic and Commercial Relations of the United States and Peru, 1826–1875." Ph.D. diss., Duke University, 1935.

Olinger, John Peter. "Dreyfus Freres, Guano and Peruvian Government Finance: 1869–1880. A Chapter in Economic Imperialism." Ph.D. diss., State University of New York at Binghamton, 1973.

Page, A. Nayland. "United States Diplomacy in the Tacna-Arica Dispute, 1884–1929." Ph.D. diss., University of Oklahoma, 1958.

Parkerson, Phillip Taylor. "Sub-Regional Integration in Nineteenth Century

South America: Andres Santa Cruz and the Peru-Bolivia Confederation, 1835–1839." Ph.D. diss., University of Florida, 1979.

Peterson, Dale William. "The Diplomatic and Commercial Relations Between the United States and Peru from 1883 to 1918." Ph.D. diss., University of Minnesota, 1969.

Phillips, Richard Snyder, Jr. "Bolivia in the War of the Pacific, 1879–1884." Ph.D. diss., University of Virginia, 1973.

St John, Ronald Bruce. "Peruvian Foreign Policy, 1919–1939: The Delimitation of Frontiers." Ph.D. diss., University of Denver, 1970.

Soder, John Phillip, Jr. "The Impact of the Tacna-Arica Dispute on the Pan-American Movement." Ph.D. diss., Georgetown University, 1970.

Wilson, Joe Foster. "An Evaluation of the Failure of the Tacna-Arica Plebiscitary Commission, 1925–1926." Ph.D. diss., University of Georgia, Athens, 1965.

Worrall, Janet Evelyn. "Italian Immigration to Peru: 1860–1914." Ph.D. diss., Indiana University, 1972.

BOOKS AND MONOGRAPHS

Albert, Bill. *South America and the First World War: The impact of the war on Brazil, Argentina, Peru and Chile.* Cambridge: Cambridge University Press, 1988.

Alessandri, Arturo. *Recuerdos de Gobierno.* 3 vols. Santiago: Editorial Nascimento, 1967.

Anna, Timothy E. *The Fall of the Royal Government in Peru.* Lincoln: University of Nebraska Press, 1979.

Arana, Julio César. *El protocolo Salomón-Lozano o el Pacto de Límites con Colombia.* Lima: Sanmarti y Compañía, 1927.

Araujo Arana, Humberto. *Conflicto fronterizo Peru-Colombia, Año 1932–1933.* 3 vols. Lima: Talleres de Litografía Huascarán, 1965.

Arguedas, Alcides. *Historia de Bolivia.* 5 vols. La Paz: Librería Editorial "Juventud," 1981.

Arias Schreiber, Diómedes. *Exposición sobre los motivos jurídicos que justifican la revisión del Tratado de Límites celebrado por el Perú y Colombia el 24 de marzo de 1922.* Lima: E. B. y B. Sucesor, 1933.

Arona, Juan de [Pedro Paz Soldán y Unanue]. *Páginas diplomáticas del Perú.* 2d ed. Lima: Talleres Gráficas P. L. Villanueva, 1968.

Arróspide de la Flor, César, et al. *Perú: Identidad nacional.* Lima: Ediciones CEDEP, 1979.

Arroyo Delgado, Enrique. *Las Negociaciones limítrofes Ecuatoriano-Peruanas en Washington.* Quito: Editoriad de "El Comercio," 1939.

Auguste, Barry B.L. *The Continental Shelf: The Practice and Policy of the Latin American States with Special Reference to Chile, Ecuador and Peru.* Geneva: Librairie E. Droz, 1960.

Barra, Felipe de la. *Tumbes, Jaén y Maynas.* Lima: Los Talleres Gráficos del Diet, 1961.

Barrenechea y Raygada, Oscar. *El congreso de Panamá, 1826.* Lima: Ministerio de

Relaciones Exteriores, 1942.

Barrenechea y Raygada, Oscar. *Congresos y conferencias internacionales celebrados en Lima, 1847–1894.* Buenos Aires: Peuser, 1947.

Barros Borgoño, Luis. *La cuestión del Pacífico y las nuevas orientaciones de Bolivia.* Santiago: Imprenta Universitaria, 1922.

Basadre, Jorge. *Chile, Perú y Bolivia independientes.* Barcelona: Salvat Editores, 1948.

Basadre, Jorge. *Historia de la república del Perú, 1822–1933.* 6th ed. 16 vols. Lima: Editorial Universitaria, 1968.

Basadre, Jorge. *Sultanismo, corrupción y dependencia en el Perú republicano.* Lima: Editorial Milla Batres, 1979.

Basadre y Chocano, Modesto. *Diez años de historia política del Perú (1834–1844).* Lima: Editorial Huascarán, 1953.

Basile, Clemente. *Una Guerra poca conocida.* 2 vols. Buenos Aires: Círculo Militar, 1943.

Bautista de Laballe, Juan. *El Perú y la Gran Guerra.* Lima: Imprenta Americana, 1919.

Belaúnde, Víctor Andrés. *Bolivar and the Political Thought of the Spanish American Revolution.* Baltimore: Johns Hopkins University Press, 1938.

Belaúnde, Víctor Andrés. *La realidad nacional.* Paris: "Le Livre Libre," 1931.

Belaúnde, Víctor Andrés. *La vida internacional del Perú.* Lima: Imprenta Torres Aguirre, 1942.

Bello C., Emilio. *Anotaciones para la historia de las negociaciones diplomáticas con el Perú y Bolivia, 1900–1904.* Santiago: La Ilustración, 1919.

Bemis, Samuel Flagg. *The Latin American Policy of the United States: An Interpretation.* New York: Harcourt, Brace and Company, 1943.

Benavides de Peña, Paquita, et al. *El Mariscal Benavides: Su Vida y Su Obra.* 2 vols. Lima: Imprenta Editora Atlántida, 1976–1981.

Bonilla, Heraclio, ed. *Gran Bretaña y el Perú: Informes de los cónsules británicos: 1826–1919.* 5 vols. Lima: Instituto de Estudios Peruanos, 1975.

Bonilla, Heraclio. *Guano y Burguesía en el Perú.* Lima: Instituto de Estudios Peruanos, 1974.

Bonilla, Heraclio, et al. *La independencia en el Perú.* 2d ed. Lima: Instituto de Estudios Peruanos, 1981.

Bonilla, Heraclio. *Un siglo a la deriva: ensayos sobre el Perú, Bolivia y la guerra.* Lima: Instituto de Estudios Peruanos, 1980.

Bourricaud, Francois. *Power and Society in Contemporary Peru.* London: Faber and Faber, 1970.

Bracamonte y Orbegoso, Alvaro de. *Leguía: Su vida y su obra.* Lima: n.p., 1953.

Burga, Manuel, and Alberto Flores Galindo. *Apogeo y crisis de la república aristocrática.* 2d ed. Lima: Ediciones Rikchay Perú, 1981.

Burr, Robert N. *By Reason or Force: Chile and the Balancing of Power in South America, 1830–1905.* Berkeley and Los Angeles: University of California Press, 1965.

Bustamante y Rivero, José Luis. *Tres años de lucha por la democracia en el Perú.* Buenos Aires: Artes Gráficas, 1949.

Cabeza de Vaca, Manuel. *Aspectos históricos y jurídicos de la cuestión limítrofe: las negociaciones en Washington y los desenvolvimientos posteriores.* Quito:

Talleres Gráficos Nacionales, 1956.

Cabeza de Vaca, Manuel. *La posición del Ecuador en el conflicto colombo-peruano*. Quito: Talleres Gráficos Nacionales, 1934.

Camacho Omiste, Edgar. *Bolivia y la Integración Andina*. 2d ed. La Paz: Editorial Los Amigos del Libro, 1981.

Cano, Washington. *Historia de los límites del Perú*. Arequipa: Tipografía Quiróz Perea, 1925.

Capuñay, Manuel A. *Leguía: Vida y obra del constructor del gran Perú*. Lima: Compañia de Impresiones y Publicidad, 1952.

Carey, James C. *Peru and the United States, 1900–1962*. Notre Dame: University of Notre Dame Press, 1964.

Carlos Martin, José. *José Pardo y Barreda: El Estadista*. Lima: Campañía de Impresiones y Publicidad, 1948.

Carrasco, José. *Bolivia ante la Liga de las Naciones*. Lima: Librería e Imprenta Gil. 1920.

Cavelier, Germán. *La política internacional de Colombia*. 2d ed. 4 vols. Bogotá: Editorial Iqueima, 1960.

Cavero Egúsquiza y Seavedra, Ricardo. *El conflicto de Leticia*. Lima: Taller de Linotipia, 1932.

Cayo Córdoba, Percy, et al. *El Torno a la Guerra del Pacífico*. Lima: Fondo Editorial, 1983.

Checa Drouet, B. *La Doctrina Americana del Uti Possidetis de 1810*. Lima: Librería e Imprenta Gil, 1936.

Child, Jack. *Antarctica and South American Geopolitics: Frozen Lebensraum*. New York: Praeger Publishers, 1988.

Chirinos Soto, Enrique. *Historia de la república, 1821-Peru-1982*. 2d ed. Lima: Editorial "Minerva," 1982.

Chirinos Soto, Enrique. *Perú y Ecuador*. Lima: Talleres Gráficos P. L. Villanueva, 1968.

Cobas, Efraín. *Fuerzo Armada, Misiones Militares y Dependencia en el Peru*. Lima: Editorial Horizonte, 1982.

Cotler, Julio. *Clases, estado y nación en el Perú*. Lima: Instituto de Estudios Peruanos, 1978.

Cotler, Julio. *Democracia e integración nacional*. Lima: Instituto de Estudios Peruanos, 1980.

Crespo, Alfonso. *Santa Cruz: El Condor Indio*. La Paz: Librería y Editorial "Juventud," 1979.

Cruchaga Ossa, Alberto. *Estudios de historia diplomática chilena*. Santiago: Editorial Andrés Bello, 1962.

Cuevas Cancino, Francisco. *Del Congreso de Panama a la conferencia de Caracas*. Caracas: Oficina Central de Información, 1976.

Davis, Harold Eugene, John J. Finan, and F. Taylor Peck. *Latin American Diplomatic History: An Introduction*. Baton Rouge: Louisiana State University Press, 1977.

Davis, William Columbus. *The Last Conquistadores: The Spanish Intervention in Peru and Chile, 1863–1866*. Athens: University of Georgia Press, 1950.

Dennis, William Jefferson. *Documentary History of the Tacna-Arica Dispute*. Iowa City: University of Iowa Press, 1927.

Dennis, William Jefferson. *Tacna and Arica: An Account of the Chile-Peru Boundary Dispute and of the Arbitrations by the United States*. New Haven: Yale University Press, 1931.

Dobyns, Henry E., and Paul L. Doughty. *Peru: A Cultural History*. New York: Oxford University Press, 1976.

Durán Abarca, Washington. *La Soberania y las 200 Millas*. Lima: n.p., 1983.

Echenique, José Rufino. *Memorias para la historia del Perú (1808–1878)*. 2 vols. Lima: Editorial Huascarán, 1952.

Egas M., José María. *El principio de uti possidetis americano y nuestro litigio de fronteras con el Perú*. Guayaquil: Imprenta Municipal, 1927.

Einhorn, Jessica Pernitz. *Expropriation Politics*. Lexington, Mass.: Lexington Books, 1974.

Encina, Francisco A. *Las Relaciones Entre Chile y Bolivia, 1841–1863*. Santiago: Editorial Nascimento, 1963.

Encina, Francisco A. *Resumen de la Historia de Chile*. 2d ed. 3 vols. Santiago: Empresa Editora Zig-Zag, 1956.

Escobari Cusicanqui, Jorge. *Historia Diplomática de Bolivia*. 4th ed. 2 vols. Lima: Industrial Gráfica, 1982.

Espinosa Moraga, Oscar. *Bolivia y el mar, 1810–1964*. Santiago: Editorial Nascimento, 1965.

Fernando Guachalla, Luis. *La cuestión portuaria y las negociaciones de 1950*. La Paz: Editorial Los Amigos del Libro, 1976.

Ferrero Costa, Eduardo. *El Nuevo Derecho del Mar: El Perú y las 200 Millas*. Lima: Pontificia Universidad Católica del Perú, 1979.

Ferrero Costa, Eduardo, ed. *Relaciones del Perú con los Estados Unidos*. Lima: Centro Peruano de Estudios Internacionales, 1987.

Ferris, Elizabeth G., and Jennie K. Lincoln. *Latin American Foreign Policies: Global and Regional Dimensions*. Boulder, Colo.: Westview Press, 1981.

Fifer, J. Valerie. *Bolivia: Land, Location, and Politics Since 1825*. Cambridge: Cambridge University Press, 1972.

FitzGerald, E.V.K. *The Political Economy of Peru, 1956–78: Economic Development and the Restructuring of Capital*. Cambridge: Cambridge University Press, 1979.

Flores-Galindo, Alberto. *Arequipa y el sur andino: ensayo de historia regional (siglos XVIII–XX)*. Lima: Editorial Horizonte, 1977.

Fontaine, Roger W. *The Andean Pact: A Political Analysis*. Beverly Hills: Sage Publications, 1977.

Forero Franco, Guillermo. *Entre dos dictaduras*. 2 vols. Bogotá: "El Gráfico," 1934.

Franco, Carlos, ed. *El Perú de Velasco*. 3 vols. Lima: CEDEP, 1983.

Galdames, Luis. *A History of Chile*. Edited and translated by Isaac Joslin Cox. Chapel Hill: University of North Carolina Press, 1941.

Galindo Quiroga, Eudoro. *Litoral Andino: Retrospección y Perspectivas en Torno al Problema Marítimo*. La Paz: Editorial Los Amigos del Libro, 1977.

García Bedoya, Carlos. *Política exterior peruana: Teoría y práctica*. Lima: Mosca Azul Editores, 1981.

García Salazar, Arturo. *Historia diplomática del Perú. Vol. 1, Chile, 1884–1922*. Lima: Imprenta A. J. Rivas Berrio, 1930.

García Salazar, Arturo. *Resumen de historia diplomática del Perú, 1820–1884.* Lima: Talleres Gráficas Sanmartí y Cía, 1928.

Gardiner, C. Harvey. *The Japanese and Peru, 1873–1973.* Albuquerque: University of New Mexico Press, 1975.

Golte, Jürgen. *Repartos y Rebeliones: Túpac Amaru y las contradicciones de la economía colonial.* Lima: Instituto de Estudios Peruanos, 1980.

Gómez, Juan Pablo. *Vida, pasión y muerte del General Mariano Melgarejo.* La Paz: Ediciones Puerte del Sol, 1980.

Goodsell, Charles T. *American Corporations and Peruvian Politics.* Cambridge: Harvard University Press, 1974.

Gootenberg, Paul. *Between Silver and Guano: Commercial Policy and the State in Postindependence Peru.* Princeton: Princeton University Press, 1989.

Gorman, Stephen M., ed. *Post-Revolutionary Peru: The Politics of Transformation.* Boulder, Colo.: Westview Press, 1982.

Guerrero, Julio C. *1879–1883: La guerra de las ocasiones perdidas.* Lima: Editorial Milla Batres, 1975.

Guzmán, Augusto. *Historia de Bolivia.* 3d ed. La Paz: Editorial "Los Amigos del Libro," 1976.

Haya de la Torre, Víctor Raúl. *El Plan de Aprismo.* Lima: Editorial Libertad, 1931.

Hellman, Ronald G., and H. Jon Rosenbaum, eds. *Latin America: The Search for a New International Role.* New York: John Wiley & Sons, 1975.

Herrera Alarcón, Dante F. *Rebeliones que Intentaron Desmembrar el Sur del Perú.* Lima: Imprenta Colegio Militar Leoncio Prado, 1961.

Hooper López, René. *Leguía: Ensayo Biográfico.* Lima: Ediciones Peruanas, 1964.

Hudson, Manley O. *The Verdict of the League: Colombia and Peru at Leticia.* Boston: World Peace Foundation, 1933.

Hunt, Shane J. *Growth and Guano in Nineteenth Century Peru.* Woodrow Wilson School Discussion Paper 34. Princeton: Princeton University, 1973.

Ireland, Gordon. *Boundaries, Possessions, and Conflicts in South America.* Cambridge: Harvard University Press, 1938.

Ingram, George M. *Expropriation of U.S. Property in South America: Nationalization of Oil and Copper Companies in Peru, Bolivia, and Chile.* New York: Praeger Publishers, 1974.

Inman, Samuel Guy. *Inter-American Conferences, 1826–1954: History and Problems.* Washington, D.C.: University Press, 1965.

Jaramillo Alvarado, Pío. *Los tratados con Colombia.* Quito: Imprenta de la Universidad Central, 1925.

Javier de Luna Pizarro, Francisco. *Escritos Políticos.* Lima: Universidad Nacional Mayor de San Marcos, 1959.

Joslin, David. *A Century of Banking in Latin America.* London: Oxford University Press, 1963.

Klein, Herbert S. *Parties and Political Change in Bolivia, 1880–1952.* Cambridge: Cambridge University Press, 1969.

Kuczynski, Pedro-Pablo. *Latin American Debt.* Baltimore: Johns Hopkins University Press, 1988.

Kuczynski, Pedro-Pablo. *Peruvian Democracy Under Economic Stress: An Account of the Belaúnde Administration, 1963–1968.* Princeton: Princeton

University Press, 1977.

Lecaros Villavisencio, Fernando. *La Guerra con Chile en sus Documentos*. 3d ed. Lima: Ediciones Rikchay Peru, 1983.

Levin, Jonathan V. *The Export Economies: Their Pattern of Development in Historical Perspective*. Cambridge: Harvard University Press, 1960.

Lincoln, Jennie K., and Elizabeth G. Ferris, eds. *The Dynamics of Latin American Foreign Policies: Challenges for the 1980s*. Boulder, Colo.: Westview Press, 1984.

López, Alfonso. *La política internacional*. Bogotá: Imprenta Nacional, 1936.

López, Jacinto. *Lecciones del conflicto entre Colombia y el Perú resultante del tratado secreto de 1922: la conferencia de Rio de Janeiro*. New York: Carlos Lopez Press, 1933.

López, Jacinto. *Los tratados de límites y la paz internacional americana: el tratado secreto de 1922 entre Colombia y el Perú*. New York: n.p., 1932.

Loveday, B. W. *Sanchez Cerro and Peruvian Politics, 1930–1933*. Occasional Papers No. 6, Institute of Latin American Studies. Glasgow: University of Glasgow, 1973.

Loveman, Brian. *Chile: The Legacy of Hispanic Capitalism*. New York: Oxford University Press, 1979.

Lowenthal, Abraham F. *The Peruvian Experiment: Continuity and Change Under Military Rule*. Princeton: Princeton University Press, 1975.

Lozano y Lozano, Fabio. *El punto de vista colombiano en la cuestión de Leticia*. Mexico: A. Mijares y Hno, 1933.

Lozano Torrijos, Fabio. *El tratado Lozano-Salomón*. Mexico: Editorial "Cultura," 1934.

Luna Vegas, Emilio. *Perú y Chile en 5 siglos*. 5 vols. Lima: Talleres Gráficos de la Librería Editorial "Minerva," 1982.

Málaga Grenef, Francisco E. *Una carta a Wilson*. Lima: Imprenta Americana, 1919.

Marett, Sir Robert. *Peru*. New York: Praeger Publishers, 1969.

Mariátegui, José Carlos. *Seven Interpretive Essays on Peruvian Reality*. Austin: University of Texas Press, 1974.

Markham, Clements R. *A History of Peru*. Chicago: Charles H. Sergel and Company, 1892.

Martinez, Miguel A. *La Vida Heróica del Liberator, Gran Mariscal Don Ramón Castilla*. 2d ed. Lima: Imprenta Santa María, 1954.

Masur, Gerhard. *Simon Bolivar*. Albuquerque: University of New Mexico Press, 1948.

Maude, H. E. *Slavers in Paradise: The Peruvian Slave Trade in Polynesia, 1862–1864*. Stanford: Stanford University Press, 1982.

McClintock, Cynthia, and Abraham F. Lowenthal, eds. *The Peruvian Experiment Reconsidered*. Princeton: Princeton University Press, 1983.

McQueen, Charles A. *Peruvian Public Finance*. Washington, D.C.: Government Printing Office, 1926.

Medina, Pío Max. *La controversia peruano-chileno*. 2 vols. Lima: Imprenta Torres Aguirre, 1925.

Mercado Jarrín, Edgardo, ed. *El Perú y la Antártida*. Lima: Instituto Peruano de Estudios Geopolítica y Estratégios, 1984.

Mercado Jarrín, Edgardo. *El conflicto con Ecuador.* Lima: Ediciones Rikchay Perú, 1981.

Mercado Jarrín, Edgardo. *Política y Estrategía en la Guerra de Chile.* Lima: n.p., 1979.

Millington, Herbert. *American Diplomacy and the War of the Pacific.* New York: Columbia University Press, 1948.

Miró Quesada Laos, Carlos. *Autopsia de los Partidos Políticos.* Lima: Ediciones "Páginas Peruanas," 1961.

Miró Quesada Laos, Carlos. *Sánchez Cerro y su tiempo.* Buenos Aires: "El Ateneo," 1947.

Moore, John Bassett. *Brazil and Peru Boundary Question.* New York: Knickerbocker Press, 1904.

Morawetz, David. *The Andean Group: A Case Study in Economic Integration Among Developing Countries.* Cambridge: MIT Press, 1974.

Morimoto, Amelia. *Los inmigrantes japoneses en el Perú.* Lima: Taller de Estudios Andinos, 1979.

Mörner, Magnus. *The Andean Past: Land, Societies, and Conflicts.* New York: Columbia University Press, 1985.

Muñoz, Heraldo, ed. *America latina y el caribe: políticas exteriores para sobrevivir.* Buenos Aires: Grupo Editor Latinoamericano/Prospel, 1986.

Muñoz, Heraldo, ed. *Las Políticas exteriores latinoamericanas frente a la crisis.* Buenos Aires: Grupo Editor Latinoamericano/Prospel, 1985.

Muñoz, Heraldo, and Joséph S. Tulchin, eds. *Latin American Nations in World Politics.* Boulder, Colo.: Westview Press, 1984.

Muñoz Vernaza, Alberto. *Exposición sobre el tratado de límites de 1916 entre el Ecuador y Colombia y análisis jurídico de tratado de límites de 1922 entre Colombia y el Perú.* Quito: Tipográficos de El Comercio, 1928.

Normano, J. F., and Antonello Gerbi. *The Japanese in South America: An Introductory Survey with Special Reference to Peru.* AMS ed. New York: Institute of Pacific Relations, 1943.

North, Liisa. *Civil-Military Relations in Argentina, Chile, and Peru.* Berkeley: University of California Press, 1966.

Ortiz de Zevallos Paz Soldán, Carlos, ed. *Archivo Diplomático Peruano.* 9 vols. Lima: various publishers, various years.

Palacios Rodríguez, Raúl. *La Chilenización de Tacna y Arica, 1883–1929.* Lima: Editorial Arica, 1974.

Palma, Hugo. *America Latina: Limitación de armamentos y desarme en la región.* Lima: CEPEI, 1986.

Palmer, David Scott. *Peru: The Authoritarian Tradition.* New York: Praeger Publishers, 1980.

Palmer, David Scott. "United States-Peru Relations in the 1990s: Asymmetry and Its Consequences." In *Latin America and Caribbean Contemporary Record,* vol. 9, *1989–90,* edited by Eduardo Gamarra and James Malloy. New York: Holmes and Meier, 1992.

Pareja Paz-Soldán, José, ed. *Visión del Perú en el siglo xx.* 2 vols. Lima: Ediciones Librería Studium, 1962.

Paz-Soldán, Juan Pedro. *El canciller Porras y sus doctrinas internacionales.* Lima: Librería e Imprenta Gil, 1920.

Pease García, Henry. *Los Caminos del Poder: Tres Años de Crisis en la Escena Política.* 2d ed. Lima: DESCO, 1981.

Pease García, Henry. *El Ocaso del Poder Oligarquico: Lucha política en la escena oficial, 1968–1975.* 3d ed. Lima: DESCO, 1980.

Pease García, Henry, et al. *Peru, 1968–1980: Cronología política.* 9 vols. Lima: DESCO, 1974–1982.

Peñaloza Cordero, Luis. *Nueva Historia Económica de Bolivia: La Guerra del Pacífico.* La Paz: Editorial Los Amigos del Libro, 1984.

Pérez del Castillo, Alvaro. *Bolivia, Colombia, Chile y el Perú.* La Paz: Editorial "Los Amigos del Libro," 1980.

Pérez Concha, Jorge. *Ensayo histórico-crítico de las relaciones diplomáticos del Ecuador con los estados limítrofes.* 2d ed. 3 vols. Quito: Editorial Casa de la Cultura Ecuatoriana, 1961.

Philip, George D.E. *The Rise and Fall of the Peruvian Military Radicals, 1968–1976.* London: Athlone Press, 1978.

Pike, Fredrick B. *Chile and the United States, 1880–1962.* Notre Dame: University of Notre Dame Press, 1963.

Pike, Fredrick B. *The Modern History of Peru.* New York: Frederick A. Praeger, 1967.

Pike, Fredrick B. *Spanish America, 1900–1970: Tradition and Social Innovation.* London: Thames and Hudson, 1973.

Pike, Fredrick B. *The United States and the Andean Republics: Peru, Bolivia, and Ecuador.* Cambridge: Harvard University Press, 1977.

Pinelo, Adalberto J. *The Multinational Corporation as a Force in Latin American Politics: A Case Study of the International Petroleum Company in Peru.* New York: Praeger Publishers, 1973.

Platt, D.C.M., ed. *Business Imperialism, 1840–1930: An Inquiry Based on British Experience in Latin America.* Oxford: Oxford University Press, 1982.

Pons Muzzo, Gustavo. *Las fronteras del Perú. Historia de los límites.* Lima: Ediciones del Colegio San Julián, 1962.

Porras Barrenechea, Raúl. *Historia de los límites del Perú.* Lima: Rosay, 1930.

Porras Barrenechea, Raúl. *El litigio peru-ecuatoriano ante los principios jurídicos americanos.* Lima: n.p., 1942.

Puente Arnao, Juan Angulo. *Historia de los límites del Perú.* Lima: Imprenta de la Intendencia General de Guerra, 1927.

Querejazu Calvo, Roberto. *Bolivia y los ingleses, 1825–1948.* Cochabamba: Editorial Los Amigos del Libro, 1973.

Querejazu Calvo, Roberto. *Guano, Salitre, Sangre: Historia de la Guerra del Pacífico.* La Paz: Editorial Los Amigos del Libro, 1979.

Querejazu Calvo, Roberto. *La Guerra del Pacífico.* La Paz: Editorial Los Amigos del Libro, 1983.

Quijano, Aníbal. *Imperialismo, clases sociales y estado en el Perú: 1890–1930.* Lima: Mosca Azul Editores, 1978.

Quijano, Aníbal. *Nationalism and Capitalism in Peru: A Study in Neo-Imperialism.* New York: Monthly Review Press, 1971.

Ramírez Gastón, J. M. *Política, Económica y Financiera, Manuel Prado: Sus Gobiernos de 1939–1945 y 1956–1962, Apuntes para la Historia Económica.* Lima: Editorial Litográfica "La Confianza," 1969.

Randall, Laura. *A Comparative Economic History of Latin America, 1500–1914. Vol. 4, Peru.* Ann Arbor: University Microfilms International, 1977.

Rebagliati, Raúl Ferrero, ed. *El liberalismo peruano: contribución a una historia de las ideas.* Lima: Biblioteca de Escritores Peruanos, 1958.

Reyes, Oscar Efrén. *Breve historia general del Ecuador.* 3 vols. Quito: Editorial "Fray Jodoco Ricke," 1967.

Ríos Gallardo, Conrado. *Chile y Perú, los pactos de 1929.* Santiago: Editorial Nascimento, 1959.

Ríos Gallardo, Conrado. *Después de la paz: las relaciones chileno-bolivianas.* Santiago: Imprenta Universitaria, 1926.

Rippy, J. Fred. *British Investments in Latin America, 1822–1949.* Minneapolis: University of Minnesota Press, 1959. Reprint. New York: Arno Press, 1977.

Rippy, J. Fred. *Rivalry of the United States and Great Britain over Latin America, 1808–1830.* Baltimore: Johns Hopkins University Press, 1929.

Rivas, Raimundo. *Historia diplomática de Colombia, 1810–1934.* Bogotá: Imprenta Nacional, 1961.

Rivera Palomino, Jaime Daniel. *Geopolítica y Geoeconomía de la Guerra del Pacífico.* Ayacucho: Universidad Nacional de San Cristóbal de Huamanga, 1980.

Rodriguez Beruff, Jorge. *Los militares y el poder: Un ensayo sobre la doctrina militar en el Perú, 1948–1968.* Lima: Mosca Azul Editores, 1983.

Rojas, Castro. *Historia financiera de Bolivia.* 2d ed. La Paz: Editorial Universitaria, 1977.

Rowe, L. S. *Early Effects of the War upon the Finance, Commerce and Industry of Peru.* Carnegie Endowment for International Peace, Preliminary Economic Studies of the War, No. 17. New York: Oxford University Press, 1920.

San Cristóval, Evaristo. *Manuel Pardo y Lavalle: Su vida y su obra.* Lima: Librería e Imprenta Gil, 1945.

San Cristóval, Evaristo. *Páginas internacionales: Antecedentes diplomáticos del tratado Salomón-Lozano; estudio crítico del tratado.* 2d ed. Lima: Librería e Imprenta Gil, 1932.

Sánchez Cerro, Luis M. *Manifesto a la nación.* Lima: La Imprenta Peruana, 1930.

Sánchez Cerro, Luis M. *Programa de gobierno del comandante Luis M. Sánchez Cerro candidato a la presidencia de la república del Perú.* Lima: n.p., 1931.

Sater, William F. *Chile and the War of the Pacific.* Lincoln: University of Nebraska Press, 1986.

Scheetz, Thomas. *Peru and the International Monetary Fund.* Pittsburgh: University of Pittsburgh Press, 1986.

Schydlowsky, Daniel M. and Juan J. Wicht. *Anatomía de un Fracaso Económico: Perú, 1968–1978.* 6th ed. Lima: Universidad del Pacifico, 1982.

Scott, James Brown, ed. *The International Conference of American States, 1889–1928.* New York: Oxford University Press, 1931.

Sharp, Daniel A., ed. *U.S. Foreign Policy and Peru.* Austin: University of Texas Press, 1972.

Smith, Joséph. *Illusions of Conflict: Anglo-American Diplomacy Toward Latin America, 1865–1896.* Pittsburgh: University of Pittsburgh Press, 1979.

Stallings, Barbara. *Banker to the Third World: U.S. Portfolio Investment in Latin America, 1900–1986.* Berkeley: University of California Press, 1987.

Stein, Stanley J., and Barbara H. Stein. *The Colonial Heritage of Latin America: Essays on Economic Dependence in Perspective.* New York: Oxford University Press, 1970.

Stepan, Alfred. *The State and Society: Peru in Comparative Perspective.* Princeton: Princeton University Press, 1978.

Stewart, Watt. *Chinese Bondage in Peru: A History of the Chinese Coolie in Peru, 1849–1874.* Durham: Duke University Press, 1951.

Stuart, Graham H. *The Tacna-Arica Dispute.* Boston: World Peace Foundation Pamphlets, 1927.

Thorp, Rosemary, and Geoffrey Bertram. *Peru, 1890–1977: Growth and Policy in an Open Economy.* New York: Columbia University Press, 1978.

Tironi, Ernesto, ed. *Pacto Andino: Carácter y Perspectivas.* Lima: IEP Ediciones, 1978.

Tironi, Ernesto, ed. *Pacto Andino: Desarrollo Nacional e Integración Andino.* Lima: IEP Ediciones, 1978.

Tobar Donoso, Julio. *La invasión peruana y el Protocolo de Rio.* Quito: "Editorial Ecuatoriana," 1945.

Tobar Donoso, Julio, and Alfredo Luna Tobar. *Derecho territorial ecuatoriano.* Quito: Editorial "La Unión Católica," 1961.

Tobar García, Julio. *Historia de límites del Ecuador.* Quito: Editorial "Santo Domingo," 1966.

Tudela, Francisco. *The Controversy Between Peru and Ecuador.* Lima: Imprenta Torres Aguirre, 1941.

Tudela, Francisco. *La política internacional y la dictadura de don Augusto Leguía.* Paris: Imprimerie OMNES, 1925.

Tudela, Francisco. *La posición jurídica internacional del Perú en el proceso de la determinación de su frontera con el Ecuador.* Lima: Imprenta Torres Aguirre, 1952.

Tyler, Alice Felt. *The Foreign Policy of James G. Blaine.* Minneapolis: University of Minnesota Press, 1927.

Ugarteche, Pedro. *La Comisión Consultiva de Relaciones Exteriores del Perú.* Lima: Imprenta Torres Aguirre, 1948.

Ugarteche, Pedro. *Diplomacia chilena, 1826–1926.* Lima: Editorial Garcilaso, 1926.

Ugarteche, Pedro. *Documentos que acusan (El tratado Salomón-Lozano).* Lima: Litográfico Tipográfico Estanco Del Tabaco, 1933.

Ugarteche, Pedro. *Formación del Diplomático Peruano.* Lima: Talleres Gráfico P. L. Villanueva, 1955.

Ugarteche, Pedro. *El Perú en la vida internacional Americana, 1826–1879.* Lima: Imprenta "Garcilaso," 1927.

Ugarteche, Pedro. *La política internacional peruana durante la dictadura de Leguía.* Lima: Imprenta C. A. Castrillon, 1930.

Ugarteche, Pedro. *Proyecto de Ley Orgánica de Relaciones Exteriores.* Lima: Imprenta Torres Aguirre, 1944.

Ugarteche, Pedro. *Sánchez Cerro: Papeles y Recuerdos de un Presidente del Perú.* 4 vols. Lima: Editorial Universitaria, 1969–1970.

Ugarteche, Oscar. *Teoría y práctica de la deuda externa en el Perú.* Lima: IEP Ediciones, 1980.

Ulloa Sotomayor, Alberto. *Congresos Americanos de Lima*. 2 vols. Lima: Imprenta Torres Aguirres, 1938.

Ulloa Sotomayor, Alberto. *Don Nicolás de Piérola: Una época de la historia del Perú*. 2d ed. Lima: Editorial Minerva,"1981.

Ulloa Sotomayor, Alberto. *El fallo arbitral del presidente de Estados Unidos de America en la cuestión de Tacna y Arica*. Lima: n.p., 1925.

Ulloa Sotomayor, Alberto. *Perú y Ecuador: Ultima etapa del problema de límites (1941-1942)*. Lima: Imprenta Torres Aguirre, 1942.

Ulloa Sotomayor, Alberto. *Perú y Japón*. Lima: Imprenta Torres Aguirre, 1943.

Ulloa Sotomayor, Alberto. *Posición internacional del Perú*. Lima: Imprenta Torres Aguirre, 1941.

Uribe, Antonio José. *Colombia y el Perú; el tratado de límites y navegación fluvial de 1922, unión de las naciones amazónicas, cooperación económica*. Bogotá: Editorial Minerva, 1931.

Van Aken, Mark J. *King of the Night: Juan José Flores and Ecuador, 1824-1864*. Berkeley: University of California Press, 1989.

Vargas Ugarte, Ruben. *Ramón Castilla*. Buenos Aires: Imprenta López, 1962.

Vega, José de la. *El conflicto colombo-peruano*. Bogotá: Libreria Nueva, 1933.

Velasco Alvarado, Juan. *La revolución peruana*. Buenos Aires: Editorial Universitaria de Buenos Aires, 1973.

Villanueva, Víctor. *El APRA en busca del poder, 1930-1940*. Lima: Editorial Horizonte, 1975.

Villanueva, Víctor. *El CAEM y la revolución de la Fuerza Armada*. Lima: IEP Ediciones, 1972.

Villanueva, Víctor. *Cien Años del Ejército Peruano: Frustraciones y Cambios*. Lima: Editorial Juan Mejía Baca, 1971.

Villanueva, Víctor. *Ejército Peruano: del caudillaje anárquico al militarismo reformista*. Lima: Librería-Editorial Juan Mejía Baca, 1973.

Villanueva, Víctor. *El militarismo en el Perú*. Lima: Empresa Gráfica T. Scheuch, 1962.

Wagner de Reyna, Alberto. *Historia diplomática del Perú, 1900-1945*. 2 vols. Lima: Ediciones Peruanas, 1964.

Wagner de Reyna, Alberto. *Los límites del Perú*. 2d ed. Lima: Ediciones del Sol, 1962.

Wagner de Reyna, Alberto. *Las Relaciones Diplomáticas entre el Perú y Chile durante el Conflicto con España, 1864-1867*. Lima: Ediciones del Sol, 1963.

Werlich, David P. *Peru: A Short History*. Carbondale and Edwardsville: Southern Illinois University Press, 1978.

Wengel, Jan Ter. *Allocation of Industry in the Andean Common Market*. Boston: Martinus Nijhoff, 1980.

Whitaker, Arthur P. *The United States and the Independence of Latin America, 1800-1830*. New York: W. W. Norton & Company, 1964.

Wood, Bryce. *Aggression and History: The Case of Ecuador and Peru*. Ann Arbor: University Microfilms International, 1978.

Wood, Bryce. *The United States and Latin American Wars, 1932-1942*. New York: Columbia University Press, 1966.

Wynne, William H. *State Insolvency and Foreign Bondholders: Selected Case Histories of Governmental Foreign Bond Defaults and Debt Readjustments*. 2

vols. New Haven: Yale University Press, 1951.

Yepes, J. M. *Del congreso de Panamá a la conferencia de Caracas, 1826–1954.* 2 vols. Caracas: CROMOTIP, 1955.

Yepes del Castillo, Ernesto. *Perú, 1820–1920: Un siglo de desarrollo capitalista?* Lima: Ediciones Signo, 1981.

Zarate Lescano, José. *Biblioteca militar del oficial no. 34: historia militar del conflicto con Colombia de 1932.* Lima: Imprenta del Ministerio de Guerra, 1965.

Zarate Lescano, José. *Reseña histórica del problema limítrofe peruano-ecuatoriano.* Lima: Ministerio de Guerra, 1960.

Zook, David H., Jr. *Zarumilla-Marañón: The Ecuador-Peru Dispute.* New York: Bookman Associates, 1964.

ARTICLES

Adrianzén, Alberto. "Estados Unidos frente al proceso peruano." *Cuadernos de Marcha* 1, 4 (November–December 1969): 67–76.

Avery, William P. "The Politics of Crisis and Cooperation in the Andean Group." *Journal of Developing Areas* 17, 2 (January 1983): 155–183.

Barnhart, Edward N. "Japanese Internees from Peru." *Pacific Historical Review* 31 (May 1963): 169–178.

Beltrán, Pedro G. "Foreign Loans and Politics in Latin America." *Foreign Affairs* 34 (1956): 297–304.

Berríos, Rubén. "Relaciones Perú-Paises Socialistas: Comercio, asistencia y flujos de tecnología." *Socialismo y Participación* 22 (June 1983): 55–63.

Berríos, Rubén. "The Search for Independence." *NACLA Report on the Americas* 20, 3 (June 1986): 27–32.

Blanchard, Peter. "A Populist Precursor: Guillermo Billinghurst." *Journal of Latin American Studies* 9, 2 (November 1977): 251–273.

Bonilla, Heraclio. "The War of the Pacific and the National and Colonial Problem in Peru." *Past and Present* 81 (November 1978): 92–118.

Borah, Woodrow. "Colonial Institutions and Contemporary Latin America: Political and Economic Life." *Hispanic American Historical Review* 43, 3 (August 1963): 371–379.

Bunker, Rod. "Linkages and the Foreign Policy of Peru, 1958–1966." *Western Political Quarterly* 22, 2 (June 1969): 280–297.

Ciccarelli, Orazio. "The Leticia Dispute, 1932–1934: A Reconsideration of Peruvian Motivations." *Southern Quarterly* 11 (May 1973): 277–296.

Coker, William S. "The War of the Ten Centavos: The Geographic, Economic, and Political Causes of the War of the Pacific." *Southern Quarterly* 7 (1969): 113–129.

Cortada, James W. "Diplomatic Rivalry Between Spain and the United States over Chile and Peru, 1864–1871." *Inter-American Economic Affairs* 27, 4 (Spring 1974): 47–57.

Cotler, Julio. "Political Crisis and Military Populism in Peru." *Studies in Comparative International Development* 6, 5 (1970–1971): 95–113.

Crabtree, John. "The Consolidation of Alan García's Government in Peru." *Third World Quarterly* 9, 3 (July 1987): 804–824.

"La cuestión de Leticia." *Boletín de la Sociedad Geográfica de Lima* 51, 2 (June 30, 1934): 1–242.

"De Jueves A Jueves." *Variedades* 22 (June 26, 1926): 3–4.

Edmonds, David C. "The 200 Miles Fishing Rights Controversy: Ecology or High Tariffs?" *Inter-American Economic Affairs* 26, 4 (Spring 1973): 3–18.

Ferrero Costa, Eduardo. "Peruvian Foreign Policy: Current Trends, Constraints and Opportunities." *Journal of Interamerican Studies and World Affairs* 29, 2 (Summer 1987): 55–78.

Ferris, Elizabeth G. "National Political Support for Regional Integration: The Andean Pact." *International Organization* 33, 1 (Winter 1979): 83–104.

Fisher, John. "Royalism, Regionalism, and Rebellion in Colonial Peru, 1808–1815." *Hispanic American Historical Review* 59, 2 (May 1979): 232–257.

Frazer, Robert W. "The Role of the Lima Congress, 1864–1865, in the Development of Pan-Americanism." *Hispanic American Historical Review* 29, 3 (August 1949): 319–348.

Furnish, Dale B. "Peruvian Domestic Law Aspects of the La Brea y Pariñas Controversy." *Kentucky Law Journal* 59 (1970): 351–385.

Ganzert, Frederic William. "The Boundary Controversy in the Upper Amazon Between Brazil, Bolivia, and Peru, 1903–1909." *Hispanic American Historical Review* 14, 4 (November 1934): 427–449.

Goodwin, Richard N. "Letter from Peru." *New Yorker* (May 17, 1969): 41–109.

Gordon, Dennis R. "The Question of the Pacific: Current Perspectives on a Long-Standing Dispute." *World Affairs* 141, 4 (Spring 1979): 321–335.

Gorman, Stephen M. "Present Threats to Peace in South America: The Territorial Dimensions of Conflict." *Inter-American Economic Affairs* 33, 1 (Summer 1979): 51–71.

Gorriti, Gustavo. "Terror in the Andes: The Flight of the Asháninkas." *New York Times Magazine* (December 2, 1990): 40–48, 65–72.

Greenhill, Robert G., and Rory M. Miller. "The Peruvian Government and the Nitrate Trade, 1873–1879." *Journal of Latin American Studies* 5, 1 (May 1973): 107–131.

Guillermoprieto, Alma. "Letter from Lima." *New Yorker* (October 29, 1990): 116–129.

Harrison, John P. "Science and Politics: Origins and Objectives of Mid-Nineteenth Century Government Expeditions to Latin America." *Hispanic American Historical Review* 35, 2 (May 1955): 175–202.

Haskins, Ralph W. "Juan José Flores and the Proposed Expedition Against Ecuador, 1846–1847." *Hispanic American Historical Review* 27, 3 (August 1947): 467–495.

Hayn, Rolf. "Peruvian Exchange Controls: 1945–1948." *Inter-American Economic Affairs* 10, 4 (Spring 1940): 47–70.

Irie, Toraji. "History of Japanese Migration to Peru, Part I." *Hispanic American Historical Review* 31, 3 (August 1951): 437–452.

Irie, Toraji. "History of Japanese Migration to Peru, Part II." *Hispanic American Historical Review* 31, 4 (November 1951): 648–664.

Irie, Toraji. "History of Japanese Migration to Peru, Part III (Conclusion)."

Hispanic American Historical Review 32, 1 (February 1952): 73–82.

Kendall, Lane Carter. "Andrés Santa Cruz and the Peru-Bolivia Confederation." *Hispanic American Historical Review* 16, 1 (February 1936): 29–48.

Kiernan, V. G. "Foreign Interests in the War of the Pacific." *Hispanic American Historical Review* 35, 1 (February 1955): 14–36.

Kuczynski, Pedro-Pablo. "Latin American Debt." *Foreign Affairs* 61, 2 (Winter 1982/83): 344–364.

Kuczynski, Pedro-Pablo. "The Peruvian External Debt: Problem and Prospect." *Journal of Interamerican Studies and World Affairs* 23, 1 (February 1981): 3–27.

Lecuna, Vicente. "Bolívar and San Martín at Guayaquil." *Hispanic American Historical Review* 31, 3 (August 1951): 371–393.

Livermore, Seward W. "American Strategy Diplomacy in the South Pacific, 1890–1914." *Pacific Historical Review* 12 (March 1943): 33–51.

Lowenthal, Abraham F. "Dateline Peru: A Sagging Revolution." *Foreign Policy* 38 (Spring 1980): 182–190.

Lowenthal, Abraham F. "Peru's Ambiguous Revolution." *Foreign Affairs* 52, 4 (July 1974): 799–817.

Martin, Percy Alvin. "The Influence of the United States on the Opening of the Amazon to the World's Commerce." *Hispanic American Historical Review* 1, 2 (May 1918): 146–162.

Masur, Gerhard. "The Conference of Guayaquil." *Hispanic American Historical Review* 31, 2 (May 1951): 189–229.

Mathew, W. M. "The First Anglo-Peruvian Debt and Its Settlement, 1822–1849." *Journal of Latin American Studies* 2, 1 (May 1970): 81–98.

Mathew, W. M. "Foreign Contractors and the Peruvian Government at the Outset of the Guano Trade." *Hispanic American Historical Review* 52, 4 (November 1972): 598–620.

Mathew, W. M. "The Imperialism of Free Trade: Peru, 1820–70." *Economic History Review* 2, 21 (December 1968): 562–579.

McClintock, Cynthia. "The War on Drugs: The Peruvian Case." *Journal of Interamerican Studies and World Affairs* 30, 2/3 (Summer/Fall 1988): 127–142.

Miller, Rory. "The Making of the Grace Contract: British Bondholders and the Peruvian Government, 1885–1890." *Journal of Latin American Studies* 8, 1 (May 1976): 73–100.

Millor, Manuel R. "Algunos Aspectos de la Política Exterior del Nuevo Regimen Peruano." *Foro Internacional* (April/May 1970): 407–424.

Nolan, Louis Clinton. "The Relations of the United States and Peru with Respect to Claims, 1822–1870." *Hispanic American Historical Review* 17, 1 (February 1937): 30–66.

Nuermberger, Gustave A. "The Continental Treaties of 1856: An American Union Exclusive of the United States." *Hispanic American Historical Review* 20, 1 (February 1940): 32–55.

O'Brien, Thomas F. "Chilean Elites and Foreign Investors: Chilean Nitrate Policy, 1880–1882." *Journal of Latin American Studies* 11, 1 (May 1979): 101–121.

Olson, Richard Stuart. "Economic Coercion in International Disputes: The United

States and Peru in the IPC Expropriation Dispute of 1968–1971." *Journal of Developing Areas* 9, 3 (April 1975): 395–413.

Ortega, Luis. "Nitrates, Chilean Entrepreneurs and the Origins of the War of the Pacific." *Journal of Latin American Studies* 16, 2 (November 1984): 337–380.

Palmer, David Scott. "Peru's Persistent Problems." *Current History* 89, 543 (January 1990): 5–8, 31–34.

Pike, Fredrick B. "Heresy, Real and Alleged in Peru: An Aspect of the Conservative-Liberal Struggle, 1830–1875." *Hispanic American Historical Review* 47, 1 (February 1967): 50–74.

Robinson, H. Leslie. "The Hickenlooper Amendment and the IPC." *Pacific Historian* 14 (Spring 1970): 22–51.

Roett, Riordan. "Peru: The Message from García." *Foreign Affairs* 64, 2 (Winter 1985/86): 274–286.

Ruiz, Juan. "Las relaciones con el Ecuador: Historia y Perspectivas." *Debate* 9 (1981): 27–37.

St John, Ronald Bruce. "The Boundary Dispute Between Peru and Ecuador." *American Journal of International Law* 71, 2 (April 1977): 322–330.

St John, Ronald Bruce. "The End of Innocence: Peruvian Foreign Policy and the United States, 1919–1942." *Journal of Latin American Studies* 8, 2 (November 1976): 325–344.

St John, Ronald Bruce. "Hacia el Mar: Bolivia's Quest for a Pacific Port." *Inter-American Economic Affairs* 31, 3 (Winter 1977): 41–73.

St John, Ronald Bruce. "Peru: Democracy Under Siege." *World Today* 40, 7 (July 1984): 299–306.

Sánchez Albavera, Fernando. "Frente al FMI: un paso adelante, tres atrás?" *Quehacer* 40 (April–May 1986): 7–10.

Saulniers, Alfred H. "The Peruvian President's Economic Dilemmas." *LASA Forum* 16, 4 (Winter 1986): 15–21.

Seckinger, Ron L. "South American Power Politics During the 1820s." *Hispanic American Historical Review* 56, 2 (May 1976): 241–267.

Van Cleve, John V. "The Latin American Policy of President Kennedy: A Reexamination: Case: Peru." *Inter-American Economic Affairs* 30, 4 (Spring 1977): 29–44.

Vargas-Hidalgo, Rafael. "The Crisis of the Andean Pact: Lessons for Integration Among Developing Countries." *Journal of Common Market Studies* 17, 3 (March 1979): 213–226.

Vazquez Ayllon, Carlos. "Política exterior del Peru." *Revista de política internacional* 158 (1978): 23–39.

Werlich, David P. "Debt, Democracy and Terrorism in Peru." *Current History* 86, 516 (January 1987): 29–32, 36–37.

Werlich, David P. "Fujimori and the 'Disaster' in Peru." *Current History* 90, 553 (February 1991): 61–64, 81–83.

Werlich, David P. "Peru: García Loses His Charm." *Current History* 87, 525 (January 1988): 13–16, 36–37.

Wilgus, A. Curtis. "The Second International Conference at Mexico City." *Hispanic American Historical Review* 11, 1 (February 1931): 27–68.

Wilgus, A. Curtis. "The Third International American Conference at Rio de Janeiro, 1906." *Hispanic American Historical Review* 12, 4 (November 1932):

420–456.

Wise, Carol. "Alan García, el disarme, Reagan y la guerra de las galaxies." *Quehacer* 39 (February–March 1986): 68–76.

Wise, Carol. "The Perils of Orthodoxy: Peru's Political Economy." *NACLA Report on the Americas* 20, 3 (June 1986): 14–26.

Worcester, Donald E. "Naval Strategy in the War of the Pacific." *Journal of Inter-American Studies* 5, 1 (January 1963): 31–37.

Wright, L. A. "A Study of the Conflict Between the Republics of Peru and Ecuador." *Geographical Journal* 48 (December 1941): 253–272.

Zook, David H. Jr. "The Spanish Arbitration of the Ecuador-Peru Dispute." *Americas* 20 (April 1964): 359–375.

NEWSPAPERS AND RELATED SOURCES

Andean Air Mail and Peruvian Times (Lima)
Caretas (Lima)
El Comercio (Lima)
La Crónica (Lima)
El Mercurio (Santiago)
La Nación (Santiago)
New York Times (New York)
El Peruano (Lima)
La Prensa (Lima)
Quehacer (Lima)
Socialismo y Participación (Lima)
El Tiempo (Lima)
El Universo (Quito)

INTERVIEWS WITH AUTHOR

Fernando Belaúnde Terry. Denver (May 16, 1969) and Lima (July 11, 1983).
Julio Cotler. Lima (July 15, 1983).
Hélan Jaworski C. Lima (July 14, 1983).
José Matos Mar. Lima (July 12, 1983).
Frank V. Ortiz. Lima (July 11, 1983).
Pedro Ugarteche. Lima (February 28, 1968, and April 29, 1968).
Alberto Ulloa y Sotomayor. Lima (June 25, 1968).
Víctor Villanueva. Lima (July 14, 1983).

Index

Abuná River, 146
Acha, José María de, 61
Acora, 39
Acre, 145, 146, 152
Acre River, 152, 153
Act of Talara, 197
Adams, Charles, 119
Adelante, 62
Aid: from United States, 189, 194, 195–196, 204
Aircraft: military, 196–197
Airfields, 181–182
Albistur, Ignacio, 75, 76
Alcorta, José Figueroa, 151
Aldunate, Luís, 121
Alessandri administration, 161, 163
Alfonso, Paulino, 154
Alliance for Progress, 194, 195
Alliances, 10, 27, 58, 76, 89, 93; with Bolivia, 48–49, 98–100, 104, 105, 106, 109–110, 115; with Chile, 75, 77; with Ecuador, 49–50
Almirante Cochrane, 99, 100, 103–104, 110
Almirante Grau, 139, 168
Alternative Development Agency, 215
Alvarez, Mariano Alejo, 26, 118
Alzamora, Isaac, 141
Amazon Basin, 224, 230; disputes over, 10, 58–59, 81–82, 148, 203; opening, 52–54; treaties on, 152–153
Amazon River, 1, 54, 146, 165, 177, 186, 211
American Popular Revolutionary Alliance (APRA), 172, 173, 174, 179–180, 181, 183, 194, 195, 206; policies of, 209–213, 227
Amonea River, 145

Ancón, 36, 37
Andean Common Market, 1. *See also* Andean Group
Andean Group, 204, 205–206, 208, 211
Andean Pact, 2, 4, 205, 211, 223, 229
Andean Parliament, 216
Andean Reserve Fund (FAR), 212
Angamos, 113
Antarctica, 207
Antarctic Treaty, 207
Anti-imperialism, 172, 198
Antofagasta, 100, 102, 116, 143; blockade of, 103–104; seizure of, 105–106
Antofagasta Nitrate and Railroad Company, 100, 102, 103–104
Antony Gibbs and Sons, 47
Apolobamba, 19
APRA (Apristas). *See* American Popular Revolutionary Alliance
Aquiles, 33
Aquiles Allier, 47
Aquiri, 144
Arana, Julio C., 168
Arcinta, 35
Arequipa, 13, 26, 29, 35, 49, 122, 123; and Peru-Bolivia Confederation, 14, 31
Argentina, 12, 13, 14, 18, 68, 75, 93, 101, 125, 138, 204, 207, 211, 212; arbitration by, 145, 146; and Chile, 141–142, 143; mediation by, 153, 182; relations with, 24, 99–100, 102, 148, 151–152; territorial disputes with, 11, 35; war with, 23, 34, 36
Arguedas, Juan Bautista, 39
Arica, 19, 27, 97, 110, 116, 143, 145,

186, 203, 210; access to, 14, 28;
control of, 98, 121, 122, 131, 133,
135, 137, 138, 142, 153, 154, 158,
160, 161, 162, 164, 179–180, 223,
224, 226; occupation of, 39, 113,
115, 117, 120
Arica Bay, 164, 179
Armies, 7, 29, 110; Argentine, 36;
Bolivian, 24, 28, 39, 80; Chilean,
32; Colombian, 9, 12, 15; Peru-
Bolivia Confederation, 36;
Peruvian, 25, 28, 39, 81
Army of the South, 38
Arthur, Chester A., 120, 122
Aspillaga, Antero, 158
Aspillaga-Donoughmore Contract,
132
Atacama Desert, 89, 97–98, 109, 124,
203, 204, 224
Atlantic Charter, 181
Audiencia of Charcas, 145
Audiencia of Cuzco, 10
Audiencia of Lima, 10
Austerity program, 201–202, 214
Authority: internal, 15–16
Axis powers: opposition to, 181–182
Ayacucho, 11, 29, 31, 206, 221

Bacourt-Errázuriz treaty, 142
Ballesteros, José Merino, 68
Ballivián, José, 39
Balmeceda, José Manuel, 120, 121,
133
Balta administration, 62, 79, 80, 81,
90; economic policies of, 83, 84–
85
Banking system, 210
Bankruptcy, 17, 90
Barreda, Federico L., 78, 79
Barrenechea, José Antonio, 82, 93
Barros Jarpa, Ernesto, 161
Beagle Channel, 204
Belaúnde Terry, Fernando, 188, 193,
195, 196, 204, 209, 229; on
economic development, 207–208;
and Popular Action Party, 194, 206
Belgium, 60
Belgrano, 207

Bello Codesido-Gutiérrez treaty, 143
Belzu, Manuel Isidoro, President, 61
Benavides, Oscar R., 153, 175, 180,
181, 184; and Ecudor, 178, 179; as
president, 156–158, 176
Beni River, 82
Bermúdez, Pedro Pablo, 29
Bermúdez, Remigio Morales, 134, 139
Billinghurst, Guillermo E., 141, 155–
156
Billinghurst-La Torre protocol, 142
Blaine, James G., 118–119, 120, 136,
138
Blanco Encalada, 103, 104, 110
Blanco Encalada, Manuel, 35
Blockades, 36, 103–104, 113
Bolivár Simón, 8–9, 14, 18, 19;
leadership of, 23, 25, 222;
opposition to, 11–12
Bolivia, 1, 13, 17, 24, 25, 29, 37, 50,
93, 101, 111, 134, 141, 151, 179,
205, 210, 215, 224; alliances with,
48–49, 75, 98–100, 115–116; army
of, 36, 80, 104; and Atacama
Desert, 89, 97, 124, 204; and
Brazil, 81–82, 145–146; and Chile,
4, 102, 104–106, 135, 143;
federation with, 19, 31; independence of, 11, 12; mediation by, 70–
71; negotiations with, 26–27, 154;
nitrate industry of, 102–104, 105–
106; Pacific access for, 10–11, 35,
123, 124, 164, 185–186, 207; and
Peru-Bolivia Confederation, 14,
36; relations with, 18, 19, 60–61,
63, 81, 117–118, 122, 144–145,
148, 152–153, 158, 171, 203, 211,
216; trade with, 27–28, 30, 225;
treaties with, 38–39, 57; in War of
the Pacific, 109–110, 112, 115,
116–117; wars with, 23, 36, 61
Borders. *See* Boundaries, Territory
Borgoño, Justiniano, 139
Borrowing, 84–85
Boundaries, 10, 12, 26; in Amazon
Basin, 52, 81, 82; disputes over, 1,
41, 51, 144–146, 151–153, 178–
179, 206–207, 223–224, 226;

issues over, 25, 34; plebiscite over, 134–135

Brazil, 12, 48, 60, 68, 101, 102, 112, 151, 152, 167, 211, 212, 224; and Amazon Basin, 52–53, 54, 58; and Argentina, 99–100; and Bolivia, 81–82, 145–146; mediation by, 153, 175, 182; relations with, 24, 82, 147, 148, 158, 204, 227; trade with, 14, 30, 225

Buck, Charles, 135–136

Buenos Aires, 67

Bulnes, Manuel, 37, 38

Bureau of Foreign and Domestic Commerce, 157

Bush, George, 215

Businesses: United States, 140, 194. *See also* Corporations

Bustamante y Rivero, José Luís, 171, 183, 229

Bustamante y Salazar, Enrique, 125

Cáceres, Andres Avelino, 117, 125, 139; administration of, 93, 131–133, 136

CAEM. *See* Centro de Altos Estudios Militares

Calama Oasis, 104

Calderón, Isauro, 173

Callao, 7, 11, 32, 69, 141, 153, 230; blockade of, 36, 113; Chilean attack on, 33, 37, 116; customs house seizure at, 135–136; Spanish attack on, 77–78

Camarones River, 116

Camarones Valley, 135

Cambio '90, 214

Campero administration, 115

Candamo, Manuel, 139

Candamo-Terrazas protocol, 144

Canelos, 58–59

Canevaro, José Francisco, 104

Capital: foreign, 205

Caquetá River, 146, 153

Caracoles, 93, 104

Carangas, 145

Carrillo, Juan Crisóstomo, 118, 144

Cartagena Agreement, 204–205, 215

Carter, Jimmy, 202

Castellon–Elías protocol, 132

Castilla, Ramón, 2, 26, 38, 49, 57, 68, 72, 90, 127, 229; and Amazon Basin, 53–54; and Bolivia, 60–61; and Ecuador, 58–60; on guano exports, 46, 48; on immigration laws, 61–62; as president, 45–46, 50, 54–55, 62–63; and United States, 51–52, 82

Catamayo-Chira irrigation scheme, 206

Catay, 152

Caudillismo, 41, 221–222, 229

Caudillos, 2, 14, 20, 23, 59, 102, 125

Cavero, Juan Celestino, 58, 59

Cayaltí, 94

Cedula of 1802, 59

Cenepa River, 186

Central America, 12, 58, 67, 211, 213. *See also various countries*

Centralism, 9

Centro de Altos Estudios Militares (CAEM), 198

Cerro de Pasco, 140

Cerro de Pasco Mining Company, 180, 228

Chaco War, 179

Charaña, 186

Charcas, 18

Charún, Agustín, 40

Chero, 134

Chiclayo, 69

Chile, 1, 12, 18, 39, 50, 72, 111, 151, 187, 205, 210, 224; and Atacama Desert, 89, 97–98, 100–101, 109, 204; and Bolivia, 4, 100, 104–106, 135, 185–186, 207; and Brazil, 100, 102; and Colombia, 142–143; debt in, 16–17, 48; mediation by, 28, 70–71; national sovereignty of, 4, 73; naval expansion of, 80–81; negotiations with, 33–34, 79, 119–122, 131, 138, 141–144, 155, 160–163, 172; nitrate deposits of, 91–92, 103, 105–106, 126–127; relations with, 80–81, 93, 99, 152, 164, 171, 179, 203, 204; and Tacna-

Arica, 10–11, 133–135, 147, 153–154, 185–186; trade with, 30, 32–33, 38, 225; treaties with, 57–58, 101; and Treaty of Ancon, 123–124; and United States, 140–141; in War of the Pacific, 110, 112, 113, 114, 116, 123; war with, 23, 34, 35–36, 37; and war with Spain, 75, 76–78
Chimbote, 119, 136, 141, 154–155
China, 94, 96–97. *See also* People's Republic of China
Chincha Islands, 60; return of, 74–75; Spanish occupation of, 69, 70, 71, 72, 83
Chinese, 54, 62, 89, 93, 94, 125
Chinese Law, 54
Chipana, 113
Chorrillos, 36
Chuquisaca, 14, 32, 36, 38
Civilismo, 92–93, 158
Civilistas, 101, 127, 139, 142
Civil rights, 9
Civil war, 29, 30, 57
Civil War (U.S.), 61
Clay, Henry, 53, 56
Coalfields, 141
Coaling station, 119, 136, 141
Cobija, 27, 28, 57, 104, 143
Cocaine trade, 213
Cochabamba, 38
Colombia, 1, 8, 9, 11, 13, 15, 16, 19, 23, 26, 34, 73, 82, 101, 112, 131, 137, 173, 204, 205, 215, 224; alliance with, 27, 76; border issues for, 12, 174; and Chile, 142–143; disputes with, 10, 25, 151, 167, 171, 172, 175; negotiation with, 153, 155, 165, 166, 176–177; relations with, 148, 153, 158, 167–168, 216; treaty with, 146–147
Colonial era, 1, 15, 32, 221, 223–224
Commerce. *See* Trade
Concha, Carlos, 178–179
Concha-Gutierrez protocol, 179
Concha-Subercaseaux protocol, 179
Confederations, 10, 31–32, 73, 115
Conference for the Maintenance of

Peace and Security, 184
Conference of Arica, 116
Conference of Non-Aligned Countries, 202
Conferences, 2, 8–9, 50–51, 72, 138. *See also by name*
Congresses, 12, 38, 39, 101; Peruvian, 11, 12, 125, 159, 229
Conservatives, 9
Consular corps, 45–46
Consultative Commission on Foreign Relations, 93, 176
Contadora Group, 208, 211, 212
Contadora Support Group, 211, 212
Continental shelf: jurisdiction over, 4, 171, 187
Continental Treaty, 58, 63, 73
Convivencia, 188, 193–194
Cooley, James, 30
Coolidge, Calvin, 162
Coolidge award, 162–163, 167, 179, 227
Cooperation: regional, 204–205, 216
Copacabana Peninsula, 19, 27, 171, 179
Copper, 196, 201
Cordillera del Condor, 186, 206
Coronel Bolognesi, 139
Corporations, 46, 47, 199, 214, 228–229
Costa Rica, 58
Cotton production, 61, 188
Coups d'etat, 194, 198, 205. *See also* Golpes
Covadonga, 75, 77, 79
Credit, 16, 59, 61, 180, 201, 210
Creoles, 13
Cuba, 4, 101, 196, 199
Cuenca, 25
Customs: revenues from, 16, 156–157
Customs zones, 144
Cuzco, 13, 14, 29, 31, 38

Daste, Bernardo, 40
Daza, Hilarión Grosole, 102, 103, 110
Debt, 34, 59, 68, 70, 84, 92, 126, 144, 225; to Chile, 16–17; external, 90, 131–132, 208, 209–210, 212; and

guano contracts, 46, 47, 48; land concessions and, 136–137; public, 201, 213

Decision 24, 205

Declaration of Bogota, 204

Declaration of Caracas, 216

Decree 90, 45–46

Decree 553, 46

Default, 17, 92, 131, 225

Deficits, 84, 90, 214

Democracy, 6, 194

Democrats, 142

Demonstrations, 153

Department of La Paz, 19, 39

Dependence, 17, 188, 200–201, 207, 208, 225, 227, 230

Desaguadero, 26–27, 186

Desaguadero River, 27

Development, 200–201, 202, 207–208, 228

Diez Canseco, Pedro, 74, 75, 83

Diplomatic corps, 3–4, 45–46, 62–63

Disarmament, 210–211, 212

Donoughmore, Earl of, 132

Dreyfus and Company, 83–84, 85, 90–91, 114, 132

Drug trafficking, 215, 216

Duties, 28, 49, 52, 115, 208

Easter Island, 62

Eastern Airlines, 208

Eastern Europe, 2, 201

Echenique, José Rufino, 52, 54–55, 56–57, 60

Echenique Gandarillos, José Miguel, 153

Economy, 5, 6, 16, 17, 92, 212, 222, 225; cooperation on, 189, 193; crisis in, 89–90, 208–209, 213–214; disputes over, 24–25; guano and, 46, 83–85, 90–91; integration of, 125, 198–199, 204; international, 215–216, 226–227; reform of, 184–185, 196, 201–202, 207–208, 214–215; revitalization of, 139–140, 210; and War of the Pacific, 126–127; and World War II, 182–184

Ecuador, 1, 4, 8, 9, 13, 15, 40, 53, 55, 58, 59, 73, 101, 143, 147, 204, 205, 210, 224; alliances with, 34, 49–50, 75; disputes with, 10, 26, 178, 182–183, 206–207; land concessions of, 136–137; mediation by, 111–112; negotiation with, 153, 154, 155–156, 166–167, 172; and Oriente, 165–166, 186–187; relations with, 2, 34–35, 58–60, 63, 148, 153, 158, 203, 211, 216; trade with, 30, 225; war with, 23, 25

Edwards, Agustín, 153, 154

Egaña, Mariano, 33, 34, 38

Eighth Inter-American Conference, 179

8th Summit of Non-Aligned States, 212

Eisenhower, Dwight D., 188, 189

Eleventh Inter-American Conference, 187

Elias, Domingo, 57

Elite, 13, 33. *See also* Ruling class

Elmore, Juan Federico, 95, 97

El Salvador, 58

Embargos, 103, 113, 146. *See also* Blockades

Emigration, 94, 96–97

Empresa Petrolera Fiscal (EPF), 197–198

England. *See* Great Britain

Enterprise for the Americas Initiative, 215

EPF. *See* Empresa Petrolera Fiscal

Esmeralda, 110

Espinosa-Bonifaz convention, 131, 136, 137

Espionage: Chilean, 204

Essequibo, 163–164

Ethnic groups, 14, 125

Europe, 8, 17, 63, 93–94, 111, 188. *See also various countries*

European Immigration Society, 93

Evarts, William, 112–113, 118

Everett, Edward, 56

Everett-De Osma treaty, 56–57

Exchange rate, 183

Export-Import Bank, 180
Exports, 30, 46, 202; Chilean, 32, 126–127; and development, 200–201; earnings on, 196, 202; Peruvian, 185, 188; United States, 156–157
Exposición documentada, 161

FAR. *See* Andean Reserve Fund
Fatalism, 126
Federación Boliviana, 19
Federalism, 9
Federation, 12, 19
Federation of the Andes, 222
Ferreyros y de la Mata, Manuel, 27
Fierro-Sarratea treaty, 102
Figueroa Larrain, Emiliano, 164
Fillmore, Millard, 56
First Expedition of Restoration, 35
First Pan-American Conference, 138, 223
Fishing rights, 187, 200, 207
Fish meal, 196, 201
Flores, Juan José, 27, 40, 55, 57, 59; expedition of, 50, 67–68
Foreign Assistance Act, 200
Foreign Military Sales Act, 200
France, 3, 17, 59, 72, 111, 133, 139, 199; guano contracts with, 47, 83; intervention by, 67, 68; mediation by, 70–71, 76, 77, 79, 116; trade with, 30, 31
Franco, Guillermo, 59
Freire, Ramón, 33, 55
Frelinghuysen, Frederick T., 120, 121
Freyre, Manuel, 80
Fujimori, Alberto Keinya, 193; economic policies of, 214–215; and United States, 215–216
"Fujishock," 214

Galapagos Islands, 60
Gálvez, Pedro, 58, 94
Gamarra, Agustín, 24, 25, 29, 37; negotiations of, 26–27, 38, 40; as president, 26, 39, 47; on trade, 27–28
García Calderón, Francisco, 117, 118, 119, 120; negotiations with, 121–122, 123

García del Río, Juan, 8, 34
García-Herrera treaty, 137
García Moreno, Gabriel, 59, 60
García Pérez, Alan: economic policy of, 209–210; on international relations, 210–213
García Salazar, Arturo, 3
García y García, Aurelio, 225; diplomatic mission of, 94–97
Garfield administration, 118, 119, 120
Georgiana, 60
Germany, 112, 125, 157
Gibbs, Crawley and Company, 47
Godoy, Joaquin, 111
Golpes, 26, 29, 33, 156, 158, 163, 168
Good Neighbor Policy, 181
Grace, Michael P., 132, 140
Grace & Company, W. R., 228–229
Grace Contract, 132–133
Gran Colombia, 9, 11, 59; treaty ratification by, 25–26; war with, 23, 24–25
Great Britain, 2, 3, 7, 13, 17, 18, 50, 67, 68, 72, 80, 111, 133, 159, 187, 207, 222; as creditor, 16, 59; guano trade and, 46, 47, 55–56, 225; mediation by, 76, 77, 79, 112, 116; trade with, 30–31
Grenada, 208
Group of 8, 212
Group of 77, 4, 199
Guano, 46, 70, 89, 111, 224, 230; contracts for, 46–48, 83, 84, 90–91, 114; control of, 100, 121, 123–124, 126; policies on, 55–56; sales of, 51, 127, 132; trade in, 60, 225–226
Guaporé River, 52
Guaqui, 186
Guatemala, 58, 101
Guayaquil, 8, 24, 25, 50, 153
Gueppi, 175, 176
Guerrilla movements, 215. *See also* Sendero Luminoso
Guido, Tomás, 9
Gutierrez de la Fuente, Antonio, 24

Hacendados, 48, 61, 93
Hague Convention, 147, 148, 223

Harding, Warren, 161, 162, 166
Harrison administration, 136
Hay, John, 147
Haya de la Torre, Víctor Raúl, 125, 172–173, 181, 194
Hayes, Rutherford B., 112
Heath River, 152
Herrera, Bartolomé, 53
Herrera-Da Ponte Ribeyro convention, 53, 81
Hickenlooper Amendment, 200
Hicks, George, 103
Holland. See Netherlands
Holy Alliance, 12
Honduras, 101
Hong Kong, 94
Hoover, Herbert, 164
Huacho, 37
Huancabamba River, 178
Huancavelica, 29
Huancayo, 38
Huanillos, 113
Huáscar, 110, 113
Huaura, 31
Hughes, Charles Evans, 161, 166, 167
Humahuaca, 36
Human rights, 185, 204, 208
Huneeus-Valera protocol, 155, 161
Hurlbut, Stephen A., 118, 119, 120–121

Ibáñez y Gutierrez, Adolfo, 102
Ideology, 5, 9, 53, 227, 229
Iglesias, Miguel, 123, 124–125
Ilo, 113, 186
IMF. See International Monetary Fund
Immigration, 54, 61–62, 89, 93–94, 222
Imperialism, 181
Imports, 17, 49
Income, 16, 48, 185
Independence, 1–2, 7, 8, 11, 12, 15, 18, 50, 221
Independence movement, 7, 9, 11, 221
Independencia, 110, 112, 113
Indians, 125, 126
Industrialization, 185, 198, 206
Industry, 205
Inflation, 213

Ingavi, 39
Inter-American Development Bank, 199, 209–210, 215
Inter-American Reciprocal Assistance Treaty, 199
International Bureau of American Republics, 138, 148
International Labour Organisation, 183
Internation law, 4, 50, 52, 101
International Monetary Fund (IMF), 184–185, 202, 209, 213, 229
International Organization for Latin America and the Caribbean (OELAC), 212
International Petroleum Company (IPC), 183, 195–196, 197–198, 200, 229
Investment, 2, 11, 202, 216, 226; foreign, 17, 116, 140, 159, 184–185, 196, 205, 215, 225
IPC. See International Petroleum Company
Iquique, 19, 35, 104, 110
Iquique, 71
Iquitos, 173
Iquitos, 139
Irigoyen, Pedro, 104
Irisarri, Antonio José de, 35
Italy, 93, 111, 116

Jacobinism, 9
Jaén, 24, 40, 50, 178, 179, 182
Japan, 214, 215; mission to, 94–96; relations with, 180–181
Japanese-Peruvians: deportation of, 181, 182
Japurá River, 152
Javary River, 52, 81, 82, 145
Junta gubernativa, 16
Jurua River, 145

Kennedy, John F., 194, 195
Kilpatrick, Judson A., 119
Knox, Secretary of State, 154

Labor force, 54, 61–62, 69, 93
La Brea y Pariñas, 197
Lackawanna, 116

La Palma, 57
La Paz, 14, 38, 118, 143, 154, 186
La Pedrera, 153
La Puerta, Vice President, 114
Larrabure y Unánue, Eugenio, 134
Larrea-Gual treaty, 25–26
Latin American Economic System (SELA), 212
Latin American Free Trade Association, 2, 189, 223
Lavalle, Hernando de, 188
Lavalle, José Antonio de: peace mission of, 104–106
Law of the sea, 4, 171, 187–188
Law of the Sea Conferences, 187–188, 223
Law of the Sea Convention, 211
Lead, 188
League of Nations, 2, 160, 171, 175, 180, 183, 223
Leguía, Augusto B., 54, 163, 164, 180; administration of, 151–155; election of, 158–159; on Oriente, 165–166, 167–168, 174–175; and United States, 159–162
León, Matías, 40
Leticia, 3; occupation of, 171, 173–175, 177
Leticia Trapezoid, 165, 168, 173, 174, 175, 176–177
Liberals, 9, 23–24
Liberation movements, 200
Lima, 7, 11, 29, 32, 37, 113, 116, 153, 230; regionalism of, 13, 14
Lima Conference, 1, 51, 222–223
Lima Conference of Jurists, 101
Linares, José María, 61
Lindsay-Corral protocol, 98, 100
Lizzie Thompson, 60
Loa, 113
Loans: foreign, 16–17, 209–210, 226; negotiations for, 8, 84, 214
Loa River, 97
Lobos Islands, 56–57, 120, 121, 123, 126
Logan, Cornelius A., 121–122
López, Alfonzo, 176, 177
López, de Romana administration, 141

Loret de Mola, Carlos, 197–198
Loreto, 52, 53, 173, 177
Lorton, 157
Lozano Y Torrijos, Fabio, 165, 177
Luna Pizarro, Francisco Javier de, 23–24

Macao, 94, 96
Madeira River, 52, 82, 145, 146
Madre de Dios, 144, 145
Magdalena, 117
Malvinas/Falklands War, 4, 207, 208
Mamore River, 82
Manifesto of Montán, 123
Manú, 144
Manuripi River, 152
Manzanilla, José Matías, 174
Maquinhuayo, 29
Marañon River, 137, 178
Marcona Corporation, 202
María Luz, 95
Mariátegui, José Carlos, 125
Martial law, 36
Martínez, Marcial, 80
Mar y Cortazar, José de la, 19–20, 23, 24, 25
Matarani, 186
Maúrtua, Víctor M., 3
Maynas, 24, 40, 50, 178, 179, 182
Mejillones, 97, 100, 104, 143
Melgarejo administration, 81
Melo Franco, Afranio de, 176, 177
Mendez Núñez, Casto, 77
Merchant marine, 95–96
Mestizos, 125
Mexico, 12, 13, 67, 68
Militarism, 29, 41, 222, 229
Military, 24, 49, 52, 189; Chilean, 80, 104, 194; modernization of, 196–197; Peruvian, 73–74, 80, 81, 83, 92–93, 104, 125–126, 139–140, 156, 175, 185, 198, 204; in War of the Pacific, 114–115, 116–117
Military government, 194–195, 198
Mineral resources, 230
Ministry of External Relations, 46
Ministry of Foreign Affairs, 62, 93
Ministry of State and External

Relations, 45
Mollendo, 110, 113
Monarchy, 8, 9, 18, 68
Monroe Doctrine, 50, 77
Montane Company, 47
Monteagudo, Bernardo, 8, 9, 10
Montenegro, 36
Montero, Lizardo, 114, 117, 118, 121, 122–123, 125
Montes, Ismael, 151
Moquegua, 114, 186
Morales, Agustín, 98
Morales Bermúdez, Francisco, 201, 205, 211; regional diplomacy of, 202–203
Morona, 52
Morro de Arica, 179, 210
Mosquera, Joaquín, 10
Mosquera, Tomás C., 26
Moyobamba, 52
Muñoz, Donato, 82
Muñoz-Netto convention, 81–82
Mutinies, 125

Napo, 52
Napo River, 146
Nationalism, 7, 14–15, 38–39, 126, 166, 171, 176, 183, 185, 198, 229; and Oriente, 165, 177
Nationalization, 48, 172, 199, 202, 210; of nitrate deposits, 91–92, 93
Naturalization: of citizens, 154
Nauta, 53
Naval base: at Chimbote, 119, 136, 141, 154–155
Navies: Chilean, 33, 80, 92, 100, 110, 113–114; French, 31; Peru-Bolivia Confederation, 35; Peruvian, 25, 33, 80, 81, 92, 127, 139; Spanish, 70, 73, 77–78; United States, 119, 136, 141, 154–155
Netherlands, 13, 111
Nevados de Palomani, 145
New Granada, 9, 25, 40, 51, 53, 55
New international economic order, 199
Nicaragua, 57, 58, 159–160, 211, 213
1922 Protocol and Supplementary

Agreement of Washington, 161, 174–175
Ninth Inter-American Conference, 184
Nitrate deposits, 105, 111, 124, 224, 230; acquisition of, 100–102; claims over, 89, 97–98; control of, 123, 155; export of, 126–127; nationalization of, 91–92, 93; ten-centavo tax on, 102–104
Nixon, Richard M., 188
Nolasco Videla, Pedro, 103
Non-Aligned Movement, 4, 193, 199, 202, 212, 229
Northern Cook Islands, 62
North Korea, 212
North Peru, 31, 36, 37

OAS. *See* Organization of American States
Odría, Manuel A., 187, 188; economic reform of, 184–185; regional diplomacy of, 185–186
OELAC. *See* International Organization for Latin America and the Caribbean
Oil production, 201, 230
O'Higgins, 104
Olañeta, Casimiro, 27, 33, 34
Oligarchy. *See* Ruling class
Oncenio, 167, 172, 226
Orbegoso, Luís José de, 28–29, 31, 33, 36, 37
Organization of American States (OAS), 1, 184, 187, 189, 199, 207, 208, 223, 229
Organization of Non-Aligned Countries, 199
Oriente, 136–137; negotiations over, 165–167, 174–175, 178
Ortíz de Zevallos, Ignacio, 19, 59
Oruro, 38
Osma, Joaquín José de, 48
Osma, Juan Ignacio de, 56

Pacheco, Toribio, 71, 76
Pacific Ocean, 1, 10–11
Panama, 211–212, 222

Panama Canal, 155, 157, 181, 199
Panama Conference, 1, 12–13, 222
Pan-American conferences, 136, 138, 147–148
Pan-Americanism, 7, 12, 14
Pan American Union, 157
Pando, José María de, 12
Paquisha, 206
Paraguay, 75, 100, 179
Paraguay River, 146
Pardo, José, 156, 157, 158–159
Pardo, Manuel, 1, 43, 100, 101; and economy, 89–90; military policy of, 92–93, 127
Pareja, José Manuel, 72, 73, 74, 75, 77
Paris Peace Conference, 158, 160
Paroissien, James, 8
Partido Civil, 89
Pastasa, 52
Pastaza River, 137, 182
Pasto region, 40
Patagonia, 102
Paz-Soldán, Gregorio, 53
Pedemonte, Carlos, 26
Pedemonte-Mosquera protocol, 26
Pelly Amendment, 200
People's Republic of China, 199, 201
Pérez de Tudela, Manuel, 12
Permanent Commission of Inter-American Conciliation, 175
Permanent Court of Arbitration at the Hague, 153, 154, 156, 177
Permanent Court of International Justice at The Hague, 183
Peru-Bolivia Confederation, 1, 23, 31, 32, 34, 37–38, 222; consolidation of, 35–36; opposition to, 13–14
Peruvian Corporation, 132, 140
Peruvian Defense Commission, 163
Peruvian Guano Company, 91, 114
Peruvian Institute for Antarctic Studies, 207
Peruvian National Antarctic Commission, 207
Petroleum. *See* Oil production
Pezet administration, 74, 80, 83; and Talambo affair, 69, 70, 71, 72
Píerola, Nicolás de, 83, 85, 101, 114,

127, 141; economy under, 139–140; and War of the Pacific, 116, 117
Pinochet government, 204
Pinto, Anibal, 104
Pinzón Luís Hernandez, 68, 69, 70, 71, 72
Pisagua, 113
Plebiscite: on Tacna and Arica, 133–135, 153–154, 163
Poinsett, Joel Roberts, 18
Polo, Solón, 163
Polo–Rivas Vicuña treaty, 179
Polo-Sánchez Bustamante treaty, 152–153
Polynesians, 62
Ponce-Castro Oyanguren protocol, 167, 178
Popular Action Party, 194, 195, 206, 208, 209
Porras, Melitón, 153
Porras-Tanco Argáez treaty, 153
Portales, Diego, 33
Portete de Tarqui: battle of, 25
Portillo, Pedro, 137
Ports, 18, 20, 33; Bolivian access to, 14, 19, 27–28, 35, 100, 143
Portugal, 52, 94, 96
Potosí, 38
Prado, Manuel, 181–182, 188, 194
Prado, Mariano Ignacio, 74, 75, 80, 83, 181; foreign policy of, 101–102; and U.S. mediation, 78–79; War of the Pacific, 110, 112–114; war with Chile, 104, 105–106; war with Spain, 76–77
Prado Doctrine, 188
Prevost, John B., 18
Protectionism, 31
Protocol of Viña del Mar, 120, 121
Puerto Rico, 202
Puga Borne, Federico, 160–161
Puna de Atacama, 135
Puno, 13, 26, 29, 31, 38, 39, 186
Purus, 144, 146
Purus River, 145, 152
Putumayo, 52
Putumayo River, 82, 153, 165, 175, 176, 177

Puyango-Tumbes irrigation scheme, 206, 211
Puymerol, Poumarrox and Company, 47

Quadruple Alliance, 75, 80
Quijos, 59
Quilca, 35
Quiroz, Francisco, 46, 47
Quiroz, Allier and Company, 47
Quito, 153

Railroads, 154; construction of, 84–85, 132, 134, 143–144, 146, 186
Raphael and Sons, 91
Reagan administration, 208, 213
Rebellions, 14, 38, 74, 94, 117, 184; in Leticia, 173–176; military, 24, 29, 38
Regency. See Monarchy
Regional Center for Peace, Disarmament, and Development, 211
Regionalism, 7, 13–14, 32, 222
Republicanism, 18
Restoration, 38
Revolutionary Government of the Armed Forces, 198
Revolutionary Union Party, 173
Reyes Ortiz, Serapio, 103, 104, 105, 106
Ribeyro, Juan Antonio, 69–70, 71
Río César A. del, 84
Rio de Janeiro, 146, 177–178
Rio Protocol, 4, 171, 182–183, 186–187, 207
Roads, 186
Robinson, Jeremy, 18
Rocafuerte, Vicente, 34
Rockefeller, Nelson, 200
Roosevelt, Franklin D., 181
Roosevelt, Theodore, 141
Rosas, Juan Manuel de, 34, 67
Rubber collection, 143
Ruling class, 4, 125, 126, 127
Russia, 95. See also Soviet Union

Salaverry, Felipe Santiago, 29, 33
Salazar y Baquíjano, Manuel, 19
Salazar y Mazarredo, Eusebio de, 69–70, 71, 72, 74
Salomón, Alberto, 161
Salomón-Lozano treaty, 3–4, 165, 167, 177
Sánchez Carrión, José Faustino, 10
Sánchez Cerro, Luís M., 172, 173–174, 175, 178
San Martín, José de, 8–9, 16, 32, 45
San Miguel River, 165
Santa Cruz, 38
Santa Cruz, Andrés, 12, 24, 27, 29; and Chilean relations, 33, 35; in exile, 38, 39; opposition to, 34, 36–37; and Peru-Bolivia Confederation, 14, 32; as president, 18–19; support for, 26, 31
Santa Rosa River, 152
Santiago River, 137
Santo Domingo, 68
Scientific expedition: Spanish, 68–69
Sechura Contract, 183
Sechura Desert, 183
Second Hague Conference, 148
Second Lima Conference, 72, 73, 89, 223
Second Pan-American Conference, 147–148
Security, 227–228
SELA. See Latin American Economic System
Sendero Luminoso, 206, 208, 215, 229
Serna, José de la, 8
Serranos, 125
17th Congress of the Socialist International, 212
Seward, William H., 72, 76, 79
Shining Path. See Sendero Luminoso
Shipping, 157, 187
Sicuani, 31
Silver deposits, 98
Sixth Pan-American Conference, 163
Socialism, 202
Socialist Party, 158
Social reform, 189
Social structure, 8, 14, 15, 125
Soldán y Unanue, Pedro Paz, 3
Sotomayor, Emilio, 103
South Africa, 212
South Peru, 31, 36, 37

South West African People's Organization (SWAPO), 212
Sovereignty, 135, 222; Chilean, 143, 153; over Lobos Islands, 56–57; national, 4, 73; safeguarding, 57, 203
Soviet Union, 2, 188, 199, 204, 207
Spain, 7, 17, 59, 214; arbitration by, 137, 144, 224; colonial policies of, 1, 52, 223–224; intervention by, 67–68, 72–73, 75, 89; as naval power, 73–74; negotiations with, 69–72, 78–80; war with, 75–78, 83
Standard Oil of New Jersey, 183
Steamships, 132, 157
Suches River, 145
Sucre, 18, 49
Sucre, Antonio José de, 11, 24, 25
Sucumbios Triangle, 174
Sugar industry, 141
SWAPO. See South West African People's Organization

Tacna, 31, 38, 97, 116, 145, 179, 186, 209; battle of, 114–115; control of, 19, 27, 98, 110, 121, 122, 131, 133, 135, 137, 138, 142, 153–154, 158, 160, 161, 162, 164, 223, 224, 226; occupation of, 39, 113, 117, 120
Tacna and Arica Treaty and Additional Protocol, 164
Tacna-Arica Accord, 4
Tacna-Arica issue, 1, 10–11, 144, 147, 156; resolution of, 155, 157–158, 163–164
Talambo affair, 69–71
Talara, 181
Tarapacá, 97, 113, 175; cession of, 19, 27, 116, 120, 123; Chilean interests in, 100–101, 121; control of, 158, 160, 161, 162; nitrates in, 91–92, 102, 105, 106, 155; occupation of, 117, 176
Tariffs, 28, 30, 33, 38, 61, 141, 206; lowering, 207–208
Tarija, 14, 35, 38
Tarma, 13

Tarqui, 25
Távara, Santiago, 55
Taxation, 48, 84, 90, 140
Taxes, 30; ten-centavo, 102–104, 105, 106
Territory, 1, 11, 35, 50, 222; disputes over, 19, 24–25, 36, 40, 41, 52, 82, 118, 145, 146, 151, 223–224; loss of, 126–127; negotiations over, 27, 203; in Oriente, 136–137, 167–168, 176–178
Terrorism, 81, 206
Textiles, 208
Third Pan-American Conference, 147–148
Third World, 2, 231. See also Non-Aligned Movement
Tigre River, 182
Tiquina, 28
Tirado, José Manuel, 53
Tirado-Moncayo convention, 55
Titicaca, Lake, 19, 132, 171, 186
Tocopilla, 104, 143
Toro, President, 180
Torre, Aníbal de la, 99
Trade, 2, 14, 17, 23, 54, 94, 216, 225, 226; agreements, 49, 135; with Bolivia, 27–28, 116, 180; with Chile, 32–33, 179; disputes over, 20, 37; with Japan, 95–96, 180–181; liberalization of, 205–206; policies of, 30–31; with United States, 33, 52, 159, 228; and World War I, 156–157
Treaties, 1, 12, 27; with Bolivia, 38–39; with Brazil, 60, 82; Chilean-Bolivian, 135, 143; with Colombia, 146–147; commercial, 33, 34, 81; defensive and offensive alliance, 57–58, 75, 98–99; Ecuador-Colombia, 147; extradition, 81–82; federation and limits, 19; friendship, commerce, and navigation, 51, 80, 82, 96, 101, 136, 181, 226; guano, 56–57; with Japan, 95–96; peace and commerce, 49; peace and friendship, 28; ratification of, 25–26; revision of, 174–175; trade,

30, 33; with United States, 52, 140
Treaty for Amazonic Cooperation, 204
Treaty of Acora, 40, 48
Treaty of Ancón, 10, 123–124, 125, 126, 127, 132, 142, 143, 145; arbitration of, 161–163, 164; plebiscite on, 13, 133–135, 153–154
Treaty of Arequipa, 28, 57
Treaty of Frontiers and Free Inland Navigation, 165–166
Treaty of La Paz, 29
Treaty of Limits, Commerce, and Navigation on the Amazon River Basin, 152
Treaty of Limits, Peace and Friendship, 61
Treaty of Mapasingue, 59
Treaty of Mutual Benefits, 97–98
Treaty of Paucarpata, 35–36
Treaty of Petropolis, 146
Treaty of Piquiza, 24
Treaty of San Ildefonso, 53, 81, 145
Treaty of Sucre, 57, 100, 102
Treaty of Tacna, 32, 36
Treaty of Tientsin, 96
Treaty of Triple Alliance, 100
Treaty of Union and Defensive Alliance, 73
Treaty of Versailles, 160
Treaty on the Conservation of Peace, 73
Trescot, William Henry: as envoy, 119–121
Tripartate Additional Arbitration Convention, 137
Trujillo, 11, 13
Tudela y Varela, Francisco, 3
Tudor, William, 18
Tumbes, 50, 178, 179, 182
Tumbes River, 178
Tuna Clipper, 200
Tupac Amaru, 14
Tupac Amaru Revolutionary Movement, 229
200-mile limit, 4, 171, 187, 200

Ugarte, Jesús, 173
Ulloa Sotomayor, Alberto, 3

Unánue, Hipólito, 8
United Nations, 3, 171, 184, 189, 210–211, 212, 223, 229
United Nations Law of the Sea Convention, 207
United Nations World Conference on Sanctions against South Africa, 212
United Provinces of Buenos Aires, 12, 48
United States, 7, 13, 17, 53, 61, 76, 77, 101, 125, 138, 181, 187, 193, 222; agreements with, 51–52, 136; aid from, 195–196, 215; arbitration by, 161–164, 166–167, 179; diplomacy of, 118–123; and drug issues, 215, 216; and economy, 156–157, 215–216, 226–227; guano, 55, 60; influence of, 2, 9, 12, 127, 147–148, 207, 208, 228–229; and Lobos Island controversy, 56–57; mediation by, 50, 70–72, 78–80, 112–113, 116, 153, 182; military aid from, 196–197; Panama invasion by, 211–212; relations with, 4, 18, 30, 63, 82–83, 135–136, 140–141, 154–155, 157–158, 159–160, 174, 180, 185, 188–189, 194–195, 200, 213, 214, 225–226
Upper Peru, 7, 11, 13, 18–19. *See also* Bolivia
Urbina, José María, 55, 111
Uruguay, 68, 75, 211
Uti possidetis, 10, 53, 59, 81, 145, 152, 224

Valdivieso, José Feliz, 40
Valle, Manuel María del, 144
Valle-Carrillo agreement, 144
Valle Riestra, Domingo, 75
Valparaiso, 33, 36, 37
Valparaiso, 100
Vargas Llosa, Mario, 213–214
Velasco Alvarado, Juan: on development, 200–201; on economy, 198–199; on foreign investment, 205–206; on regional cooperation, 204–

205
Velasco Ibarra, José, 186–187, 204
Venezuela, 9, 26, 53, 55, 73, 76, 101;
    cooperation with, 204, 205, 216
Vera Cruz, 67
Viceroyalty of Buenos Aires, 145
Viceroyalty of Peru, 10, 145
Vidaurre, Manuel Lorenzo, 12
Vientimilla, José Ignacio, 111
Vigil, Enrique A., 168, 173
Vilque, 29
Vitor, 134, 135
Vivanco, Manuel Ignacio de, 74
Vivanco-Pareja treaty, 74–75, 76, 80
Vivanco revolution, 60

Wagner, Allan, 211
Walker, William, 57
War of independence, 7
War of the Pacific, 1, 2, 102, 109,
    224, 226; actions in, 113–116;
    impacts of, 125–127; mediation of,
    111–113, 119–123
Wars, 23, 106, 179; with Argentina,
    34, 36; with Bolivia, 39, 61; with

Chile, 34, 35–36, 105; and
    economy, 83–85; with Ecuador, 25,
    182; with Gran Colombia, 24–25;
    with Spain, 75–80; Spain and
    Portugal, 52–53. See also Civil War
Webster, Daniel, 56
William Joseph Myers and Company,
    46–47
Wilson, Belford H., 37, 38
Wilson, Woodrow, 157–158, 159
World Bank, 209, 215
World War I, 226; Allied support in,
    157–158; and trade, 156–157
World War II, 1, 2; impacts of, 181–
    183

Yanacocha, 29
Yavarija River, 152, 153
Yavarí River, 152
Yungay, 38
Yuruá, 146
Yuruá River, 145, 152

Zañartu, Miguel, 28
Zarumilla sector, 182

About the Book
and the Author

Since Peru gained independence in 1824, its foreign policy has been shaped by the conflicting demands of independence and interdependence. Ronald Bruce St John systematically analyzes the strong link between the external and internal concerns that determine Peruvian foreign policy, demonstrating that domestic objectives and political considerations strongly influence—perhaps actually dictate—many aspects of the nation's international posture.

With violence an integral part of the Peruvian political system, internal conflict has frequently disrupted external policy, and the latter has often become largely a reflection of the former. Other factors, including the country's geographical size and location, the export-led nature of its economy, and the socioeconomic and political relationships it has developed with regional and extraregional powers, have exerted a strong influence as well.

Approaching Peru as a case study in Third World foreign policy. St John also draws from its rich history conclusions that aptly can be applied to other nations.

Ronald Bruce St John received his doctorate from the University of Denver's Graduate School of International Studies and is the author of numerous books and articles, including several on Peru and its neighbors.